WGR

Out of Print

S0-BGM-988

BOOK PUBLISHING: INSIDE VIEWS

compiled by
Jean Spealman Kujoth

The Scarecrow Press, Inc.
Metuchen, N.J.   1971

Copyright 1971 by Jean Spealman Kujoth

ISBN 0-8108-0420-4

Library of Congress Catalog Card Number: 76-155284

This book is dedicated with appreciation to
Dr. Ralph Robert Shaw, Mr. Albert W. Daub, Mr. Eric Moon,
and others of the Scarecrow Press,
and to Mr. Al P. Nelson, Wisconsin teacher of writing.

Introduction and Acknowledgments

This anthology of recently published articles by people engaged in and concerned with book publishing, helps to fill a conspicuous gap in the literature.

In it, publishers discuss what it's like to be a publisher; ethical dilemmas that influence a publisher's decisions; and memorable experiences they have had working with authors. Editors discuss what it's like to be an editor; the editor's role, aims, and problems; and the nature of the editor-author relationship. Notable authors discuss their experiences with book publishing; whether it's important to establish and maintain a public image; and the writer's relationships with editors and with readers. Artists, literary agents, and book promoters tell of their respective roles in, and experiences with, book publishing. And various specialists on book publishing discuss issues and trends; the economics of book publishing; how book publishing has been changed by the paperback revolution, publishing mergers, technological innovations, and government aid; and the publishing of such special types of books as art books, children's books, textbooks, scholarly books, encyclopedias, and reprints.

In short, this book has something to offer anyone, novice or expert, who is interested in book publishing.

The compiler expresses sincere appreciation to the authors and publishers who so kindly made it possible to include their articles in the book, and to the libraries that made the material accessible.

Jean S. Kujoth
Milwaukee, Wisconsin

Table of Contents

vii

PART I: MEET . . .

A. The Publisher

The Publisher and His Conscience

By Robert J. R. Follett, Vice President, Follett Publishing Company.

Reprinted (with permission) from School Library Journal 9:111-2, October 1962, copyright © R. R. Bowker Company. Adapted from a talk presented before a joint meeting of the Children's Reading Round Table and the Society of Midland Authors, April 9, 1962.

Let me assure you that the publisher does have a conscience, an invisible guide that shows itself in the responsibilities it serves. In publishing, the major responsibilities are threefold, for publishing is at once a business, a profession and an art.

As a businessman, the publisher is clearly responsible to his stockholders, his employes, his customers, his community--and his business. These, of course, are the responsibilities of any businessman. But the publisher bears additional burdens; secondly, he is responsible to the profession of publishing.

As a professional, the publisher must honor the standards and ethics of publishing. These are not codified, but they are known by all responsible publishers. Penalties are inflicted on those who ignore accepted standards of book selection, production and distribution; and on those who ignore accepted ethics in author, customer and company relations. I am sure most of us measure a publisher more by his acceptance of professional responsibilities than by his attention to business responsibilities.

Finally, the publisher is responsible to his art. A simple definition of "an artist" is one whose products are characterized by imagination and taste. Whether the products are paintings, songs, sonnets, buildings or books, we call them artistic when they are conceived and executed with imagination and taste. The most respected publishers

13

have always accepted this standard, and their publications
consistently reflect imagination and taste.

Business, profession, art: a publisher's conscience
must balance this trinity of responsibilities.

Now what are some of the dilemmas that invoke the
publisher's conscience? Put yourself in the publisher's
shoes, if you will, for the first dilemma.

You have discovered and nurtured an author. He has
produced for you two excellent books, both critical and
financial successes. Now he presents a third manuscript.
Perhaps he has written this one in haste or in the heat of
emotion. Whatever the reason, the manuscript is wretched.
Yet the author believes it is a valid effort worthy of publication; in fact, he hints that another publisher is interested
in this manuscript and in all future manuscripts. What do
you do?

You can publish the manuscript. The previous reputation of the author and a concentrated sales effort will
probably make it pay off. Or you can reject the manuscript
with full expectation that future good writing by this author
will go to another company. You must search your conscience for the right decision.

There is a variant of this dilemma. Someone sub-
mits a wonderful first chapter and charming art roughs.
You announce a publication date and train your full battery
of promotion and sales guns on the market. Then personal
problems, professional pressures or other factors cause the
author or artist to finish with a whimper instead of a bang.
What do you do?

You may meet your promised publication date; or you
may postpone or cancel the book.

Here is another type of dilemma. You receive a
manuscript for a history of Europe. It is pungent, incisive
and provocative. It immediately marks the author as someone with a distinctive contribution to make both to history
and to writing. However, as you examine the chapters on
Luther and the Reformation, you are convinced that certain
Catholic groups will be immediate and vocal in condemning
the author's viewpoint. Then as you read about Loyola
and the Counter Reformation, you can anticipate the outraged

cries of some Protestant groups. And further on, some
forthright comments on the roles of the Jews seem to invite
attack by Jewish pressure groups. Thus within one book you
have the danger of provoking attacks by three major religious
groups. What do you do?

You have several alternatives. You may reject the
manuscript despite its obvious quality. Or you may ask the
author to tone down his book. (In doing this you risk
eliminating the pungency and provocativeness that make the
book valuable. You also risk antagonizing the author.) Or
you can go ahead with publication, aware that the voices of
the pressure groups will be raised not only against the book
but against you, your company and all its works as well.

There is still another kind of dilemma you may face
as a publisher. Some years back you began a major publishing project in the textbook field. With your approval,
a philosophy and organization were agreed upon. Outstanding authors began work. But now a new research group,
sponsored by the Federal Government, has just published an
examination of the field. With the aid of top names and lots
of money, the group has completely revised the philosophical
basis and organizational premise that once governed the field.
You are not sure that the findings of the Government-
sponsored research group will be universally accepted, but
its prestige and heavy financial support make your position
look shaky. What do you do?

You can abandon the project, thus alienating those
whose hard work you once so earnestly solicited and thus
discarding all the time, effort and money that have been
invested so far. Or you can finish up the project and publish it. This will satisfy your commitment to the authors,
but you will now be throwing money and energy into a
project that has very reduced chances of success.

Finally, let me introduce one of the most common
dilemmas of the publisher. You have planned to publish an
outstanding book. Manufacturing specifications have been
set, an artist has been chosen, a promotional and sales
effort has been launched. But now the production department
reports a rise in manufacturing costs. The artist finds the
job more complicated than he imagined and demands more
money for its completion. The promotion department warns
that estimates of their campaign costs will have to be revised upwards. And the sales department advises that a

raised price on the book is sure to harm sales. What do you do?

You can use cheaper paper, have less art or ease back on promotional efforts in order to cut costs. Or you can continue with your original production and promotion plans but raise the price of the book.

These are some of the dilemmas the publisher faces daily. There are no set answers to any of them. If there were set answers, the publisher would not need his conscience.

What is the future of the conscience in modern publishing? In these days of Wall Street money, mass merchandising and monster mergers, will the committee and the computer replace the conscience? I do not think so.

All problems eventually pass from committees to a single individual who must search his conscience for the solutions. Computers may serve to sharpen our view of the alternatives, but in the end a single individual must grope within himself for the answer.

This single individual, whether he is at the top of a small company or somewhere in the middle of a big company, is the person we must call publisher. As the publisher, he will always have to face up to his threefold responsibilities. There is only one way he can do so--by searching his conscience and letting his conscience be his guide.

Authoring Success; A Conversation with Bennett Cerf,
author, wit, and co-founder of Random House

By Sterling G. Slappey, Associate Editor, Nation's Business.

From Nation's Business 56:74-8, January 1968. © 1967,
Nation's Business--the Chamber of Commerce of the United
States. Reprinted by permission.

In his own mind, Bennett Cerf's two most important
successes are making publishing a paying proposition and
finding and developing talent.

A score of the finest novelists, biographers, historians, essayists and poets of our time either first saw the
light of day under Mr. Cerf's imprint, or were led to new
heights by him.

Being successful in one career has not been enough
for this bubbly, imaginative, outrageously witty man. He
has written 11 books of his own. He does a daily syndicated humor column for nearly 200 newspapers. He was one
of the big stars of the long-running television program,
"What's My Line." He gives scores of lectures each year
and he has served on several corporate boards of directors.

He has initiated dozens of innovations during his more
than 40 years in publishing.

Bennett Cerf, by any standards, is getting on in years.
He's an unbelievable 69.

But he acts, talks, thinks, bounces about and works
as if he were 39.

He is a leader deluxe. He and his partner, Donald
Klopfer, founded Random House in the 1920's and built it into a giant of publishing.

Another success Mr. Cerf is prideful of is his fam-
ily--a wife he has been married to "since long before time
began" and his two sons.   One son is finishing Harvard University and will soon join Random House.   The other is now
one of Random House's highly valued editors.

Mr. Cerf's wife also is a Random House editor, and
Mr. Cerf gleefully lauds the benefits of nepotism.

In the following interview, Mr. Cerf candidly talks
about the practices of his industry and traces his own varied
and unique career.

Mr. Cerf, what makes a book sell?
        That's a question that people have been arguing about
since the publishing business started.   Is it word of mouth?
Is it fortuitous circumstances?   Is it book club choice?   Is
it good publishing exploitation?   Or is it advertising?

All the advertising in the world will not sell a book
that has not gotten some kind of start for itself.   Like a car
stuck in the mud.   If it is really stuck, 10 people can't get
it started.   But if it is moving just a little bit, one man can
push it.

When can you tell a book is beginning to move?
        Of course, if you have a book by an author who is
well known, you are in before you start.   It doesn't require
any great skill to make a best seller from a book by John
O'Hara or James Michener or Truman Capote.   The publisher who is worth his salt is the one who can take one unknown, find a handle for the book and put it over.   That is
the exciting part of publishing, discovering some new talent
and watching the new talent burst on the scene.   Then watching the author change overnight.

Who are some of your writers and some of their best works?
        The first great author Random House had was Eugene
O'Neill.

When we combined with a firm called Smith and Hass
it brought us a small but beautiful list headed by one of the
giants of American literature, William Faulkner.

Next thing that happened to us was that a very wonderful editor, Harry Maule, came to us, and brought with
him Sinclair Lewis, William MacFee and Vincent Sheehan.

Editor Albert Erskine brought us Robert Penn Warren. So now we really were off and running. Then we began developing some young authors of our own. We published Budd Schulberg's What Makes Sammy Run, The Young Lions by Irwin Shaw. Then came Truman Capote and his memorable Other Voices, Other Rooms.

Two of our most important authors now are John O' Hara and James Michener.

Some authors wait eight or nine years between books. But not John O'Hara or Michener. When they finish one book, they are ready to start another one.

William Styron was another four-star addition to the Random House cast. His Confessions of Nat Turner in two weeks became number one on the best seller lists. ·This is one of the great books of our time. This is one of the reasons that I am so happy being a book publisher. Just to have a book like that with my imprint on it, by God, that is exciting.

What percentage of books bought are read?
That depends largely on the type of book. I guess one of the most profitable authors we have had is Dr. Seuss. Theodor Geisel is his real name. His The Cat in the Hat is the most successful children's book ever published in this country. It has sold a couple of million copies. A copy of a book by Dr. Seuss you can bet is read not only once but by 50 kids before it exhausts itself.

A novel by John O'Hara, I would say 90 percent of the people who buy that read it. A novel by Michener, the same. But then you come to books that have prestige value. Because the reviews are superb, people buy them.

Doctor Zhivago got a great amount of front-page publicity when Boris Pasternak, the author, wasn't allowed by the Russians to take the Nobel Prize. I would say a good half of the people who bought that book put it on their library table and didn't read it.

Would you recommend book publishing to any young man who has reasonably decent prospects of succeeding in anything else?
I would recommend it if he loved books and writers of books as much as I did when I was a kid. I decided in my second year of high school that book publishing was for me.

I have never seen anybody go broke in the publishing
business. Some of them have cried a lot about publishing.
I have seen their tears bounce off the decks of their private
yachts.

Your office here, do you know how many books you have?
Yes. In this room are about 3,000 books.

And you have read them all?
I certainly have not.

Are you a fast reader?
Yes, I can read a manuscript of a novel in one evening.

I just came by it naturally. Maybe this is one of the
reasons that I love books, because I always found them easy
to read. You have to have good retention. When the author
comes in the next day he is suspicious and gives you a quiz.
One trick is to ask you about an episode that is not in the
book. You say "Yes, that was damn good," and he knows
you are faking.

Is book writing a proper vocation for a bright lad?
You can't make a writer. I am on the faculty of the
Famous Writers School in Westport, Conn., which I think
is the best mail-order writing course that has ever been developed in this country. But I keep telling anybody who
writes me that this school doesn't pretend to teach people
writing. It can only tell a writer how to polish his work.

Is fiction dying?
Not at all. It is just that the ratio has reversed itself. When I started in the publishing business 40 years
ago, fiction outsold non-fiction four to one. That ratio is
now exactly reversed.

The reason is the world has become such a wildly
exciting place that the novelist is hard put to keep up with
the front page of the daily newspaper.

Has TV hurt fiction?
TV has hurt a certain kind of fiction, what we used
to call hammock reading. Some novels, light fiction or light
love stories, mystery stories, westerns, have been hurt by
TV because all you have to do is turn a knob and you will
see four westerns, four mysteries, spy stories--along with

ads about bad breath, underarm odors and dirty sinks.

But good books have not been hurt by television.

Some books are published and you never sell another copy after the advance sale. In fact, you get back some of the copies you sell in advance. They are born to blush unseen, and waste their fragrance on the desert air. Sometimes they are darn good books too! Another first novel will come along not much better than six others that have failed, something happens and suddenly it is in.

It is like a horse race. A 50-to-one shot comes in once in a while.

Would you describe the process of buying a work and bringing it to the marketplace?
An important author today, with the competition in its present keen state, can get almost anything he wants as an advance.

Sometimes it is wise for a publisher to take a book on terms that he knows can never allow him to break even, because there are other advantages in having that book. A publisher may want to have a book by a distinguished citizen on his list to lend it distinction. He is willing to lose money on that book because he is getting publicity to compensate.

Ledgers of publishers are full of advances that were paid for books which were never delivered. One publisher told me he has paid out over $1 million in the last 20 years for manuscripts he never saw, for books that never arrived, for authors that vanished.

But the man today who won't take a chance is dead.

Tell us about the founding of Random House. Incidentally, isn't that a rather strange name?
It is an accidental name.

My partner, Donald Klopfer, and I got to know each other at Columbia in a music appreciation class. Only lazy fellows like Don and I knew about the class. We got credit for listening to a fellow play pieces on the piano. It was wonderful.

We became good friends and then we bought The Mod-

ern Library together from Horace Liveright. That was in
1925. For about a year we were busy making back the
money we had paid for The Modern Library, since some of
it was borrowed. As soon as we found ourselves free and
clear, we wanted to do some other things.

The Modern Library was profitable but not terribly
exciting. We were publishing the successes that others had
made. We wanted to publish successes of our own. One
day I walked into the office and said, "We are going to do a
few books here and there at random. Why don't we call it
Random House?"

At that moment Rockwell Kent, who was then the most
popular artist in America, was sitting at my desk and said,
"That's a good name. I'll draw you a trademark." In a-
bout five minutes he drew this house, which is still our
trademark. The bigger we got, the angrier he got for giving it to us for nothing.

What did you pay for The Modern Library?
            Two hundred and fifteen thousand dollars. That was
a lot of money in 1925.

I was working for Liveright and I wanted The Modern
Library. Many times I said, "Why don't you sell me Modern Library?" For my pains I would be thrown out of his
office, and rightly.

One day I was going to Europe and Horace Liveright
treated me to lunch at a place called Jack and Charlie's,
since renamed "21." He was wishing me bon voyage. He
liked me. I was a worshipful kid and he was a great publisher to me. He began moaning about personal debts he
had incurred. And for about the fourteenth time I said,
"Why don't you sell me The Modern Library?"

This time to my astonishment, he said, "What will
you give me for it?" We finally hit upon this figure of
$215,000.

We made it back in exactly two years. The Modern
Library is the keystone today of Random House.

How is your acquisition by RCA coming along?
            Oh, that has been a very happy thing for everybody
concerned. We, of course, got a fair price for our stock.

I don't have to worry every night about whether Random House stock is going up or down. Whenever it declined I took it as a personal grievance and was afraid to show my face in public, for fear people would say, "Look at that dope; his stock went down." And, indeed they did.

It was a pleasure to get under the umbrella of a huge corporation like RCA.

A lot of publishers today are tying up with big companies. RCA and Random House are only one example. CBS bought Holt, Rinehart. Xerox bought American Education Publications.

It is the educational part of the publishing business that interests these great companies. In the next 10 or 12 years, desks of school kids are going to look like miniature computer centers with all kinds of machines on their tables and desks. They will take their examinations on something that looks like a typewriter, and the grades will come back from a central location in a matter of minutes.

I think that is great, because now teachers spend about half their time on examinations and fighting with the parents about the marks they gave little Willie.

The production of these machines will not cut down on the people needed. It's Parkinson's Law. By the end of the year you have more people and twice as much machinery as you had before, but of course you get much more information and you get it quickly.

These machines we call the hardware. The publishers are going to supply the software, the material that is fed into these machines. Without software, machines aren't worth anything. It is like a man who buys a beautiful Rolls-Royce. If he hasn't got gasoline in there, it won't move.

How do you see yourself in the intellectual world and business world?
                    I must admit I am not an intellectual. People think I am more of an entrepreneur, or playboy, as I have been called. This is by angry competitors who resent the fact that I enjoy my life much more than they do.

Publishing is one part of my life. I ham it around on television. I enjoyed my years on "What's My Line" more than I can possibly tell you.

I now consider myself an actor out of work, and I am dying to get back on.

Since then a week doesn't go by but one or two shows are offered to me. One, so far, worse than the other.

I also write. I went through Columbia School of Journalism and was the editor of a paper there. But I didn't do any real writing until World War II when it seemed to me many people needed laughter very badly, just as they do today.

I proposed to the publishers of "Pocketbooks" that I do a book of war humor. This sold about two million copies. Suddenly I was an author.

I did another book, this time anecdotes, always about people I had met. I have always gone around with stars in my eyes. When it was finished it was to be another paperback, but it also became a hard-cover book.

I suggested the name, Try and Stop Me. It was published in the middle of the war, and I think it was the number one best seller for about 10 months. We sold about a million hard copies.

So that established me as a collector of humor. I started doing a column for Saturday Review called "Tradewinds" and a column for This Week magazine called "Cerfboard." Then King Features said, "We have got hundreds of papers signed up. Why don't you go ahead and do a daily humor column."

So to this day I do a column for the newspapers called "Try and Stop Me."

A story I've told a thousand times is about a fellow I met up in Bridgeport, Conn., a gynecologist, about 82. He has delivered about 2,500 babies. He charges either $100 or $200. I asked him, "How do you decide how much? Do you look up their bank account?" He said, "I couldn't care less. Whenever I deliver a baby, I go down to the waiting room where the father is pacing up and down. If the fellow asks, 'Is it a boy or girl?' I charge him $200. If he asks, 'How is my wife?' I charge him only $100."

Well, when you hear a story like that, that is a nug-
get. That goes into the back of my little head, to be used
on any necessary occasion.

Your lecture fee is about $1,500?
It's quite high, I admit. But the gross for a week
like that (sometimes I'll do eight talks in one five-day span)
is so big it pleases the ham in me. A good part of it goes
to the agency and the rest to the United States government.
But the urge of earning this money just for talking is so
fantastic. My wife, Phyllis, rolls on the ground with laughter. She says, "If these folks only knew that you would pay
them for the privilege of talking."

Book Publishing Today; An Interview

By Michael Bessie, President of Atheneum Publishers, inter-
viewed by R. W. Apple, Jr., Writer for The New York
Times and NBC Television.

From the New York Herald Tribune, 1962. Copyright ©
1962, New York Herald Tribune Inc. Reprinted by permission of R. W. Apple, Jr.

Q. How do you go about finding books to publish?
     A. You open the door with a publisher's sign on the
outside and manuscripts fall in. Some of us think that there
are several thousand manuscripts in semipermanent circulation among publishers. Two or three of the books that have
done very well for us, including one that has won its author
several prizes and earned a considerable amount of money,
were turned down by half a dozen major publishers before
they came to us. Some of our other books were written by
authors that Haydn, Knopf and I had been responsible for in
the houses where we formerly worked. They were either
close enough to us, or liked us well enough, or whatever, to
leave security for a question mark. But most of our books
have come to us from agents or writers we've known--
writers who hadn't published before, or who had had gaps in
their publishing careers.

Q. Do you spend a good deal of your time--to use a slightly offensive word--cultivating writers?
     A. You spend a good deal of your time, partly by
interest and partly by professional necessity, living with
writers. If you're interested in publishing, you're interested
in writing; if you're interested in writing, you're probably interested in writers; if you're interested in writers, you spend
time with writers. Some of my best friends are writers.

Q. For instance?
     A. Jan de Hartog, who is one of my closest friends;
Teddy White, Alfred Hayes, Robert Ardrey--these are all

friends as well as writers. I've just made a contract for
an autobiography by my oldest friend, a very distinguished
and successful writer whom we've never published--John R.
Tunis.

Q. Exactly how do you choose a book?
A. I think you want to publish a book for as simple
a reason as you like one car better than another or prefer
one painter to another. These are things you can talk a-
bout, but when you come down to it, you're apt to say you
like this better than that because its lines are prettier.
This is a very subjective statement, and so it is with books.
You read the book, and while you're reading, you're making
two judgments. As compared to other books you have read
or published, how much do you like it? At some point you
cross the line. You like it well enough to want to publish
it, which means that you like it enough to invest in it, to
put your time into it, to put yourself and your house behind
it. In other words, to be proud of it, to sponsor it.

You're also making an estimate of how well you can
sell it. This is the vaguest and most unreliable of factors.
When I read The Last of the Just, in French, in proof, before it had been published--and I remember this with great
clarity, because the book impressed me enormously--I came
into the office and announced to my partners that here was
a book we had to publish, although I was afraid there was
little hope that it would sell very many copies. Aside from
the extraordinary quality of this book, I said, it is another
novel about the persecution of the Jews and the concentration
camps, and God knows we've had plenty of those. I did not
think it was going to be a best-seller.

Q. What do you yourself look for?
A. The simplest answer to that is to look at what
I have caused to be published here, and at Harper's before
that. I haven't--and maybe a publisher should--I haven't the
mind and the preferences of a critic. I tend to be interested
in fiction, and in the kind of writing that has undertones. I
tend to be interested in serious writing. I tend to be interested in the kind of writing that suggests the qualities I admire in those writers of the past whom I turn to when I have
time for reading, and that stretches from Stendhal to E. M.
Forster.

Q. Who is your favorite among the novelists writing now?
A. If he's still writing, E. M. Forster. If not, I

think the novel published in recent times by an American
which I admire most is The Ides of March by Thornton
Wilder, and I should think that Wilder would come very close
to being my favorite living American writer.

Q. Haven't you ever published a book principally to make
money?
          A. The question reminds me of the story about the
ambassador to a Middle Eastern country who cabled the State
Department, "Call me home. They're getting close to my
price." The temptation is certainly there. So far we
haven't succumbed to it. I hope we don't.

Q. What is the editing process, as you see it?
          A. The editor reads, and selects what he likes, as
I have said. He either likes the book as it is, and says I
will publish this as it is--and that does happen--or he likes
it enough to think that with some work it can be in the
shape it ought to be in. He attempts to make out what the
author's intentions are, and to try to help him find his way
to the fulfillment of them. In other words, what you really
are is a first critical reader. It's not your job, or it
shouldn't be, to write the book, or rewrite the book, or lead
the author in ways of your choosing and not his. What you
should be doing is pointing out the things he intended to do,
or should have intended to do, and hasn't done. That's the
editorial process.

Q. Do most manuscripts need this kind of treatment?
          A. I should think, as Bernard DeVoto once said,
that every manuscript, indeed every published book, falls far
short of what the author had dreamed. The saddest contrast
in a writer's life is the contrast between the book he dreamed
and the book he published. Most manuscripts I've had
anything to do with, or knowledge of, have been worked on
between the time they were accepted and the time they were
published, and by worked on I mean worked on by the writer.
It's rare, despite the going prejudice that American editors
are busy monkeying about with manuscripts when they
shouldn't be--the English are fond of saying this--it's rare
that a very great deal is done to a manuscript.

Q. Then you do very little blue-penciling or rewriting yourself?
          A. I think that this is likely to happen more where
the book is by someone who is not a full-time writer, where
the person is an expert in a given field but not an experi-

enced writer. The process of working with an established
writer, on the other hand, is really a conversational process. I don't put pencil to manuscript except to write a note
in the margin saying, "Here's something I want to talk to
you about." When you talk with the writer you react to what
he's written, and you hope your reactions to what he's written will help him get it the way it ought to be.

Q. You would not put in a phrase or a sentence, then, and
say, "This is the way I want it"?
          A. Oh, no, no, no, no. A book belongs to the
writer. Our contract form says that we believe that books
belong to the people who write them. Well, that's a glorious phrase, but we really think so. It's his book, it's his
name that's on it. Very few people are aware of the publisher's imprint on a book.

Q. What makes a good editor? Is it the same thing that
makes a good writer?
          A. No. Most emphatically not. A writer should be
someone who goes through life, however selfishly, collecting
material for his own book. An editor should be someone
who goes through life looking for writing he would like to see
published and if possible improved. Not by himself but by
the writer.

Q. What are the main weaknesses in the manuscripts that
come your way?
          A. I share the often-expressed view that lots of
American writing tends to be vigorous but sloppy, sloppy
stylistically. Words are used imprecisely. You wish frequently that the language had been more at the service of the
writer, that he'd mastered it more thoroughly. I also think
most books are too big. And there is a tendency to let research fascinate to the point where it dominates the writing.
It should be the other way around.

The Economics of Publishing,
or Adam Smith and Literature

By Dan Lacy, Managing Director, American Book Publishers'
Council; author of Freedom and Communications and of numerous articles on the problems of libraries and publishers.

From Daedalus 92:42-62, Winter 1963. © American Academy of Arts and Sciences. Reprinted by permission.

Between the artist and his audience stand the media
of communication through which he must reach them: the
opera companies, the theater managements, the broadcasting
networks, the galleries, the publishing houses. To a degree, this has always been true. Throughout history an entrepreneur of some kind has assembled the artist's audience
and given him the chance to be heard. Victorian authors as
well as ours had to rely on publishers to disseminate their
books; Mozart and Beethoven received the patronage of
princes who were in a sense impresarios; Shakespeare wrote
with both eyes on the needs and demands of the commercial
theater of his day; and when Homer smote his lyre it was
to satisfy a courtly market for flattering epics. But the
media have grown so vast--armed with the technology of
high-speed presses, television cameras, and broadcasting
towers, all organized into complex industries--that they now
assume an almost wholly new role.

They can offer an artist audiences and financial rewards beyond any earlier imagining. The nineteenth-century
publisher or theater manager could count in thousands the
audiences he could find for a successful author or playwright.
Today a novel--or a Rise and Fall of the Third Reich--that
is fortunate enough to be a book-club choice and a successful paperback as well as a best seller may be read by millions. A television show may be seen by tens of millions.
Indeed, it is said that more people witnessed a single televised performance of "Hamlet" a few years ago than the sum
of all the audiences that had seen it enacted on all the stages

30

of the world throughout the centuries since its opening night.
The financial rewards may be fitted to this scale of
audience.   Though only a few dozens or hundreds of unsal-
aried writers and composers may make enough from their
work to live on, the occasional creator whose work meets
the highest criteria of success in the mass media may gain
great wealth in a single stroke.   The author of a smash
best-selling novel may possibly receive from royalties and
from book-club, reprint, and motion picture rights a million
dollars or more.   The role of the media of communications
matters now to a degree it never did before.   One book finds
an audience of 2,000--another, through televised adaptation
as well as book sale, one of 30,000,000.   Their suitability
to the mass media is what determines the difference.

The role of the media matters also in another sense.
The communications industries have become vast and largely
autonomous enterprises, often imposing their own criteria
upon the material they disseminate--criteria that may be unrelated either to the impulses of the creator or to the needs
of the audience.   The medium here tends to become the instrument of neither.   Rather it may exist to serve its own
ends, the principal one of which may be to return profits to
an entrepreneur, primarily by attracting an appropriate audience for advertising.   The medium thus may cease to be a
mechanism existing in order to link a creator to an audience; rather the writer or composer may be hired to produce
something to the medium's specifications that will aid it in
assembling and "conditioning" an audience for an advertisement.   What the writer or composer is able to disseminate
and what the audience may be able to see or hear may hence
be determined not by their own desires or interests, but by
extraneous criteria imposed by the needs of the media.

These needs of the media in turn reflect the facts of
their technology and their economic organization.   Contrary
to a general impression, they do not often reflect the personal idiosyncrasies of their owners.   No publisher or rec-
ord-company president or broadcasting-station owner can
successfully or continuously impose his own tastes or views
on the material disseminated through his medium in defiance
of the requirement of the medium itself.

Particularly do the economics and technology of the
media affect what is widely or massively available to the
public.   It is true that almost any writer with any trace of

perceptible merit can get into print in some way, even if he
has to have his book published at his own expense. And it
is true that a determined inquirer can ultimately get to read
or hear almost anything that has been printed or performed.
But it is the media themselves that determine which authors
or composers have access to the mass audience and, in
turn, what the cultural fare of the mass audience will be.
It may hence be worthwhile to look at one of the communications industries--in this case book publishing--in order to
explore the relations between its economics and the actual
communication between authors and readers in the United
States.

     We may begin by asking what a publisher does, what
is the essential element in publishing. A publisher may hire
authors to write books to his direction, and he may own a
press on which to print them and bookstores in which to sell
them. But in these activities he is being an author or a
printer or a bookseller, not a publisher. The essence of
publishing is pure entrepreneurship. The publisher contracts
with an author for the right to issue his book; contracts with
a printer and binder to have it manufactured; and then under-
takes to promote it to the general or a special audience, to
place it in the hands of wholesalers or bookstores where it
will be sold, or to sell it by mail directly to schools or libraries or individuals. The publisher pays the costs and
assumes the risks of issuing each book, and hence he occu-
pies a highly speculative position. His role is somewhat
analogous to that of a theater producer, or an independent
film producer; but the investment required in publishing any
single book is far less than in producing any single film or
play. His economic role is quite different from that of a
manufacturer, whose activities are based on his owning a
factory for the physical production of a commodity, or from
that of a newspaper publisher or broadcaster, whose power
to decide what is disseminated to the public is derived from
his ownership of a large and expensive physical plant.

     Important consequences flow from this specialized,
entrepreneurial role of book publishing. In the first place,
one can become a publisher with a very small capital in-
vestment--at least, as compared with the cost of entering
any of the other communications industries. No investment
in physical equipment is necessary beyond office furniture.
If one wishes to publish so few books that shipping and storage space cannot be economically used, it is quite possible

to contract for shipping and warehousing too, and many rather large publishers do. If the size of the business will not
justify a full-time sales force, one can engage the services
of "commission men" who represent several publishers, or
even arrange with a larger publisher to handle the entire
sales and distribution operations. Similarly, a publisher
too small to employ a full-time book designer or production
department or a separate publicity staff can engage those
services as well on an "as needed" basis.

    The result is that almost anyone with a few thousand
dollars who wants to "publish" a book may do so, and anyone with a capital of $100,000 or even less can establish a
"publishing house." New ones in fact are started annually,
and there are several hundred firms in the United States
that can properly be called book publishers, not to mention
the hundreds or perhaps even thousands of business firms,
foundations, churches, schools, committees, and citizen
groups that issue books and pamphlets from time to time incidentally to their main activities. Hence, while there are
only three major networks, two major press services, and
in most cities only one newspaper publisher and not more
than two or three television stations, there are hundreds of
publishers to whom an author may turn. Each of these may
expand or contract his output flexibly to respond to demand.
If there is a demand none of them fills, new houses arise
to meet it. Nor is publishing confined, as urban newspaper
publishing or telecasting necessarily is, to men of great
wealth with major investments to protect and hence with a
bent toward the economic and political views of their class.
All sorts of houses--commercial firms of widely ranging
sizes, purely personal publishers, church and university
presses, committees with a "cause," and others with varying motivations--compete for attention.

    There are, of course, small magazines, small news-
papers, and small radio stations. But the unique characteristic of small book publishers is that even the smallest has
access, like the largest, to the entire national audience.
Nothing published in the rural newspaper or the little magazine or broadcast by a small-town radio station can in that
form reach beyond its local or previously defined special
audience; but books published by very small publishers indeed may achieve very large sales. An outstanding example
was the sale of more than 250,000 copies of Arthritis and
Common Sense, published by the Witkower Press in Hartford,
Connecticut. Such best-selling novelists as Frank Yerby,

Frances Parkinson Keyes, Grace Metalious, and James Baldwin are or have been published by houses that, though well established, are small in comparison with the giants of the industry.

Nor is a small publisher at an insuperably competitive disadvantage. There are undoubtedly economies in warehousing, shipping, and sales force that accrue to the larger publisher, as there may well be in overhead for the smaller publisher. But the competitive advantages of bigness that establish an almost irresistible trend to centralization and oligopoly in most manufacturing industries--the economies of mass production and mass advertising--are absent or are mitigated in publishing. Competition for efficiency in manufacture is between printers rather than between publishers, and the large publisher and the small publisher may well use the same printer and benefit from the same efficiency. Similarly, in publishing one advertises the book, not the publishing house, and budgets are geared to the size of the edition, not the size of the publisher. Studebaker cannot possibly be advertised as Chevrolet is, but a book with an estimated sales potential of 20,000 copies is likely to have the same advertising allotment regardless of the size of the publisher.

In the number and variety of competing units, the ease with which they enter or leave the market place, and the flexibility with which each competitor can respond to changing demand, book publishing perhaps corresponds more closely than almost any other to the models of the classical economists who assumed perfect competition among atomized firms. It is Adam Smith's kind of industry.

Like the contractual relation with printers and binders, the publisher's contractual relation with authors providing for payments on a royalty basis has a major effect on the industry's communications function. In newspaper writing, in writing and composing for films and television, and in a great deal of magazine writing, the author or composer is an employee, hired on a salary or for a fixed fee to create a product to the specifications of the entrepreneur. In most book publishing, however, the author is not an employee but an independent partner of the publisher, sharing the publisher's risks and gains. He owns and controls his own work, which cannot be altered without his consent. And the dissemination of the author's work in the form in which he wants it is the object of the enterprise.

All the foregoing observations have been true of original publishing in free countries generally.   What are the particular characteristics and dimensions of book publishing in
the United States today?   In the first place, it has grown
very rapidly in recent years.   Surveys done for the American Textbook Publishers Institute and the American Book
Publishers Council, which between them embrace almost all
book publishers of consequence in the United States, report
an increase in the net sales of publishers from $501 million
in 1952 to $1,240 million in 1961, an increase of about 15
percent in nine years.   Though the prices of any given form
of book have increased over those years, the average price
of all books has remained rather stable, because of the higher proportion of paperbounds and inexpensive children's
books in the total output.   The total number of individual
books sold has hence increased in about the same proportion
as the net sales in dollars.   The American people and their
institutions are buying, even on a per-capita basis, about
twice as many books as they were ten years ago.

As communications industries go, the book industry
is now a big one, and it is probably growing faster than any
of the others.   Of this rather large complex, however, only
a minor part is devoted to the original publishing of general
books for the adult reader.   The image of publishing as the
handmaiden of literature is only a very small part of the
comprehensive picture.   The two biggest sectors of industry
are rather the publication of textbooks (elementary, high
school and college) with total receipts in 1961 of $385 mil-
lion, and the publication of encyclopedias, with the rather
startlingly large volume of $345 million.   Other categories
are small by comparison.

Book clubs are the next largest with receipts of about
$115 million, representing something over 75 million books.
Then come children's books, with sales of $103 million rep-
resenting 227 million books.   Nearly 175 million of these
books, bringing in about $35 million, are inexpensive chil-
dren's books, the majority of them sold in supermarkets and
similar outlets.   Specialized and professional books (reli-
gous, law, medical, business, scientific and technical) are
another big segment of the industry, with total sales of about
$85 million.   Paperback sales are about $97 million, representing about 305 million books.   Of these, about 26 million books, selling at publishers' prices for $16 million, are
the higher priced "trade" paperbacks, usually published by

general publishers and sold primarily through magazine outlets.   About 280 million books selling for $81 million are
the usually less expensive paperbacks sold primarily (though
by no means exclusively) through the same outlets as magazines.   University presses represent about $12 million, and
miscellaneous books not otherwise classified about $10 mil-
lion of the total.

Of the whole complex of book-publishing enterprises
in the United States, therefore, only about $87 million, or
7.5 percent, represents hard-cover, adult "trade" publishing.   This roughly defines the area of original publishing of
general books for the adult--the novels, biographies, histories, popular works on science, politics, and economics,
the discussions of current issues, poetry and essays.   This
is what we think of traditionally as "publishing," yet it represents only about 1/15 of the book publishing industry in
the United States.

It is the economics of this small segment of the industry, however, that determines the character of the literature published in the United States, and it is worth examining in some detail.   It will be useful to illustrate this by setting forth the specific economic pattern of the publishing of
a single book.   That pattern will not be exactly alike for any
two books, varying as it will with price, size of edition, and
methods of sale; but perhaps a sort of composite can be presented.   Let us imagine a novel, retailing at $5.00, of which
about 6,500 copies have been printed.   Let us suppose the
publisher was lucky and sold about 6,000 of those, and that
he was even luckier in that only about 1,000 of these were
returned by the bookstores as unsold.   His total income, assuming an average 40 percent discount, would have been
$15,000.   What would his costs have been?   Production
costs, including composition, paper, printing and binding,
would probably have been about $6,000.   Authors' royalties
would probably have come to $2,500, leaving a cost for the
books themselves of $8,500, or a gross margin of $6,500.

Out of this a wide variety of expenses must be met.
Editorial costs for work with the author and revising and
copy-editing the manuscript, together with a pro-rata share
of the costs of reading and rejecting the dozens of unpublishable manuscripts that must be gone through to find one that
is suitable, would come to about $1,250--assuming an author
who took little time in conference and produced a clean,
easily handled manuscript.   The book might have an adver-

tising and promotion budget, including its share of overhead
costs of the advertising and publicity department, of about
$2,200--too little really to do any good, but too much in
fact for the publisher to afford. Salesmen's commissions
and other selling costs would come at least to another $750.
An equal amount would be consumed in warehousing and shipping. Salaries of administrative personnel--bookkeepers,
clerks, the comptroller, etc., employee benefits, rent,
taxes, and other general overhead, when pro-rated among
all the titles published--would come to another $2,250.

The arithmetically minded reader will have noted that
the expenses to be met out of the $6,500 gross margin have
totalled $7,200, for a loss of $700. How does the publisher
stay in business--especially when we consider that our hypothetical book was on the whole a very fortunate one? Its
sales were modest, but it did sell while many books sell only a thousand or two. Returns were only 20 percent of net
sales, when often they run twice as high on new novels.
And the shrewd hypothetical publisher did not overprint, or
splurge on a big advertising campaign for an unsalable book,
or make any of the other mistakes that invite major loss.

He stays in business for several reasons. Frequently, even usually, he has a juvenile department or a textbook
line, or a paperback series, or any one or more of other
specialized divisions that are more dependable money-makers
and that carry part of the overhead of the trade department.
And while he has many books that will lose a lot more, he
hopes to have a few that are really major sellers and that
can bring large profits. It need cost no more to select and
edit a book that sells 100,000 copies than one that sells
5,000. Composition costs will become negligible, and printing and binding costs will be much less per copy because of
the greater efficiency of longer printing runs. Royalties will
run higher per copy, as most contracts provide that the royalty will increase from 10 percent of the retail price to 15
percent as sales increase. But all other per-copy prices
will be markedly less, and the profits to the publisher as
well as the returns to the author will be substantial.

The third and often the most important factor enabling the publisher to stay in business is the income from
subsidiary rights, especially from book clubs and from paperbound reprints. His contract with the author will always
provide that the publisher controls the reprint of the book in
those forms. The income is normally evenly shared with the

author. The author may convey to the publisher or reserve
for himself or his agent various other rights, such as dra-
matization, film, broadcast, serialization, or translation,
and sometimes British Commonwealth rights for publications
in English. If these rights are conveyed to the publisher,
his share of the income from them is usually less than half
and may be only 25 percent or, in certain cases, even 10
percent. When one reads of the sale of movie rights to a
book for $100,000 or more, the transaction is almost always
directly between the agent, acting for the author, and the
film producer. The publisher is rarely involved in such
bonanzas. Though confined generally to the more modest
reprint rights--whether hardbound, paperbound, or book
club--subsidiary rights income plays a major role in the e-
conomy of trade publishing.

On the average, it probably runs something over 8
percent of the income from the sales of hardcover books.
Our hypothetical book's share would hence have been $1,200
or a bit more for the publisher and an equal amount for the
author, enough to provide a thin edge of profit (about $500)
for the publisher and to increase the author's income from
the book by half, from $2,500 to $3,700. But in practice
the income from subsidiary rights is not distributed in this
even manner. Most books are never reprinted at all and
produce no subsidiary income, while a few books may hit a
jackpot. The sale of rights to a major book club will produce from $60,000 to $100,000 to be shared with the author.
A modestly successful--even an unsuccessful--reprint in a
mass-market paperbound series will bring in from $3,000
to $5,000; guarantees of a minimum income of $100,000 are
no longer great rarities for major books, with the actual
earnings more often than not being much larger; and guarantees have gone as high as $400,000.

These windfalls of book-club and reprint payments
come, of course, to the books that also achieve success in
the trade. To those that have shall be given. The consequence is that the economics of trade publishing somewhat
resembles that of a shrewd and informed bettor at the race
tracks, whose loss of a number of small bets is offset by an
occasional substantial win. Probably the great majority of
new "trade" books are published at a loss--which is usually
not a great one unless the publisher has grossly overestimated its sales potentials and overinvested in printing or advertising. The continuation of the whole flow of books is
thus dependent on how frequent and how "big" are the suc-

cesses that by their income from large trade sales and large subsidiary rights serve to create a profit margin offsetting the more frequent small losses.

It would be logical to suppose that this dependence on "best-sellers" with substantial subsidiary-rights income would cause publishers to confine their offerings to works that had a good chance of achieving that kind of audience, and to refuse to publish the works that, whatever their merit, offered little hope of large sales. Possibly there is a marginal effect of this kind. Certainly the statistics that indicate that American publishers issue many fewer new titles every year than those of Japan, Great Britain, or Western Germany are often quoted to suggest such a limitation. But these statistics are largely illusory, being based on differing methods of defining "books" and on the exclusion from the American figures of government publications. Probably the differences are minor and, where they exist, are in the area of highly specialized technical, scientific, and professional publications. There does not appear to be any reason to believe that fiction or poetry or essays or histories, biographies, and works on public affairs or science addressed to the layman, or any other "trade" books of any conceivable merit fail of publication. On the contrary, an examination of any considerable part of the more than 2,000 new novels published every year suggests not only that all with any perceptible merit are published, but that hundreds appear without that justification.

How do we escape such a constriction in the number of books issued? Why do publishers continue to publish so vast a number of books when any consideration of the economics of their industry would suggest that it would be very much more profitable to publish many fewer titles with a high average edition sold of each? One reason is an engagingly persistent if unwary optimism on the part of publishers. When there are several dozen different trade publishers to whom a novel may be submitted, it is not difficult to find at least one whose hopeful eye may see possibilities not apparent to others. And who knows, the public favor can fall on odd choices; if it does not sell, the loss will not be very great; and just maybe . . . .

A second reason is that if overhead costs are allocated pro rata among all titles published, as in our hypothetical case, most of them will be found to be unprofitable. Most publishers, however, will assume that they must in

any case rent space, pay a management, support editorial,
promotional, and sales staffs, and maintain warehousing and
shipping facilities. If a new manuscript being considered
promises to meet its direct costs and to contribute anything
at all toward these general overhead items--even though that
contribution may be less than a pro rata share--its publication may seem desirable. In economists' terms, publishers
are likely to measure the returns from any new manuscript
against the marginal or incremental cost of publishing it
rather than against the total costs.

Finally, the competition among hundreds of publishers
for publishable manuscripts is so great; the number of publishers (university presses, church publishers and the like)
having some freedom from the necessity of pursuing profits
is so large; and it is so relatively easy to establish new
houses to issue worthy manuscripts that may fail of publication elsewhere, that any vacuum that may be left by the lim-
iting practices of any single company or any number of companies is readily filled by others.

The economics of publishing hence permit the issuance of a most wide and varied range of writing, from comic books to the purest expressions of literature, from 25¢
infants' picture books to treatises on the most arcane area
of physics, from political tracts to prayerbooks. Its economics also makes publishing exceptionally hospitable to all the
winds of political and economic belief and to the unpopular
new forms of literary expression. This is true in part for
a reason already pointed out: that anyone may, at relatively little cost, gain access to the national market. A Com-
munist-oriented book-publishing house is, for example, quite
practical, while a Communist daily newspaper is impractical
and a Communist broadcasting station would be impossible.
But it is also true for a number of other reasons. The organization of the publishing industry makes each publisher a
broker between a variety of authors and their audiences rather than his being the spokesman for a point of view, as is
the publisher of a newspaper or magazine. A single publisher may well publish political figures of the right, the
left, and the center, hack writers of formula fiction as well
as the most sensitive of poets, and sexy stories as well as
manuals of chemical engineering. Hundreds of houses, each
actively searching for every possible opportunity to make a
dollar by bringing an author's product to an audience, even
a small and specialized one, assure that no voice for which
there is any listener is unheard. In the intense profit-seek-

ing drive of a highly competitive, atomized industry there is
a guarantee of the freedom of the press as effective as any
in the Constitution.

Moreover, the economics of the industry permits a
publisher to make money, or at least break even, if he can
find an audience of, say, five thousand purchasers for a book
over a two-year period. A general magazine, attempting a
broad national circulation, could hardly make do with less
than 100,000 people prepared to purchase every month at
least; a nationally broadcast television program in prime time
would have to assemble an audience of 5 million or so every
week. Hence books are able to cater to minority tastes and
interests in a way impossible to those media whose economics compel them to seek a larger audience. Nor do books
have to take into account the needs of their advertisers, as
do magazines, newspapers, and broadcasts. So long as it
offers some chance of returning the modest cost of publishing, a book can be issued solely on its own merits without
having to consider whether its purchasers make up an appropriate audience--in terms of size, interests, buying power, and mood--for the advertisement of a commodity. In
magazines, for example, the most inconsequential, hack-
written pieces on boating, stamp-collecting, bee-keeping, or
hi-fi receivers will be in active demand, because people interested in those subjects make up in each case a homogeneous market to which advertising can be profitably addressed
and hence for whom numerous magazines can be published.
But magazine outlets for a poem are limited, because people
interested in poetry do not make up a homogeneous market,
like people interested in stamp-collecting. From these pressures book publishing is happily free.

It is also remarkably free from the pressures of
censorship. Economic pressure on a book publisher can have
little effect. He is not exposed and vulnerable as a local
newspaper or broadcasting station is. He cannot be boy-
cotted, like a motion-picture theater. The censor's only
means of pressure against the publisher himself is to refuse
to buy the book, and the sort of controversy that accompanies such organized refusal is likely to stimulate so much interest as to sell far more copies of the book elsewhere. (I
am referring here to trade publishing; textbook and encyclopedia publishers are necessarily somewhat more exposed to
pressure.) Even if a publisher can be pressed into refusing
to publish a book, there remain hundreds of others, many of
whom will be prepared to consider it. The economic organi-

zation of book publishing thus equips it admirably for the issuance of writings of the widest possible variety, for the
smallest and most specialized audiences, and with the greatest freedom from pressures of conformity or censorship.

When we turn to the actual distribution of these publications to the people, however, the situation is quite different; and for the great majority of titles distribution is
limited, ineffective, and costly. In part this weakness in
distribution is a direct consequence of the strength of the industry in issuing materials. The very facts that about
15,000 new editions of the most diverse sorts appear annually, and that about 150,000 different titles are in print create the magnitude and difficulty of this task of making the
whole range of American publishing available to more than
180 million people in thousands of cities, towns, and villages
across the country. If it were harder to get a book published, it would be easier to get it distributed.

The traditional pattern of book distribution is, of
course, through bookstores. The publisher, through a sales
force and through advance advertising in trade publications,
tries to get bookstores to stock a book for sale. He then
tries to call public attention to the book in three ways: by
advertising to the public; by sending liberal numbers of free
review copies to newspapers, magazines, and technical journals; and by publicizing the book and its author as much as
possible in all the media of communications. The bookseller in turn tries to promote books he considers salable
by local advertising and direct mail (the cost of which may
be shared by the publisher) and by such methods as window
displays and word-of-mouth recommendations.

This method has severe limitations, both in scope and
in cost. In the first place the number of bookstores in the
United States is pitifully small. How many there are depends on what one calls a "bookstore," but there are perhaps
1,400 that stock a fairly wide representation of new hardbound books. Contrary to the general impression, the number of bookstores is increasing rather rapidly, but it remains completely inadequate to the effective national distribution of books. This is particularly true in small towns
and rural areas. Indeed, save for a few university communities and resort areas, it would be rare to find a good
bookstore in a city or town of less than 50,000.

Even where there is a bookstore, and a good large one, it can rarely stock more than 3,000 to 4,000 titles, of which half or more may be standard older titles. This is likely to mean that even in a good bookstore there is only about one chance in ten that a new book will be in stock and perhaps one in a hundred that an older one will be. Still more discouraging is the fact that even when a bookstore exists, and even when it stocks a book on its shelves, it will be exposed to only a tiny fraction of the population. I would guess that hardly more than 1 percent of the adult population are regular patrons of a bookstore.

The same kinds of limitation apply to advertising and promotion. The fact that each one of the thousands of titles every year must be separately advertised imposes almost insuperable obstacles in the way of effective national advertising. It is as though General Motors for each tenth Chevrolet had to change the name, design, and characteristics of the car and launch a new national advertising campaign to sell the next ten cars. We have seen how pitifully small must be the advertising budget for the average single title, with the consequence that only for a very limited number of books is anything possible beyond one or two modest insertions in media with a relatively limited circulation, among a specially interested audience of book buyers. The advertising problem (except perhaps for encyclopedias and book clubs) is thus wholly different from that of the advertiser of a single brand that remains on sale indefinitely. As compared with other industries, publishers spend an extraordinarily high proportion of their total revenue on advertising that has a regrettably small impact.

The same thing is true of reviews. Even The New York Times, which reviews many more books than any other journal addressed to the general public, covers only about 20 percent of the annual output. Many books of major importance in specialized fields go entirely unnoticed in such general media, and it is by no means unknown for even National Book Award winners to go unreviewed in the major national journals.

The real problem is with the solid, meritorious book that is neither a best-seller nor a major book-club choice and that is not reprinted in a mass-market paperbound edition. Thousands of such books are published annually, and in their myriad diversity and range of content is the triumph of publishing. Yet, in consequence of all the difficulties de-

scribed above, I suspect that for a typical book of this sort,
one would find that in the overwhelming majority of counties
in this country no copy had ever been seen in any bookstore
or library, and that it had never been reviewed or even mentioned in any local newspaper or in any magazine or broadcast regularly read or seen. All the manifold intellectual
and cultural resources offered in the vast annual flow of
books passes unnoticed by the great majority of Americans
and indeed unknown to them.

The fact that this method of distribution is ineffective
does not make it inexpensive. Most of what a customer pays
for a book in a bookstore goes not to get it written or printed
or published, but rather to get it distributed to him. Trade
books are usually sold to a bookseller at a discount that begins at 40 percent for multiple-copy (and some single-copy)
orders and may rise with the size of the order to 46 percent or even 48 percent, and they are usually sold under the
condition that the bookseller may return them for full credit
if he does not succeed in selling them. In other words, of
the $5.00 a customer may pay for a novel, the bookseller
may get $2.00, the printer about $1.00, the author about
75¢, and the publisher about $1.25. But of the $1.35 or
$1.40 expenses the publisher must meet from this (see a-
bove!), many are essentially distribution costs--sales, shipping, advertising and promotion--so that actually well over
half the five dollars goes for distribution. And yet it is
needed. Except for fast-moving best-sellers and some high-
priced items, the bookseller's 40 percent probably does not
meet his actual costs.

To break through these limitations, publishers have
resorted to three major devices: book clubs, paperbounds
sold through magazine wholesalers and other mass-market
channels, and direct sales. Direct sales have been remarkably successful. These have taken two forms: house-to-
house or office-to-office selling and mail sales. The former
is actually one of the oldest forms of book-selling in the
United States, and it was commonplace in the nineteenth century for complete sets of major authors and other important
works to be sold in that manner, often by subscription in advance of publication. Today, however, the need for high returns to salesmen permits this type of distribution only for
expensive sets or specialized volumes like encyclopedias and
medical and law books. More than one-fourth of the dollar
volume of book sales goes through this channel, but it is irrelevant to the distribution of general books.

Mail sales have been more versatile. A conventional
practice is to sell specialized, usually scholarly, books to
potential buyers who can be readily identified and easily
reached through specialized mailing lists or by relatively inexpensive advertising in learned or other specialized journals. Many university-press books are sold in this way.
When the potential purchasers of a book cannot be narrowly
defined as any specific professional group, the costs of selling by mail rise sharply. It is usually possible to meet
these costs in selling to the general public only if the work
is rather expensive (usually $10 or more) and if it offers
something more to the buyer than the pleasure of reading it:
for example, pride in a handsome and expensive possession
like an art book or some aid to advancement. Neither method of direct sale is feasible for bringing most general books
to the general public.

Book clubs and paperbounds were both adapted from
the two principal magazine distribution techniques. The book
club distributes books to subscribers through the mail, like
magazine subscriptions. The mass-market paperbound in
fact uses for its distribution the very same national distributors, local wholesalers, and individual newsstands used by
magazines for their individual-copy circulation. Both these
methods have been overwhelmingly successful in enlarging
the audience for books and increasing the number distributed.
Last year about 39 million hardbound adult "trade" (that is,
general) books were sold outside book-club channels, together with 26 million higher-priced "trade" paperbounds sold
primarily through bookstores. This contrasts with about 280
million paperbounds sold primarily through mass-market
channels and nearly 80 million books distributed through book
clubs. This means that of approximately 425 million general
adult books sold in the United States last year, about 360
million went through book club or mass-market channels.
And only 39 million of the 65 million moving through traditional channels were hardbound. When it is further considered that a very considerable proportion of this 39 million
copies was bought by libraries, it becomes evident that four
general books out of five bought by or for individual American adults come to them through book-club or mass-market
channels. And many of the remaining fifth come as gifts
rather than as purchases by the consumer himself.

These methods of sale have succeeded because they
have surmounted the physical constraints of the bookstore and
lessened the barriers of inertia. Rather than decide on a

book and seek it out, one does nothing and the book club
brings it. Paperbounds lie across one's daily path--on the
newsstand, in the drugstore, in the grocery, at the cigar
counter, in the bus terminal, at the railway station.   They
have also succeeded because they have sharply reduced the
price of books, particularly in the case of the mass-market
paperbound editions, which may sell for as little as one-
eighth or even one-tenth the cost of an original hardbound
edition.   Indeed, the two go hand-in-hand: the ubiquitous display would be impractical for a book priced above the level
of impulse buying; the price would be impossible except for
mass distribution.

      Why, then, not publish all or most books--and espe-
cially new books for the general audience--in paper bindings
and with the same low prices achieve the same mass sale?
A glance back to the analysis of the price structure of hardbound books should give the answer.   Remember that of the
price of a popular $5.00 book, from 50¢ to 75¢ goes to the
author and only about $1.00 to the manufacturer and most of
the rest to distribution costs.   It is obvious that the sorts
of savings achieved in mass-market paperbound editions must
come primarily from the manner of distribution, not the
manner of binding.   Indeed, if books could be manufactured
absolutely free, a $5.00 book would still be a $4.00 book
unless other costs were reduced as well.   Of course, the
use of paper instead of board-and-cloth binding saves money;
so do glueing in place of sewing and the use of smaller type
and less expensive paper.   So especially does printing
100,000 books at once on high-speed rotary press.   Only
books that can sell that many copies fairly quickly can a-
chieve that kind of savings.   Royalties come down too.   On
the fifty-cent edition they will be about 3¢, not the 75¢ of
the popular $5.00 edition, and the author will normally get
only half of that if it is a reprint.   Editorial costs go way
down, because most paperbounds are reprints that have already been edited, and the selection process is far less costly.   So, of course, do administrative, shipping, warehousing, and accounting costs per copy, when they are divided
by the millions of copies flowing from the press.

      But the principal savings must be found where the
principal costs are found--in distribution.   A mass-market
paperbound must be sold with a cost for retailing of no more
than 8¢ to 15¢ per copy and generally with only an infini-
tesimal cost for per-copy sales, advertising, and promotion.
This means that the books must essentially sell themselves.

They must be books of the sort that 100,000 or more people will buy on impulse if they see them displayed, either because the book or the author is well-known or because the subject or theme commands interest. And there must be an opportunity for exposure, because books can be sold in this way only to the extent that they are displayed in high-traffic locations for buyers to see. It is also obvious that with so small a return to the retailer, he cannot ordinarily afford to maintain and check extensive stocks or to order for a customer individual titles he does not happen to have in stock at the moment. Except in some bookstores specializing in paperbounds, the customer is dependent on the more or less accidental content of the racks at any given outlet at any given time. The lower price of mass-market paperbounds is hence not due primarily to its binding, or even to the lower cost of manufacture in general, but to savings in editing, introducing, and distributing it. These savings in turn are possible only for certain kinds of books, and only for a number of books not greater than can receive adequate exposure in available outlets. It has been possible through mass-market paperbounds to distribute billions of copies of thousands of titles to a much wider audience than could be reached by other means; but it is not possible to solve the problems of books in general merely by binding them in paper.

Many of the same observations apply to the higher-priced paperbacks usually published in much smaller editions (typically 5000 to 20,000 copies) and distributed through conventional trade channels. The higher price not only permits a smaller edition; it also allows a much larger per-copy return to the bookseller. This in turn permits more selective stocking, personal assistance to customer, and special ordering (usually with a small added service charge) of books not in stock. Many more titles can be accommodated in this pattern of distribution, and new series appear frequently. A recent sampling shows that slightly more than half of the 2,500 paperbacks issued in a three-month period were in this $1.00 to $3.00 range. These so-called "trade" paperbacks are, however, like mass-market paperbacks, dependent in large measure upon impulse buying of copies on display. The number in print has now far outrun the capacity of the largest paperback bookstore even to stock, much less to display. In consequence, paperbacks are beginning to encounter some of the same distribution problems as hardbacks. As soon as the savings of the largely automatic distribution of a reasonably small number of titles, from among which the user has only a limited choice, begin to diminish, costs begin to rise. When it becomes necessary to finance a distribution mechanism that will allow a user to take realistic advantage of the fact that nearly 20,000 books are available in paperbacks, the price of paperbacks must go up. This is indeed happening and, though production costs have also increased, higher distribution costs are perhaps the principal explanation of the recent trend towards higher paperback prices. The more broadly the paperbound format is used for general publishing, the more nearly do its price structure and distribution problems approach those of hardbound publishing.

The consequence of these economic factors is that American publishing functions responsively, even brilliantly, in meeting national needs for the issuance of books; but it is able to distribute effectively only those for which the audience is either very large or else very specialized and clearly defined. It can do a very good job for the scientific, technical, scholarly, or professional book whose potential buyers are reached through specialized journals or mailing lists. And it can do a good job with the classics and very popular books for which the potential audience can justify large-scale advertising and stocking in bookstores and distribution by book-club or paperbound methods. It is the great body of books in between, for which there is neither a mass audience nor an identifiable specialized audience with which, relatively speaking, we fail. And yet it is in making just such books available that book publishing can perform its most distinctive function, providing a communication service that can be given by no other medium.

Publishing and book distribution are in a period of very rapid change today. Some of those changes have been viewed with apprehension as further emphasizing a limited number of intensively sold, commercially profitable books to the derogation of the broader flow of literature. Among these changes are the merger of a number of publishing houses into larger aggregations, and the transformation of a number of others into publicly held corporations in which there is substantial outside investment presumably interested only in financial returns. The effect of the mergers on trade publishing has been generally overestimated. Most recent mergers have involved bringing together units from different areas of publishing, not competitive with each other, into a horizontally integrated company, or else have not in-

volved trade publishing at all.   Only two or three mergers
of consequence have coalesced companies both of whose prior
interests were primarily in trade publishing.   And these
have been offset in part by the rise of new companies.

Less easy to evaluate is the consequence of "going
public," since publicly held corporations have previously been
almost unknown in trade publishing; but it will almost certainly be small.   Even if it should have an effect in curtail-
ing or redirecting the trade publishing activities of any single
house, it can hardly affect the output of American publishing
generally.   Dozens of substantial trade houses remain under
personal or family ownership, new houses are steadily being
established, and any books refused as a result of new policies in one house can be quickly accepted by another.   The
greater size and strength of publishing houses may indeed
have quite the opposite effect of providing new venture capital and enlarging the capacity to publish and distribute a
widely diversified list.

Also feared has been the rise of discount-selling of
books.   Though this has been widespread only in some metropolitan areas (notably New York) and has been confined to
limited numbers of best-selling titles, it has been viewed as
the death-knell of general bookstores.   Undoubtedly it has
cost many bookstores some considerable numbers of sales of
certain titles to which they could have normally looked for a
major part of their profits.   But the impact seems not to be
as large as one might have feared.   As we have noted, the
number of bookstores is, in fact, growing rather rapidly on
a national basis; and sales seem to be rising even in some
of those quite near large discount houses.   Other trends toward a broadening of the market for a wide variety of titles
and a lessening of emphasis on a few "best-sellers" may
help to offset this situation.

Much more important are the hopeful trends.   One of
the most important is the rapid growth of library service.
This is not only important in itself, as bringing a wide diversity of books to people throughout the country, including
small town and rural areas, but also as providing the publisher with a market for many serious books addressed to a
small but general audience, which it might not otherwise be
possible to publish at all.   This is not the place to discuss
library development, but it is a very large and important
factor in the economy of publishing as well as in the enrich-
ment of education.

Also very hopeful are the educational developments that have led directly to a far wider and more varied demand for books at every level, from elementary school through college, and which in time should lead to a general elevation of the intellectual interests and book-buying habits of the American people. It has been a principal factor in the rapid growth of paperbound publishing and the broadening of its scope.

The larger and more varied the book market, the better it can be served. With each major increase in book-buying, more titles can progress to each level of book distribution. The doubling of per-capita book purchases in the last decade for example, has already made it possible to keep in print in paperbacks not merely a few hundred mysteries, westerns, and romances--as was the case at the beginning of the period--but nearly 20,000 titles covering every aspect of literature and scholarship. The same market growth has made it possible to expand book-club distribution from a few dozen broadly popular general titles a year to the many hundreds that can now justify distribution through one of the nearly one hundred specialized book clubs. It has made possible the opening of the paperback and general book departments in the hundreds of college stores already mentioned. The proliferation of serious titles in such fields as science, public affairs, and international relations is another consequence.

There is every reason to suppose that the market will continue to grow rapidly and will double again within the decade. Simple increase in the adult population will accomplish much of this. The postwar crop of babies which has accounted for our population boom has not yet affected the market for adult books, but it will have an enormous impact on that market within the decade. So will the explosion of college enrollments, which will add an additional 3,500,000 to 4,000,000 students within the decade. The effect of this will be immediate in the books that students buy for themselves and in those that are bought for new or enlarged college libraries. It will be even greater in its effect on the educational characteristics of the future population. We shall soon have twice as many well-to-do college-educated adults as we have now.

The effect of this vastly increased book market not only on the size but also on the character of book publishing and distribution will be great. Books that can be published at all now can then be published in editions two or three times as large, with accompanying economies in manufacture and distribution.   Small bookstores can become larger, and towns with no bookstores will be able to afford them.   Mass distribution can be achieved for many titles that can now have only limited sale.   There is a vicious circle in much publishing now; small markets leading to small editions, high costs, and inefficient distribution, ultimately restricting the market even further.   The past decade has shown that for hundreds, even thousands of titles, a larger market can transform this into an upward spiral in which larger editions lead to lower costs and more and more efficient distribution which breaks through into even larger markets.

There is every reason to hope that over the next ten to twenty-five years an even more rapid increase in demand can effect such a transformation in the economics of publishing on a yet broader basis, embracing the whole of 'book publishing.   If so, the consequence in enriching and diversifying the intellectual and cultural resources realistically available to Americans generally could be beneficent beyond measurement.

Book Publishing's Hidden Bonanza

By Curtis G. Benjamin, Consultant to McGraw-Hill, Inc.
and former President and Chairman of the McGraw-Hill
Book Company.

From Saturday Review, pp. 19-21+, April 18, 1970. Copyright 1970 Saturday Review, Inc. Reprinted by permission.

The division of the book world most readily recognized by the general public is between textbook publishing
and general (or "trade") book publishing.   Indeed, the U. S.
book industry has for many years divided itself in this way
by maintaining two trade associations: the American Book
Publishers Council for producers of general books, and the
American Educational Publishers Institute for producers of
textbooks and related teaching materials.   But this dichotomy loses validity every year as educators continue to move
sharply away from the traditional one-subject-one-book teaching practice.   In fact, most publishers today, foreseeing a
sure meeting of the twain, think their two trade associations
should be merged; this move seems imminent.

Another division, and a more natural one, is between
what are known within the industry as literary books and
non-literary books.   The first category includes fiction, biography, poetry, drama, and general literature.   The second encompasses several classifications of practical and professional works in such subject areas as agriculture, business, economics, education, law, medicine, science, and
technology; and it includes a multitude of handbooks, manuals, directories, statistical reports, sets of numerical
tables and data, and "how-to" guides.   Most textbooks, by
nature as well as subject matter, fall into this second category.   The classifications of the respective categories have
been used since the turn of the century by the Publishers'
Weekly annual statistical reports.

This division represents two worlds of publishing,
each quite different and separate, and sufficient unto itself.

There is, in fact, a far greater distinction between literary and nonliterary houses than between textbook and nontextbook houses.

During the 1960's, there occurred an astonishing explosion of nonliterary books. This unexpected development was doubly astonishing in that it was within the hardcover realm, and it came at the end of a long and little noticed sea change that began some forty years earlier. Although the explosion was a big one, not many people heard it, or even heard about it. This was because it occurred in the hidden part of the book-industry iceberg, the much larger part that is all but invisible to the general public, and that is not much celebrated within the industry itself.

In the early years of the century, newly published literary works outnumbered nonliterary works by two to one. Then, starting with the 1930s, there came a change in this imbalance; the production of literary works declined, while that of nonliterary works increased in proportion. The decline of the former was caused presumably by restricted spending for nonessentials during the Depression.

In the following decade, the 1940s, literary works declined a little more, while nonliterary works climbed a little higher. Then both categories climbed sharply through the 1950s, and by the end of that decade the two were almost even. Happy days were here again for all kinds of literary books, and for fiction especially. Income from sales of reprint, book-club, and motion-picture rights gave novels a new lease on life, and restored their production to an interesting level of profitability.

Then came the 1960s and the spectacular leap ahead in the production of nonliterary works. In that decade alone, the number of such works produced annually increased by 164 percent, while literary titles increased by only 29 percent. The imbalance of the earlier years was completely reversed, and by 1969 new nonliterary works outnumbered new literary works by more than two to one.

The long-range change over this forty-year period was even more striking: Annual nonliterary book production increased by some 380 percent, while literary production increased by only 40 percent.

The story is dramatically revealed in Chart I. What

NEW TITLES

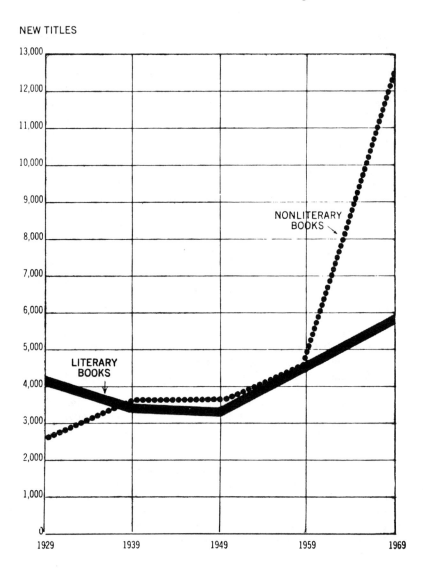

cannot be revealed as simply are the more subtle mutations
in the health and behavior of the book industry that came
with the change.   Certainly, the industry as a whole became
more stable, more vigorous, more venturesome, and more
prosperous.   Also, it grew enough in size and affluence to

to be recognized nationally as a moderately important area
of commercial enterprise and financial speculation.   How
much each of the subject-matter components contributed to
the nonliterary explosion can be seen in Table I, which
shows the historical thrust as well as the total surge of the
category.   Note in particular the astonishing records of books

Table I: Books Published Annually--by Subject

Literary Books	1929	1939	1949	1959	1969
Biography	738	628	595	776	1, 161
Fiction	2, 142	1, 547	1, 644	2, 437	2, 717
General Literature	572	584	535	836	724
Poetry & Drama	727	657	574	499	1, 254
	4, 179	3, 416	3, 348	4, 548	5, 856

(Increase 1969 over 1929: 1, 677 titles,
or 40. 1 percent.)

Nonliterary Books					
Agriculture	82	129	191	129	260
Business	213	357	306	422	683
Education	317	315	254	417	842
Sports & Games	130	219	235	259	734
Home Economics	53	148	263	181	314
Law	116	160	267	302	525
Medicine	402	431	450	590	1, 190
Sociology & Economics	484	854	548	625	4, 462
Science	424	523	676	1, 033	2, 353
Technology	359	461	455	736	1, 035
	2, 580	3, 597	3, 645	4, 694	12, 398

(Increase 1969 over 1929: 9, 818 titles,
or 380. 5 per cent.)

in the social sciences and in the natural sciences and technology.

      It is amusing to note the aloofness of certain lofty-
minded literary publishers and commentators who like to describe many kinds of nonliterary works as "nonbooks."   The
publishers of these books laugh all the way to the bank over
this disdainful characterization.   They know that these "non-

books'' are in great demand, that they have high societal
value, and that they are of large importance to the overall
resources and economy of the book industry.   They know,
too, that in many a large, multi-interest publishing firm,
the profit earned by nonliterary titles bankrolls the whole
house; that more often than not this profit provides large
sums for investments in glamorous but uncertain literary ventures of great worth and prestige--ventures of the very kind
that always are warmly applauded by the literary buffs.

Another possible division of the book publishing world
is the paperback/hardcover bisection.   This division actually is not as sharp or as meaningful within the industry as it
is in the public's mind.   Strangely, one of the most persistent of current myths about book publishing is that the two
kinds of books are locked in a battle for survival.   Indeed,
many people on the fringes of the publishing world now believe firmly that paperbacks are in and hardcovers are out.
This belief has gone so far that many students today suspect the value of any book that has not been reprinted in
somebody's paperback series.   I, myself, often have to suffer the pity of certain of my young friends when I insist that
hardcover books are here to stay.   To them paperbacks have
a high public visibility--at bookstores, newsstands, drug-
stores, supermarkets, railroad stations, bus terminals, and
airports everywhere.   Besides, they have had the truth of
the matter from their teachers and from numerous reporters,
columnists, lecturers, TV commentators, and book reviewers.

As an example of how the public can be misinformed
about the fortune of paperbacks and the fate of hardcovers,
a statement in The New York Times of January 31, written
as background to a review of a recently published history of
the Houghton Mifflin Company, read:

> The economics of publishing today has reached
> such a stage that the hardcover book is almost
> a liability to the man who brings it out.   Since
> all the money is in the subsidiary rights, in
> what can be spun off in the form of movie op-
> tions, stage adaptations, paperback rights, di-
> gests and the like, the publisher wishes the
> hardcover would go away and leave him alone.

Imagine with what dismay this statement was read by
those insiders who know for certain that in recent years

hardcover books have provided almost 90 percent of our industry's sales and about 95 percent of its profits. Naturally, the question arises why the public fancy has been so far misled. Why has the paperback "explosion" been so over-celebrated? Why has its supposed impact on hardcover publishing been so overstated? The answer, of course, is that large segments of the general public, and some people in book publishing as well, want it that way. Indeed, they want it that way so badly that they refuse to believe hard facts and figures. They simply will not believe that mass-market paperback publishing is, economically speaking, only a small part of the total publishing world. Nor will they believe that the paperback explosion actually has been more helpful than hurtful to hardcover publishing.

The foregoing observation should not be taken in any way as a denial of the status of paperback publishing. Everyone knows that the paperback explosion of the 1950s had large importance of its own. Everyone recognizes that paperbacks, and especially mass-market paperbacks, also have high and special societal values. The insider knows, too, that paperbacks have made a large indirect contribution to the overall prosperity of the U. S. book industry. He sees that they serve to hook thousands of new readers every year who would never have started on the hardcover stuff. Thus, he knows that the importance of the many millions of paperbacks sold each year is far greater than the dollar income and profit derived from their sale.

In this light, it is especially regrettable that paperback publishing had several difficult years in the second half of the 1960s. Although between 300 million and 350 million copies of mass-market paperbacks were sold annually, some of their major producers had rather rough going. The trouble came not from a lack of buyers, but rather from excessive payments for reprint rights and from costly competition for market outlets. Some of this trouble was offset by newfound success with what have been dubbed "instant paperbacks"--meaning quick reprints in large quantities of certain public documents of wide popular appeal, such as the report of the Warren Commission. These quick reprints, in some instances, have put paperback books into fairly direct competition with the news media, and thus have given a "new dimension" to the book industry.

In fairness, the quotation from the Times is true of fiction; still, fiction represents less than 10 percent of the

present annual output of new books. In any case, it appears
that the Times reviewer, like most other outside observers
of the publishing scene, was totally unaware of the great
hardcover explosion that had occurred on the nether side of
his world.

The striking aspect of the book market as a total aggregate is that, while the annual production of new books of
all kinds increased by only 40 percent in the three decades
that ended in 1959, the increase in the subsequent ten years
was over 100 percent. It was inevitable, of course, that
there would come with this sharp increase an intensification
of the perennial cry that too many books are being produced.
Unfortunately, this cry has been repeated through even the
years of the book industry's greatest and soundest growth.
It comes from certain breast-beating publishers who loftily
call for "fewer and better books." What they plainly want,
of course, is to cut out the other fellow's trash. Often they
want also to eliminate all those dull "non-books" that no one
ever sees.

Nearly all these advocates of fewer and better books
are literary buffs. Observing the publishing scene narrowly, they look no deeper than the rising total numbers of
books produced annually, and then declare positively that the
market cannot possibly absorb so many new titles. Often
they wail, correlatively, that quality is being sacrificed for
quantity, that bad books are driving out good books, and
that the book industry is going to hell in a crassly overload-
ed handbasket. Such talk has always been popular with literary audiences and with reporters looking for stories about
the charismatic world of publishing. Yet, it has never made
sense, and it never made less sense than in the 1960s. For
example, how could the great increase in scientific and technical books have anything whatever to do with the quality of
the new fiction of the decade? And did the slowdown in published general literature really improve its quality? No,
the postulate of fewer and better books patently has no general value as a working principle for the industry.

Far from being choked up in recent years, book markets have actually been expanding rapidly in size and recep-
tivity. In fact, sales of almost all kinds of books climbed
sharply through the 1960s. In that decade, total dollar volume of industry sales increased by almost 150 percent,
from $1.106-billion to $2.760-billion. Much of this gain
came, to be sure, from higher prices and inflated dollars--

about a fourth of it, roughly. With an adjustment for this
inflation factor, the real ten-year gain was about 110 percent. In the same period, the country's Gross National
Product, after application of the same kind of implicit de-
flators, grew by only 50 percent. It is clear, then, that the
book industry's growth was far greater than that of the nation's economy as a whole.

In the longer view, looking back through the earlier
years of sea change, the book industry as a whole in a way
scored a truly remarkable long-term growth record, but in
another way it seemed not to keep up with its true potential.
Some interesting comparative figures on forty-year growth
trends appear in Table II. According to these figures, the
book industry in sales growth again far exceeded the long-
term growth of the national economy. (The dollar figures
for both book sales and GNP are adjusted to 1929 values--
and who won't be shocked to see that the 2.760-billion of
1969 sales dollars converts to only 1.290-billion of 1929
sales dollars?)

Table II: Comparative Growth Figures

	Number of Titles Published Annually	Value of Book Sales* ($Million)	Value of U.S. GNP* ($ Billion)	Number of College Graduates (Million)
1929	10,187	$ 199	$ 104.4	1.7
1939	10,640	178	108.7	3.4
1949	10,892	NA	167.9	5.3
1959	14,876	675	244.3	8.3
1969	29,579	1,290	368.3	13.8
1969 over 1929 Actual	190 percent			712 percent
1969 over 1929 Adjusted		548 percent.	253 percent	

*Stated in 1929 dollars

On the other hand, looking at the long-term growth
in the nation's population of college graduates, one can ask
whether the book industry has not failed to make the most of
its growing opportunity. Assuming that college graduates
represent the country's hard core of book buyers, it appears
that publishers have not kept up with the natural growth of

their markets.   (In the forty-year period, the college graduate population increased eightfold, while book sales increased only sixfold.)   Indeed, it can be fairly said that the
industry as a whole has been riding rather than making the
long wave of its good fortune.

        The publishers of educational and reference books
rode high on the wave through the 1960s.   The injection of
massive federal funds into education and library budgets
caused a soaring of sales that reached a truly dizzying
height in 1966: In that year, an aberration in government
disbursement practice caused most of the funds for two federal fiscal years to be spent in the one calendar year.   In
the following three years, there was a disappointing slacken-
ing in the sale of textbooks and related instructional materials, and of encyclopedias, dictionaries, atlases, etc.   Still
the publishers of such works, always more prosperous than
general book publishers, never had it better.   In the decade,
their sales increased by 156 percent.   Their net profits
failed to soar proportionately, largely because the costs of
intensified competition exacted a heavy toll as more and
more firms rushed to what was for them a newfound and unfamiliar mother lode.

        Many inside observers were bemused by one particu-
lar behavioral response of educational publishers in the
1960s.   This was the alacrity and enthusiasm with which
many reputedly turgid textbook firms answered the call of
educators for more and larger multi-unit instructional packages.   When teachers began some years ago to move away
from the conventional textbook as a monolithic instructional
instrument, many textbook publishers pushed to the head of
the parade.   Sure, they could supply rather quickly the needed multi-unit packages containing core text materials, supplementary readers, laboratory manuals, workbooks, tests,
and whatever else was wanted.   Some could, and did, supply
even larger and more costly multimedia packages (including
films and tapes), which were scooped up by the more affluent school systems and certain government-financed special
programs.   All this explains in part the juiced-up growth in
the educational publishers' sales volume.   It also explains
how many an old-line textbook firm quickly acquired a re-
freshing stimulant and a higher sense of professional responsibility.   Thus again did progress and prosperity go hand
in hand.

        The curious phenomenon that helped to produce in the

1960s an inordinate increase of scientific and technical books had a powerful effect on publishing through many years; I have called this, by analogy, the "twigging phenomenon." It can best be described as the continual furcation and fractionation of scientific and technical knowledge, and, hence, of the subject matter of books in these fields. Naturally, this endless fractionation has resulted in the publication each year of hundreds of highly specialized books for groups of readers that are no larger today than they were ten or twenty years ago, despite the fact that our total population of scientists and engineers has almost quadrupled in the past two decades. The specialists need and write books on proliferated and refined subjects; the technical publisher who properly serves his clientele must, of course, publish them in proliferated numbers.

In my analogy, the subjects of such books represent the twigs on the tree of scientific and technical knowledge. Although the tree itself is perhaps five times as big as it was twenty years ago, the twigs are still the same size-- and so are the markets for the specialized books. This phenomenon explains in large part why publishers of scientific and technical books have had to scramble to keep up with their markets, and why these particular markets have so readily absorbed the greatly escalated numbers of new titles published in the past decade.

Finally, another, but not so subtle, phenomenon that worked with force on the book industry in the 1960s was the wide impulse for corporate mergers and for related marriages, in some instances, between the electronics industry and book publishing. Many of the mergers were impelled by "cross-media" marriages, and all the latter were inspired by rationalized dreams of synergistically induced extra-dividend happiness. The industrial giants (hardware grooms) happily took to wife many carefully selected bedmates among the available book firms (software brides). "We have the hardware, they have the software," General Sarnoff is reported to have said when RCA acquired Random House in 1965.

Then what happened? It is, of course, too early to say for sure, but two things now seem quite obvious to insiders.

First, the hardware-software marriages, though widely celebrated in the press and greatly feared by many in the

book industry, have been tried and found wanting. The syn-
ergistic effect has not come off as expected; to date, the
unions have been disappointingly unproductive of profitable
hybrids.   Clearly, computers and books have not mixed so
readily and effectively as many people believed they would.
Consequently, some high-powered grooms already have been
heard to grumble about their brides, many of which were
bought at quite fancy prices.   At the same time, many relatively low-powered book publishers have unexpectedly been
enjoying life as millionaires.   Thus, by the end of the decade, the miscegenetic marriages were rapidly going out of
style.   Maybe we shall see some annulments or spin-off di-
vorces in the 1970s.   Even so, many publishing houses will
have been provided, meanwhile, with more adequate working
capital and more progressive management.

Second, the many mergers and cross-media marriages
have not resulted, as widely supposed, in a baneful concentration of book publishing in the hands of a few large and
powerful corporate complexes and conglomerates.   To be
sure, many independent houses, both large and small, have
become operating units in a wide variety of much larger corporate structures.   But, at the same time, many new and
growing firms have come along to take their places in the
ranks of the independents.   In fact, contrary to popular belief, these ranks have been more than filled every year.
Actually, there were more independent book houses in the
United States at the end than at the beginning of the 1960s,
just as there were more at the end than at the beginning of
the 1950s.   Anyone who doubts this statement can be self-
convinced by counting the number of independent firms listed
in Literary Market Place (Bowker's annual guide to book publishing) for certain years.   He will find that there were 508
in 1949; 638 in 1959; and 675 in 1969.

No, the book industry is not about to be gobbled up
or monopolized by a few large and sinister industrial octo-
puses--not, at least, for some time to come.

Myths About Publishing

By John Fischer, Editor-in-Chief, Harper's Magazine.

Copyright © 1963, by Harper's Magazine, Inc. Reprinted from the July, 1963 issue of Harper's Magazine by permission of the author.

Geoffrey Wagner, a British novelist now living in this country, announced recently in an English magazine that, "American publishing has become big business." In his view, this is a calamity. "Most small publishers of interest," he says, are being swallowed up by a few big firms. The survivors, he claims, are adopting a "blockbuster technique" which has "resulted in astronomical pre-publication deals, movie tie-ins, etc." Although "the killings are much bigger than they used to be," Mr. Wagner believes this is a bad thing, especially for novelists. It helps nobody but the insolent and materialistic publishers, "gloating over [their] stock exchange listings."

This lament is simply an echo of rumors which have been rustling around in the American (and British) literary world for several years. So long as they were confined to this milieu--notoriously flighty and gossip-prone--they could do little harm. About 1961, however, they reached Wall Street, which is even more susceptible to rumors, fads, and hunches. Soon a lot of supposedly hardheaded brokers, speculators, and investment counselors convinced themselves that publishing really was becoming a big business, with an extraordinary growth potential.

The upshot was that a good many people got badly burned. They started buying publishing stocks--the relatively few available to the public on the stock exchanges and over-the-counter--with no more discrimination than they had shown a little earlier, when they plunged into the so-called space-age and electronics industries. Prices shot up, in spite of warnings from several worried publishers that there

was no rational basis for such enthusiasm.   The boom was
brief.   In 1962 publishing stocks dropped as swiftly as they
had risen, to an average of less than half of their previous
highs.

At this writing, however, they are beginning to creep
up again.   Brokers are issuing surveys of the publishing industry; some investment funds are showing an interest; and
even a few authors--inspired perhaps by accounts such as
Mr. Wagner's--have recently bought into publishing firms.
Consequently it might be of some use to try to sort out the
facts from the myths about publishing; and to look at the various parts of the business--such as textbook, paperback,
juvenile, and "trade" publishing--which operate in quite different ways.   (It would be unfair to expect Mr. Wagner to
do this.   After all, he specializes in fiction.)

To begin with, is publishing actually Big Business?
In comparison with other industries--steel, chemicals,
automobiles, air lines, or even the ladies' garment trade--
it is quite small.   The total sales of all American book publishers climbed above $1 billion a year only in 1960--and
that includes all texts, encyclopedias, reference books, and
paperbacks, as well as trade books: i.e., ordinary hardbound fiction and non-fiction sold through bookstores.   For
the last decade book sales have been growing at a steady but
unspectacular rate of about 10 percent a year; they may total
close to $1.5 billion in 1963.

Do a few big firms dominate the industry?
Again, no.   Publishing is one of the most competitive
of all businesses.   Nobody can be quite sure how many firms
are engaged in it, since anybody can bring out a book now
and then for only a modest investment.   But if you count only those firms which published at least five books in 1962,
you would find (according to Publishers' Weekly) 470 of them.
No one company published as much as 3 percent of the total
number of titles.

Are "most small publishers of interest" being swallowed up
by their giant competitors?
Far from it.   Every year some companies disappear,
through bankruptcy or merger, but new ones constantly take
their place.   Today there are more firms in the business
than ever before--and some of the liveliest and most "interesting" are only a few years old.

The representative firm--if one can speak of such a thing in so diverse an industry--probably has got bigger (in sales volume and number of titles published) in recent years. In part, this is due to the natural growth of population and of the whole economy.   Then, too, rising costs of paper, printing, postage, and everything else have forced publishers to look for every possible economy; and some savings do result from large-scale operations.   As a consequence, many houses have tried to round out their line with paperback, juvenile, and other departments, in addition to the traditional trade books.

This seems, however, to be a self-limiting process. Publishing is a peculiarly personal business.   Whenever a firm gets so big that it can no longer give constant, intimate attention to each author--if it begins to turn out books like so many cans of beans--then it probably is on the verge of a decline.   Its writers will soon drift away to smaller, nimbler, more imaginative publishers.   It is astonishing how quickly a publisher can gather a stable of first-rate authors. If he can show them that he is primarily interested in them and their work . . . in producing the best possible books, rather than the fastest possible buck.   For this reason, every successful publisher has been editorial-minded--in some sense, a professional man.   He must of course be a competent businessman as well; but if his business grows to the point where he has to worry more about management than about writing, he is in trouble.   Hence it is most unlikely that any one company will ever dominate publishing, in the way that General Motors and U.S. Steel dominate their industries.

How about those financial killings?
Another myth.   Publishers had a pretty good year in 1962, but on the average they probably earned only about 4 percent on their sales after taxes.   The best houses (not necessarily the largest) did somewhat better; many did worse. Indeed, any publisher considers himself lucky when he barely breaks even on the bookstore sale of his general list; for any profit, he looks to subsidiary income from reprints and book clubs, and to specialized works such as juveniles and textbooks.   Contrary to common belief, the publisher seldom gets a share of any film, TV, or magazine rights income; ordinarily all that goes to the author.

Those "astronomical pre-publication deals, movie tie-ins, etc." are exceedingly rare--much rarer than they were

in Hollywood's heyday. In fact, most publishers refuse to
make pre-publication reprint deals, for an obvious business
reason: if a book sells well in its original hardbound edition, it will fetch a better price from the reprint houses
than it could when its sales potential was untested. The
same thing holds for film rights--although occasionally an
established popular novelist does make a movie sale before
his new book is published, or even written.

**Well, then, why is Wall Street taking over the publishing
industry?**
        It isn't.   Thirteen publishing companies are listed on
the New York Stock Exchange.   About two dozen more are
publicly owned, with stock traded over-the-counter.   The
great majority of firms--more than four hundred of them,
including some of the largest--are still privately owned, by
individuals, families, or small groups operating in effect as
partnerships.

      Most of the houses that have "gone public" in recent
years did so for one of three reasons:

      1.   To facilitate a merger--as, for example, when a
trade publisher joins forces with a textbook firm, to offer a
more complete line of books and more effective marketing
than either could offer alone.

      2.   To raise capital for expansion.

      3.   To avoid destruction by inheritance taxes.   If a
firm is owned entirely or in large part by one man, his
heirs might have to liquidate the business in order to pay
the inheritance taxes.   Consequently the founder of a publishing house may--as he gets on in years--convert it into a public company, in order to spread the ownership and to get
cash in advance for the tax collector.   Or, as in one recent
case, he may prefer to merge with a company which already
is publicly owned, and whose publishing policies he respects.

**Is public ownership, even on a small scale, a bad thing for
literature?**
        In theory, it could be.   David Dempsey sug-
gested a few weeks ago in the Saturday Review that:
"The fact that it is publicly held changes a company's viewpoint.   The head of a firm can no longer afford to indulge
quite so many of his personal whims.   A very considerable
number of great authors--Conrad is the supreme example--

got their start on the poor business judgment of their publishers. With the old family-owned houses, this could be
done, and we were all the richer.   But when stockholders
expect an operating profit, year in and year out, it becomes
more difficult. "

     This apparently is what bothers Geoffrey Wagner.   In
his article he complained that "today, books are published,
not authors . . . few younger novelists can count on being
followed through a number of books in the way not only possible but probable a century ago."   In other words, if a
fledgling novelist writes two or three books which the public
refuses to buy, his publisher may not be eager to bring out
a fourth.

     True enough.   Most publishers now probably will not
carry an unprofitable novelist at a loss for quite as long as
they would have done before World War II.   The reason,
however, may be different from that cited by Mr. Dempsey
and Mr. Wagner.

     For fiction has been losing ground to non-fiction for
at least forty years.   Back in the 'twenties, readers bought
roughly two novels in their original editions for every one
non-fiction book; today the reverse is true. *   So in those
days, a publisher could afford a bigger gamble on a young
novelist, because if he eventually turned out to be a Scott
Fitzgerald, a Hemingway, or a Harold Bell Wright, the losses on the early, unsuccessful books would eventually be recouped.   Today the chances of this happening are much smaller.   For example, the average sale of Wright's nineteen novels was more than half-a-million copies each, while one of
them reached 1,650,000.   Nowadays a sale of 50,000 is often
enough to put a novel at the top of the fiction best-seller list;
and the author's next book cannot by any means be sure of an
eager, automatic audience of the kind that Wright and scores
of other novelists once commanded.   Moreover, it cost less
to gamble on a novelist in the old days; a publisher could then
break even if he sold some 1,200 copies--while today he would
have to sell at least five or six times as many.

    *In paperback reprints the trend is in the same direction,
but slower.   Best-sellers Directory reports that in 1956 a-
bout 14 percent of such reprints were non-fiction; by 1960 the
figure had risen above 26 percent.

Personally I have not yet seen any hard evidence that publicly-owned publishing firms are becoming less venturesome--but they are now, I think, more likely to gamble on non-fiction projects than on novelists. So are privately-held companies. And this change seems to be related to a shift in public taste, rather than to the financial structure of the industry.

Why are readers turning from novels to non-fiction?

Any answer is at best a guess; but these are the explanations heard most frequently around publishers' lunch tables:

1. The rising level of education and America's increasing involvement with the rest of the world have led to a growing interest in serious non-fiction--particularly history, biography, politics, and international affairs. This kind of subject matter, for the same reason, is attracting many of the best writers.

2. The real world has become more exciting, and sometimes more fantastic, than the world of fiction. When men are exploring sunken cities beneath the sea, preparing journeys to the moon, building mega-death weapons, creating new nations by the score, cruising under the polar ice cap, and staging rebellions every other weekend, it is hard for a novelist--short of genius--to compete. As Philip Roth recently said: "The actuality is continually outdoing our talents, and the culture tosses up figures daily that are the envy of any novelist . . . . The world we have been given, the society and the community, has ceased to be as suitable or as manageable a subject for the novelist as it once may have been."

3. Many former buyers of light fiction--romance, Westerns, mysteries, adventure stories--now get the same commodity on television, free.

4. Among serious fiction writers, one large group now seems (in the words of a veteran publisher) to be "more concerned with self-expression than with entertaining the public." Wagner defines them as the poetic novelists. With them, and with most of the critics who make "serious" literary reputations, storytelling has become disreputable. Their main concern is with sensibility, with the inner drama of the psyche, not with the large events of the outside world.

Often they are accomplished craftsmen. Their style is lu-
minously burnished . . . they write on two levels, or even
three . . . their work contains more symbols than a Chinese band . . . it may plumb the depths of the human soul
. . . it may be (in Felicia Lamport's phrase) as deeply felt
as a Borsalino hat. But all too often it just isn't much fun
to read.

If such exercises in occupational therapy don't sell
very well, the author has small grounds for complaint. He
has written them, after all, primarily to massage his own
ego and to harvest critico-academic bay leaves. Since he
isn't interested in a mass audience, why should it be interested in him?

Does this mean that less fiction is published nowadays?
Strangely enough, it does not. Publishers remain in-
corrigibly hopeful; last year they brought out 1, 787 new nov-
els--an all-time high--even though they probably lost money
on a majority of them. (A first novel, for example, is lucky
to sell more than three thousand copies; while the publisher's
break-even point is about seven thousand.) They keep trying
because there is always a chance that the next unknown novelist will turn out to be a Richard McKenna. His first book,
The Sand Pebbles, won a major prize novel contest, was
serialized in the Saturday Evening Post, became a book-club
selection and stood for many weeks at or near the top of the
best-seller list. Then, too, every good publisher brings out
some novels every year which he knows will lose money,
simply because he believes in the book's quality or the author's not-yet-fully-developed talent.

If he is a sensible businessman, why doesn't a publisher
take on only best-sellers?
Some have tried; but they have been no more successful than the horseplayer who bets only on favorites. Nobody
has yet figured out a system for predicting with certainty
how a novel or general non-fiction book will sell, or whether
it may be a book-club selection, or what appeal it may have
for reprinters. The successful trade-book editor still has
to operate on an indefinable mixture of taste, experience,
hunch, and personal conviction.

Against such unpredictable odds, how can a publisher survive?
If he depended only on trade books, his chances would
make an actuary blanch. But, although such books get most
of the public attention and practically all of the review space,

they make up only a small part of the book business--less
than 8 percent of total sales. Consequently the prudent publisher usually tries to hedge his bets by developing other
lines. For example, textbooks or juveniles or paperbacks,
each of which brings in more money for the industry as a
whole than hardbound trade books do. (In the case of textbooks, nearly four times as much.) Moreover, juveniles
and textbooks are the fastest growing segments of the business. Paperback sales seem to have leveled off--for the
moment, at least--except for the higher-priced, more intellectual reprints. This is hardly surprising, since the reprinters have run through three thousand years of literature
in twenty-five years, and now have to depend heavily on the
current output of the original hardbound publishers.

In these lines, too, nobody has discovered how to pick
a winner every time. But the odds are a bit less daunting
with textbooks, juveniles, and reprints than with trade books,
and the profit margins are not so thin. Therefore, the publisher who spreads his bets over the whole field is less likely to be wiped out by a few bad guesses.

Why should any investor put his money into such a chancy
business?

A hard question. The enthusiasts point to the steady
rise in total book sales--a growth somewhat faster than that
of the American economy as a whole, and not much affected
by business cycles. They argue that this growth is likely to
continue, because the number of schoolchildren keeps increasing; so does their demand for textbooks, since new
knowledge is developing rapidly in many fields; and every
year more students go on to higher education. Moreover,
better-educated people read more books, throughout their
lives.

So long as you look only at the total figures, all this
is true. But any individual book is a gamble--and sometimes a very expensive one. A publisher may invest several
hundred thousand dollars in a textbook project, only to find
that a competitor beats him to the market with a better one.
Or, on his trade list, he may have a half-dozen best-sellers
one year and none the next. Furthermore, a publisher's
chief asset is his ability, and that of his editors, to find
good manuscripts--a highly intangible asset, and one remarkably hard for an outside investor to judge. With this peculiar talent, the successful firm must also combine, somehow,
a special kind of managerial ability; for each book pub-

lished is a different product, requiring its own special treatment in editing, manufacturing, advertising and marketing--
through a distribution system which is still far from ideal.

Consequently an investment in publishing is not like
an investment in the utilities industry, which provides a
standard product to a predictable market.   Nor is it like the
electronics industry, which is likely to make spectacular
profits from time to time by scientific breakthroughs.   It is
not the best place, therefore, either for the widow who wants
maximum safety, a steady return, and a minimum of bother;
or for the speculator looking for a quick killing.   For the
moderately venturesome, who will take the trouble to study
the individual firms in the industry with considerable care,
it may offer its rewards; and it does provide (for some of
us, at least) a fascination which no other business can match.
But before anyone even thinks seriously about putting his
money into it, he would do well to forget the current myths
about publishing, and to soak himself thoroughly in the pro-
saic facts.

Speaking Tetrahedrally: The Relationship Between
Authors, Publishers, Booksellers
and Librarians

By W. Gordon Graham, Managing Director, McGraw-Hill
Publishing Company Ltd.

From the Library Association Record 70:58-61, March 1968.
Reprinted by permission.   Substance of an address given to
the annual meeting of the Berkshire, Buckinghamshire and
Oxfordshire Branch of the Library Association, Oxford,
March 18, 1967.

Barabbas, the bandit whose release from custody by
Pontius Pilate and a fickle mob was an accessory to the
Crucifixion, was said unkindly, either by Thomas Campbell
or Lord Byron or both of them, to have been a publisher.
Mark Antony stole an entire library from Pergamon as a
gift for his mistress Cleopatra.   What on earth was the librarian doing when this happened?   Did he go with the ab-
ducted library to Alexandria or was he left contemplating his
empty shelves?   Julius Caesar, an early example of the
military man turned author, was assassinated.   His counterparts today live well on their royalty cheques.   According to
the poet Horace, the prototype of the bookseller in ancient
Rome was a place where trained slaves copied manuscripts
for sale to the public.   Some booksellers may feel that their
status has not improved markedly in the intervening centuries.

Obviously, the early representatives of the four professions were too busy saving their skins to develop much of
a relationship.   Yet even today is this tetrahedron as solid
as it should be?   I can think of four reasons--the whole subject seems to be tetramerous by nature--why this question is
worth examining.   One, the interdependence of the four parties has never been greater than it is today.   Two, the communication between them is uneven and spasmodic and may
well be too slight for their common good.   Three, they face
common perils which ought to overshadow any internal dif-

ferences.   And four, they have to strengthen their combined role in a society which holds books in progressively lower esteem.   Let us examine these four aspects--interdependence, communications, common perils and combined role--consecutively.

So that my contribution will be as tetrahedral as possible, I shall try to look at these issues not only as a publisher, which I now am; but also as a writer, which I once was; as a librarian, which was the start of my commercial career; and as a bookseller, which I hope one day to be--for which of us who loves books does not dream of ending his days dispensing knowledge from a quiet and scholarly book store, provided, of course, he does not have to depend on it for his living?

First, I must document my claim to experience as a librarian, which, although brief, left a deep mark upon me. I had the good fortune to be born and grow up in the city of Glasgow, between the wars, in what history will doubtless call the twilight of the Gutenberg era.   The printed word was still the dominant influence on human thought.   Plain living was a necessity and high thinking an almost inescapable virtue.   I thus grew up not too late to experience the impact of a book on a mind which surrenders entirely to it. In those days a book was less beautiful, but more revered. Recently I told John Knox, the distinguished doyen of Glasgow booksellers--to his pleasure, I think--of the reverence with which as a bare-legged laddie I first ventured into John Smith & Son to buy a Collins Pocket Classic for two shillings.   Reverence, too, would describe the moment when John Buchan--what a hero he was to every Scottish schoolboy!--handed me at a school prize-giving the Historical Romances of Conan Doyle.   No disrespect to Sir Arthur, but I would rather have had an autographed copy of The Thirty-nine Steps from the hands of this small man with the whimsical mouth and distant eyes.

And it was certainly something akin to reverence that attended my twice weekly visit to the Public Library, a mile from my home.   I used to make the journey on a vehicle called a scooter--do they still exist?--on which one rested the right foot and pushed oneself along by plopping the left foot at regular intervals on to the pavement.   Since both hands were needed for steering, the book which I was taking to or from the library had to be strapped on the frame.   On one occasion I was stopped and surrounded by a jeering gang

of contemporaries who wanted to fight me on the grounds
that there must be something unhealthy about a boy who was
forever scooting up and down the road with a book lashed to
his handlebars.   There was no fight, but I developed at that
moment the sour and threatening look which I still use on
those whose attitude to a book is less than reverential.

The library I patronized--so gloriously free of charge,
so delicious with its papery smell, so solemn with its creaks
and whispers--engendered in me the ambition to start a library of my own.   By this time I had sufficient Collins Classics, with the entire works of Stevenson and Scott as a solid
core, to justify such an ambition.   I also had strong views
on what my friends ought to be reading.   The labour of covering all these books in brown paper saved from parcels,
and ruling, in pencil, slips which would permit each book to
be borrowed thirty times, was considerable.   My only cash
investments were a date stamp and a bottle of gum.   I en-
rolled all my friends free of charge and announced that they
could borrow the books at a half-penny per week.   To my
dismay, the scheme was successful and as a result I spent
many hours mourning the spaces on my shelves and worrying
about my absent children.   Then, to my relief, summer-
time came and the enterprise passed into limbo.   No one reminded me about it next winter and I was glad.   That was
the total of my experience as a librarian and it taught me
that I was better at borrowing than at lending.

It also taught me by inference that a library is much
more than a place from which books are lent.   Many of us
forget, after our student days are over, the role of a library
as a study centre.   What educated person does not have in
his history a library to which he owes a debt that money cannot repay?   This, I believe, is the essential role of the library: to bring books into the lives of people who need them
and thus help to bring both the people and the books to ma-
turity--a role not changed by the vision of the automated library of the future, when librarians will be called information scientists and will be experts in the use of electronic
devices.

Interdependence greater than ever before
Which brings me to the first theme of my tetralogy--
the high degree of interdependence among our four parties--
because if there's one word that makes authors, publishers
and booksellers clutch their skirts about them and run appre-
hensively into one another's arms, it is the word "electron-

ics. " All three depend now, as never before, on libraries
which are bigger and richer--or at least less poor--than
ever before, to buy a major part of the first printings of
new books.   This applies especially to technical and scientific books, the cost of manufacture of which has risen 100
percent in the past twenty years, but the numerical market
for which has not increased, unless they are textbooks.   It
can cost Ł 2, 000 to compose an advanced technical book,
which is one shilling a copy--if 40, 000 copies are printed.
But such has been the fragmentation of scientific knowledge
in the past two decades that possibly there are only 2, 000
libraries that can buy the book.   And that's Ł 1 a copy, for
composition only.   At the prices consequent on such costs,
only the libraries can be counted on to buy copies for sure,
and here the publisher has reason to be grateful for the
growth of specialized, university, and industrial libraries.

The bookseller, too, depends ever more heavily on
the library market because, on the one hand, book prices
have climbed more steeply than the public's idea of what a
book is worth and, on the other, the library market has
multiplied to the point where it is now around Ł 15 million
a year--nearly one-fourth of the market for all books in the
United Kingdom.   As a corollary of this dependence, the
book trade looks to the library more than it has in the past
to educate its patrons into the habit of book purchase.   That
is one of the reasons why the National Library Week is so
called.   Libraries are undoubtedly used by people who could
afford to buy books and would benefit from buying them, but
don't.   The well-heeled lady who gushes to the author that
she would love to read his novel but there is a waiting list
of fifty at the library, is no joke.   She exists by the thousand.   Who can educate her?   We can all try, but the library is closest.

The bookseller is the most vulnerable flank of the
tetrahedron.   Imagine trying to sell drugs available free under the National Health Service!   Caught between budget-
conscious libraries, discount-conscious publishers and a public which spends 30s. per year per adult head on books, the
booksellers of Britain are fighting for their lives.   More and
more towns are going to be without bookshops.   And book-
selling will polarize into financially strong groups plus those
highly individualistic booksellers who venture aggressively into specialized selling, taking the books, in one way or another, to their customers, instead of merely waiting for the
customers to come to them.

Authors, on their side, are certainly closer to publishers now than ever before, because publishers are wooing
them under the pressure of competition. The proportion of
proposals coming unsolicited to publishers is declining. The
number of books written at publishers' suggestions is increasing. As a result, the publisher enters more into the
formulation of a book than he used to, and in some cases
the editor and the author work in something close to a partnership as the book is written.

Speaking tetrahedrally, three parties of our four--
those who make, or hope to make, money out of books--are
bound to increase their pressure on the fourth party, which
spends money on books. And of the three, it is the author
who has the greatest claim on the library. Some form of
public lending right seems likely to be established soon. It
seems to me that the principle of payment by usage has always been defensible and that now it is becoming practical,
because the library user is more affluent. Everyone who
reads a book owes the author something and to say that he
is a ratepayer does not discharge this debt. On the other
hand, the concept bristles with puzzling questions of both administration and justice. Should only British authors be
benefited? Should academic libraries be subject to the levy
as well as public libraries? Are scientific writers, who are
generally not dependent on their writing for an income, to
be treated in the same way as fiction authors?

This increasing interdependence begins to sound like
that of the crew of a leaky boat in a howling gale. But as
a philosophical crew-member would remark under such circumstances, "It's one way of learning what the others are
really like." Which brings me to the second aspect: the degree of communications among our four constituents.

The need for more and better communication

Authors, by and large, communicate little with the other three groups and I believe this is as it should be. The
Society of Authors is more protective than promotive in purpose. Authors, as we publishers know, are highly individual. Their motivations for writing run the gamut from philosophical to political to psychological to personal to pecuniary,
although even the most philosophical do not fail to cash their
royalty cheques. Every author after all has a relationship
with his own publisher as close as that of a pregnant woman
to her obstetrician, on a mental plane, and the publisher
learns to cope alike with the slow-writing perfectionist who

will not part with his manuscript and the slap-dasher who is
ready to part with it before he should.   Nor is there much
reason for authors to communicate with booksellers except
to complain that their books are not displayed.

Booksellers and publishers, by contrast, like their
counterparts all over the world, are engaged in an eternal
duet with recurring themes of "terms" and "service."
"Terms" are a British euphemism for "discounts" which
booksellers generally feel should be "more liberal," which
is a euphemism for "higher." "Service" refers to the publishers' apparent inability to deliver quickly to the bookseller
precisely the books that he orders.   This ostensibly simple
process gets more difficult all the time.   In my own company, for example, we have 7,000 different titles, a million
books in the warehouse, and about 4,000 different bookseller
customers, many of whom order the books one at a time.
But this is no excuse for us or anyone.   A few British publishers are giving good service.   Most are not, and the book
trade has a justified complaint, though it has to bear in mind
that the cost of carriage, which most publishers bear, is
getting higher year by year, and when a satisfactory standard of service is attained, it's going to use part of the same
pound of publishers' flesh that the book trade would like to
have as additional discount.

This forever dialogue between booksellers and publishers is governed by unwritten ground rules which allow
the bookseller to be the more aggressive party, the publisher
being inhibited by the fact that he wants the bookseller to buy
more of his books.   Their relationship is a little like that
of the Scots and the English who might not get along so well
with each other were it not for the fact that they have to
live on the same island.   The occasions when either party
strays beyond the unwritten ethic are so rare that when they
occur they are startling.   I had an instance the other day.
A leading bookseller wrote to an author whose book we were
about to publish and advised him that he would have done better to sign with a "British house"--a British house, moreover, granting "more liberal terms."   The author referred
the letter non-committally to me and must have been rather
bewildered to receive in response a two-page snarling letter
which on the one hand condemned nationalism in publishing
and on the other, rather illogically, emphasized that McGraw-
Hill has been established in Britain since 1899.   It also included a gratuitous lecture on the economics of publishing
and bookselling.   Anyway, apart from giving me the kind of

cathartic that publishers, constipated with the self-righteous-
ness of their own cause periodically need, the incident
served only to confirm by its rarity that booksellers do leave
author communications to the publisher.

But what of librarian communication? At this end of
the book's life-cycle there has been until recently a puzzling
hiatus. Even the book trade, which sells Ŀ 15 millions'
worth of books to libraries, has not worked as closely with
library organizations as their mutual interests might have
justified. Possibly communications have been pre-empted by
the library suppliers. Some booksellers who contribute their
rates to the maintenance of local public libraries feel strongly that these libraries should buy from them, but they also,
for the most part, recognize that in order to get the local
business they have to give a service equal in cost and efficiency to that of the library suppliers.

Between publishers and librarians, too little has been
said, with the result that they often have distorted concepts
of each other. Librarians are critical of book prices. They
are critical of what they find to be the unsuitable form and
content of publishers' promotion material, and weary of its
endless flow and frequent duplication. They are critical of
the delays and mistakes in service which booksellers and library suppliers report to them, in most cases truly, as
publishers' peccadilloes. Some librarians also believe that
publishers wilfully bring out books which are identical in content with other books.

Publishers, on their side, can never understand why
librarians do not acquire every book they publish. They are
not enthusiastic about inter-library lending. They wonder
why public librarians are mostly unwilling to receive their
representatives. And they reluctantly admire the enthusiasm
with which a specialized library can lay claim to a library
licence on the ground that a member of the public once wan-
dered in and was not ejected.

There is a clear need for more communication here
and both sides have been doing something about it. The
Publishers' Association has recently formed a Public Libraries Committee. There have been numerous constructive
bookseller-librarian-publisher conferences in the past two
years, the School of Librarianship of the North-Western Poly-
technic in London being particularly enterprising. In my
own company we had the idea of inviting all librarians with-

in a 30-mile radius of Maidenhead to come and confer for a
day, and to our pleasure 40 out of 60 accepted. So much
wisdom is now filed away in dozens of conference papers and
minutes that perhaps it is time to take stock and distil what
has been said and agreed into a handy form for everyone to
read.

I would hope that such a document would include one
grudge of long standing that all publishers, authors and booksellers have against the leading libraries in the country.   I
refer to Section 15 of the Copyright Act of 1911, which requires publishers to give away six free copies of every book
they publish, five of them to the richest libraries in the
United Kingdom--the British Museum, the libraries of Oxford and Cambridge and the national libraries of Scotland and
Wales--and the sixth to a library in another country which,
except where such largesse is concerned, is at pains to emphasize its independence. Publishers are incensed over this
piece of legalized robbery, which costs my own company between L7,000 and L8,000 each year. Authors get no royalties on these books and booksellers lose sales which are
rightfully theirs. We can estimate--though only the six bene-
ficiary libraries could confirm--that publisher and booksellers are being deprived of their profits, and authors of their
royalties on about L250,000's worth of books each year by
an antiquated law paralleled in no other country in the world.
Even if as few as 25 copies of a book are imported, five
have to be given away, the National Library of Wales being
content to levy only when 100 or more are imported. Publishers hope that the day is not distant when this Section of
the Copyright Act will be repealed with the exception of requiring a single copy of each new book to be sent to the
British Museum.

Dangers: present and future
But there are larger perils that our four constituents
face. No. 1 surely is the low per capita purchase of books
in Britain, particularly among those who could afford to buy
books but choose not to. When I returned to this country
four years ago after 21 years abroad, one of the first things
I had to do was buy a house. In looking at houses for sale
I was invariably astonished to find them inhabited by cultured people with a high standard of living who apparently
found it possible to live without books--unless they had them
in trunks in their attics--yet who had obviously used books
in their formative years. We book people could do sillier
things than try to talk the building industry into incorporat-

ing bookshelves in their house designs, just to give people
the idea that books have a place in their home. We could
spend more money in sillier ways than producing an illustrated booklet called "Books in your home," to be given a-
way by libraries and bookshops, which would not only speak
of the artistic and cultural value of books, but would give
practical information about the installation of bookshelves.
Too much of the laudable work of the National Book League,
the National Library Week and other co-operative efforts
seems to amount to preaching either to the converted or the
unconvertible.   Most of the non-book-buyers in this country
are hopelessly lost to other media.   Their capacity to absorb information and their will to seek it are fully taken up
by the popular press, television, comic strips, football cou-
pons, cereal packets, etc.   But there is a sizeable minority
which is affluent enough and educated enough and receptive
enough to the idea of a book to be a worth-while target.
These people are not reached by injunctions to "read a book"
but rather by persuasive invitations to "read this book."
Our best missionaries in this direction are the paperback
publishers who assault the non-book-buyer from many directions without straining his pocket-book; the non-fiction trade
publishers who are creating a new market for hard-cover
books at a medium price level; the book clubs and direct
mail houses; and not least those aggressive booksellers who
reach out into their local markets.

    No. 2 is the economics of publishing, which is put-
ting a severe squeeze on publishers and booksellers, and also on some authors whose books have to be rejected not because unworthy of publication, but because they would not
command a big enough market at the price which the number
printed would dictate.   Here I am talking mainly of advanced
treatises, monographs, handbooks and symposia--books of a
genre important to libraries and already criticized by some
librarians for their high prices.   Paradoxically, it is hard
to avoid the observation that the British publishing industry
is over-producing.   Twenty-nine thousand new titles a year
is an horrendous number and could not be supported without
Britain's £50 million export market--if, indeed, it is being
supported; only inventory managers and remainder houses
could reveal this secret.   I am not in a position to criticize
this enormous flow since McGraw-Hill's British company is
currently adding to it at the rate of five new books a month.
All I can say is that I couldn't make money publishing some
of the books my competitors are bringing out, but I expect
they are saying the same about mine.

No. 3 is the apparent reluctance of national and local government authorities to ensure that sufficient public funds are spent on books for education.   University libraries are often underbudgeted.   University students are given Ł 35 a year to spend, mostly on books, but in practice they spend less than Ł 10.   There is no government machinery to compel students to spend these public funds for the purpose for which they are entrusted to them.   Nor should the libraries, either public or university, be expected to lend students textbooks for the purchase of which the students have been given public funds.

The situation in schools is even more grave.   The capitation, or equipment, allowances, from which school textbook purchases are made but which include other items as well, are below 30s. a year in some primary schools. The Plowden Report estimates that it would take between Ł 500,000 and Ł 1,000,000 just to bring the underbudgeted primary schools up to a satisfactory minimum.   One cannot help feeling that some national standards, to which local education authorities would be required to conform, are needed, since as a result of local autonomy some schools are much worse served than others.   School textbook publishers on their side are naturally inhibited by the low capitation allowances.

No. 4--completing our tetragon of perils, and one of truly tetrahedral concern--is the threat to the principle of copyright.   In McGraw-Hill we have changed our copyright notice from a simple,

© 1967 McGraw-Hill Publishing Company Ltd.

to read as follows:

© 1967 McGraw-Hill Publishing Company Limited.
All rights reserved.   No part of this publication
may be reproduced, stored in a retrieval system,
or transmitted, in any form or by any means
electronic, mechanical, photocopying, recording
or otherwise, without the prior permission of Mc-
Graw-Hill Publishing Company Limited.

This is a sufficient commentary on our apprehension over the inevitable increase in photocopying, whether done with or without permission, whether done with or without payment. There are those who may see no harm in multi-copying for

private use.   There are those who may see no harm in co-
operative copying service among libraries.   The answer to
these copy enthusiasts is that if wholesale copying were to
become customary, editions, particularly of advanced books,
would get smaller and smaller and their prices would get
higher and higher until instead of publishing a mere 3,000
copies at 100 shillings, the publisher would be bringing out
100 copies at 3,000 shillings each--if he were still in business.

A secondary current threat to copyright comes from
certain governments that take the view that copyright should
be waived or diluted so that their educators and librarians
can reproduce copyrighted material to a limited extent without paying for it, as a kind of economic aid from the copyright holders.   And of course the U.S.S.R. has not yet altered its stand about paying for translation rights, except
under certain circumstances, to authors in roubles.   And
our Chinese friends on Formosa are still in the piracy business.   All of this is a multiple erosion of the rights of authors and publishers in their own property, in fighting which
they seek the understanding and support of librarians and
booksellers.

Co-operation in the common cause
Standing foursquare (tetrapodically?) on the principle
of copyright would be one illustration of the potential power
of unity, the need for which is my fourth and (naturally) final
plea.   What is at stake?   As we gaze into a future of data
centres, computerized libraries, microfilms, teaching machines, television by satellite and as yet unrevealed developments of these, it is just possible that it is the book itself
as an institution which is at stake.   I am not suggesting that
the book could wither and die, but I am suggesting that its
purpose could change radically under our noses and that we
could be left promoting an outmoded concept, pre-empted by
technicians of the new media.   The proceedings of a convention of harness-makers about the year 1908 would be salutary reading for us book people today, because our means of
idea communication are surely facing as great a revolution
as that which overtook our means of locomotion with the on-
set of the automotive age.

The signs are plentiful.   The eagerness with which
the big electronic companies of the United States--IBM,
CBS, RCA and so on--have bought their way into the publishing business, is matched by the willingness of the book pub-

lishers to be bought, apparently confident that this is the way
to further growth.   In McGraw-Hill, books and magazines
are now only about two-thirds of our business.   We sell
tapes, records, flashcards, motion pictures, filmstrips, data
systems, psychological testing devices, subliminal projectors, educational toys, programmed learning devices, and information services of many kinds.   Our most recent acquisition was a company manufacturing planetariums.   Last year
at the Frankfurt Book Fair we had live rats and chameleons
in the midst of our books--samples of materials sold along
with our biology textbooks.

    Nor is Europe the least bit behindhand in this impend-
ing revolution.   One of the most eye-opening experiences for
a traditional publisher is to visit the biennial Didakta Fair
(the next one will be at Hanover in 1968), where educational
materials from all over Europe include devices quite as
sophisticated as those in the United States.   But in Europe
the revolution is less evident because the new media are being developed for the most part by specialist rather than
multi-media enterprises.   This could delay developments
here because in the United States it seems, so far, that the
use of books as educational tools--which is today their principal use--is growing with the help of and not in spite of the
new media.   The book, no longer the teacher's only support
apart from his own talk and chalk, becomes the centrepiece
of a package which is transmitting knowledge with new standards of efficiency in the face of the continual multiplication
both of the knowledge and the pupils to whom it is to be im-
parted.

    Even Professor Marshall McLuhan, the Canadian
apostle of instant knowledge, whose book Understanding
Media: the Extensions of Man (McGraw-Hill, 1964) challenges
our whole concept of what communication is, nowhere proph-
esies the decline of the book, although he classifies the
printed word as a medium of more historical than contemporary significance.   But he refers to the imminent end of the
"Gutenberg era." "The electric technology," he says, "is
within the gates and we are numb, deaf, blind and mute a-
bout its encounter with the Gutenberg technology, on and
through which the American way of life was formed." He is
perhaps himself not sure what is going to happen but sees
enough to prophesy profound change.   And he doesn't think
much of our readiness to cope with this change.   On page
82 of Understanding Media, he says:

It is true that there is more material written and
printed and read today than ever before, but there
is also a new electric technology that threatens
this ancient technology of literacy built on the
phonetic alphabet.   Because of its action in extending our central nervous system, electric technology
seems to favour the inclusive and participational
spoken word over the specialist written word.   Our
Western values, built on the written word, have already been considerably affected by the electric
media of the telephone, radio, and TV.   Perhaps
that is the reason why many highly literate people
in our time find it difficult to examine this question without getting into a moral panic.

If change is coming, we who write, produce, market
and disseminate books must be the first to be aware' of it.
One of the demands of this awareness will be an ascension
from national to global thinking, because the electric technology is non-national.   If the book is to maintain, in an
electrically homogenized society which doubles its knowledge
every decade and demands instant access to any particle of
it, a place at all comparable with its place in the Gutenberg
era, then the four constituents of the book must nurture their
relations with one another as never before.   In a word, what
we need is tetravalence, and we need it now.

Black Marks: A London Book Publisher's Awards

By T. M. Farmiloe, of Macmillan & Company, Ltd.

From English 15:105-6, Autumn 1964.   Copyright 1964 by
T. M. Farmiloe.   Reprinted by permission.

For all sorts and conditions of badly presented manuscripts, from the dog-eared to the illegible, which are alike
in doing their utmost to come between author and reader.

For indecipherable hand-writers, particularly those
who occupy Chairs and should know better.

For 'authors,' especially the religious and political
cranks and doctoral-thesis writers, who visit us without any
warning, carrying their unpublishable manuscripts, and, having insisted on speaking to an editor, keep him engaged for
half an hour.

For authors, editors, and publishers who apply for
permission to reprint material that is out of copyright or
covered by the law of fair dealing or not published by us--
or all three.

For books, particularly novels, which abruptly stop
selling in any quantity the very day that the printers start
to machine the reprint which we have ordered in the confident expectation that the sales will continue at a reasonable
rate.

For copies of books published elsewhere which arrive
without any hint of why they have been sent to us.

For correspondents who address the firm, and not an
individual, and fail to quote the reference requested of them:
particularly such foreign-language correspondents whose letters are translated before it is realized that the person for
whom the letter is intended can read the language in question.

For former protectorates and colonies, such as Nya-
saland and the Gold Coast, which change their names on at-
taining independence, thereby necessitating costly alterations
to the type or plates of our publications.

For freelance proof-readers whose letters of application for work contain spelling mistakes (the record for one
letter is four).

For indexers whose entries appear out of alphabetical order.

For literary agents who write obsequious letters and
get most of their facts wrong.

For literary editors who, when specially asked to
mention that a book is available in a paperback as well as
a hard-cover edition, fail to do so.

For members of the public who send in copies of
books, sometimes not even published by us, and ask whether
they are first editions and how much they are worth, and expect us to return the books with the required information at
our own expense.

For reviewers, as ignorant of the law and practice of
publishing as--judging by some of their comments on prices
--they are of its economics, who criticize us for not restor-
ing material to print or for not publishing it in paperback
when the copyright-holder has refused persistent requests on
our part to do exactly this.

For students who write in for bibliographical and biographical information that is readily available in the usual
reference books, demand a reply by return of post as their
examination is next week, and do not bother to thank us.

For those who contrive to mis-spell the names of
London publishing houses, e.g. 'Cassel' for 'Cassell,'
'Gollanz' for 'Gollancz,' 'Harrop' for 'Harrap,' 'Heineman'
for 'Heinemann,' 'Longman' for 'Longmans,' 'MacMillan' for
'Macmillan,' 'Weidenfield and Nicholson' for 'Weidenfeld and
Nicolson,' and, inevitably, 'Hart Davies' for 'Hart-Davis'
and 'Peter Davis' for 'Peter Davies.'

For the imperfect copy of a book--perhaps the only
one in a printing of several thousand--which, at least since

the days of Lewis Carroll, has always insisted on getting into its author's hands.

State of the Art of Computers in Commercial Publishing

By John Markus, Manager, Information Research, McGraw-Hill, Inc., New York.

Reprinted from, and by permission of, American Documentation, April 1966, v. 17, p. 76-88. Copyright 1966 by the American Society for Information Science (American Documentation Institute), 1140 Connecticut Avenue, N.W., Washington, D.C. 20036.

Introduction

This paper starts with a dream. In this dream there is a huge room, filled with hundreds of blondes, brunettes, and redheads. They are all retyping manuscripts in rhythm, to the tune of the Stars and Stripes Forever, on tape-punching typewriter keyboards. Nobody worries about justification, punctuation, widows, rivers, or the other little details of typography that plague a Linotype operator. The typewriter hard copy is proofread, correction tapes are punched, and all the tapes are fed into a computer at 500 or 1,000 characters per second.

The computer justifies and hyphenates the copy as per typographical specifications. It also inserts repetitive words, supplies headings, makes up pages, eliminates bad breaks, calculates total length, and even spreads out or squeezes together the lines to eliminate blank pages in the last printing form.

The final output tape of the computer is error-free, because our computer does not make mistakes. The output display machine, equally error-free, converts this tape into negatives or positives, ready for offset or letterpress plate-making. Since this dream system makes no mistakes, there is no need for galley proofs or page proofs. This means no more printer's alteration charges, because authors will no longer get a chance to rewrite their manuscripts on galleys or page proofs.

Sure this sounds like a dream.   But technologically, without too great an investment, we could make this dream come true today for practically any printing job, if we wanted to.   Now I must sound a warning: Pushing technology too fast could change our dream into a nightmare.   As many of you have noticed, quite a few parts of this dream are fuzzy.   For instance, I didn't say whether these girls were in the publisher's office, a printing plant, a central service bureau, or a huge and drafty old castle in England. I didn't say where the computer was.   Likewise, I didn't say who had the output machine, or what it was.   All I did say is that we ended up with negatives or positives that were ready for conventional plate-making and printing.

Now let's see why we have to be so vague--why we need answers to so many questions before the ultimate role of computers in publishing can be pinpointed.

System Design

The chief problem in computerized publishing is that there are so many different types of equipment and so many different techniques, each with advantages and drawbacks, for each part of our system.   From these many variables, we must find the optimum system combination that will meet specific present and future publishing needs, reliably and economically.   The glamour and publicity of new computer hardware must not lure us into premature action.   This system design problem divides into four parts:

1. Input hardware, which converts the manuscript into machine-readable form.

2. Computer hardware, which does the creative part of the printing process.

3. Computer software, including programs that provide for the production of proofs, correction of errors, and updating of subsequent editions.

4. Output hardware, consisting usually of a photo-composition machine that converts the computer output tapes to negatives or repro copy for printing.

Input Hardware

A computer will accept editorial copy only in machine-readable form.   This can be punched cards, punched

tape, magnetic tape, or scanner-readable typed characters.
Our manuscript must therefore be retyped, or rather key-
boarded, first. Here we have three basic choices:

Tape Perforators

Most computer composition systems in operation today use tape-punching typewriters as input hardware. Flexowriters and Dura machines built around standard IBM electric typewriters are the most popular. Prices range from
$1,500 to $2,500 each. There are also tape perforators
without printing facilities, such as the Fairchild TTS perforators used in many printing plants. At least one of the
machines should also have a tape reader to permit checking
the performance of the machine by running punched tape
through the reader and checking the hard copy produced from
the tape.

The choice of tape-punching typewriters is difficult.
On the Dura Mach 10 tape-punching typewriter, high typing
speeds are possible because shift and unshift codes are
punched automatically when the typist hits the conventional
shift keys. On Friden Flexowriters each shift code must be
punched separately by the operator. Unfortunately, some
Dura machines get out of adjustment and occasionally lose a
shift code when typists work at their maximum speed. Slow-
ing down the typists eliminates this malfunction, but output
is then down to that of Flexowriters. This leads to the conclusion that there is as yet no ideal tape-punching input machine for computer composition.

Punched paper tape for computers is often called idiot
tape by printers, because it can be produced by ordinary
typists without years of special training. This input tape
contains nothing more than code equivalents of typed characters, without hyphenating or end-of-the-line indications, and
with a minimum of special control characters for designat-
ing type font changes.

A typewriter keyboard has many advantages over the
Linotype or Monotype keyboards currently used in printing
plants. First of all, ordinary typists can be used for keyboarding of composition, after no more than a few hours of
additional training. These typists can generally turn out at
least 20% more work than is ordinarily obtained on keyboards
of hot-metal casting machines. One reason is that a typist
has only 44 keys to hit, while a Linotype operator has more

than twice as many. Another reason is that typists do not have to slow up for the end-of-line justification or hyphenation decisions. The typewriter also gives hard copy immediately for proofreading.

Keypunches

Our second input possibility is a standard keypunch, driven by an essentially standard typewriter keyboard. The punched cards produced here can be imprinted either simultaneously with punching or in a separate machine to provide a line of printing across the top of the card for proofreading. Keypunching is viewed as an interim input measure for use with computers that have only punched-card input equipment, however, because it is slower and more expensive than punching paper tape.

Scanners

Controlled-font typewriters can be teamed up with a character-reading scanner for use as input hardware. Here editorial copy is retyped on an electric typewriter having a special font of all-cap characters that can be read accurately by a photoelectric scanning machine, such as the Farrington and Control Data Corp. scanners. Special controlled-font balls are now available for the IBM Selectric bouncing-ball typewriter.

Scanners generally deliver magnetic tape, ready for use as computer input. The scanner approach is attractive, but the all-caps limitation of the lower priced scanners is a drawback for input typing and for proofreading the hard copy.

An example of book composition as it might be typed for an all-caps scanner, in Fig. 1, shows how function codes might be used to obtain the desired typography. Note that the all-caps input lines do not end on the same words as the final typeset copy, because the computer ignores typewriter carriage returns. Note also that the computer has adjusted the spaces between words to achieve justification (lineup at the right). It could also hyphenate words whenever necessary to avoid excessive space between words.

It is possible today to purchase a scanner that will read both caps and lower case typing, in regular or controlled fonts. Cost is much more than for an all-caps scanner, however, and accuracy is still open to question. One of

COMPUTERS AND PEOPLE BY POSTLEY MCGRAW—HILL

⊢C ⊿B ⊐ DECISION MAKING ⊿R IS AN ACTIVITY WHICH HAS HISTORICALLY BEEN
PERFORMED BY PEOPLE. THESE PEOPLE, INCLUDING YOU AND ME, SEEM RATHER
DEFENSIVE ABOUT THEIR EXCLUSIVE PREROGATIVES TO PERFORM THIS ACTIVITY,
THAT IS, THEIR PREROGATIVES TO "MAKE DECISIONS." ⊢2 ⊿T ⊐ A
DEFINITION OF DECISION MAKING ⊢1 ⊿R ⊢P THE PROCESS BY WHICH ONE ARRIVES
AT CONCLUSIONS—MAKES DECISIONS—IS INTERESTING TO EXAMINE. IN THE FIRST
PLACE, WHILE THESE CONCLUSIONS ARE USUALLY SAID TO DERIVE DIRECTLY FROM
A SET OF "FACTS" IT ALMOST ALWAYS DEVELOPS THAT THESE SO—CALLED "FACTS"
ARE IN REALITY AN ⊿I ESTIMATE ⊿R OF THE TRUE FACTS

⊢	FUNCTION CODE COMMAND
⊢C	START NEW CHAPTER
⊢P	START NEW PARAGRAPH
⊢1	1 LINE SPACE
⊢2	2 LINES SPACE
⊿	FONT CHANGE COMMAND
⊿B	CAP AND SMALL CAP
⊿T	BELL GOTHIC BOLD SUBHEAD
⊿R	NEWS GOTHIC BODY TEXT
⊿I	ITALICS OF BODY TEXT
⊐	CAPITALIZE NEXT LETTER
.	PERIOD FOLLOWED BY SPACE MAKES NEXT LETTER CAP

DECISION MAKING is an activity which has historically been performed by people. These people, including you and me, seem rather defensive about their exclusive prerogatives to perform this activity, that is, their prerogatives to "make decisions."

A definition of decision making

The process by which one arrives at conclusions—makes decisions—is interesting to examine. In the first place, while these conclusions are usually said to derive directly from a set of "facts," it almost always develops that these so-called "facts" are in reality an *estimate* of the true facts

Fig. 1. Example of book composition as typed for Farrington scanner (top), final output copy (lower left), and meanings of control code characters used by typist.

these, the Retina machine made by Recognition Equipment Corp., is being tested by Perry Publications in Florida for setting newspaper classified ads. Philco scanners have multi-font as well as lower case capability at correspondingly higher prices.

When a scanner for ordinary typing becomes available at a reasonable price, the pages of an author's manuscript could be fed directly into the scanner without retyping for conversion to magnetic tape. Colored pencil marks could be made at points where editing is desired. These would make the scanner read editing changes and corrections that have been typed between the lines or generate a code that tells the computer to take the desired change from another source.

Computer Hardware
Many different general-purpose computers are suitable for electronic processing of manuscripts. The IBM 1620 general-purpose computer leads the picture here, with several dozen being used in printing plants as well as in newspaper applications. Software for newspaper composition on this computer is available from IBM. Next in popularity is the RCA 301, for which computer typesetting software has also been made available by the manufacturer. Other general-purpose computers used for composition include the Honeywell 200, Digital Equipment PDP-8, several Control Data models, the IBM 1400 series, and NCR 315. A few of these are used exclusively for composition, but in most installations the primary application is accounting. Composition work, for books in particular, is generally run during idle time on second or third shifts.

Choice of a particular general-purpose computer will generally be based on such factors as availability of the necessary operating time, availability of some or all the necessary software from the manufacturer, and availability of compatible input and output composition hardware for the computer. Size of the internal storage and speed of the input and output hardware are other factors to be considered. The output paper-tape punch speed is particularly important because it is generally operated on-line. A fast line printer is another asset; even better is one having a cap and lower case chain.

In general, the sum of the times required for the input reader, line printer, and output punch to handle their re-

spective total characters will closely approach the total computer operating time for a particular composition job. The
actual processing runs involving only magnetic tape handlers
take a small percentage of the operating time on modern
high-speed, general-purpose computers. This fact makes it
possible to estimate composition run times with a high degree of accuracy, assuming availability of debugged programs, a good computer room operating staff, and an input
that contains the correct control codes needed for proper
processing by the computer.

Service bureaus offering computer composition include
National Computer Analysts, Rocappi, and Documentation,
Inc. These firms operate in competition with commercial
printers because up to now only a few printers are using
their computers for composition.

Special-purpose computers for composition include the
Mergenthaler Linasec, Compugraphic DTP, three Harris-
Intertype computers, and the Fairchild Comp/Set. These
are intended chiefly for newspaper and printing plants, for
use with tape-controlled hot-metal or photocomposition machines.

The most expensive of the three Harris-Intertype
models provides a combination of logic and magnetic-drum
dictionary lookup for automatic hyphenation. A simpler model uses only logic for hyphenation, so it occasionally inserts
hyphens by guessing when logic fails. The simplest and
cheapest model stops automatically whenever it reaches a
point where a word must be hyphenated to allow a human operator to make a decision on where the hyphen should go.

Software Problems
A computer can only follow the instructions that are
stored in its electronic memory. These instructions are
known as software. Each program of instructions must allow for all possible combinations of input problems, yet
must fit into the available core storage.

Computer software and computer hardware together
serve to convert low-cost keyboarding by a typist to whatever is needed for driving the output composition machines.
To do this, the software must include one or more of the
following composition functions: (a) format and typography
control; (b) justification; (c) hyphenation; (d) page make-
up; (e) code conversion for the output hardware.

The control codes that specify line widths, indentations, type fonts, italicizing, bold-facing, subscripts, superscripts, leading (vertical spacing between lines), tabulating, and other parameters of composition must be converted by computer software into the units of length on which the computer bases its running width total of the characters already set in each line. To do this, the computer must be given beforehand the exact width of each character, in each of the fonts being used in the job being run. For justification, the computer must also be given the range of word spacing that will be permitted when justifying lines for a particular composition job. The greater the range, the less will be the need for hyphenating words. When the computer comes to a word that won't fit in the specified line width, it must reject that word and increase the spaces between words to fill the line.

A refinement of the justification program involves rearranging words in previous lines in a paragraph whenever a line cannot be justified within specified limits without hyphenating. The computer tries to transfer words from the end of one line to the start of the next, working back to the beginning of a paragraph, and staying within the word spacing limits, to see if a different arrangement of words can be achieved that will eliminate the need for hyphenating. This technique naturally works best for wide columns such as are used in books.

So far, software programs for computer composition have been written for specific jobs. This means that they must generally be revised rather extensively when changes in format, typography, or content are desired. At the present time, however, both RCA's Graphic Services Division and National Computer Analysts are working on programs that will be more or less universal, so as to permit reasonable changes in format. These programs are much more costly to produce, but will be cheaper in the long run because their costs can be spread out over a number of users of computer composition.

Hyphenation

The software goal envisioned by many in computer-controlled typesetting is the introduction of hyphens correctly at ends of lines by means of a program that involves only logic, with no dictionary lookup of exception words. Perfection will never be achieved here as long as dictionaries are

BIL-LOWY	BIL-LOWY
BIL-LY	BIL-LY
BI-ME-TAL-LIC	** BIMETALL-IC
BI-MET-AL-ISM	** BIME-TAL-ISM
BIN	BIN
BIND	BIND
BIND-ER	BIND-ER
BIND-ING	BIND-ING
BIN-OC-U-LARS	BINOCULARS
BI-OG-RA-PHER	BI-OG-RA-PHER
BI-O-GRAPH-I-CAL	** BIO-GRA-PHI-CAL
BI-OG-RA-PHY	BI-OG-RA-PHY
BI-O-LOG-I-CAL	BI-OLOGI-CAL
BI-OL-O-GIST	BI-OLO-GIST
BI-OL-O-GY	BI-OLO-GY
BIRCH	BIRCH
BIRD	BIRD
BIRD-CALL	BIRD-CALL
BIRD-IE	** BIR-DIE
BIRD'-S/EYE	BIRD'S/EYE
BIR-MING-HAM	BIR-MING-HAM
BIRTH	BIRTH
BIRTH-DAY	BIRTH-DAY
BIRTH-PLACE	BIRTHPLACE
BIRTH-RIGHT	** BIR-THRIGHT
BIS-CUIT	** BIS-CU-IT
BI-SECT	BISECT
BISH-OP	** BI-SHOP
BISH-OP-RIC	** BI-SHO-PRIC
BIS-MARCK	BIS-MARCK
BI-SON	BISON
BIT	BIT
BITE	BITE
BIT-ING	BIT-ING

Fig. 2.   Early test of automatic hyphenation by logic a-
lone.   Left column shows hyphenation of Merriam-Webster
Unabridged Third Edition and right column shows hyphenation by National Computer Analysts logic routines.   Asterisks
indicate misplaced hyphens.   Hyphens omitted by computer
were not counted as errors here, but newer test program
counts both omitted and erroneous hyphens.

used as hyphenating guides, because proper names and many
ordinary words in dictionaries do not follow logical rules for
hyphenation.   Scientific words derived from proper names
(such as wattage, hyphenated watt-age because named after

James Watt) are another headache, as also are words that are spelled the same but hyphenated differently depending on pronunciation. Worse yet, dictionaries do not agree on hyphenation. Even the Second and Third Editions of Merriam-Webster's Unabridged Dictionary differ from each other.

One program is available today that can equal or better the accuracy of human hyphenation while relying entirely on logic. This was written at National Computer Analysts in Princeton for an RCA 301 computer, and has been rewritten for Control Data and Univac computers. In developing this software, the computer was programmed to hyphenate test words in every possible position, compare its work with hyphenation as given in the Third Edition of Merriam-Webster Unabridged, and place asterisks ahead of each word having a hyphen in a wrong position. The resulting printout, part of which is shown in Feb. 1, was then used as a guide for further refining the hyphenating logic.

Here is a suggestion. Why not line up a stable of experts in linguistics, logic, typesetting, and proofreading to establish a consistent set of rules for hyphenation that are compatible with computer processing? A computer program could then be written from these rules to produce a word list showing the new and logical hyphenation for every word in the English language for publishing as the new standard hyphenating guide. Could we agree on a basic standard for hyphenation, based only on logic?

The majority of computer-controlled typesetting operations today are using a combination of logic and dictionary lookup for hyphenation. Here, when the computer reaches a word that must be hyphenated, it first looks in its internal dictionary of problem words that have been stored with hyphens in all possible positions. If the word is found there, the computer chooses a hyphenating position that places the line within the specified justifying limits. If the word is not in the internal dictionary, the computer then applies its stored rules of logic, based on common word endings and common combinations of letters, for placing the hyphen. If the word is one of the exceptions for which logic rules do not apply or have not yet been written into the program, the computer can arbitrarily place the hyphen after an odd-numbered letter, because statistics show that most hyphens fall after the 3rd, 5th, 7th, etc., letter in a word. In one program, when none of the logic rules applies, the computer in effect flips a coin and places the hyphen arbitrarily before or after a convenient vowel.

A third hyphenating alternative, which no one has tried as yet because it calls for more internal memory capacity than is available in any computer, would involve storing all of the words in the Merriam-Webster Unabridged Dictionary with all hyphen positions, for complete dictionary lookup. With a sufficiently large capacity in random-access disk file or other large memory, it is not inconceivable that this approach may be tried in the future.

Finally, at the other extreme is manual hyphenation, wherein we have computer software that stops everything and sounds an alarm when a word is reached that requires hyphenation. An operator must then look at the word as shown on the computer display or as typed out by the computer and indicate where the hyphen should go. This manual operation is at present used only with small special-purpose computers, because it fails to utilize the hyphenating capabilities of a computer. On the other hand, with wide-column book composition an appropriate justifying program could reduce the need for hyphens to less than one line in 100. Here it may be more economical to use this combination of automotive and human procedures.

For page makeup of books, the available newspaper composition programs need to be expanded to cover handling of illustrations, computation of book length, and elimination of bad breaks such as widows, rivers, and heads at the bottom of a page or column. The preparation and testing of suitable programs for publishing requirements could be costly and time consuming for an individual publisher. Standard composition programs are now being prepared by some service bureaus for the benefit of all of their publisher clients.

Error Detection

IBM is already carrying out research on the use of a computer to detect errors in spelling and typing of editorial copy. One obstacle here is the size of the computer internal storage required for holding all of the words in the English language, with high-speed access to each word so the process does not appreciably slow up computer processing. Another drawback is that some typing errors create acceptable different words.

Photocomposition Control Codes

The last part of the software for computer-controlled typesetting is a program for converting the code format of the computer to that required by the composing machine and adding the necessary machine control codes. Computer manufacturers have developed this conversion software for the Teletypesetter tape required for hot-metal newspaper composition, and will presumably have conversion programs for photocomposition machines eventually.

Proofreading

Normally, typeset material is proofread twice, on galley proofs and on page proofs. Computer composition will undoubtedly change this. Here are some of the possibilities that we must explore to determine the optimum proofreading procedures for each system from the standpoint of economics, accuracy, and acceptance by editors and authors.

Proofreading of the hard copy produced on input tape-punching typewriters could be the only proofreading needed in an error-free computer system, if we could count on the typewriter and its punches to work perfectly. We can't yet. Furthermore, the hard copy at the input is not typed to final column width, hence there can be no checking of hyphenation, widows, and the other factors that determine high-quality composition. The hard input copy will be cap and lower case, however, and can have code characters to indicate italics, bold face, special characters, and other desired typographic changes.

The hard copy that is produced as a by-product of tape-punching is thus quite useful for detecting human errors in keyboarding. It will not show up machine errors occurring between the fingertips of the typist and the magnetic tape of the computer, however, so we need at least one more proofreading. How do we get it?

Use of a computer's own line printer to produce a display for proofreading is one logical answer. A major drawback, however, is that most line printers have only capital letters. Special programming is then needed to identify the letters that must be capitalized in the final output.

One method of indicating capitalization is based on the fact that three characters must be punched on paper tape

```
<H>ABCOCK <R>ELAYS <D>IV <B>ABCOCK <E>LECTRONICS <C>ORP
<M>R <C L M>ARTIN, <V P M>KTG                3501 <H>ARBOR <B>LVD
<C>OSTA <M>ESA                    <C>AL

<B>ABCOCK <7 W>ILCOX <C>O <R>EFRACTORIES <D>IV
<M>R <M J T>ERMAN, <M>KTG <M>GR          161 <E >42ND <S>T
<N>EW <Y>ORK 17          <N Y>

<B>ACON <I>NDUSTRIES, <I>NC
<M>R <E>LDON <H F>AY, <S>ALES <M>GR       192 <P>LEASANT <S>T
<W>ATERTOWN 72          <M>ASS
```

Fig. 3. Use of lesser-than sign to indicate shift to caps and greater-than sign to indicate shift down to lower case as required for proofreading accurately from line printer proofs.

Fig. 4. Method of using open lozenges to indicate true capital letters on line printer proofs.

```
                    ACCT NUMBER 2063758      DATE 04/26/65

ACCT# 2063758  A 251 1(01) CURTISS-WRIGHT CORP ELECTRONICS DIV
             □                  □       □                 □

   (02) 35 MARKET ST                        (03) E PATERSON
            □                                    □□□

   (05) PASSAIC                (06) 07407 (07) 201 791-0100   (08)
        □

   (11) S BRINSFIELD, PRES          MAIL TO  MR R A JOHNSON
        □ □          □    □□□□□              □□□□□□□□□□□□□□□□□□□□□□

PROD# ADV    INS   AD REFERENCE PAGE NUMBER       PROD# ADV

677757                                            678755
```

each time a typist hits a capital letter. First comes the
upper-shift character, produced when she touches the shift
key. Next is the actual character, followed by the down-
shift character that is punched when she releases the shift
key. These shift characters can be converted to lesser-
than and greater-than signs surrounding the letter or letters
that are true caps on line printer proofs, as in Fig. 3. (Yes,
we do get complaints from proofreaders with this approach.)

Another method involves more programming to re-
move the two shift characters from the printout and, instead, place an open lozenge or other special character on
the line below, directly under each cap character, as in Fig.
4. This makes proofreading much easier but doubles line-
printer running time. This method is better from the stand-
points of proofreading accuracy, proofreader morale, and
labor vs. machine-time costs.

A cap-and-lower-case printer would give a more readable proof, but special characters would still be needed for
italicizing, bold-facing, and characters not on the chain.
The cost of this chain and the additional computer circuitry
required must be weighed against the value of the lower-case
printout for proofreading and its value in other applications.
As one example, this cap-and-lower-case chain might be
used to produce more readable repro copy for indexes at low
cost compared to photocomposition or hot-metal typesetting,
though at a serious penalty in characters per inch since the
letters are uniformly spaced. Also, for a given level of
readability, the cap-and-lower-case printout cannot be reduced in size as much as an all-caps printout and will therefore require more printed pages per job.

Proofreading of output photocomposition from Xerox
copies of paper repro proofs or from blueprints of negatives
is the ideal solution, though probably the most expensive.
Here we see exact equivalents of conventional galley and page
proofs showing all formats and all fonts of type called for.

Corrections

After errors have been caught by proofreading, paper
tapes for the corrections must be punched with appropriate
record, field, line, or other identifying codes. These correction tapes are fed into the computer for updating the master tape file, since this will be used for subsequent editions.
Five procedures are now available, depending on the nature

and amount of corrections:

1. Use the computer to punch output tapes only for lines requiring change, run these through the photocomposition machine, and get corrected lines for stripping into the negatives or pasting on the repro positives. This is generally the preferred procedure.

2. Use the computer to punch the entire output tapes over again for a second complete run through the photocomposition machines. This costly procedure will probably be preferable when there are drastic changes, such as might occur when a publisher allows an author to rewrite his manuscript on galley or page proofs.

3. Reperforating the punched paper input tape, with manual typing only when an erroneous word is reached, to obtain a perfect new tape for use as computer input. Chief drawback here is almost a doubling of input keyboarding time with no assurance that new errors won't be made.

4. Splicing of corrections into the original tape. This requires a person who can read punched characters, hence is rarely done.

5. Merging of correction tapes with the original tapes by operator switching of two readers. This takes even more input operator time than the third procedure and can give new errors if readers are not switched back and forth at the correct instants.

Output Hardware

Output hardware includes everything needed to convert output magnetic tape of the computer to hot metal or to photographic negatives for plate-making. When the output machine requires punched paper tape, the computer itself or an off-line converter must drive a highspeed tape punch. With output machines like Photon ZIP and the forthcoming CBS-Mergenthaler Linotron, which will take magnetic tape directly, mag-to-paper conversion will not be needed. In commercial publishing, the punching of output paper tapes is generally done on-line, even though this means many more hours of computer time.

Hot-metal Output

Many Linotype and Intertype casting machines will operate from punched paper tapes. The chief drawback to a hot-metal output machine, however, is the inherent mechanical error rate of the machine. In general, a machine malfunction will cause an error in about one out of every 50 cast slugs even with the best possible machine operation and maintenance. Until this error rate is eliminated, the trend in computer-controlled typesetting will logically be toward photocomposition machines, because these can theoretically operate without error.

Photocomposition Output

Machines currently available for photocomposition from punched paper tape include those made by Photon, Harris-Intertype, ATF, Mergenthaler, and Alphatype. More are undoubtedly under development. These use a punched paper input tape to control the exposure of a film negative, character by character, with precise positioning of characters and precise control of spacing between lines, as determined by the codes produced during computer processing. The choice of a machine must be based on cost, speed, reliability, quality, the number of fonts of type required, the convenience of obtaining special characters, and the availability of backup machines if breakdowns occur.

ZIP

The high-speed Photon ZIP machine installed at the National Library of Medicine is the only machine that today takes computer magnetic tape directly. Its successful performance in producing Index Medicus is being closely studied by publishers and printers. The price tag today is $200,000, with the user furnishing his own computer. This first ZIP is setting about 300 characters per second, which means that it can expose all the negatives for a 100,000-word book in less than an hour. This is equal to about 30 Linotypes. ZIP holds 264 characters at a time, and these can be changed by sliding in a new set of glass matrices.

The quality of the output of ZIP is satisfactory for indexes and directories, but most book and magazine publishers require better work. Chief defects are erratic vertical positioning of letters and variations in letter density.

Each line on the negatives for Index Medicus is exposed across all three columns, because their computer also does page makeup.   The internal memory or external disc file must therefore have enough capacity to hold the contents of an entire page, in addition to the required working storage capacity.

The second model of ZIP is being used experimentally by Western Electric Co. for printing daily and monthly changes in some New York City telephone directories, for use by operators.   The third is scheduled to go to England. There is real hope that an improved ZIP will take the magnetic output tapes of the computer directly and give graphic arts quality in a variety of type fonts.

With a high-speed photocomposition machine that accepts magnetic tape directly, there may be less of a cost penalty for using the machine to produce proofs.   The machine is so fast that it would likely be idle part of the time on second or third shifts, if not on the first shift.   It is then logical to use the machine for producing either paper prints or film negatives for proofreading, since the out-of-pocket extra cost is only for the photographic proof paper.

Photon 713

A few of the new Photon 713 photocomposition machines are now in the field.   Early reports indicate that this machine has real promise for producing composition of graphic arts quality from punched paper tapes of computers.   The specifications definitely offer advantages over other photocomposition machines available today.   Speed is about 20 characters per second, with a choice of 720 characters or eight full fonts in eight type sizes, in producing either negatives or repro positives from punched paper tape.   Price is about $50,000. Photon is also offering, for $15,000 additional, the same capability working directly from the magnetic output tapes of a computer.   This version, if it performs reliably, will be of high interest to printers and service bureaus because it eliminates the slow and costly extra step of using a computer to convert magnetic tape to punched paper output tape.

Fototronic

Another promising photocomposition machine for punched paper output tapes of computers is the Harris-Intertype Fototronic, now selling for around $55,000. This has the same rated speed as the Photon 713, but actual through-put varies with the number of type size and font changes re-quired on a given job.

Cathode-ray Photocomposition

Many cathode-ray character-generating systems have been proposed for direct operation from magnetic tape, but as yet none is on the market in commercial form. The Government Printing Office awarded jointly to Mergenthaler Linotype Company and CBS Laboratories a $2,185,000 con-tract to produce two such machines, called Linotrons, for 1966 delivery. Speed varies with type size, because it takes longer to make an electron beam create a larger character from a pattern of fine lines, but is expected to be much faster than ZIP. For making paper proofs, which can be lower in quality as long as they are readable, the Linotron can run at up to 5,000 characters per second. Linotron will give a choice of 256 characters in one basic font that can be changed electronically to any of eight different sizes ranging from 5 to 18 points. Resolution is claimed to be better than Linotype hot-metal work but not quite up to Linofilm photo-composition quality. A price of $500,000 is being quoted for a commercial model.

Other firms working on the cathode-ray approach in-clude the RCA Graphic Services Division, Alphanumerics, K. S. Paul & Associates in England, and Rudolf Hell in Ger-many.

The role of costly, high-speed cathode-ray machines in commercial publishing is as yet unknown. Smaller and slower machines can share the work and back up each other. A fast machine is economically unsound unless it can be kept busy or can be justified on the basis of its high speed for a few specific jobs.

Line Printer Output

With proper adjustment and operation of a high-speed line printer, using a high-quality new nylon ribbon and a high grade of paper, repro copy can be obtained directly from a computer. This can then be reduced in size photographical-ly to produce plates for offset printing of indexes, directo-ries, and other types of reference books. Alternatively, pa-per masters can be produced directly on the line printer if the original large type size is acceptable.

The two chief drawbacks of line printers are the waste of space inherent in uniform spacing of characters on a line printer and the objections of users to the all-caps print-out of most line printers.   The cap-and-lower-case chain that is available for the IBM 1403 line printer gives improved readability in the new typewriter-like font, but the spacing is still the same.   In one case, for Index Medicus, this cap-and-lower-case printer is backup for the Photon ZIP, but an emergency issue produced on the line-printer will take twice as many pages.

The line printer is envisioned only for jobs where less than graphic arts quality can be tolerated and space require-ments are not critical.   Indexes, book-form library catalogs, parts lists, and some directories are examples of work for which a line printer should be considered.

Economical Applications

Although real progress has been made in computer composition, there are today very few economical commer-cial applications that provide graphic arts quality.   One rea-son for this has been the lack of photocomposition machines suitable for computer composition.   Another is the lack of completely versatile software.

Production costs drop most spectacularly when print-ing jobs make maximum use of the data processing capabili-ties of computers, as with indexes and directories.   Here are some job characteristics that favor use of computers:

1. A need to explode information so a given item of input is duplicated many times by the computer.

2. A need to sort items of information, so they ap-pear in one or more desired sequences regardless of the order in which the items enter the computer.

3. A need for updating the information, by cumulating corrections and new material with old material, so the computer can be used to eliminate rekeyboard-ing of the unchanged older material.

4. A need for speed that overrides cost considera-tions.

One publication that met these characteristics was the annual <u>Electronics Buyers' Guide</u>. This McGraw-Hill publication tells who makes the components and equipment that constitute the electronic industry. The input data for this directory is the equivalent of 300 pages in print, while the output or final directory is almost 800 pages in print--a tremendous explosion of information. There is a real requirement for data processing here also; the input from questionnaires requires three alpha sorts. Just before the cutoff deadline for input, the entries of advertisers must be changed to bold face type and sequenced separately. And finally, there is the requirement for updating once a year by incorporating any changes in the manufacturer's name and address, phone number, corporate data, addresses of representatives, or products made. The potential for saving by computer was so attractive that a decision was made to produce it this way for the first time in 1965.

Since there was no precedent for producing a directory of this size by computer, many decisions had to be made in conjunction with an exhaustive systems study. While describing the procedures finally adopted, the problems and options will be covered for guidance in planning similar jobs. Here are the main steps:

1. <u>Assign Code Numbers.</u> First of all, the 7,000 manufacturer names were arranged manually in the desired alphabetic sequence and fed into a computer for automatic assignment of 6-digit manufacturer code numbers, with a spacing of 125 between the numbers. This permits insertion of new names in correct alphabetic sequence in future years. Each new name is given a number halfway between the numbers of adjacent names to leave room for inserting further names. Product headings were similarly tape-punched and given 5-digit codes.

When assigning codes, the computer also adds a check digit at the end of each number to permit automatic computer detection of errors in typing of code numbers. If an error is made in a code number, the computer will get a different check digit and thus detect the errors.

2. <u>Prepare Typographic Specifications.</u> This is a much bigger job than it sounds. Rules must be established for each detail of type size, style, special characters, punctuation, indents, capitalization, handling of turnover lines, column widths, spacings between lines, leader dots, rules

for breaking an address when it will not all go on one line, etc. The entire input must be divided into logical fields, and the maximum number of characters in each field must be specified. Fields were made as small as possible; examples of fields are the corporate name, street address, city, state, ZIP code, phone number, and number of engineers employed. The importance of establishing specs and field lengths before-hand cannot be emphasized too much, because changes in computer programming can be very costly.

The column width was 200 units of 6-point type, which came out to be 14.1527 picas. Character widths were specified to thirds of a unit, so each line was made up of 600 increments. The width of each character in increments had to be determined and fed into the computer first.

Instead of justifying right-hand margins of columns by changing word spaces and hyphenating, the first lines of an entry were left short when the next field wouldn't fit. For the last line of each entry, leader dots were specified to make the phone number or state abbreviation come out flush right. The illusion of justification does not look too bad, as can be seen in Fig. 5.

3. Choose a Computer. The decision here went to a 24K Honeywell 200 computer in the McGraw-Hill Data Processing Center in Hightstown, New Jersey, used with a Honeywell 500-character-per-second paper tape reader and a 100-character-per-second paper tape punch.

4. Choose Output Machines. Here the choice was the American Type Founders B-8 paper-tape-driven photocomposition machine, which is reliable even though painfully slow (about as fast as an average typist, at 5 characters per second). The slowness is an asset, however, because the four machines required to meet the production schedule provided backup for each other in the event of trouble. Special 176-character type discs had to be designed and made to get the variety of type fonts and sizes required (6-point c & lc, 6-point b-f caps, and 8-point b-f caps).

5. Select Programmers. Programming was contracted to National Computer Analysts in Princeton, New Jersey. This firm was chosen chiefly because their programmers had heavy experience in computer composition.

6. Punch Input Paper Tapes. This input punching

Pa   W I Duncan & Assoc. 5452 Charles St, Phila....744-6110
Tex   Cain & Co, 435 Bainff Airways Bldg, Dallas....357-8645
Wash Stanley Enterprises, 127 S River St, Seattle 723-3320

WHEELER LABORATORIES INC, 122 CUTTER MILL RD
GREAT NECK, N Y.....516 482-7876
H WHEELER, PRES., EMP 111, ENG 62, $1,000-2,500M

WHEELOCK SIGNALS INC, 273 BRANCHPORT AVE
LONG BRANCH, N J.....201 222-6880
R NEWMAN, SLS MGR, EMP 153, ENG 18, $1,000-2,500M
Ala   Emory Design & Equip, 404 Dexter Ave
      Birmingham .....TR 1-1369
Ariz Stepco. Box 3109, Scottsdale 945-4925
Cal   Web Electronics Assoc, Box 45734
      Los Angeles 671 8297
Cal   R A Banks Sales, 1000 Acacia Ave, Los Altos....941-0900
Colo Stepco. 216 Clayton St, Denver.....388-9302
Conn Hatch-Hutchinson Assoc, Box 12
      Manchester.....MI 3-0863
Fla   NBS Inc, 3524 Devonswood Dr, Orlando.....423-4856
Fla   NBS Inc, 3931 SW 5th Terr, Miami.....444-1118
Ill   Electro-Comp Sales, 5129 W Devon
      Chicago.....RO 3-3636

Pa   Power - Tronic Systems Inc, 10-12 Pine Ct, New Rochelle...N Y
      Radio Corp of America Broadcast & Communications
      Prods Div, Front & Cooper Sts, Camden.....N J
      Spring City Electrical Mfg Co, 5 Main St, Spring City.....Pa
      York Metal Products Inc, 34-20 12th St, Long Island City...N Y

HUMIDITY INDICATORS See INDICATORS--HUMIDITY

HUMIDITY RECORDERS See RECORDERS--HUMIDITY

HYBRID JUNCTIONS--MICROWAVE

BUDD-STANLEY CO INC, 175 EILEEN WAY
  SYOSSET.....N Y ADV PGS 746, 747
DORNE & MARGOLIN INC, 29 NEW YORK AVE
  WESTBURY.....N Y ADV PG 618
Adams-Russel Co, Inc, 280 Bear Hill Rd, Waltham.....Mass
Ainslie Corp, 531 Pond St, Braintree.....Mass
Aircom Inc, 48 Cummington St, Boston.....Mass
Airtec Inc, 264 Columbus Ave, Roselle.....N J
Airtron, Div of Litton Industries, Inc, 200 E Hanover Ave
  Morris Plains.....N J
Alford Mfg Co. 299 Atlantic Ave, Boston.....Mass
Allied Research & Engineering Co, 10300 Glasgow
  Los Angeles.....Cal
Alpha Microwave. Div Alpha Industries Inc, 381 Elliot St
  Newton Upper Falls.....Mass

Fig. 5. Typography of Manufacturers Section (left) and Product Section (right) of 1965 Electronics Buyers' Guide, as produced by running computer-produced paper tapes through ATF model B-8 photocomposition machines. Computer is programmed to insert exactly the correct number of leader dots ahead of phone number and state fields to make these line up at right, giving effect of justification.

was farmed out to the programming firm to achieve single responsibility for establishing and punching the necessary control codes.   Here it was found that the hard copy did not always correspond to the punches made by the two Dura Mach 10 tape-punching typewriters.   Accordingly, the tapes were fed back into the readers of the Duras to produce new hard copy for proofreading against the questionnaires.   Error correction required very little additional keyboarding, because only the manufacturer code, the field number, and the new corrected wording for the field had to be punched.   The average length of a directory field is only about three words.

7.   Produce Line Printer Proofs.   Batches of the punched tape were fed into the computer along with the correction tapes for converting to magnetic tape, merging corrections, sorting records into final sequence, making validity checks of code numbers, counting characters to make sure no field was longer than the maximum length provided for it, and printing proofs.   Since the line printer could print only capital letters, some means of identifying true capital letters had to be used.   The decision to print an open lozenge under each true capital letter, as in Fig. 4, worked out very well from the proofreading standpoint, even though it doubled the line printer running time.

8.   Punch Output Paper Tape.   After coded instructions for bold-facing of advertisers had been punched and inputted, the computer selected the fields of data needed, processed these as required for the final sequences in the two sections of the directory, and added the necessary control codes for the photocomposition machines.   Output tapes were then punched for the Manufacturer's Section in 21 hours of Honeywell 200 computer time and for the Product Section in 35 hours, to give a total of about 28 miles of 8-channel paper tape.

9.   Convert Tapes to Repro Positives.   The output of paper tape was run through three ATF B-8 machines to get paper prints in about 20 days of three shift operation.   (An additional machine was kept in the publisher's plant for making last minute corrections and to serve as backup for those in the printer's plant.)   The paper repro prints were dummied along with ad proofs, then photographed to get page negatives for making offset printing plates.

Next Edition.   The magnetic tape reels containing the input data were stored, for two purposes: (a) to produce

IRRIGATORS, Soil

Allen W D Mfg Co 650 S 25 Av Bellwood Ill
Canvas Kid—See Canvas Products Co
Canvas Products Co 2115 Locust St St Louis 3 Mo
Hastings Canvas & Mfg Co Hastings Neb
Jons Mfg Co St Matthews SC
Research Products Corp 1015 E Washington Av Madison 10
   Wis
Rose Soak Rod—See Allen W D Mfg Co
Soakeze—See Jons Mfg Co
Soil-Soaker—See Hastings Canvas & Mfg Co
Spot Soaker—See Research Products Corp
Turfgrass Farm 4961 E 22 St Tucson Ariz
Wagner Awning & Mfg Co 2658 Scranton Rd Cleveland 1
Water Bubbler—See Turfgrass Farm

IRRIGATORS, Sub-Soil

Allen W D Mfg Co 650 S 25 Av Bellwood Ill
Anson Tool & Mfg Co Inc 4750 N Ronald Av Chicago 31
Birch Mfg Co 1521 Sedgwick St Chicago 10
Hubbard Mfg Co 2668 Territorial Rd St Paul 14 Minn
★ Preen Products Co 9 & Grayson Sts Berkeley 10 Cal
Root-A-Gators—See Anson Tool & Mfg Co Inc
Root Feed—See Wilson Plastics Inc
Root Irrigator—See Allen W D Mfg Co
Ross—See Ross Daniels Inc
Ross Daniels Inc 115 SW 8 St Des Moines 9 Iowa
Specialty Mfg Co 2356 University Av St Paul 14 Minn
★ Waterspike—See Preen Products Co
Wilson Plastics Inc Div Foster Grant Co Inc 400 Broadway San-
   dusky O

ISOLATED LIGHTING PLANTS—See Lighting Plants Farm
   Electric

JACK HANDLES—See Handles Logging Tool

JACK KNIVES—See Knives Pocket

JACK PLANES—See Planes

Fig. 6.   Typography of Hardware Age as produced by a
Photon 513 from computer-processed information. Bold-faced
lines preceded by star indicate advertisers.   Cross-references for trade names are alphabetized in same sequence
with manufacturers.   This directory has only a product section.

---

individual questionnaires for acquiring data for the next edition, with addresses in correct positions for window enve-
lopes; (b) to repeat unchanged material in the next edition
without additional keyboarding. Customized questionnaires
make it easy for manufacturers to check what they had in
the previous directory and mark the changes desired. It is
estimated that only about 50 pages of new input will be key-
boarded in 1966 to get 800 pages of output.

Other Directories. Chilton's Hardware Age directory was produced on a computer in 1965, using the facilities of Rocappi in Philadelphia. The hardware consisted of Dura Mach 10 tape-punching input typewriters, an RCA 301 computer, and a Photon 513 output photocomposition machine. The end product was 329 pages of composition in 6-point type, having the typographic format of Fig. 6.

Book Catalogs for Libraries

Computer composition techniques have made it possible for many libraries to replace their catalog card files with much more convenient book-type catalogs. These are usually updated annually, and cumulative supplements for new material are issued quarterly. The catalogs can serve a number of main libraries as well as all branch locations.

One example is the combination catalog serving the medical libraries of Yale, Harvard, and Columbia, produced by computer under the direction of F. G. Kilgour of Yale.

Another significant example is being produced by Documentation, Inc., for the Baltimore County Public Library. There are three hardbound annual volumes, for Title, Author, and Subject, containing 1,500, 1,500, and 1,700 pages respectively to cover 50,000 titles. Press run is about 100 sets. Here the cap and lower case printout of an IBM 1403 chain printer is reduced photographically to 8-point for off-set printing to give the format shown in Fig. 7. Punched cards are used for input. Processing is done on an IBM 1401, as also are sorting, breakout, and cumulating of the paper cover quarterly supplements.

Other computer processed book catalogs include those of the University of Toronto Library and the Florida Atlantic University Library. A number of special industrial libraries are using the same computer techniques but using the line printer printouts directly in binders, because the three or four copies produced in this way are adequate for their needs.

Summary

Computer composition is economical today for many types of directories, indexes, cumulated bibliographies, and other works involving significant amounts of sorting and other manipulation of input information.

For straight text that requires only justification and

```
INFANTS--CARE AND HYGIENE
  Prudden, Bonnie  How to keep your child fit
  from birth to six  c1964
  0165-13515                               136.7 P
INFORMATION SERVICES
  Cossman, E. Joseph  How to get 50,000 dollars'
  worth of services  free, each year, from the
  U.S. Government  1964
  0365-16495                               015.73 C
  Kent, Allen  Centralized information services
  1958
  0265-15398                               010.78 K
INFORMATION STORAGE AND RETRIEVAL SYSTEMS
  Foskett, D. J.  Science, humanism, and
  libraries  1964
  0265-15102                           Ref 020 F
  0165-14385                           Ref 010.78 W
  Jonker, Frederick  Indexing theory, indexing
  methods and search  devices  c1964
  0165-12676                               029.5 J
  Conference on libraries and automation, Airlie
  foundation, 1963.  Libraries and automation  1964
  0365-16479                           Ref 010.78 C
  Licklider, J. C. R.  Libraries of the future
  1965
  0365-17100                               010.78 L
  Metcalfe, John Wallace  Information indexing
  and subject cataloging  c1957
  0165-13195                           Ref 025.4 M
  Perry, James Whitney  Tools for machine
  literature searching  c1958
  0165-13441                               010.78 P
  Perry, James Whitney  Machine literature
  searching  1956
  0365-17368                               010.78 P
  Simonton, Wesley C.  Information retrieval
  today  1963
  0165-13882                               651.8 S
  Western Reserve university, Cleveland.  School
  of library science  Information systems in
  documentation  c1957
INFORMATION STORAGE AND RETRIEVAL SYSTEMS--
DICTIONARIES
  Honeywell, inc.  Glossary of data processing and
  communications terms  1965
  0365-16903                           Ref 010.78 H
```

Fig. 7. Portion of October 1965 supplement to printed book catalog that now replaces catalog card files in Baltimore County Public Library system, as produced from IBM 1403 line printer having cap and lower case chain.

---

hyphenation, it is much more difficult to promise cost savings at this time. Here also there is a major technological problem--the inability to produce at computer speeds a printout that will be acceptable to proofreaders, editors, and authors in place of conventional printed galley proofs. The cathode-ray approach to character generation does offer promise here as a proof printer. Cost and speed of the ma-

chine should approximate that of a line printer, but it must
be able to give easily readable proof prints in a wide variety of type faces, sizes, and special characters.

Another important deterrent to widespread adoption of
computer composition is the high cost of software. Work
on basic compiler programs having sufficient flexibility to
handle different jobs without reprogramming is now under
way.   Costs are high, well up into six figures.   If these
programs can be made sufficiently universal to permit amor-
tizing cost over a large number of jobs, the number of economical applications for computer composition should increase tremendously.

Input hardware problems are being solved at a satisfactory rate with a variety of keyboard units that punch paper tape with or without hard copy.   Some keyboard units
even produce magnetic tape, but the higher cost per machine
may preclude widespread use.

The output photocomposition hardware picture also
looks more encouraging in 1966, now that Photon 713's and
Harris-Intertype Fototronics are in actual use in printing
plants.   These machines sell for about four times the price
of an ATF B-8, but provide a greater variety of type fonts
and sizes along with higher operating speeds.

Cathode-ray photocomposition machines are appearing
also this year in Europe as well as this country, but it remains to be seen whether they can consistently and reliably
provide the graphic arts quality required by most book and
magazine publishers.

Bibliography

1.   Austin, Charles J.   1965.   The MEDLARS Project at
     the National Library of Medicine.   Libr. Resources
     & Tech. Ser. , 9:94-99. Winter issue.

2.   Quinn, Hugh J.   1965.   Computer Magic.   Printing
     Magazine/National Lithographer, 89 (11):42-44, 47,
     64.   Directory production.

3.   Roadblocks to Computer Composition; Editing and Proof-
     reading for Computer-Processed Books.   1965.
     Book Production Industry, 41 (9):58-63.

4. Hard Copy Proofs; What Authors Need to Know to Work with Hard Copy. 1965. Book Production Industry, 41 (6):53-57.

5. Computers in Composition 1965; The Debate Grows on Hyphenation. 1965. Book Production Industry, 41 (4):53-59.

6. Santarelli, P. F. Computer Prepared Text: A Real-Time/Time-Sharing Multi-Terminal Publication System. IBM Technical Report TR 00.1263, April 20, 1965. Poughkeepsie: Systems Development Division. 36 pages.

7. Hattery, Lowell H., and Bush, George P. 1965. Automation and Electronics in Publishing. Washington: Spartan. 206 pages. Sixteen papers from American University 1965 symposium, plus 211-item bibliography.

8. Strauss, Victor. 1965. The Printing Industry. Washington: Printing Industries of America. Chapter II, Section 6 contains 32 pages dealing specifically with computerized composition.

9. Proceedings of International Conference on Computerized Typesetting, March 2-3, 1965. Washington: Research and Engineering Council of the Graphic Arts Industry, Inc. 157 pages. Nineteen papers plus discussions.

10. Computerized Typesetting: Interest Runs High. Publisher's Weekly, April 5, 1965, pp. 52-68. Report on Mar. 1965 Research and Engineering Council Conference on Computerized Typesetting.

11. Mathews, M. V., and Miller, Joan E. 1965. Computer Editing and Image Generation. AFIPS Conference Proceedings--Fall Joint Computer Conference, 1:389-398. Washington: Spartan.

12. Proceedings of Computer Typesetting Conference, London University, 1964. 1965. London: Institute of Printing Limited. 245 pages.

13. New Equipment and Trends in Automated Composition. 1964. Book Production Magazine. 80 (12):36-39.

14. Bennett, David. The Case for Unjustified Typesetting. British Printer, October 1964. 5 pages. Reprinted by Composition Information Services, 1605 N. Cahuenga Blvd., Los Angeles.

15. Gardner, Arthur E. The Age of Computerized Typesetting . . . Phase 2. 1964. Printing Production, 95 (10):48-53.

16. Getting Started in Computer Composition. 1964. Book Production Magazine, 80 (9):52-54.

17. Weinstein, Edward A., and Spry, Joan. 1964. Boeing SLIP: Computer Produced and Maintained Printed Book Catalogs. Am. Doc., 15:185-190.

18. Ohringer, Lee. Computer Input from Printing Control Tapes. A paper presented at the 16th Annual Meeting of the Technical Association of the Graphic Arts, Pittsburgh, Pa. June 3, 1964. 13 pages.

19. Barnett, Michael P., Moss, D. J., and Luce, D. A. 1964. Computer Generation of Photocopying Control Tapes. II. The P C 6 System. Am. Doc., 15:115-120.

20. The (R)evolution in Book Composition. Part 3: What's Ahead for Computers; Part 4: The Systems Concept --Key to Computer Profits, Management and the Computerized Future. Book Production Magazine, 79:55-61, (April 1964) and 67-73 (May 1964.)

21. Seybold, John W. 1964. The ROCAPPI System for Computerized Composition. Book Industry Magazine, 1 (3): 42-45.

22. Holliday, Alan S. Computer Controlled Composition for Books. Part 1: Concepts, Systems, Machines, Manning, Problems, and Solutions; Part 2: Applying the RCA 301 Computer to Book Typesetting. Book Industry, 1: 22-25 (Feb. 1964) and 28-31, 78. (Mar. 1964).

23. Computers: Their Impact on Book Composition. Special 32-page report reprinted from Feb. 1964 Book Production Magazine, containing five articles: "Computers in '64: Year of Transition from Theory to Practice"; "Kingsport and Computers: A Book Manu-

facturer's Experience in Composition Research";
"What's Ahead for Computers?"; "Computers Are
Here--What Now?"; "The Systems Concept--Key to
Computer Profits."

24. An Introduction to Computer Typesetting. Part 1:
Basic Computer Principles; Part 2: The Automation
of Typesetting in Application. Print in Britain, 11:
20-22. (Jan. 1964) and 11: 27-32 (Feb. 1964).

25. Buckland, Lawrence F. The Recording of Library of
Congress Bibliographic Data in Machine Form. May-
nard, Mass.: Inforonics, Inc. 43 pages.

26. Duncan, C. J 1964. Look! No Hands. Penrose Annual, 57: 121-167.

27. Typesetting in the Computer Age. 1964. Print in
Britain, 12:8-page supplement.

28. Gardner, Arthur E. 1964. Computerized Typesetting
--A Management Report on the State of the Art. 11
pages. Composition Information Services Newsletter,
Los Angeles, Calif.

29. 29. Duncan, C. J., Molyneux, Eve L., Page, E. S.,
and Robson, M. G. 1963. Computer Typesetting:
An Evaluation of the Problems. Printing Technology,
133-151 (Dec. 1963).

30. Bozman, William R. 1963. Phototypesetting of Computer Input. NBS Technical Note 170. Washington:
U. S. National Bureau of Standards. 6 pages.

31. Barnett, Michael P., and Kelley, K. L. Computer
Editing of Verbal Texts. Part 1. The ESI System,
Am. Doc., 14: 99-108 (April 1963); 15 (2):115-120
(April 1964).

32. Smith, Frank H. 1963. Computers and Composition.
Mod. Lithographer, 31 (1):37-44.

33. North, Arthur. 1963. Quality Typography from Computer Data. 12-page booklet. Washington: U. S.
Patent Office. Covers computer conversion of all-
caps input of directory names and addresses to cap
and lower case output.

Automation: Rosy Prospects and Cold Facts

By Daniel Melcher, President, R. R. Bowker Company

Reprinted from Library Journal, March 15, 1968, published
by the R. R. Bowker Company (a Xerox company). © 1968
R. R. Bowker Company.

Several years ago--in 1963, to be exact--I drafted an
ad in which Bowker announced that any of its book information could be had in any form, including punched cards,
punched paper tape, magnetic tape, or any other machinable
form.   The ad was repeated once or twice--but the only responses that came to it were from branches of the IBM Company.

The offer was bona fide.   We were already using
punched cards and punched paper tape in various ways, and
we were prepared to deliver whatever anyone might want at
a nominal rate, just to lend a hand with any experiments.

Four years have passed since that announcement and
the future is still very much where it always was.   We were,
at one point, supplying the data on Forthcoming Books to the
Library of Congress for mag-tape conversion.   The idea was
to help alert LC to books announced for publication but not
yet received for cataloging.   So far, any actual use of this
data in this way is still also in the future.

In another experiment we started supplying inventory
control data to 40 college stores, covering Paperbound Books
in Print.   Some of the data went out in the form of punched
cards, some in other forms.   It was, and remains, an "interesting experiment"--which is the conventional euphemism
for "unsuccessful experiment."

I don't want to give the impression that we are disil-
lusioned about the ultimate potential of the new technologies,
but it is awfully easy to read the literature and the conference reports and get the idea that things are further along

than they are.

I could tell you that we now have the capability of
creating cross-references from author-title input; or, in a
spirit of greater candor, I could tell you how, on one run,
the computer assigned each subject heading to the preceding
title, thus misclassifying 44,000 titles on a single pass.

The latter, however, I shouldn't be telling you.   The
rules of the computer game are that you talk only about what
you are going to do, never about how it turned out.   This
is a science in which you publish the results of your experiments before you make them.   I have tried to get and to
publish stories of the sad aftermath of many noble experiments, but the trouble is that the victims won't talk.   This
is a pity, because much wisdom can be gleaned from the
records of failure.

Let me leave to McLuhan the consideration of what
things will be like in 1984 and here take the narrow view,
reviewing how things are right now, with respect to the use
of computers in the publishing process.

Most large publishers now have computers, and many
small ones use computers.   They use computers for the
most part, however, in exactly the same way other industries use them--for billing, accounting, inventory control,
and sales analysis.   Very few report net savings resulting
from conversion to computer, and most went through agonies
in the conversion process.   They all hope for tangible economies in the future--though it is a bit puzzling to note that
$5 million companies seem to expect those economies when
they reach $10 million, and the $10 million companies think
there might be economies when they reach $20 million, etc.

The tangible results of computerization as they affect
the publishers' customers and authors are easier to identify.
Computers have unmistakably lengthened the time it takes to
fill an order, and have made it almost impossible to understand a royalty statement or get an intelligent answer to a
complaint or query.

The biggest advantage always cited in support of this
business department automation is that it will provide management with far more extensive operating information, and more
promptly.   To the extent that this becomes effective, presumably publishers will be out of stock less often.   Unhappily,

the near-term result often seems to be that information formerly available by means of a phone call to the order department is reported as unknowable until the computer makes
its next periodic report.

Of more interest than the automation of clerical procedures is the automation of functions peculiar to publishing,
notably type composition, indexing, directory compilation,
SDI (selective dissemination of information), and machine
translation.

So far the computer has made only modest contributions to the economics of typesetting. Quite a few printers
are using small computers to relieve human compositors of
their so-called "end of the line" decisions, that is, where to
break the line, whether to hyphenate, and so forth. It is
fair to say, however, that thus far there has been no great
breakthrough. Somebody still keyboards the manuscript at
some point. Only in certain kinds of directories and cumulations does the computer offer a means of getting multiple
outputs from a single input--as, for example, in the case of
Books in Print where a computer can itself make the title index by inverting and resequencing the author entries.

I recently read how some firm of systems analysis
said they had found a way to cut typesetting costs by 80 percent. One had to read the fine print to realize that the
promised composition savings depended on getting the author
to do the work of the compositor and, further, on getting him
not to make corrections in proof. If you could achieve those
things you could make spectacular savings, with or without
the computer.

It is true that some spectacularly high-speed composing machines are becoming available, beginning with the
Photon Zip, first used for the Index Medicus, and now including even faster machines such as the RCA Videocomp,
the Linotron, the Harris-Intertype, and Alphanumeric's
Photocomposition System APS-2. These promise a radical
improvement in the quality of computer composition, though
no breakthrough in the general run of book composition.
They may help keep down the costs of such cumulations as
Books in Print and perhaps enable corrections to be made at
a later stage in the publication process.

Automatic indexing is another way of using computers
in the publishing process. Some progress has been made,

but if you have ever tried to use a KWIC index you know that computers have much to learn about indexing.

Machine translation of, say, Russian into English has been explored rather thoroughly. The results have been interesting, but to date the human brain still scores an easy win over the computer in this area.

There is, nevertheless, no doubt that computers are here to stay. They are creatures of their time, and they come because they are needed. Four factors, in my opinion, are working together to put a computer in your future and mine, even if their full promise is yet to be realized.

The first factor is the steady rise in the cost of human time. With each upward boost in salaries and fringe benefits, new laborsaving devices become more practical and former luxuries become present economies.

The second basic kind of change is the declining cost of machine time. Computers cost less, or do more. Other machines also cost less or do more. The cost of offset printing plates drops from $1.50 a page to $1 a page to ten cents a page, even to five cents a page--in an almost unbelievable series of technical breakthroughs.

The third big change, as I see it, after the rise in the cost of human time and the decline in the cost of machine time, is the enlargement of the market. Where once only the biggest reference libraries would have bought certain kinds of new reference tools, now even the high schools become prospects. There are more users among whom to divide costs.

A fourth change is in our attitude toward time. We have become impatient with abstracting services that are two years behind and national bibliographies that are up to five years behind. We want to learn more promptly about what's coming or is now ready, and we want to get it more promptly once we learn of it, and get it into service quickly once it arrives. The pace is quickening.

Out of these changes emerge many opportunities for improving information services, not all of which have been exploited by any means. In effect, in today's world, name it--and you can probably have it. Out of these changes has come the reprint revolution which has brought long out-of-

print items back into print in droves--the title count for the
latest Books in Print is up from 190,000 to 240,000. There
also has come the possibility of reprinting not merely editions of 1000 or more, but even editions of 100, or 25--or
even editions of one. Out of it all has come new interest
in microforms--though there is precious little in the reprint, mini-, or micro-technology that wasn't rather clearly
set forth 30 years ago in Robert C. Binkley's classic Manual on Methods of Reproducing Research Materials. Out of
these changes have come timesaving devices like the enlarged Forthcoming Books, which now not only looks five
months ahead but provides cumulative information on everything published since the latest revision of Books in Print.

It must be noted, however, that as yet the utilization
of computers to meet these changing needs has been massively disappointing. When an eminent Australian librarian
came here in late 1965, enthused by the rosy projections of
library automation in the library literature, he was forced to
report that almost nothing of the promise had come to pass
--or even seemed imminent ("American Automation in Action," by Harrison Bryan, LJ, January 15, 1967, p. 189-
96). He found just one seemingly effective automated system for claiming missing serials, and just one example of
reasonably efficient, overall library automation, though even
the latter depended on punched card technology more than on
computers.

The glamor, let's face it, is in the computers, but
the breakthroughs are elsewhere. It ought to be big news
when one publisher bucks the trend and provides same-day
shipment on all orders received before 3 P.M. ("Behind
the Scenes at Britain's 'Best Shipper,'" by H. Fred Scott,
Publishers' Weekly, October 23, 1967, p. 27-29). It would
be if he had used a computer to do it--but he didn't.

The computer is a marvelous machine, and it does
some things extremely well, such as handle airline reservations. But all too often we find ourselves invited to applaud
computer applications that are somewhat in a class with the
dog who played the violin--not that it was done well, but
rather that it was done at all. A shining exception was a
recent brief news item in Library Journal (October 15, 1967,
p. 3584) in which it was candidly reported that a three-
month experiment with a telefacsimile link between two South
Carolina libraries was discontinued because of "excessive
cost" and "infrequent use."

You hear that a certain encyclopedia is to be indexed by computer. You find later that this was, indeed, tried, but was given up. You hear that one of the book wholesalers has automated. Of course, his service goes into a tailspin, but ultimately straightens out. Did he get the bugs out of the system? Not a bit of it; he finally threw out the system.

I talked to one wholesaler who had really made his automation work, but who had wound up with costs a good deal higher than a competitor's. I asked whether he really thought he could get his costs down. He said: "No, but I think the other fellow's costs will rise--he's automating, too."

And I've always liked the story that was told of one of the larger corporations. Back in the days when you couldn't hold up your head in big corporation circles unless you had a computer, they went right along with the rest. But they were unusually well-advised on procedure and they recruited and trained an inside team of systems analysts and gave them a full two years to prepare the way for the computer. At the end of that time the company was able to report that the computerization program had already shown greater savings than had been anticipated, even though the computer itself had not yet arrived.

We began quite early at Bowker to inquire about the possibilities of computerizing our bibliographies. Ordinarily, the computer people would announce, almost before looking around, that their equipment was ideal for our needs and could save us much time and money. After study they would report that they could produce Books in Print in so many months for so much per page. I would then have to break it to them that, just using our old-fashioned methods, we were already producing it in half that time and at half that cost, with greater legibility to boot.

Times change, of course. I keep inquiring every year or so to see whether the rising hourly cost of people has yet crossed the descending unit cost of computers, with respect to any of our projects.

It is interesting to watch the action at the interface between the computer world and the printing world. I have a little gambit I like to use on hardware people when they begin bragging about how fast their machines can go. I say,

"Yes, but your output is so slow."

They bridle a bit and point out that even the least of their impact printers can knock out 600 lines a minute. I look sorrowful and say that we have a printer who can turn out better than two million lines a minute. They don't believe me, of course, but they ask me what kind of printer that is. I tell them it's an ordinary printer with a printing press. And it's true. The web offset press which does Books in Print delivers 20,000 signatures an hour, each containing 32 pages with 200 lines to the page!

The real glamor of the computer is at its chromium-plated best, however, when the talk gets around to real-time access to central data banks, to the end that an inquirer can get answers almost instantly, either on a television screen or in the form of hard copy made from the image on the television screen.

I am as fascinated by this concept as anybody. I wonder, however, what proportion of library patrons are going to value this kind of speed enough to be willing to pay its cost. I get the impression that the fellow who is vaguely resolved to take out a copy of War and Peace, if he can ever find one on the shelf, is getting lumped in with the surgeon who has a patient hanging between life and death and needs quick information from the National Library of Medicine.

Console Cookery

Some time ago I attended a seminar on technological progress in publishing and found myself eating breakfast with one of the speakers, a man who was in charge of research at General Electric. He had told us the evening before that he thought books would be obsolete within a decade. I told him I suspected he didn't really believe it himself but was simply trying to needle us. With an absolutely straight face, he said that he did, indeed, mean it.

I tried to kid him out of it. I said it seemed likely to me that, ten years hence, or 20 years hence, or 30 years hence, if my wife got up in the morning and felt like making a batch of raisin bran muffins she would still feel that the simplest approach was to reach for her trusty copy of Rombauer's Joy of Cooking.

My companion at the breakfast table implied that while
there might be some problem about retraining my generation,
the generations coming up would learn to present not just
some problems but any and all problems directly to the
household's communications console.   I asked him to give
me a rough idea how he saw this working in the case of the
raisin bran muffins.

He said I would go to the console and tap out the
word "muffin."   I asked him if perhaps keyboarding itself
wasn't already obsolete, and he apologized for overlooking
this point and agreed that it was.   He started afresh by saying that I would go to the console and simply say: "It's
muffins that I want to talk to you about."   The screen of the
console, he said, would then promptly flash a legend such
as "I have information on muffins, history; muffins, nutri-
tion; and muffins, recipes.   Which aspect did you have in
mind?"

I reminded him that he'd told us the night before that
reading itself might be obsolete, thus making it impractical
for a future generation to read anything off a screen unless
the message were pictorialized.   He conceded the point and
amended his example to presuppose that the choices would
be pictorialized or verbalized.   But he forgot about this a
moment later and had the screen showing me the table of
contents of a cookbook and then any selected page from the
book.

Well, I don't know.   I have a feeling that, ten years
from now, not only will my wife still have a copy of Rombauer in the kitchen, but so will my son's wife.   If nothing
else, it would surely be cheaper, even if interrogations of
the console came as cheap as telephone calls--which seems
unlikely.   Cost is a problem that is often glossed over in
the world of automation.

I see no reason to doubt that all of the promised electronic miracles are technologically possible.   But I have the
gravest doubts about how soon they are going to be really
practical or desirable except in very special circumstances.
In a very high proportion of current library inquiries, even
our old-fashioned library methods provide fast and satisfactory answers.   Of the remainder, some would probably go
unsatisfied in any case, and the residue might well survive
modest delays rather than warrant involvement of heavy hardware.

Consider, for example, the number of librarians who are right now talking in dead earnest about real-time, on-line access to the holdings of other libraries, while at the same time accepting substantial delays on access to their own holdings. Consider the libraries which are right now accumulating orders for weeks instead of placing them daily, and are accepting four-week delays in delivery of books by the wholesaler, six-week delays in processing, and 12-week delays in binding serials--while trying for real-time access to data in other libraries where similar backlogs exist.

I don't want to sound pessimistic, because I'm not. Actually, one can cite many nice little breakthroughs. At Bowker we began by just putting our information about Forthcoming Books on punched cards, using one not-very-terrifying keypunch. We then started reshuffling the cards to get better statistics. Then we got a second keypunch. But we were still sending out the cards to a service bureau for listing.

Then, one fine day, we discovered to our delight that we were, technically speaking, computerized; that is to say, the service bureau put our cards through its computer in-stead of through the far simpler card lister formerly used. The result was no different, and they charged us three times as much--but it made us feel kind of big league.

Then we decided something had to be done about the horrid ALL CAP type you get out of computers. It was a-bout 20 cents a page for the ALL CAP stuff, and $5 a page for taking the same computer output and feeding it through a Linotype.

However, we made a few more calculations and con-cluded that if we operated our own Justowriters we could get a really legible page for under $1 with real bookface type. So we plunged. We bought two Flexowriters that would take punched tape from the computer and give us back book pages ready for offset.

On those machines we not only did Forthcoming Books but also two catalogs of children's books. We got the hang of inputting by Flexowriter and proofing from computer list-ings. We marveled at how we could put in material in scrambled sequence and have it come back neatly sorted by author, title, subject, and publisher--sometimes with im-personal little reproving messages from the computer, like

"You goofed--price omitted." Our next step up was to the
Photon Zip--it was either that or buy 20 Justowriters.

To be candid about it, however, I think that we could
have done all this if anybody had wanted it, even before the
invention of the computer. There are cases where you can
do things that you couldn't otherwise have done at all, but
there are many more where the computer represents only a
small step forward, if any, in speed, economy, or other advantage. And there are probably even more cases where
the most efficient way of doing something by computer would
show no gain at all unless the comparison was with some
former method that was hopelessly inefficient by old-fashioned standards.

I realize that all this has a sort of negative sound.
On the other hand, the computer enthusiasts can point with
pride to Index Medicus, Science Citation Index, and the current awareness publications of Chemical Abstracts Service,
and I am going to point with pride to the latest Paperbound
Books in Print. Without a doubt, publishing is going to be
revolutionized by the computer. To this point, though, it
has been affected even more by such other revolutionary developments as cold-type, lowered offset costs, xerographic
copying, microtechniques, wire transmission and, yes, the
spread of library service itself.

Although Bowker's ventures into the world of computers have thus far been few and unsophisticated, we have
still made our full share of mistakes and have taken our
quota of punishment. Tuition in this school comes high. If
I think back over things I wish I had known sooner, several
points come to mind.

Advice to Automaters
          In the first place, I have long since ceased to ask
any computer man whether a thing can be done. The answer
is always "yes." Anything can be done, I guess--but that
isn't the issue. What matters is whether anyone in his right
mind would choose that way of doing it. If I hadn't been
through it, I wouldn't have believed the idiotic advice you can
get out of systems analysts who should know better. One
man, after extended discussion of whether certain data could
be got into two lines instead of three, suggested, in dead
seriousness, leaving out the spaces between words. One
man brushed aside a problem involving incompatible formats

--you could convert to anything, he said.   Yes, I guess you
can, if you can find the equipment, or if cost and delay are
no object.   But it can easily cost more to convert than to
re-keyboard.

My second piece of burnt-child cynicism has to do
with reliance on outside consultants.   It goes almost without
saying that no reliance whatever is to be placed on any advice you get from a hardware salesman.   In this situation,
as in others, advice that is free of charge, but not free of
motivation, is worth about what you pay for it.   But the situation is nearly as bad when it comes to independent outside consultants--nor can they really be blamed for it.   The
fact is they do not--and could not--know your problems,
and they are no more likely to be able to pick up what they
need to know about your problems in a series of interviews
than you are likely to pick up what you need to know of their
expertise in the same brief exposure.   There is no substitute for inside expertise, and developing it is inevitably going to be a slow process, whether you try initially to find
it inside or outside the staff.

My third lesson comes from watching others fall on
their faces.   This commonly results from scrapping the old
methods before the new ones are really proved out.   Any
conversion plan that does not provide either for parallel op-
eration--or for gradual rather than all-at-once conversion--
is an invitation to trouble.   In most conversions, there
seems to come a false dawn.   The temptations to try and
fly before you can crawl are legion, but I hope I can go on
resisting them.

Another lesson that I feel I am just beginning to appreciate, is: Don't try to clean up an inefficient manual
situation by a direct jump to automated methods.   Clean up
the manual methods first.   It may seem double work but,
without it, there is grave danger of blanketing waste motion
into the automated plan.   I know one big school system
which uses five times as much time, money, and paper to
place an order as is remotely necessary.   But instead of
eliminating the red tape, they are automating it!

The worst pitfall in computerizing, in my opinion, is
batch processing.   You don't hear about it in the beginning.
Only later do you find that while your computer could do
what you want done, it vastly prefers to do things its own
way--with delays all along the line.   It can delay your or-

ders, delay your deliveries, delay your payments, and cut
you off from ready access to your own data.

Books--let it be repeated--are not obsolete.   Not all
inquiry is for easily tagged, isolated facts.   Much is for
browsing, review, enlightenment, inspiration, entertainment
--for most of which uses the book is a supremely efficient
package.

Nor is reading obsolete.   Reading, as a means of
input to the mind, is several times as fast as listening.
The interaction between mind and book is "on line" and
"random access."   For best use of computers we are told
to avoid situations where the computer is "input-bound,"
that is to say where its capacity to process data is bottle-
necked by its capacity to take in the data to be processed.
The same logic can be applied to the mind.   In a vast variety of situations the book--and only the book--can provide
input to the mind fast enough to stretch the mind.

B.   The Editor

The Editor As Publisher

By Ed Victor, a Director of Jonathan Cape.

From the Times Literary Supplement no. 3429:1087, November 16, 1967. Copyright by Times Newspapers Limited. Reprinted by permission.

For people outside publishing circles, the meaning of the term "editor" ranges from the lowly back-room boy with a blue pencil to the legendary father-confessor figure epitomized in the literary history by Maxwell Perkins of Scribner's in his relationship with Thomas Wolfe. The role of the editor encompasses both ends of this scale, and in his work on one book he may leap from the most menial sub-editorial chores to suggesting a total rewrite. Moreover, with the breaking-up of the rigidly hierarchical family firms (where the head of the firm was the publisher, the man with "taste," and the editorial staff provided little more than a technical service), editors in London are beginning to emulate their more powerful and autonomous counterparts in New York. The leading British editors now build up their own "lists" of authors within the larger structure of the house's imprint; they assume overall responsibility for the presentation and promotion of the book; they may sell paperback, translation and occasionally even film rights; they effectively determine what the author shall be paid for his work, and once it has been decided to publish him they fight to make him known and successful in an increasingly overcrowded literary scene.

Because of the editor's emergence as, from the author's point of view, the most important figure in the publishing house, authors are becoming more attached to their individual editors than to the institution of the house; and, as traditionally happens in America, when an editor leaves, the author is now likely to follow.

The editor's field of activity can be divided into two main areas. First, he finds books suitable for the list by selecting a very few titles from the literally thousands of manuscripts which are offered by agents or sent in directly by authors (in the case of Jonathan Cape, ten to twenty new authors are taken on out of two to three thousand submissions in any year). Other books will come to the house because the editor has specifically pursued them. Secondly, once an author has been taken on, the editor sees the book through its various stages of production to publication. The first of these tasks is largely a matter of taste; the second of technique. Another obvious split in the editor's role arises in the very different judgments and methods used in the selection and editing of non-fiction as opposed to fiction. In some firms there is a strict division of labour between these two fields, but surprisingly often the same editor is responsible for both genres.

It is impossible to generalize about the selection of fiction when so many publishing houses judge novels by totally different criteria. At one extreme, there are a number of houses primarily interested in publishing literature (although in England there is no purely literary house that maintains the consistently high standards of, say, Suhrkamp in Germany), while at the other there are quite a few houses whose fiction lists consist mainly of novels that have no literary merit whatsoever.

An editor at a literary house would claim that he will publish a novel on outstanding critical merit alone, regardless of commercial prospects. Alas, this principle is rarely tested, and, normally, the editor is involved in balancing literary and commercial values in whatever proportion is characteristic of his particular house. It is this balance which creates (or maintains) the imprint's identity. At Jonathan Cape, for example, the majority of novels are accepted more for their literary than for their commercial value. But in a few titles each year we look for considerable commerical possibilities so that the publication of these books, in effect, subsidizes all the books on the list which are likely to make a loss.

Although the individual editor recommends the acceptance of a book, his proposal is usually ratified by some kind of "Editorial Committee." The editor will then negotiate the terms of a contract with the author himself or with a literary agent acting on his behalf (the latter being in-

creasingly the case). Once the contract has been signed,
the editor goes through the manuscript slowly and with great
care (the first reading is never sufficiently detailed), looking for everything from weaknesses in the plot or the characterization to minor stylistic points. He will then meet
with the author to discuss any suggested changes. However
strongly an editor may feel about what he considers to be
flaws in a novel, he should only recommend--and never insist upon--changes. When the author and editor disagree
about something there are no convenient outside arbiters;
the author's name is on the book and his must be the last
word. It therefore becomes a question of the editor's per-
suasiveness in putting his points to the author, and the author's faith in the critical acumen of his editor.

When the final form of the book (and the title--which
frequently an editor is able to improve) has been basically
agreed, the manuscript is passed to those who prepare it for
the printer and put it into House style (most publishers have
evolved their own peculiar variations on the Oxford rules).

Since the editor is normally the main point of contact
between the author and the publishing house, it is up to him
to sponsor the author within the house, by trying to assure
that his book is handsomely produced, effectively launched
and well sold. He will discuss the design of the book and
the jacket with the production department; he will try to make
the sales department share his enthusiasm for it; he will
talk to the publicity department about promotional material
and review lists; and, of course, he will also talk about the
book to influential people outside the publishing house--col-
umnists, literary editors, even reviewers. All this activity,
both within the house (where the book competes for attention
with all the other books on the list) and outside the house
(where the book competes for attention with the roughly
25,000 other titles which are published in any given year),
is aimed at creating the best possible climate for the book
to be taken seriously and, if it is as good as the editor believes, to succeed. Literary editors of newspapers and journals for example, are notoriously and often rightly suspicious of publishers' editors who attempt to draw a book to
their attention. Unfortunately, too many editors "push" the
books on their list indiscriminately. This makes it difficult
for an editor who enthuses about only those books he really
cares for.

Frequently, the effort which an editor puts into the publication of a novel bears little relation to its potential profitability.   This is because he is far more concerned with the writer's long-term success than with the immediate success of any particular book.   The editor's relationships with his writers comprise probably the most crucial aspect of his job.   These should be full-time relationships, and not just ones which spring up as and when each new manuscript is delivered.   There are authors who desperately want to talk about what they are writing; there are those for whom mere talk would be disastrous.   Although the editor may run a tremendous risk by asking to see a portion of a work in progress (an unfavourable response could make it impossible for the author to continue) it is sometimes important that he do so, since his early editorial advice could be vital.   Even the most successful and established writers can go through periods of shattering insecurity, and often it is only the editor's encouragement and enthusiasm which will help.   A corollary of this proposition occurs when an editor feels that a book is such a mistake that he must advise the author simply to put it away--the extreme test of the author/editor relationship.

This relationship is not usually so deep or dependent in the field of non-fiction, where books tend to be made rather than born.   Today, the majority of non-fiction books for the general market are either commissioned in advance from the author on the basis of a short synopsis, or else written in response to an idea put up by the publisher himself.   The non-fiction editor, therefore, must have talents very different from those of the fiction editor.   By having a good working knowledge of recent bibliography in a large number of fields, he can put forward ideas for books to fill significant gaps.   Combined with this general knowledge, he should have a wide range of contacts in both academic and journalistic circles, so that he can "marry" the right author to the right ideas.   In fact, he is something of an impresario, not simply in a creative sense but in a business sense, in that, when the book is his idea, he will try to buy all the foreign rights in it from the author, and then sell them on a grand, international scale--giving the author a percentage, of course. The non-fiction editor must also be able to attract authors with their own ideas to the house and to evaluate their projects on the basis of only a short synopsis and perhaps one or two sample chapters.   This kind of very early decision-making (the fiction editor rarely commits himself before reading the whole book) requires him to be an expert in finding experts to help him, as well as a quick learner, so that he can acquire enough knowledge of any given field to discuss the synopsis intelligibly and intelligently with the prospective author. This is one of the principal differences between the two genres from the editor's point of view. While the non-fiction editor is open to advice and suggestions from many outside sources, the fiction editor relies almost entirely on his own judgment.

Editors are frequently asked why they don't write themselves. It should be clear that an editor's job is a full-time one, if not, indeed, a way of life. The fact that a man can devote much of his energies to working on someone else's writing does not mean that he is a frustrated writer himself. On the contrary, the editor is a skilled professional who can find satisfaction within the terms of his own job-- a job which has, today, developed to such a point that he is, in effect, the publisher.

The Editor's Trade

By John Fischer, Executive Vice President and Editor-in-Chief, Harper's Magazine.

Copyright © 1965, by Harper's Magazine, Inc. Reprinted from the July, 1965 issue of Harper's Magazine by permission of the author.

So far as I can discover, nobody has yet written a good book on editing. And, for reasons to be noted in a moment, it is quite possible that nobody ever will.

This may seem odd, since how-to-do-it books on everything from golf to sex pour out of the printing plants in an ever-swelling stream. Moreover, in fields closely related to editing, the supply of books is copious. At least once a week somebody turns out a new meditation on writing; and a few of them--for example, E. M. Forster's Aspects of the Novel or Eudora Welty on the short story--are indispensable to anyone interested in learning the craft. About once a month we get another book on advertising. Some--such as David Ogilvy's Confessions of an Advertising Man--make excellent reading, while others--notably Rosser Reeves's Reality in Advertising--offer a useful, if rather chilling, glimpse of the way a supersalesman stalks his prey. Perhaps once in five years somebody produces an illuminating book about publishing, such as William Jovanovich's recent Now, Barabbas.

Yet it is extremely rare for anyone even to try to write intelligibly about the editor's trade. Although there are plenty of manuals on the technical details, such as copy editing and English usage, I don't know of any that attempts to explain its essentials. When James Thurber sat down to record what he knew about the founding editor of The New Yorker, he turned out an entertaining memoir, a postmortem on a complex personality and a treasure vault of anecdotes. But he never told us what Harold Ross actually did.

When you finish reading The Years with Ross you know all
about his drinking habits, views on sex, and contempt for
Alexander Woollcott; you have no idea how Ross handled his
job.   Somehow he managed to make The New Yorker monu-
mentally successful, while scores of other editorial ventures
--often started more auspiciously and with stronger financing
--failed.   Why?   Thurber can't tell us.   Nor does he give
us a clue for distinguishing a good editor from a bad one.
(I don't think Thurber knew.   Like most writers, he had only the dimmest notion about what editors are up to, and really didn't care.   Which probably is a good thing; the world
is poorer for every minute Thurber devoted to thinking a-
bout anything except his own writing.)

        Similarly, W. A. Swanberg's recent biography of The-
odore Dreiser gives us every significant fact except one:
How could a man who lived such a messy and disorganized
life, and whose mind was so muddled that he could cheer for
the Communists and the Nazis at the same time, contrive to
edit the Butterick fashion magazines with reasonable competence?   Autobiographies aren't much help either.   Few editors have written them, and I know of only one--William
Allen White of the Emporia, Kansas, Gazette--who conveyed
a little useful information about his operating methods.   Even
that is fragmentary and scattered through several books.

        Since I've been trying to edit something--newspapers,
books, or magazines--most of the time since my teens, the
subject is one of pointed interest to me.   Because I couldn't
learn much about it from books, and since trial and error
is a suicidally expensive method of education (one bad error
and you are out of business), I tried to pick up what I could
by watching veteran editors.   I've had the good luck to work
under three superb ones, two who were abysmally bad, and
a dozen or so in between; and naturally I spend many an evening talking shop with other editors of all sorts.

        The main conclusion I've reached from some thirty
years of such tuition is that most editors are utterly incapable of explaining what they do, or why.   This doesn't mean
that they don't know; it is simply that they can't put it into
words which will convey much to outsiders--just as my old
friend Wiley Post could not have told anyone how to pilot an
airplane.   Like the early aviators, editors generally seem
to fly by the seat of their pants.

        To put it another way, the primary piece of equip-

ment for a good editor probably is an instinct, or hunch,
which tells him what people will want to read a month, a
year, or a decade from now.   (Books often are contracted
for years ahead of publication, and even daily newspapers
have to plan their major projects months in advance.)   In
addition to this hunchability, a trait always hard to explain,
an editor needs to persuade the right authors to produce the
copy he wants--on time.   Equally important, and often harder, he has to keep out of print those things which in his
judgment don't belong there.

Is there a recipe for developing these rather specialized skills?   I am not at all sure; and if there is, I'm not
confident that I understand it.   Certainly I no longer have
much faith in certain formulae that I accepted as gospel
some ten or fifteen years ago.   Nevertheless I do think it is
possible at least to spot some of the ingredients that go into
the making of an editor; perhaps I am especially conscious
of those I know I lack.

An obvious one is curiosity, in abnormal quantity.
(I don't know whether people are born with this characteristic, or whether it can be developed, like a biceps.)   All of
the good editors I have known have been intensely inquisitive
about almost everything, from oceanography to Hollywood
starlets.   Once I worked with a night editor in the Washington bureau of the Associated Press who would spend the
quiet hours before dawn reading the encyclopedia--not dutifully, but with avidity.   Another man on the same staff used
his spare time in preparing a commentary on James Joyce,
simply because he was curious about both the way Joyce's
mind worked and the Dublin of his day.

Such an inflamed curiosity no doubt contributes a lot
to the Essential Instinct.   If an editor is passionately eager
to know all about, say, birth control in India, then there is
a good possibility that a lot of readers may feel the same
way.   But wait a minute. . . Six months from now, when
an article might conceivably be ready for the press, will potential readers still be interested?   Maybe by that time they
will have heard all they want about India's population problems?   Maybe the subject will have been covered, to the
point of boredom, by the newspapers and TV documentaries?
Or, horrid thought, maybe nobody else ever was anything
like as curious about it as the editor himself.   (In the latter
case, he had better become a demographer or go to work for
the Planned Parenthood Federation.)

This knack for projecting into the future, for estimating what people will be eager to read at some remote date,
seems to be associated with three characteristics.

One of them is a certain ordinariness. A good editor reacts, in his bones and belly, the same way as most
of the people in his audience--whether it is large or small,
general or specialized. He will have much the same range
of interests, the same values, the same kind of enthusi-
asms, a capacity for indignation at the outrages which stir
them. A prime example is DeWitt Wallace, the founder and
still the presiding genius of The Reader's Digest. Because
he is a sort of human litmus paper, anything that interests
him is almost certain to interest at least thirty million other
Americans, plus millions overseas. Anyone who knows him
realizes that he has gathered the biggest readership of any
periodical in history, not by cold-blooded analysis of mass
tastes, but simply because he is himself the quintessential
middle-class American citizen.

For even the most specialized publications, the same
rule holds. The editors of Seventeen, Scientific American,
and Partisan Review must each be tuned to vibrate to the
chords which will stir his particular audience. A really
great editor is one who vibrates a little ahead of time. As
they turn his pages, the readers' reaction will be "How
true! Why didn't I think of that myself?" or "That's what
I've always believed, really, but I could never put it into
words." Such an editor becomes a Leader of Opinion. But
he dare not take too long a lead, for once he gets out of
sight his following is likely to trail off after some other
Pied Piper who is not quite so avant-garde. Publishing history is littered with the dead logotypes of brilliant periodicals which were too far in advance of their times.

Also with those which lagged behind. H. L. Mencken
presents a classic case history. During the 'twenties his
raucous cynicism expressed a mood which was widespread
but which had remained latent until The American Mercury
gave it a voice. Almost immediately Mencken rallied an astonishing following of disenchanted intellectuals, rebellious
youngsters, and dissenters from the smug crassness of
Boom-time America. But in the 'thirties the Depression and
the approach of war brought a change of mood. Mencken
failed to sense it. (He predicted that even a Chinaman could
beat Roosevelt in 1936--the year FDR carried every state but
two.) In any case he would have scorned to refocus his

Weltanschauung to accommodate a mere shift in popular tem-
per.   So by 1933 his editorial career was finished.

In addition to curiosity and an intellectual companion-
ship with his constituents, a good editor usually has the enthusiasm of an adolescent in the spasms of first love.   Often
he actually is young; a surprising number of editors--includ-
ing Henry Luce, Harold Ross, Horace Liveright, and Frank
Harris--made their marks before thirty.   Others have just
been emotionally retarded, like Horace Greeley, who all his
life chased fads with childlike eagerness, his snowy whiskers
flapping in the breeze.

There is no substitute for this kind of enthusiasm,
to fetch the best authors (who usually value appreciation as
much as money), to attract a vigorous staff, to make the
printed page twitch with life . . . and to keep the editor
himself (as Thurber tells of Ross) tinkering away on recal-
citrant manuscripts till all hours, to the neglect of family,
friends, and blonde actresses.   It can't be faked.   A reader
will become passionately concerned with a publication only
when its editors believe, truly and passionately, that they
are trying to do something important.   If they don't, their
lack of enthusiasm will show on every page--in the uncombed
syntax, the jaded idea, the unweeded cliché, the routine caption, the perfunctory proofreading.

Such dispirited editing has become commonplace a-
mong American newspapers during the past generation, as
competition has disappeared from one city after another.
When all the papers in town, plus the broadcasting stations,
are owned by one firm--and especially when that firm is
dominated by businessmen who have no vocation for journalism and regard their media simply as money-machines--then
most of the incentive for good editing and writing is likely
to evaporate.

This has happened to two newspapers where I once
worked: the Amarillo, Texas, Globe and the Oklahoma City
Daily Oklahoman.   They used to be edited, respectively, by
Gene Howe and Walter Harrison--both skilled journalists with
a fanatic devotion to their trade--and when I was learning
the rudiments of reporting under their harsh direction, both
were up against rough competition.   Howe and Harrison saw
to it that no reporter could turn in a sloppy paragraph without rebuke, or produce a better-than-ordinary piece of copy
without praise.   The result was two newspapers full of

bounce and human juices. In addition, Harrison (who was the better teacher) trained scores of men who moved on to become editors and writers of some distinction for wire services, magazines, and metropolitan dailies. Today the two papers, having absorbed their competitors, are plump but plodding; they still deliver a fair amount of news with routine competence, but (to my nostalgic eye, at least) most of the old zing is gone.

Perhaps it is no coincidence that the old-fashioned 110-proof Marse Henry Watterson editorial zeal shows up most often nowadays in the ferociously competitive worlds of book and magazine publishing. A current instance is The New York Review of Books, edited by Robert Silvers, formerly of this magazine. Armed with nothing except enthusiasm, youthful energy, taste, overconfidence, and the absolute minimum of financing, he and a few associates (mostly unpaid) launched their venture two years ago in a field which everybody knew was already hopelessly overcrowded. Its odds for survival were about those of a twelve-foot sloop in a hurricane. Yet it not only has survived, but has established a national reputation for thoughtful (if sometimes a mite overearnest) literary criticism.

At the other extreme, Playboy seems to demonstrate the same point. Whatever you may think of it in other respects, its editors' enthusiasm for girlies has been established beyond all doubt.

A third trait common to most successful editors is simple ruthlessness. Happy is he who is born cruel, for if not he will have to school himself in cruelty. Without it, he is unfit for his job; because the kindly editor soon finds his columns filled with junk.

"I know too many people," Harold Ross once remarked--and every editor knows just what he meant. Hardly ever does an editor go to a dinner party without acquiring a manuscript, thrust into his hands by some sweet old lady who was always sure she could write--"I feel it here!"-- if only someone would give her a little encouragement. It happens on the street, too. A London cab driver once produced four hundred pages of a novel from under his seat the moment I asked him to drive me to the office of a well-known publisher. And just last summer I came away from a college commencement with three manuscripts, slipped to me by a pretty undergraduate, a professor, and a parent. All

are nice people, and only a brute could refuse to publish
their work.

In addition to such windfalls, a typical magazine office will get through the mail at least twenty thousand manuscripts a year.   It can publish perhaps one per cent of
them.   Among the rest will be many articles and stories
which are entirely publishable--but not quite as good as
something else in sight.   Each of them represents a heavy
investment of the author's efforts and emotions.   A surprising number will be accompanied by a note or phone call
from one of the editor's friends, or a valued contributor,
or an advertising executive, or a dear old aunt.   With or
without such endorsement, every manuscript has to be examined carefully--because it just might disclose a fresh talent, which is the lifeblood of any publication.

But in the end, at least 19,800 of the year's inflow
will have to be rejected heartlessly, regardless of broken
friendships, crushed ambitions, and the tears of charming
poetesses just out of Vassar.   This is the hardest lesson of
all, and one I have not yet mastered.   I still waste far too
much time salving bruised egos and writing what I hope are
comforting notes explaining why this piece won't quite do.
But I'm learning; I get meaner every day.

Yet somehow the indispensable ruthlessness must be
combined with a genuine liking for writers, a wide acquain-
tanceship among them and their agents, a sympathy for their
problems and respect for their work.   The best editors--
Frederick Lewis Allen, for example, and Maxwell Perkins--
seemed to blend the two qualities effortlessly and unconsciously.   They couldn't have told you how they did it because (I suspect) it was not a learned skill but a part of
their character.   Lesser editors suffer from recurrent
schizophrenia.

During the last sad months of Collier's magazine, a
series of miracle workers was brought in to save it.   One
of them told his friends confidently that he hoped to do it
within six months by building a new staff and a new stable
of writers.   He didn't last six months, but if he had his
methods probably wouldn't have worked.

For, so far as I can observe, a wise editor doesn't
try to "build" anything.   He doesn't think of writers or the
members of his staff as so many chunks of masonry, to be

chipped and hammered into his design.   Instead he thinks
rather in the manner of a Japanese gardener.

This can be most easily understood by contrast with
Italian gardening.   For 2,500 years the Italians have been
preeminent builders, and they don't really like nature--for
reasons explained by Luigi Barzini in his recent, splendid
book, The Italians.   So when they want to build a garden,
they begin by shoving nature around.   They lay out geometri-
cal paths, align the flowers and shrubs into formal patterns,
clip the trees into topiary shapes, channel the water into
cascades and fountains.

All of which would horrify a Japanese.   His object is
to make a garden look as natural as possible--but better than
nature could manage without his help.   His method is not to
construct an artificial design, but to guide and encourage
natural growth.   To this end, he places a clump of bamboo
where it will thrive best, sites an azalea bush to complement
it, plants moss between them, and then tries to make sure
that everything gets just the right amount of water, food, and
sunshine.   He may move a rock, redirect a stream, or by
gentle weights and pressures encourage a pine branch to develop into a more graceful shape.   But in each case he is
striving, not to make the rock or the pine into something different, but to make the most of its own essential nature.

In much the same way the editors I admire most have
worked both with writers and with their junior associates.
They don't try to change a novelist into a reporter, or to
push a sociologist into the style of a poet; nor do they attempt to "build" a natural-born fiction editor into an economist.   Instead--if I understand their methods correctly--they
seek to bring together talents of many sorts, place them into harmonious relationships with each other, and then provide the conditions under which each can flourish best.   It
is a slow process--but in the end it may produce a well-
balanced publisher's list or a periodical of character.

Yes, I know this sounds pretty high-flown.   But then
I told you to begin with that nobody finds it easy to explain
the editor's trade.

The Joyful Challenge

By Ursula Nordstrom, Vice President and Publisher of
Harper Junior Books.

From Saturday Review 50:39-40, November 11, 1967. Copyright 1967 Saturday Review, Inc.   Reprinted by permission.

A long time ago, when I had been publishing children's books for Harper for several years, a representative
of management took me to luncheon.   With great ceremony
he told me that since I had learned how to publish children's
books quite successfully, perhaps it was time I be given an
opportunity to publish books for adults.   He was thoroughly
surprised at and slightly wounded by my outrage.   It had
never occurred to him that publishing children's books by
creative authors and artists, and doing everything you can to
get those books to the children (most of whom are also creative) is a most exciting experience.

The wonderful way children react to good books is one
of the rewarding aspects of my life as a children's book editor.   Letters come every day to Laura Ingalls Wilder, author of the classic "Little House" books.   To these children
Laura, long since dead, will never die.   "Oh Laura, if I
was you I would have kicked Nellie Oleson in the leg when
she was so mean to you!"   A mother who had read E. B.
White's Charlotte's Webb to her son told me that when the
family moved to an apartment so spacious that it contained
a guest's room and bath, her son asked eagerly, "Now can
Mr. White come and stay overnight with us?"

Adults who stand between the creative artist and the
child have a tremendous responsibility.   It is hard for us
not to sift our reactions to a children's book through our
own adult experiences.   But we must try.   Some years ago
a librarian told me she hadn't liked Emily Neville's book
It's Like This, Cat, and when I expressed regret and inquired why, she said that "young people should respect their

parents, and that boy didn't show his father respect." The
adult world is full of myths that adults would like children
to believe. But children know that ugliness exists, that
fears are not always overcome, that not all children respect
their parents, that one is often lonely, and that people can
be mean and cruel.

When we published Maurice Sendak's Where the Wild
Things Are, some adults, at first, were appalled by the
"monsters." But the children took this story of rebellious
Max and his adventures with the Wild Things to their hearts,
and now they send Mr. Sendak drawings of their own crea-
tions three times as horrible and monstrous as those an
adult might imagine.

The reception of that book by children, and soon after by discerning parents, has been heartwarming. I remember the day that an article in the Library Journal, by
Suzanne Glazer of the Brooklyn Public Library, came to my
desk. Miss Glazer told of a four-year-old girl in a day-
care center in Brooklyn. The child would not speak, except
for an occasional indistinct word. She was lethargic; her
eyes were almost closed. In a storytelling group she began
to show slight improvement. Then, for the fourth program,
the teacher chose Where the Wild Things Are. The child
listened intently. Afterwards she approached the teacher and
uttered her first sentence in five weeks: "Can I have that
book?" Since that time, Miss Glazer wrote, "K. has become a different child physically . . . Her participation with
the rest of the group has improved . . . she runs to me and
hugs my knees waiting for me to bend down for a kiss. During story programs she is the most attentive child. K. is
now without doubt a lover of books." The day we read that
article in our department was a beautiful one for all of us.

Letters frequently ask about our "criteria" for accepting manuscripts. We don't have any rules. We simply try
(and it is really not so simple to try) to find and recognize
creative people and then let them write or draw the way that
they want to. In 1945 we published Call Me Charley by
Jesse Jackson, a young Negro writer. It was a story about
the only colored boy in a white school. We had not asked
Mr. Jackson to deliver a "message," and he had not tried
to write one. He simply wrote the book out of his own experience. In 1963, almost twenty years later, I met a young
woman at a library convention. We began to talk about race
problems. She told me that she'd been raised with certain

stereotyped racial attitudes.   But in the fifth grade she had
read a book that had made her aware of some of the problems Negro children faced and, she said, "You hear about
a person being changed by a book, and it sounds silly, but
that book really did change my whole attitude.   The book
was Call Me Charley."   She hadn't even known that it was
a Harper title.

We are not looking for certain kinds of books.   But
our search for talent never ends.   I know that a young person is often nervous when he comes into my office for the
first time.   If he could only know how nervous I am, hoping that I will be perceptive enough that day, that very minute, to recognize talent!   We certainly make mistakes.   We
may think we discern great talent, and we may be wrong.
But when we are right, we must trust the creative one.
Any suggestions for revision, for expansion of an incident,
or cutting a chapter are made only because we want what is
in the writer's head.   I've said to more than one sensitive,
touchy young person who has arrived at a point of self-defeating obstinacy over, say, any more work on the confusing
eighth chapter, "Look, I only want what is in your head.   I
don't want what's in my head.   I want what's in your head
to get to the children."

So we trust the creative person.   We distrust the author who asks us what to write, who doesn't want to "waste
the time writing" without a guarantee of success.   Children
respond to what is fresh and original and honest.   We
search for this as our primary requirement, and often it can
be found even in a few tentative pages of manuscript or in a
few rough drawings.   Talent and honesty are the telling factors.   Anything less is not good enough for a child.

"A Few Men and Women;" An Editor's Thoughts
on Children's Book Publishing

By Margaret K. McElderry, Editor of Children's Books,
Harcourt, Brace & World, Inc.

From the New York Public Library Bulletin 65:505-16, October 1961. © 1961 the New York Public Library. Reprinted by permission. This paper, the sixth Anne Carroll
Moore Lecture on Children's Books and Reading, was read
at the Donnell Library Center of The New York Public Library on April 19, 1961.

The title of this paper comes from Anne Carroll
Moore's statement, "It was to come to me quite clearly in
later years that civilization has always rested and will continue to rest on the dreams and fancies of a few men and
women and their power to persuade others of the truth of
what they see and feel." Perhaps no better way will ever
be found to make known the dreams and fancies of a few men
and women than through books. Their power to persuade is
given scope and permanence and unlimited availability in
books . . . .

Let us look at children's book publishing as it now exists in this country, and examine some of its purposes,
some of its problems, some of its rewards. Publishing is a
business, a commercial venture, which must succeed in selling the books it chooses to publish in order to continue to
choose and publish more books. It cannot exist without paying its way; it is not an altruistic venture. An editor may
be given his head to choose what he believes in, but he will
also--in time--lose his head, figuratively speaking, if his
choices too often end up in the red on the publisher's balance sheet. And yet, dollars and cents are by no means the
total picture of publishing. It is a profession as well as a
business--books are more than a commodity--and as such,
publishing has certain responsibilities which it must accept.
In no phase of the publishing industry are the responsibilities
more exacting than in the field of children's books. For

here one is dealing with the fresh, eager, developing minds and spirits of children, the ultimate inheritors to whom we in time turn over this world and its vast problems and for whom we should give of our best to help them to achieve their best.

If one faces these professional responsibilities squarely, it is not enough as an editor and publisher of children's books to find something that sells well, something that is merely popular, and to sit back and say, "Fine, no need to worry further." Safe mediocrity and mass appeal should not be the goal. It is essential to strive with consistency and force to choose and help to create and then to launch books which one believes have some special qualities to justify the expense and effort which publication entails, some claim to excellence, some right to a place in a child's experience, some contribution (in the broadest sense) to make. ·

In this highly competitive field, filled with many pressures, how does an editor function, how do books come into being? To judge from observation and from self knowledge, a children's book editor--and we come from many different backgrounds, of bookselling, of library work, of teaching, among others--a children's book editor must combine a number of traits. He (or more often she, as things are presently) should have a deep feeling for literature and books of all kinds, a responsiveness to life's experiences, a vast interest in people and an ability to work closely with them, and a deep concern with the world of childhood and the ways of children. He should have the ability to read something in manuscript and be able to envision it as a finished book. He should have a clear business head to deal with budgets, contracts, and the cost problems of book manufacturing; he should be able to administer a department, and--absolutely essential--he must have a sense of humor.

As a librarian, I used to be amused at people who thought librarianship meant nothing but "reading good books all day." As an editor, I am also sometimes amused at people who think editorial work means nothing but reading manuscripts quietly all day in an atmosphere of genteel peace and going to "elegant" literary cocktail parties quite often. Instead, an editor's daily life is a rough and tumble one, if you will--a continual involvement with telephones, people from the staff, writers and artists, and a host of others. The hopeful composer of music for children who to demonstrate his wares will burst into song the moment he enters

the editor's office, the confirmed egotist who prefers to take
an hour of an editor's time telling of what a superb book he
will write rather than to sit down and try to write it, the
would-be illustrator who wants to know what type of picture
is most popular today and who claims he can use any style
if the editor will only tell him which--these are, alas, the
perils of the day.

Above all, the editor's daily life is filled with detail
and decision. Each stage of each book must be checked
carefully and constantly to be sure that the many parts will
fit into place properly when the book is at last ready to be
launched. There is no dearth of material submitted to a
children's book department. In our own case, where we
publish about forty books a year, we receive for consideration between 1200 and 1300 manuscripts annually. As you
might deduce from the two sets of figures, a large percentage of the material sent in should never be given public exposure, but it is all considered carefully. Occasionally,
something new and exciting turns up--the magic moment of
discovery. The manuscript or artwork may come directly
from the author or artist, or from an agent, or through another writer or artist. After reading so much that is unim-
pressive, the editor immediately doubts his reaction if
something seems good, and worries that it is good only by
comparison. Once, when Carl Sandburg had finished speaking to a group of English teachers, one of them asked him
if he would give them a list of qualities which would enable
them always to recognize a classic as soon as they read it!
Mr. Sandburg's comments in telling of this later were pithy
and not for publication! If any editor, or any person, anywhere had this infallible gift of spotting a classic, his fortune would be made. So far, judging a manuscript and its
potentialities remains a highly subjective, individual business.
Thank goodness! How dull and cut-and-dried it would be
otherwise.

Every bit of experience an editor has had, all the
knowledge and wisdom (if any) he has acquired, all the sen-
sitivity he can muster are--quite unconsciously, of course--
brought into play when deciding on a manuscript. No decision to publish should be made unless the editor feels real
enthusiasm for the work under consideration. In making a
decision, the classifiable elements are a guide--good writing,
narrative pace, sound plot construction and rounded characterization in fiction, lucid exposition plus worthwhile content
in non-fiction. But it is conceivable that a manuscript may

have all these qualities and the editor still feel only lukewarm toward it.   If on subsequent readings the editor feels
the same, then the chances are he should not undertake that
one, for without a sense of excitement about a manuscript
at the beginning of its journey toward publication, the long
months of detailed work that go into the fashioning of a book
may become a chore and that would be fatal!   Belief in a
writer and an artist by an editor is essential, and the same
is equally true in reverse.   It is my opinion that such belief brings out the best in writer, artist and editor and creates an atmosphere in which all three can function most happily and well.   That atmosphere in turn touches everyone
else who has to do with the making of the book, so that, by
the time it reaches the crucial moments of sales conference
and, ultimately, publication, an attitude of confidence and
anticipation prevails.   This is highly subjective, I realize,
but I most ardently believe it.   The relationship of editor
and author or illustrator is--at its best--immensely close
and personal, for one is dealing with the elusive stuff of
creation closest to the creative person's heart--and such a
relationship must be one of mutual confidence, respect and
enjoyment.   Conversely, if a book is tackled with some
reservation on the editor's part, the reservation may very
well spread, and good final results will be harder to achieve.

An effective editor is a sounding board for a writer;
often that is all the writer needs.   But an editor must also
be able to recognize the potentialities of deep revisions or
effective cuts when an author has lost perspective on a manuscript.   Without mutual trust and respect, it would be impossible at times to broaden an author's view of his own
manuscript so that he may judge it better both in its detail
and as an entity.   All editors, at some time or another,
have shared the harrowing experience of watching an author
depart hurt and sometimes angry over carefully thought-out
suggestions and criticisms, followed by the heart-warming
relief of a call or a letter in a few days to say that--after
the heat of the argument had died down--the author had decided the editor was right, at least 70% of the way!   What
a happy moment for both concerned!   In reality, the editor
is a mid-wife who assists the author in bringing the manuscript to life as a book.   It is the writer's gifts that make
a good book good, a great book great.

Once a manuscript has been decided upon, and even
while the author may be re-working parts of it, the editor
is translating the manuscript into a physical book, pondering

its general size and shape and the kind of illustrations it
should have. With the staff designer, the details of the
forthcoming book are then worked out, usually in the following order which has a technical logic of its own--who the
artist will be, what type face should be used in what size,
how many pages there will be in the book, how many type
lines to a page, how much room for pictures, whether or
not there will be running heads, where the page number will
go, what display type will be used, how the chapter openings
will be handled and the title page and so-called front matter,
how many colors will be used in the jacket and whether it
will be printed by letterpress or offset. Once the many details are settled, they must then be executed with care and
precision and merged into a schedule in which many titles,
in various stages of editing, design, or manufacture, are
moving toward individual publication dates. Now the procedures become more and more complex, involve more and
more people, create more and more opportunities for problems to arise. And it is here that a flexible, knowledgeable
administration comes into play--necessarily accompanied by
the essential sense of humor described earlier.

The illustrators of books for children, particularly
in the field of picture books, are an immensely important
part of the whole. We, in America, are especially blessed
by having fine artists--not only from this country but from
all over the world--to call upon. There is a wealth of outstanding graphic work created for children and--as with the
writer--the best work comes when the artist is left as free
as possible to make his own individual statement, not forced
to conform to a concept established arbitrarily, but--within
certain bounds of color and printing technique imposed by
economic realities--left to interpret the text in his own way
for the quick and appreciative eyes of a child, who is often
much less conservative in taste than his parents.

Picture books present to the publisher even greater
problems of design and production, as well as large financial investments, than do books composed mainly of text and
with only occasional illustrations; but picture books are well
worth any amount of trouble encountered. Let us follow the
history of one particular title as an example. A few years
ago, we decided we would like to make a picture book from
a small collection of Christmas carols selected by the musi-
cologist and singer, John Langstaff. Four carols--all hundreds of years old--were chosen, but what artist would best
catch the traditional flavor, the color and gaiety and variety,

of these joyous and lasting hymns? For a long time we had
been hoping to use the work of a remarkable artist, Antony
Groves-Raines, who lives in Northern Ireland and who had
never heretofore done a book. This then was the perfect
opportunity. When the many intricate details about format
and technique had been decided upon, Mr. Groves-Raines
settled down to a more than two-year stint of sketching,
drawing, and--at last--painting, in southern Italy where the
architecture, the quality of light, the overall mood were
close in spirit to the medieval carols. Working from nine-
inch models of the major figures in each intricate composition, draped so that every fold, every shadow, every highlight would achieve grace and realism, he painted in the manner of a medieval Flemish miniaturist and fashioned pictures of beauty and depth and enchanting, authentic detail.
These were then sent to a Dutch printer of repute who photographed them and supplied us with film positives from which,
in turn, an American printer produced the book. The artist's unstinting labor of love, which went far beyond what
many would consider more than adequate effort, deeply impressed all who saw his work so that, in turn, all concerned wanted to do more than their normal best. Thus,
almost four years later, On Christmas Day in the Morning
came into being.

The things that can go wrong in printing and producing picture books make hair-raising publishing sagas. One
of our own now classic dramas involved a lovely Swiss picture book we were publishing--Pitschi by Hans Fischer. The
book had been done on lithograph stones--one stone for each
color in each picture--and printed in seven colors in Switz-
erland. We were supplied with pulls (or proofs) from each
stone and prepared our edition here, determined to make it
as beautiful as the Swiss one. All went well; color proofs
showed only a minimum of adjustment necessary; the large
sheets on which the book was printed, were off-press. And
then--two days later--we discovered that the green was offsetting. In less technical but equally grim words, on every
sheet the green was smearing. That was a never-to-be-for-
gotten day in our publishing history! But the ingenious--
and desperate--printer hired what he called "a crew of eras-
ers" (to this day we think of them as some special sort of
gnome!) and they were able to clean up enough sheets so
that we could publish on schedule--but with a greatly reduced supply of books on hand! Every publisher can tell
such tales, and when publishers gather they often do.

While the production of the book is in process, the editor--together with the promotion, sales, and advertising departments--must be developing plans to launch the book. Should it have a mailing piece to buyers and clerks in book stores? Should there be a special letter about it to school and public libraries? Would a poster be effective? How will the advertising be handled? This is an important phase involving ingenuity within the bounds of honesty, financial risks that once committed cannot be recalled. It makes the difference, as William Shirer recently put it, between printing a book and publishing a book.

The only thing that makes effective all this activity-- which sometimes seems rather disorganized--is a staff that functions happily and efficiently together, each taking part in carrying the publishing process along to completion. Every finished book has required the combined efforts of many individuals, many more indeed than the casual reader could possibly guess.

So it goes, with book after book, each one traveling along on its own special path toward that glorious moment when, smelling most beautifully of printer's ink and glue, it comes to hand right from the bindery, to be looked at, lingered over, and discussed in technical terms and with critical inspection far greater than any reader would render. And while one book may have arrived at this terminal point, others are in progress, some just starting the initial phase. The only thing one can be sure of as an editor is that there will never be an idle moment--and, one hopes, never a dull one.

The publishing seasons are usually two a year, spring and fall, each one prefaced by a sales conference. At this awesome event within a publishing house, the editorial and sales staffs gather, drawn in from all parts of the country, together with the advertising agency people and those con- cerned with all areas of promotion and publicity. Each edi- tor must then present the books to be published within the next six months, hoping to convey to the salesmen and the advertising people the values, the excitements, the challenges of the books he has been deeply concerned with for so long. "Awesome" is indeed the word, but my own initial dread of these events was greatly allayed some years ago. We were to publish Harry Behn's first book of poetry for children, The Little Hill.   A day or two before the conference our sales manager went over the list of new titles with me.

"There's only one turkey on your list," he said, "that book of poetry. No one buys poetry." Out of deep conviction, but with an attempt at humor, I replied that he'd live to be proud of The Little Hill. At the sales meeting I gave the book the very best send-off I could, then turned to our sales manager and--foolishly--said, "So much for your turkey!" Whereupon, he called the salesmen, one by one, in turn. Each stood up and recited a poem by Harry Behn which he had memorized, leaving me overwhelmed--and overjoyed. Time has never dimmed our pride and pleasure in Harry Behn and The Little Hill.

For the editor--and for the authors and artists con-cerned--there comes always an alarming period, the time when the finished book has been sent out to the reviewers and opinion-makers throughout the country. After so many months of detailed attention and intense concern, there is for the time being nothing more to be done. It is now up to others--the adult purchasers and the children themselves-- to complete the picture. Only when reviews begin to come in, and letters from librarians, expressing approval and pleasure or doubt and criticism, does that time of suspense end and the people principally concerned begin to feel the life process of the book has been taken up once more.

So much for the practical details of bringing a book into being. What are some of the wider aspects? We find ourselves today in a period of immense expansion in chil-dren's books both in number of titles and in their sales; this is due in major part to an unprecedented increase of population and, therefore, of schools and libraries, facts with which you are all familiar. From a quiet, steady but unspectacular part in publishing, children's book departments have rocketed into an important position in the industry. This is not the unmixed blessing it might at first seem, for publishing prominence, like prominence in all walks of life, brings with it certain dangers. And to tread a wise path through the surrounding dangers is not easy.

Let us first consider the market for children's books. The "population explosion" (already a cliché in our language) plus a new emphasis on the value of school libraries and the use of general children's books as well as textbooks in the individual classrooms, mean that many more books are be-ing purchased by schools than ever before. Parents, made increasingly aware that it is important for their children to read well to enhance their chances of success in later life, are buying more books or borrowing them in increasing numbers from public libraries.   Emphasis on books is also currently increased by the serious scrutiny directed at the teaching of English and of reading in our schools and by the deep concern expressed because of revealed inadequacies.   Many school people, who in the past have had little to do with general children's books, are now in a position to purchase them for supplementary reading; yet they must face this task with a severe shortage of trained professional people to turn to for help in book selection, and often with too few opportunities to examine books before acquiring them.   Parents, too, are understandably sometimes at a loss in choosing soundly from the welter of books available.   In the resultant confusion, the garish, the obvious, the loudly touted, deceptively packaged and merchandised book is frequently taken up, whereas further search--or experienced advice--might often lead to something clearly superior in content and style, perhaps more challenging for the child and certainly of more lasting value.

In such a situation, inevitably some in the publishing world are tempted to make a quick killing, to "get in fast" with a kind of book for which there is a known and easy market; and certain writers are equally willing to participate.   The almost incredible advances in science in today's world provide an excellent example of just such an exploitable area.   The hue and cry is on--"Science, science, science!"   So, of course, publishers' lists are filled with science books in all branches for all ages.   New publishers come into being to produce only science books for children.   Much of the material now available is excellent; much is shoddy, cheaply conceived, cheaply executed and unworthy of a child's attention.   But as long as an avid buying public exists, such ephemeral, made-to-order-in-a-hurry books will continue to be published.

"Never in our history has there been greater need for men and women of vision and power to persuade.   These qualities may, and assuredly do, take form and clarity from the facts of science but they live only in literature and in the aspirations of the human heart."   This statement, so apt for our time, was made by Anne Carroll Moore in 1920, almost half century ago.   She also spoke of "sadly confused theories concerning children's reading; to inform, instruct, or improve rather than to awaken, enlighten, and enlarge the minds and hearts of children."   And she went on to say, "We are tired of substitutes for realities in writing for children--

above all, with the commonplace in theme, treatment and
language--the proverbial stone in place of bread, in the name
of education." She recognized in its incipience what has become evident to us in such grimly current fashion, namely
that technological and scientific advancement, no matter how
breathtakingly fast or sweeping, cannot benefit man and
man's descendants unless these great developments are applied by the knowledgeable mind and the understanding heart.

In the 1960s, the confusion persists, intensified.
Never were more books of facts and information available to
young readers. There are series encompassing almost every
phase of knowledge one can think of. The postwar years
have been most marked by the spate of such books. Some
of them are of the highest quality--in conception, presentation, and illustration, and fully deserve high honors and long
life. Some are useful and adequate until something better
comes along. Some are carried only by the impetus of be-
longing to well-advertised series.

Increasingly, it is difficult for the truly individual
voice to be heard, to find a publisher and, once published,
to survive in the turmoil of thousands of other books. The
creative piece of work that fits no established pattern has
a more perilous course to follow than perhaps ever before.
But happily, there is still a sufficient body of parents and
teachers and librarians, people of deep involvement and concern everywhere, who value well-written, well-illustrated,
well-designed and produced books for children, and who buy
them, so that the books can then be used by their ultimate
readers and most honest audience--the children themselves.
And what real joy it brings to an editor, author, or librarian to have a child say of a new book, with eyes shining and
his heart in his voice, "This book is great!" That is a
real reward.

The predominant output of publishing activity, worthy
though it may be, in demand though it may be, is not in itself quite enough. The supreme moments of immense excitement that illumine the publishing process as a whole and
make it seem infinitely worthwhile, are those rare ones--
extremely rare--when the easy classifications of material,
the assured profit motive, the known areas of approval, are
dismissed in the certain recognition of something wonderful-
ly new, vigorous, untried, that captures the editor's imagination, that glows with highly individual expression, that cannot be denied as a work of art, that must be given a chance.

In such decisions, an editor may move into areas where controversies center. This is the realm of intangibles, of esthetics, of the evaluation of quality. There are no rules, no concrete criteria. Time alone is the final judge of such an enterprise--and, for the final decision, time of such length that neither author, artist, editor, nor publisher may survive to know the result. The oncoming generations of children will. These are judgments that will be made in the far future, but they concern us deeply in the present. The pursuit of such experimental excellence, to give it a name, is perhaps the most hazardous, but the greatest adventure in publishing, for it is concerned with dreams rather than with dollars, perfection rather than profit. If we do not open our eyes and minds to it today, it may never survive to become a vital part of tomorrow and to join the expanding universe of the human spirit.

Hence, how vital it continues to be to seek out, find, and foster the expressions of "a few men and women." Consider some of the great and much loved books of childhood which are a rich experience for today's children. Beatrix Potter wrote and painted, not to produce something quickly that would sell, but to amuse and please young friends. Kenneth Grahame and A. A. Milne had in mind their own beloved sons, just as Lewis Carroll was writing to delight a favorite little girl when he penned Alice in Wonderland. Each of these, when new, was an adventure in experimental excellence.

The children's books that last, that go from one generation to the next, are written because the author has something he wants to say--a story to tell, an emotion he is bound to share, a belief he holds dear. These are the books, written with loving conviction, with great skill, with no self-conscious tailoring in mind. These are the books--whether fact or fiction--which today's school curriculums should-- and will--we hope, be flexible enough to accommodate, which publishers and editors must continue to seek and publish without having to trim and mould in an effort merely to accommodate the curriculums. These are the books that will reach and stretch and fill a child's imagination and spirit, that will open whole new realms to his eager questing.

As an editor, one of the things most clearly realized is the fact that each book that stems from a true creative impulse, a true desire to share knowledge or humor or adventure or joy in life and people, is endowed like a human

being, in that it has its own particular life story, each as
different and individual as are people.   As an example, I
think of Mary Norton's books even though they are contemporary.   For those of you unfamiliar with the Borrowers, they
are tiny people no taller than a pencil who live, mostly, in
old quiet houses where they are unlikely to be seen and
where they exist by borrowing from the larger world around
them.   An aspirin bottle top makes an excellent washbowl,
for instance; a bit of red blotting paper makes a sumptuous
rug.   For years, Mary Norton had pondered the mystery of
how things disappear--safety pins, buttons, stamps; one
moment you have them, the next they're not to be found.
Out of this commonplace wonder slowly grew her memorable,
most beautifully conceived and written stories.

She was working on her third book while living in a
remote cottage on the North Devon coast, and each Saturday
night took a batch of handwritten manuscript pages to the
neighboring village where she'd meet her typist, a retired
Royal Navy Chief Petty Officer, at the local pub.   There she
would go over her handwriting with him--quite unselfcon-
sciously, until she realized one evening that the local farm-
ers, who were there also, were beginning to look at her
strangely and were obviously wondering whether a new kind
of animal invasion was about to descend upon them since
Mary and the petty officer were talking earnestly of creatures climbing down the drains, and making their homes behind baseboards!   And then one day in America came a letter from Mary Norton announcing that the typing was completed and that she had brought the manuscript home from
the village, together with other supplies, in a wheelbarrow,
through the woods which were, as she put it, "awash almost
drowned, in bluebells."   What a picture--and what a life
story that book has had since!

It is this individual order of book that elicits equally
individual comment from perceptive reviewers.   Louise Sea-
man Bechtel, writing in the New York Herald Tribune about
The Two Reds by Will and Nicolas, an unusual and controversial picture book when it first came out, said in part:
"This restores one's faith in the experimental daring of
American publishers"--a statement full of much needed encouragement for editor, author, artist, and buying public a-
like.

And what of the authors, with whom each book begins
and without whom there would be no publishing industry?

They are as varied in personality as their books, but they share a common knowledge--that writing is a solitary and a lonely occupation. Into it, the author must put his best effort--his heart and his imagination and his mind. He cannot stint of his efforts, he must believe in what he is doing, he must have the ability to write directly and lucidly, without affectation or condescension, so that children coming to his book will be caught and held by the power of his imagination, his vitality, and his ability to communicate.

The rewards of writing for children--apart from the purely monetary, which can be substantial--are great. For if children love and delight in a book, there is no more loyal or appreciative audience, and such a book will proudly meet the test of time and have a full life for many years.

These, then, are some of the thoughts and beliefs and experiences of one editor of books for children. If I may choose one point to re-emphasize, it is this: The most important responsibility today--and no doubt in the years to come--for those of us involved in this remarkable and stimulating enterprise of providing many books for many children is to keep our minds and hearts open and receptive to the new and the untried ventures whose creators will perhaps join that band whom Anne Carroll Moore described as "a few men and women who can persuade others of the truth of what they see and feel."

How to Present the Negro in Children's Books:
An Editor Sweats Out the Problem

By Jean Poindexter Colby, Children's Book Editor, Hastings
House Publishers, Inc.

From Top of the News 21:191-6, April 1965. Published by
the American Library Association. Reprinted by permission.

I was seated at my desk yesterday, editing busily.
The manuscript under scrutiny was Miss Betty of Bonney
Rock School by Barnett Spratt, to be published next fall.
Miss Spratt, a southerner, is, at the age of eighty, an exciting addition to my list of authors. I like the way she
writes and what she writes about because her material is
forcefully expressed and comes from real life, the south of
her childhood and her ancestors.

Her first book with me, Tom and the Redcoats, was
based on the events related to her grandfather by his grandfather when Lord Cornwallis took over the family farm in
South Carolina during the Revolutionary War. The new book
is again on an aspect of war--the Civil War this time--and
again based on actuality, the diary of Miss Spratt's aunt,
who taught a field school called Bonney Rock during the last
terrible years of the war.

My editorial enthusiasm grew as I read: the pathos
of those children, the courage and ingenuity of the young
teacher fired me. Yet even as I read, engulfed in that time
and place, I reached for my editorial pencil and began to
write in the margins, "Tone down." "Is this necessary?"
"Can you re-word?"

What was I marking? The words "slave" or "body
servant" or "stable boy" et cetera, et cetera. Suddenly I
threw my pencil on the desk and stared at the manuscript.
Why should I change this script? Why should I alter its viv-

162

id presentation of the South at that time? Why couldn't I
let it tell its true story as an historical document? *

You librarians already know the answer. You are my
greatest market because you buy most of the children's
books nowadays, and you wouldn't buy this because of possible criticism by civic groups, church groups, and Negro
organizations. It presents the Negro as a slave and as a
deserter. (Most of the Negroes in the book are fine people,
but it is true that many slaves who perhaps were not so ad-
mirable deserted to the northern forces during the last
months of the war.) Slavery has been practically taboo for
many years now as a subject in children's literature, and
depicting the Negro as anything but perfect is not welcome
either. White children and adults can be bad, but Negroes
cannot.

So my job is and has been to tone down or eliminate
such people and situations even though it often irks me as a
publisher and hence supposedly a disseminator of the truth.
There is no point in publishing a book that won't be bought.
An unread book carries no message, enlightens no readers,
and buys no food for the author.

But when can we lift the shroud from truth? We are
inching toward it, but at the rate we are going, a generation
of children will grow up as ignorant adults because of these
areas of historic vacuum we are leaving in their education.

Because items that are eliminated do not come to the
attention of anyone, I thought it might interest some of you
to hear some examples of what is done to toe this particular
editorial line before you receive the books. I expect other
editors have had similar experiences or they may not have
had any--I speak only for myself--but here, for what they
are worth, are some of mine.

My first encounter with this kind of censorship came
in 1946 at Houghton Mifflin Company when, as children's
book editor, I inherited from Lee Kingman the publication of
U. S. Means Us by Mina Turner. This is an excellent little

---

*Let me say right now that most of the editing which is done
to establish the Negro as a dignified, law-abiding, desirable
member of society I agree with. He has been mistreated
in our literature, even as late as World War I. Some of
the songs of that conflict are in dreadful taste.

book on life in the United States which sold well and is still
selling.   It almost didn't sell at all, though, because a terrible picture was discovered in it on a page depicting a variety of employment in the U.S.A.   Lloyd Coe, the artist,
had shown a Negro porter!   As you know, there were and
still are Negro porters--in fact, I have never seen a white
one--but that makes no difference.   Negroes cannot be shown
in a menial position such as porter-ing even though many
porters make a very good salary.

Anyway Lloyd Coe was called in and met the challenge beautifully.   I suggested he take the shaded piece of
Benday off the man's face but, as I have said before, porters aren't white and we did need a Negro doing something,
so Lloyd simply changed the hat to an ordinary flip-brim job
and there he was: a white-collar worker.   Just like that!

I wish my other problems with Negroes who cropped
up in stories or nonfiction could have been handled so easily.
I agree that dialect should be toned down and that is not
hard because the inclusion of a word or two can color a
whole page.   It is not necessary to have all the words spelled
phonetically.   Still I hate to have any uneducated person
(white or colored) in any book speak Oxford English, because they don't.   My solution in most of the dialect situations is to have them not speak at all!   Or as little as possible.

For instance, on page 85 of Deborah Remembers by
Lillie V. Albrecht, a runaway slave and her baby are hidden
in a cellar with two little white girls while a group of slave
hunters search in the house for them.   All the young Negro
mother says is, "Dear Lord, don't let him cry."

That wasn't what came in on the original manuscript
but the author agreed on the necessity for change.

Actually, that one sentence, although not in the dialect in which it would have been spoken, is very effective.
At least I think it is.

A more drastic change was made in The Leprechaun
of Bayou Luce by Joan Balfour Payne, published in 1957.
This southern gem is laid in Miss Payne's homeland of Mississippi, and Joss Turnipseed, the hero, was a little Negro
boy when the story came to me.   Joss is not a rich boy and
we first meet him swinging a string of catfish he has just

caught. He meets the Major on horseback on the way home
and gives him a couple of fish. All is pleasant, but in order to publish the book without criticisms from the same organizations I had encountered before, the man on horseback
would have to be Negro and Joss would have to be white. It
was simpler just to change Joss's race. He became white,
and I honestly don't think the book lost anything as a result
of the change. The author was goodhearted about it, too.

My next change of a similar nature hurt both the author and me, however. It took place in the book A Summer
To Share by Helen Kay, with illustrations by Polly Jackson.
This book, based on the idea of the Fresh Air Fund of the
New York Herald-Tribune, is about a country girl who asks
a city girl to visit her in the summer. The city girl was
originally Negro--in fact, the artist had made the preliminary dummy and started the final art work when I had a discussion in the late summer of 1959 at our New York office
about our spring 1960 list. (By that time galleys on all the
books had been set and art work was in preparation.) I told
the salesmen present about the book and immediately encountered such opposition that I felt we either had to cancel
the book entirely or change the book to an all-white cast.

I wrote apologetically to the author and artist, explaining the situation. They were both cooperative and the racial
switch was made. It seemed to all of us most unnecessary.

Phyllis Whitney, a mutual friend of Helen Kay's and
mine, put the situation forcefully. She wrote in a letter
dated April 24, 1960, "It broke my heart that it (Summer To
Share) had to be published with such a major change in the
whole idea. I know you weren't for that, and I do hope
you'll get a later edition printed as it should be, presenting
the real story. I feel that your salesmen were mistaken on
this and it's too bad for the sale of the book that they had
to be listened to. Now it will be just another charming little
country story, nicely written and illustrated . . . ."

The book has sold well, but it is a shame that it
couldn't have been published as intended because it would
have been most timely and might have encouraged some
thinking toward integration, if nothing else.

That was 1960. I continued on my peculiar editorial
way, changing or omitting what Negro characters said, often
lightening the color of their skins. (Isn't it appalling that I

would have such a right?)

Came 1961 and two manuscripts of definite worth landed on my desk, both about Negroes and whites. One of them, Another King for Christmas by Joan Balfour Payne, had great literary distinction but involved a small Negro boy in Mississippi going for Christmas to the plantation where his grandmother worked as a housekeeper. She was beloved and enjoyed many liberties and the little boy had a wonderful time, especially at the end. The denouement is so very lovely and unusual, as in the other writings of this author, that I was tempted to publish it and let the chips fall where they may, but something stayed my hand; it was the second manuscript: A New Boy in School by May Justus.

This is a story of a Negro boy in a new school where he is placed in a grade that has all white students. The book is not a literary epic, but it puts over a point that had not been made in children's books. It showed that a Negro boy is just like a white child in being afraid of new situations and making new friends. It showed that white children can cooperate and be friendly, but the Negroes must accept this friendliness and help themselves.

I was able to put across the publication of this book with the help of May Justus' name and my own determination. Actually I received little opposition at our editorial meeting. That was to come from other sources.

I got Joan Balfour Payne to illustrate it and in the meantime sent her Another King for Christmas to the Horn Book, knowing they often published a Christmas story in their December issue. Ruth Viguers took it right off, which made me feel better, also the author.

At sales conference time, after presenting New Boy in School to our salesmen, I was pleased to have our West Coast salesman say that he thought the book should be sold just as any other story about a new child in school. Any child, no matter what the color, is scared when he has to go to a new school, he said. The southern salesman did not agree. He didn't expect to sell any. He said that in many places he wouldn't even show it. *

---

*"New Boy was offered to two other publishers previous to Hastings House. Both companies wanted Southern stories. They both liked New Boy very much, but were simply afraid it wouldn't sell in the South. . ." M. Justus in a letter to the author.

At that time the book was only in galleys, with a few
sample illustrations, and I needed some backing badly.   So
I took the book to our local public library.   The new head
of the school libraries was a Negro and she agreed to read
it.

She called me in a few days later and really blasted
it.   In the story the father puts his son to bed after a disturbing first day at school and sings him a reassuring little
song while strumming a banjo.

A banjo, she said, signified the plantation Negro, an
image which they (Negro leaders) were working to eradicate.
Couldn't the father play the piano?   Well, this particular
family couldn't have afforded a piano, and if they had one,
it wouldn't have been in the bedroom.

At the end of the book the little boy and his new white
friend combine in a kind of duet of this same song that the
father sang.   The white boy whistles the tune as Lennie, the
Negro boy, sings it.

This was wrong according to modern Negro standards,
said the librarian, because it presented the Negro as an en-
tertainer, an image they wanted to correct.   Well, again if
you know children in first grade, you realize how hard it is
to put over the idea of friendship, of working together, of
helping each other without something like this.   Music to a
little child is a natural, easy thing, and it was important
that Lennie do something his father and mother would be
proud of.

Anyway, I wasn't encouraged by this criticism, but
New Englanders are odd people.   Sometimes the more opposition we get, the more determined we are to go ahead with
our ideas if we think they are right.   So, battered but un-
bowed, I took myself and the galleys to a Negro pastor I
knew.   I respected his judgment and his mind and I had
talked with him several times about children's books.   He
was immediately interested in the problem and said he would
have the galleys read that day in the first grade of Sunday
School, and would give me his and the teacher's frank opinion.

They were both enthusiastic, thank goodness.   The
teacher said it was an excellent book for first and second
grades and a much needed one.   She thought white children

who read it would not realize that this was a story promoting integration, but they would get the idea that Negro and
white children could play and work and have fun together.
Then when they grew older, they would have a background
of elastic, cultured thinking on the subject not from this one
book, of course, but there were bound to be others, now
that the ice had been broken.   She didn't mention the entertainment or banjo image but she did say a very different
thing.   She thought Negro children should read it as well as
white because, "it shows, Mrs. Colby, that lots of times
we go almost looking for trouble.   Lennie imagined that all
those children were against him when they weren't.   Of
course, some children do make fun of Negroes but most of
them don't, and up here in Massachusetts in another few
years white children will take Negroes in their classes for
granted and vice versa.   Many of them do already."

I decided to pursue that lead a little further and took
the galleys to Duxbury, where there are quite a few Negroes
in the public schools.   My friend, Mrs. John Arnold, read
the book to her son, a second grader, and said, "It's a
good story for this age.   Of course, George didn't pay any
attention to Lennie's being black.   There are several Negroes in his class and he just takes them for granted."

The book has been a success saleswise* and as a
"useful"** book.   It took its time getting started, but then
good reviews began to come in: from the Library Journal,
the Christian Science Monitor, the New York State Library,
Dept. of Education; the Chicago Tribune, Commonweal, the
Bulletin of the Parents League in New York, Elementary
English, the Bulletin of the Children's Book Center, Childhood Education, and many others.   It was included in the
"Books of the Year" of the Child Study Association and was
one of the New York Times' "One Hundred Best Books of
the Year."   Several southern newspapers reviewed it favorably and quite a few reviews came in from newspapers and
magazines that do not usually review children's books and

---

* Its sales have not been spectacular in the South but they
have been good in the rest of the country.   One large reading circle selected it, and several city school departments
have bought quite large quantities.

** A term used by Patricia Allen of School Library Journal in a recent panel discussion on reviewing at a meeting
of the Children's Book Council in New York City.

to which we had not sent review copies.   Alice Dalgleish, in
the Saturday Review, gave praise with some reservation.
The Horn Book never reviewed it, but I understood this because I never considered it to be a great literary achievement.

I do believe, however, that it was a thought-provoking achievement and I would have been proud to have published it even if it had not been acclaimed over the country.
I also hope this article, though unimportant in the instances
it cites, may be thought-provoking to you.   You are now the
directors of publishing trends much more than you realize,
perhaps.   We editors are trying to publish what is timely
and worth while.   Given good taste, how close will you allow us to come to the truth?

Editor and Author in a University Press

By Dan Davin, Assistant Secretary, The Clarendon Press.

From the Times Literary Supplement no. 3432:1191, December 7, 1967. Copyright by Times Newspapers Limited. Reprinted by permission.

Last April a crowded meeting of the P. E. N. Club debated the proposition that "the power of the publisher's editor has increased, is increasing, and ought to be diminished." Presumably those present were all more or less agreed that, in this context, the term "editor" carried much the sense so ably discussed in the recent article by Mr. Victor (See pages 133-7); someone who is "the main point of contact between the author and the publishing house."

What, then, was causing the embattled authors concern? From the discussion as reported in the P. E. N. Club Newsletter, it seems to have been the fear that the publisher's editor may tend to behave in the way that goes with the other senses of the term--in particular the sense in which an editor prepares someone else's, often a dead man's, papers for publication; in other words, that he will act as arbiter of what should be the ultimate form of the book and impose his views without consulting the author or in spite of him.

It is widely believed, with what justice one does not certainly know, that something of the sort has been happening in America. If it were to happen here, the anxiety of authors would certainly be justified. One hopes and believes, however, that Mr. Victor's account of the matter is the right one, at least in all reputable publishing houses.

Much, indeed most, of what Mr. Victor says applies also to the practice of a university press, but it may be helpful to supplement his article with a few observations about the role of editor in relation to author in the special conditions of university press publishing. (I would like it to be clear that what follows is based on a wide experience, direct and indirect, of many university presses, but should not be regarded as necessarily expressing anything but a personal view.) The term "editor" is accepted for convenience in this article since it is not easy to find another suitable word; accepted reluctantly, however, because of the possible confusion with its other more widely established senses. These other senses--editors of journals, of series, of classical texts--are the ones that first come to mind in a university press when the term is mentioned.

It will be convenient also at this point to establish one or two principal points of distinction between a university press and what one may call, without pejorative intent, a commercial publisher. The latter is engaged in publishing primarily to make money for the owners of his business. In the United Kingdom and indeed elsewhere, this is quite compatible with publishing works of a general character which are contributions to knowledge and of high academic quality. Nor will a commercial publisher necessarily refuse a particular book because he thinks it unlikely to make money. He may have a good reason for being prepared to lose money in the special case: a personal allegiance to a subject or an author, for example; prestige; the hope of attracting more profitable books in the same field by the same author or by another author; or the wish to signalize his bona fides as a reputable publisher moving into the academic field which has with the development of education, become so much more commercially attractive.

None the less, such a publisher's object will be ultimately a commercial one. He will be in pursuit of the best not for its own sake but for legitimate commercial reasons and his ultimate standard will be the profitability of his enterprise. It will always be open to him to decline a book on the ground that it is not likely to be profitable.

For a university press the position is rather different. Its primary aim is to advance the purposes for which the university itself exists; to promote knowledge and learning by publishing good books. If the books themselves are profitable, so much the better; and the university press, subject to its different basic purpose, should aim at least to match its commercial rivals in standards of business efficiency, quality of production, effectiveness in sales and promotion and so on. Yet the editor in a university press must never lose sight of that ultimate criterion, the quality of the book itself.

Nor will he be the sole, or even the main judge of
quality. A good commercial publisher will normally, where
an academic book is concerned, take advice from a specialist before undertaking to publish. But he is not bound to do
so and it is ultimately only the prestige and profit of his
own firm which is at risk. The university publisher, on the
other hand, will always have in the back of his mind the
fact that the good name of his university is involved. Moreover, the decision whether or not to publish will rest not
with him but with an academic committee of some sort--
Delegates, Syndics, or the like. The members of this committee will probably be scholars of distinction in one or
more fields and first-rate administrators. They will need
full evidence to be put before them before they will reach a
decision.

It follows from this that the editor in a university
press will be very much a middleman between author and
publishing committee. He will be unable to commit himself
in advance completely to backing his hunches and handing out
cheques to an author. His commercial rival will often be
able to cheer on his author over the sherry in a much more
unbuttoned way and with an open cheque book: for if the
book that finally emerges has to be declined he can always
regret that it turned out to be different from what was expected, and commercially unviable, something "more suitable
for a university press" and consider his lost cheque a risk
worth taking. A university press editor has no such ready
escape. If the book is not to be accepted, he will have to
communicate the decision of his superiors and, however polite the formula, it will have to convey that the book was unacceptable on grounds other than the commercial.

It might be supposed in these circumstances that the
only safe course would be for an editor to wait until books
were offered him unsolicited. But perhaps 75 per cent of the
books so offered are likely to be of unacceptable quality. A
publisher, university or commercial, who waited to be approached would soon perish. Publishing is one profession
where it is not only legal but essential to solicit, even in the
street. The academic market is a highly competitive one.
University laboratories and common rooms are thronged with
publishers' talent scouts. The university editor must be a-
mong them if his press is to flourish. Indeed, much of his

energy will go in the refutation of rumours spread by some
of his rivals: that a university press is all very well for
the book that no one else would publish but is too slow, too
unbusinesslike, too reluctant to pay royalties, too unskilled
in publicity and so on.   He will have to be active in refut-
ing these recurring stories and in pointing out that his press
is not only competitive in all these respects but superior in
its loyalty to books which have ceased to sell a commercial
minimum of copies for years, in its devotion to quality and
in its general identification with the best interests of both
scholars and scholarship.

     Our editor, then, must be freely accessible both in
his office and out of it.   He must be reasonably well briefed
in the current developments and scholarship of many fields
(for it will not do to tell a promising crystallographer met
at a party that he must talk to a colleague better informed).
He must be alert for new men and have enough confidence in
his judgment to risk encouraging a man or an idea of promise.   He must be able to live at once dangerously and dis-
creetly.

     He will probably live in the university of which his
press is a department and this will have considerable advantages.   He will meet his academic colleagues frequently and
be on terms of friendship with many of them.   He will get
into the habit of regarding his friends as authors and advisers, or potentially such.   This will have its dangers.   He
will be likely to forget that ink is thicker than water and
royalties stronger than loyalties; that, qua author, a man is
an author before he is a friend.   Nothing should be taken for
granted; once the friend is in fact his author he must be
treated with the same porcelain solicitude as a stranger.
Friendship may produce the offer of a book.   If that book is
in the end refused, it can be all the more painful a transac-
tion because of the friendship between the parties.

     Again, he must be prepared to suffer for his advan-
tages.   He will be well advised to have a liver of leather.
Hepatic derangements are an occupational hazard; for information, gossip, is the oxygen of publishers, reputations their
stocks and shares.   To know who are the up and coming men,
who is the best man to write this or that book, who is the
best person to give advice about another book, the editor
must be out and about but never down and out.   Unfortunately, the itch to impart information is usually at its most active where good food and drink are being consumed and it is

there that the editor must be, however great his longing for
the solitary fireside and the chance to read in peace one of
his own books.

And at every party he attends every conversation will
sooner or later introduce the phrase "Do you mind if I talk
shop for a moment?"   In circumstances inimical to sober
judgment, he will have to advise his vis-à-vis about his relations with another publisher, or about an idea for a book
which may or may not be viable, or a grievance which must
be remembered and remedied.   And through it all he will
have to retain not only his memory but his discretion: he
will have to remember what to forget and what not, and at
the same time will have to decide what information can be
prudently vouchsafed in return for further information that
will fit usefully somewhere into the mental jig-saw puzzle
with which his inner mind is continually tinkering.

He will have to develop a mental vision that is bi-
focal: for he will live in the university as in a parish and
always subject to its pressures.   But if he does not look beyond it, to the intellectual world at large, through the distant half of his lenses, his range will be too contracted.
The best in authorship, the best in advice, must be sought
wherever it is to be found.   Nothing would be so disastrous
to the true interest of his university, Oxbridge or wherever,
as to imagine that the best could be found only within its
confines.

He will have to endure in silence much misunderstanding and when he does speak, even if he speaks with the
tongues of angels, he will still have to fight with one tongue
tied behind his back.   For the advice upon which his own
judgment, and that of his committee, rests will normally be
confidential.   Anonymity in advice is a condition of candour
and the candour of advisers is indispensable.   He will seldom be free to explain all the reasons behind the decisions
for which he will be held responsible even though he has not
taken them: it is easier for the critic to blame an individual than an institution.

And blame will not be lacking.   In the tradition of
English universities, as in English history, there will always
be a Prince Rupert and an Ironside, a Sir Hudibras, a Zeal-
of-the-Land Busy, a Praise-God Barebones, all seeing an institutional press which by its nature must often be secretive

as a dragon worthy of its St. George. And the severe discipline, which constrains a scholar in his own subject never
to write even a truism without a hedging "perhaps" or a
phalanx of authority, makes him succumb the more impetu-
ously to the temptations of attack in fields other than his
own where his evidence is hearsay from partisan sources,
or a plausible presentation from a single side.

All the editor can do is to preserve a meek and civil
front, give the truth such chance to prevail as may be compatible with discretion, and choke down whatever talents and
taste he may himself have by temperament for controversy.
The effort will sometimes be great and he will often lie a-
wake at night writing in his mind the letters he would like
to send but may not; and, dealing with men whose energies
often delight in polemic, try to reserve his own as best he
may for getting on with the routine work that is at least in
the end more productive, murmuring perhaps, "I do not like
thee, Dr. Fell, especially as I cannot tell."

There will be sometimes also the solace of confi-
dences, too, in quiet offices if his judgment comes to be accepted and respected. A colleague recalls how a great scholar once paused and said "I suppose we ought not to be discussing like this people who are, after all, our friends and
colleagues." And then after a silence, the great scholar
said: "But then, more truth has been spoken in this room
than in the whole of the university. So we may as well continue."

There are satisfactions, too, especially for the intellectually omnivorous. At a university press the editor is at
the growing point of many intellectual disciplines. On the
other hand, he must resign himself to being only a dilettante
of these disciplines, at once a Casanova doomed to a life of
flirtations and a midwife to other people's children; for his
daily office routine, his correspondence with authors, his
preoccupation with production problems, publicity problems,
problems of royalty and other negotiation, will be so press-
ing and manifold that he will seldom have time to read the
manuscripts which his activity has attracted. And it is the
irony of publishing that, though it is a man's interest in literature that usually brings him into the profession, it is the
literary side of his temperament that lives nearest to starva-
tion. He will blow other men's trumpets before other Jeri-
chos than Oxford's. His only paean will be an echo, anony-

mous in another's Preface.   Alphabetical entry in Acknowl-
edgements will be his epitaph, mute memorial to the in-
glorious mutation by which the grub that might have been a
butterfly became confused in the chrysalis, changed its image, and emerged a working bee.   But though the handker-
chief that wipes his brow will never be a sudarium and his
only relic will be an under-pensioned widow, he will at least
have worked for scholarship and not for shareholders.

Sometimes, of course, he will be drawn into "editing" in the narrower sense.   An author whose native language is not English will sometimes require help (as the late
Isaac Deutscher did before he acquired his ultimate mastery
of style).   Sometimes a friend will make a point of asking
that one read over a typescript and make suggestions, however drastic.   And sometimes the editor will have special
knowledge of a special field which will give his interventions
and opinion authority.   But a sensible editor will never regard himself as other than auxiliary, even when there are
good reasons for the changes proposed.   They will be for
consideration, not mandatory.

To one "editor" at least, then, the fears of the P. E. N.
Club authors seem to have little foundation.   A really efficient and busy "editor" will be a servant of the lamp by
which other people write.   But he will have little time to
"edit."   Nor in a university press should he normally want
to do so.   In the publishing world at large it may be that
the "editor" has become a sinister figure; if so, it is because in our decadent time so many "literary" people are
simply not literate.

The academic author, however, will usually have had
some training in the arts of presentation.   Moreover, he
will be trying not so much to express himself as to express
his contribution to knowledge.   He will therefore be free
from at least those vanities that we associate with the "creative" author.   He will not be able to argue that obscurity
is the condition of his writing or wish to confuse the exhibition of his personality with the statement he is trying to
make.   He will be in search of clarity, lucidity, concise-
ness, and open to any persuasions that seem to make for
these.

Finally, since he is a specialist, he will not be particularly interested in the views of his editor about his book.
He will respect criticism only from his equals or his superi-

ors and the task of the editor therefore will be not to attempt himself to criticize but to find the outside adviser whose contribution to the book, whether in suggestions for revision or simple endorsement, will help make the book as good as it can be.   And when he has any criticisms it is he, the author himself, who will be expected to deal with them. And if he does not agree and yet cannot produce satisfactory counter-arguments he will always be free to approach another publisher.

Relations between author and editor, then, should begin with a synapsis of interest and sympathy and should aim at developing these into symbiosis.   Like marriage the association should ideally be for richer or for poorer, in sickness and in health, for better and for worse.   And it should reach beyond the grave.   For books, like metaphors, are never quite dead.

C.   The Author

So You Want to Write a Book

By Paul R. Reynolds, well-known New York literary agent; author of The Writing and Selling of Nonfiction and other books.

From Saturday Review 46:48-50, July 13, 1963; adapted from The Writing and Selling of Nonfiction, by the Author. Copyright © 1963 by The McCall's Corporation. Reprinted by permission of Paul R. Reynolds, Inc., 599 Fifth Avenue, New York, N.Y. 10017.

The segment of the book industry that sells books in hard covers through bookstores has changed little in the last 100 years. The business is custom-ridden and is managed on old-fashioned and unscientific lines. Nevertheless, it can be the road to fame and money for the author.

It can be, but often is not. Take the case of the ordinary nonfiction book one buys in a bookstore. Here, the reasons for success or failure are so complex, and in many cases so obscure, that few authors themselves fully understand them. In varying degrees, they involve the reviews, advertising and publicity, the peculiar nature of the best-seller lists, the physical appearance of the book--and, finally, what the book itself has to say. It is difficult to describe all these factors adequately, or even suggest all the rewards and pitfalls of the writer.

A total of 16,448 new books were published in 1962, of which 7,822 were nonfiction. Ninety-five per cent of them were first published in hard covers and sold primarily through bookstores.

I have estimated the earnings of the nonfiction book writer on the basis of my own experience with the business affairs of authors, and on the basis of the estimates made by publishers. Nonetheless, the reader must take these figures as a guess, although possibly an educated guess.

181

Authors of the 7,822 nonfiction books published in 1962 will average more than $3,500 a book, so that the total earnings of all these books will exceed $27,000,000. This will be distributed somewhat as follows:

50 authors earned or will earn more than $50,000 from one book;

250 authors earned or will earn more than $20,000 from one book;

2,000 authors earned or will earn more than $4,000 from one book;

5,500 authors earned or will earn less than $4,000 from one book.

Obviously, five out of seven of these writers will be poorly paid for the time and labor expended. This is characteristic of the writing trade in all mediums.

Lack of success with a book is often a severe emotional blow to the author. Publication day is the start of what the author hopes will be mass distribution of his product. The day arrives for the author like any other day. His publisher may telegraph congratulations, giving him something to paste in his scrapbook. The author's friends are ignorant of his book unless his wife has talked about it, and none of them has read it or will read it. As the days go by, reviews trickle in from various parts of the country. In every case the reviews are short, sometimes just a mention of the book; usually they are favorable. Perhaps the publisher takes one small advertisement in the New York Times Book Review. The author waits and hopes; nothing more happens. The author blames his publisher for not advertising his book ("How can my book sell if no one knows about it?"). And he blames his publisher because on a trip to Chicago, he found three bookstores that did not have a single copy of his book.

Six months or more after publication the author receives a royalty statement. Only 1,904 copies were sold to bookstores. Of these, 402 were returned by bookstores to the publisher; the total number of copies sold to the public was thus 1,502. There is an earned royalty of about $750. Since the author was paid $2,000 in advance, there is no money due him and there never will be. He does not blame the quality of his book or the whims of popular taste; he puts the blame mildly upon his agent, strongly upon his publisher.

This gloomy progression of events is reproduced several thousand times each year. It is a sad picture, but not as sad or as pointless as the author imagines. Let us suppose he wrote the book in his spare time, working an average of ten hours a week for a year. He therefore devoted some 500 hours to researching and writing the book. His rate of pay was $4 an hour. But through his book he has also added zest to the adventure of living and enriched his life in other ways than with money. I have met hundreds of writers who were angry at their publishers because of the small sale of their books, but I don't remember ever meeting one who regretted the weary labor of writing or the excitement or sorrow of publishing a book, even though its sale was microscopic.

A book can be unsuccessful, or it can be a best-seller. What is a best-seller? It is, at best, a loose term. The New York Times and various other newspapers get reports from bookstores on what books sold in the largest quantities during the previous week. From these reports best-seller lists are compiled. The bookstores are inaccurate in their reports, partly because they rarely collate their sales figures week by week, partly because accuracy does not seem to them important.

Despite the inaccuracies, the books on the top of the New York Times best-seller list are the books being talked about and being sold in large quantities. The Rise and Fall of the Third Reich sold 348,107 copies in the bookstore edition from October 1960 to September 1962. It was on the New York Times best-seller list for eighty weeks and held top place for thirty-nine weeks.

What causes a book to be at the top, have an enormous sale, be a best-seller?

Favorable reviews in themselves do not sell books. Most reviews are favorable. Over and over again books are published, are reviewed prominently and in glowing terms, and sell only 3,000 copies or so. Nor will publicity in itself sell a book. In March 1960 a really fine book entitled This Is Where I Came In was published. Because of the au-

thor's close friendship with the heads of both the Associated
Press and the United Press, and because of the timeliness
of the book itself, feature articles praising the book ran in
nearly every daily paper in America, many of them starting
on the front page.   The sale of the book was 1,718 copies.

If reviews or publicity will not sell a book, advertising cannot be expected to.   Publishers have tried advertising
over and over again without success.   Advertising in itself
will never sell a book.

What can a publisher do to sell a book?   He can
package his product well, go through the publishing motions
efficiently, and hope for the best.   A good title, an effective
jacket, a strong sales force, and suitable publicity and advertising will increase the sale of any book.   But, in themselves, they will never make any book a best-seller.   Perhaps a book that has been produced haphazardly and distributed inefficiently will sell 2,000 copies, whereas, properly packaged and handled, it would have sold 4,000 copies.
With best-sellers the sales ratio between a good publishing
job and a poor one is not as great, although the difference
in copies sold is much greater.   Perhaps a good publishing
job can sell 75,000 copies of a book that would otherwise
sell 50,000.   The publisher's activity by itself never makes
a best-seller.

But what does make a book sell?   The major factor
is a book of such a nature that one person who reads it recommends it to another.   Mrs. Smith asks Mrs. Jones,
"Have you read The Rise and Fall of the Third Reich?"
Word-of-mouth recommendation may occur a few hundred
times with a resulting modest sale, or it may occur thousands and thousands of times and result in a best-seller.
Word-of-mouth recommendation may continue for a year or
more, or it may die within a month.

The quality of the book, what is between the first page
and the last, is the big factor in a successful sale.   The
publisher has a limited role.   Just as a bad surgeon can
save a patient's life and a good surgeon can lose a patient,
so it is with publishers.   No matter how bad the publisher,
a book with the requisite qualities will sell; the best publisher in the country cannot sell a book that readers do not recommend to each other.

Do publishers recognize a best-seller when they read

the manuscript?   No, but by publication date the publisher
knows whether he has either a failure or a book that will
earn its way but not sell in large quantities, or a best-
seller.   The reaction in the trade can be wrong but usually
is not.   One can almost smell a best-seller.

     The author of a successful nonfiction book tends to fol-
low a pattern.   The author has awakened one fine morning
to find himself famous.   He is elated.   The letters, the telephone calls, the requests for him to speak, to autograph
copies, to meet other well-known people, to do this and that
keep him pleasantly occupied for several months.   His
friends congratulate him.   A few even read his book and
wonder secretly how he was able to write it.   Much as he
hoped for success, the rewards in acclaim and in money are
far greater than he ever dreamed of.   If his contracts are
properly drawn, he is carried financially for two or more
years, the length of time depending upon whether there was
a book club selection, a big magazine sale, a large paperback reprint deal, or even a motion picture, or perhaps just
depending upon how many copies were sold through bookstores.

     But no book remains on the best-seller list forever.
Royalties ultimately cease, and the author, if he is to support himself, must continue to write.   He researches and
writes a second nonfiction book, for which he has already
received a contract from his publisher at attractive terms.
The publisher accepts the new book without waxing overen-
thusiastic.   It is published.   Perhaps the second book sells
20,000 copies.   Compared to most other books it is a success.   Compared to the author's previous book, the best-
seller, it is an out-and-out failure.

     However, such an author writes a third book, and
then a fourth, and many after that.

     Books can be failures; many are.   Books can also be
successful; more are than authors realize.   But the careers
of most books, and hence of most authors, are not at the
top or at the bottom.   Books sell in quantities ranging from
under 2,000 to over 500,000 copies.   Half or more of all
published books are modest successes, make some money for
author and publisher, do not make the author rich or famous,
but appreciably add to his income and his prestige.   A book
on flower arranging will probably have only a modest sale,

but the author may be reasonably well paid for her efforts, and acclaim may reach her in the form of numerous requests to speak before garden clubs. The author has become an admired expert in something that women are interested in. Moreover, the large number of writers who make a modest success may always strive for something higher with the next book. There is no ceiling to possible success.

Every writer has three problems that are common in every walk of life but are accentuated in the world of the written word. The first problem is for the writer to make himself work. Some writers live in an atmosphere of compulsion. Once they are started, an inner force drives them to research, write, research, write. Winston Churchill in a speech said:

> Writing a book is an adventure; to begin with
> it is a toy and an amusement, then it becomes
> a mistress, and then it becomes a master, and
> then it becomes a tyrant; and the last phase is
> just as you are about to be reconciled to your
> servitude--you kill the monster and fling him . . .
> to the public.

Nearly all writers feel this compulsion occasionally, perhaps when they are on the final chapter of a book. But the average day for most writers is one in which they would like to loaf, do anything but research, organize, write and rewrite.

Some writers get lazier and lazier, and often, with the help of drink, ruin their lives. The majority learn the art of self-whipping.

The second problem of the writer is to keep up with the times, keep in tune with the ever-changing thoughts, hopes, fears, beliefs, accomplishments, and failures of mankind. This is necessary for the writer's own creativity. The good writer is usually an avid reader, a good and constant listener, ever seeking different types of people. Often he is an assiduous traveler. The writer who plays bridge every Friday, golfs every weekend, sees in rotation the same people, and scarcely leaves his house for a night except at Christmas when he visits his old mother, such a writer is heading for trouble. The successful writer is a dynamo of energy in his work and a constructive loafer in his play, which he continually varies.

The third problem for the book writer is how he shall direct his energies.   The article writer is directed by the needs and dictates of magazine editors.   The book writer must direct himself.

Writers are subject to two dangers.   Depression and discouragement are the first danger.   Egotism and a swelled head are the second.   These dangers exist in all occupations. But the writer, whose work is so lonely, is peculiarly liable to depression and discouragement, and when he is success- ful, he receives so much publicity that he is especially vul- nerable to the threat of egotism and a swelled head.   The biggest factor in success is to learn one's trade and then in- dulge in that old-fashioned virtue of hard work over a long and continuous period of time.   As for the danger of a swelled head, that affects only the highly successful, and while it is hard to live with, it is still one of life's minor troubles.

What Does a Writer Expect of an Editor?

By Phyllis A. Whitney, Instructor of Juvenile Writing at
New York University; children's book reviewer; author of 34
published books for children and adults.

Reprinted (with permission) from School Library Journal 10:
107-8, October 1963, copyright © R.R. Bowker Company.

Late last year I was asked to be one of a panel of
writers discussing "what a writer expects of an editor" before an audience of book editors. Out of my appearance on
the panel came this invitation to put my views on paper.
They are, as I gave them that night and as I give them here,
my own; but I suspect they may represent the views of a
good many other writers as well.

The basic requirements a writer has of an editor are
two. The first need of the average writer is expert criticism. It would be lovely, I suppose, if we could simply
write and have it all approved, but I don't think that is the
way to get good books published. Most professional writers
know, as editors do, that there is no such thing as a perfect manuscript; it can always be improved. The writer's-
eye view is necessarily narrow, and the editor who can tell
the writer what is wrong with his story and give suggestions
that will make it better is the editor to be treasured and listened to.

Such criticism must be both sound and specific. Unfortunately there are editors who do not have the knowledge
of fiction techniques to make their criticism down-to-earth
and exact. I have seen the vaguest criticism come back
from editors: "There's something wrong here, but I don't
know exactly what it is;" "There's an awkwardness about
these pages;" "I have a feeling this needs tightening." This
sort of thing leaves the writer floundering and confused.
Quite legitimately he doesn't know what is being asked of him
because the editor hasn't really asked anything.

Many a young editor (and perhaps some older ones) could profit by taking a practical course in fiction writing. This is not a frivolous statement. Some actual writing would be good for him, whether it succeeded or not, because it would help him to achieve more empathy in working with a writer. Such a course also would give him professional practice in the positive criticism of manuscripts--to show a writer how to build up his story.

Criticism must of course be given without destroying a writer's faith in his story, and the editor must know where to stop. There is a "point of no further profit" past which the writer goes at his peril. He can arrive at a wooden state where, if he continues to revise, he will injure rather than improve his manuscript. The more professional the writer, the more revision he is usually able to do. It takes a certain sixth sense on the part of the editor to know when the time has come to stop revising.

I am not, of course, advocating blind acceptance by the writer of all criticism or judgment given by an editor. The writer too needs a sixth sense. The final judgment is his and sometimes when he and the editor find themselves in opposition, it is a tricky thing to know which of them is right. Most editors are very sensible about this and, unless the matter is so serious as to destroy the whole book, the editor will have the forbearance to let the insistent writer try it his own way.

Editors, like writers, are not infallible. I remember very well a book I wanted to write some 16 years ago. My editor objected to the story idea. She didn't think I could do it. She doubted that it would sell, and she didn't want to publish it anyway. In this case I was stubborn about it. I knew I had to write that book, even if it failed completely. So I went ahead, alone and in the dark except for a promise from another editor to read it when it was done. The book was called Willow Hill. It won a contest prize and has sold more copies than any other juvenile I've done.

An editor's criticism, when it is sound, can help the writer to a completely new view, help him to resee his story so that he can go to work and bring out the best that lies in material which is still imperfect--without causing a loss of self-confidence.

This brings me to the second and equally important need every writer has of a good editor. It is an emotional need, and a very real one. Each of us who writes needs someone who can extract from us more than we knew we had in ourselves to give. Emerson said it well a long time ago: "Our chief want in life is someone to make us do what we can."

The writer sitting at his typewriter lives, in one sense, in a lonely world. While it is so peopled with the characters of his invention that he sometimes forgets he is alone, there are times when his belief in himself as a writer grows very shaky indeed. Family and friends may think everything he writes is remarkable but, since they may not be qualified to judge, their belief, while pleasant, means little to him. Especially when the rejection slips come in.

The reader of books has little notion of the uncertainties that beset beginner and professional alike. I have had students in my classes say to me wistfully, "But you don't have to worry; you know you'll be published." Do I? You'd be surprised. I suppose by now I really do expect that somehow or other I'll be able to come up with another published book. But there are always times when the outlook seems extremely bleak. There are times when I suspect that I've bitten off more than I can chew, that my theme is too big for me, my plot too complicated or my characters lifeless. Sometimes the machinery sticks so badly that I grind to a stop. All my joy in the story is as dead as my characters seem to be. I wonder how in the world I ever managed to have a book published in the past. Will I ever learn to be a writer? This wailing is characteristic of every writer at one time or another. If at such times a writer can turn to a trusted editor, he (and his book) can be saved. Perhaps the writer would pull through all by himself, granted the determination, but it's far better when he can find that critic-with-a-heart.

A second aspect of the emotional function of the editor has to do with his critical approval. I remember a book of mine over which I had worked especially hard. I sent it off rather fearfully, hoping I'd done what I wanted to do, but not at all sure that I had. No one else had seen it. I waited with the impatience of a beginner for the verdict. My editor phoned me rather quickly to suggest certain revisions. I agreed. We covered a few business details and I knew she was about to hang up. So I plunged in hastily, "But do you

like the book?" There was the silence of astonishment at
the other end of the wire. After a moment she said, "Why,
of course! We all like it. It's a very good story."

But she had forgotten to tell me. She regarded me
as a businesslike professional and it never occurred to her
that there would be any question about this in my mind. She
didn't understand that I still glowed with love for these particular characters. They were friends whom I knew better
than I know the people who live on my own street. I had
created them. I had thought up this whole wonderful story
and was riding high on that fine pink cloud that is the writer's
real reward for what he does. Yet at the same time I
couldn't be sure. I wanted someone to tell me I could stay
up on that cloud a little while longer because everything was
all right, the story was good because of this and this and
this, and the children would like it.

It is, I believe, an important part of an editor's obligation to a writer to fulfill this need for approval when it is
deserved. And not just to keep us up there in the rosy
mists. If we are to grow as writers, if we are not to stand
still doing the same old thing (or even deteriorating), we
need to know not only what is wrong with a story, but what
is right. By knowing exactly how we brought it off and
where, we are guided and helped in our future writing. We
can see the ways in which we are growing as writers.

It is difficult, perhaps impossible, for an editor to
babysit with every one of his writers. Nevertheless, this is
what our best editors seem to do. Their work is highly
creative, both in their criticism of a manuscript, and in
their handling of the author. They tear us down with good
criticism and they build us up and make us feel we can do
even better. The editor who manages these two things well
is usually the editor who publishes the best books.

A Writer's Public Image

By James Michener, author of Hawaii, Tales of the South Pacific, and other best sellers.

First published in Esquire Magazine 64:150+, December 1965. Reprinted by permission of William Morris Agency, Inc., on behalf of author. Copyright © 1965 by Esquire, Inc.

This letter continues a conversation between Mr. Michener and Elaine Dundy (author of The Dud Avocado) which began at a dinner party in Madrid in 1961.

> Pipersville, Penna.
> May 28, 1961

Dear Miss Dundy,

Quite the intellectual highlight of my trip to Spain was the discussion I had with you over the statement of Gore Vidal's that he regretted and indeed sometimes lamented that he had not been fortunate enough to have established early and strong a public image of himself. This has given me more food for contemplation than anything else I have heard for a long time, and I keep coming back to it.

My initial reaction, as you know, to the Vidal statement was one of confusion. I was unable to see why a writer with his talent and success would worry about this apparently trivial problem, and I pointed out that so far as I was concerned I would much rather be Vidal with no public image but with his talent than a couple of other writers I mentioned who had a damned strong image but very trivial talents. This, of course, is an impeccable position.

But then I thought about the good luck that Truman Capote had in getting that early image strongly fixed on the public and of the adroit manner in which he capitalized on this to his great advantage. Granted, he had a considerable

talent with which to fortify the haunting image, but I did have
to agree that he profited in an honest way from the luck that
had befallen him.   At this point for the first time I realized
what Vidal was talking about, and I saw some merit in his
position.

A writer, painter or actor is indeed fortunate when a
public image of himself as an artist is established early and
is one whose confines he has the talent to fulfill.   All sorts
of advantages must accrue to this position in the public eye,
and they are by and large honorable ones; for this business
of making a living in the arts is terribly difficult, and one
needs all the help he can get.   So, fundamentally one must
agree with Vidal and honor his position.

But the more I thought about this the more I was
driven into what one might call my "first position."   It
seemed to me that what we were discussing in Vidal's statement was a basic problem of all artists and one which has
historically been answered in one of two ways.   There is the
Ernest Hemingway solution whereby the artist is consciously
built up into a public figure whose image stands for something almost concrete with the public and whose life work
fulfills that image.   And there is the equally honorable method followed by James Gould Cozzens who permits and encourages no image whatever and who lives wholly outside the public gaze, writing to fulfill some inner-generated image of
himself in relationship to his particular world.   (I suppose
there is an immense third group into which most of us fall:
that of the people who would like to have an image they could
call their own but who have neither the talent nor the inventive genius to support such an image.)

I would argue facilely rather than profoundly that most
popular histories of literature focus primarily on the first
group, the image-makers, whereas most lasting analyses of
an age's literature focus primarily on the second group,
those who are strong enough to survive without the aid of an
image.   I am sure that this dichotomy would not hold up under hard inspection, but there is enough truth in it to provide an avenue into the problem.

Thus one cannot drive from his mind the image of
Edgar Allan Poe, who is almost the beau ideal of the image-
gang and who was also a rather dreary poet; but if he tries
one cannot conjure up an image per se of Herman Melville,
who is the archetype of the kind of writer who can exist with

an image and who was also a most impressive novelist.
Who carries with him an image of Jane Austen, Edmund
Spenser, Stephen Crane or Robert Penn Warren?   Who fails
to carry an image of Percy Shelley, Mark Twain, Henry
Wadsworth Longfellow or Arthur Miller?   I tend very strongly to prefer the work of the shadowy figures and I watch with
some amusement the struggles of the imagists to perpetuate
themselves.

Yet at the same time I must confess that public life
would be very dull indeed without the presence of the image-
makers.   It sometimes seems to me as if society required
a small percentage of its citizens to be visible artists--
never mind whether they are real artists or not--simply to
reassure that society that it is paying at least lip service to
the cause of the arts.   I have long suspected that any contemporary society that was in good health (and by that I
mean working to extend its frontiers and more or less eager
to go to war) had little use for living artists and damned little need for them either, but that in the nagging rear of its
collective mind it remembered that all the great civilizations
of the past are remembered primarily because of what their
artists accomplished, and that therefore, to hedge one's bets,
a civilization ought to have a quota of kept artists on hand
merely to insure its position in the future.

Now such artists ought to look like artists, ought to
be immediately recognized as such.   Thus Salvador Dali and
Pablo Picasso serve very important roles in our contemporary society.   So did Oscar Wilde and Edgar Poe in theirs.
So do Truman Capote and Edith Sitwell.   So do Hemingway
and Françoise Sagan.   They remind an art-indifferent society
that it too has certain hedges against obscurity.   But whether
this role fulfillment has anything to do with art in the long
perspective I doubt most seriously.   It is a religious-ritual-
istic propitiation and the persons involved are best thought of
in the role of acolytes furthering a cabalistic cause, although
I must admit that classifying Miss Sagan as a vestal virgin,
which she is, causes me some discomfort.

I once observed an almost perfect example of what
I'm talking about.   When the United States Occupation Forces
sprawled all over Japan they automatically came into contact
with one of the world's most prolific producers of artists.
There were literally hundreds of them, many of them men
with true genius.   But the American military was never altogether happy with these scraggly artists, yet at the same

time everyone knew that a conquering army ought to patron-
ize the arts. No one knows quite how to do this, for the
artists who were worth patronage were a pretty nondescript
lot: little men in black sack suits who were working hard to
make a living and who often needed glasses or dental work.
So no communication was possible between the conquering
military and the honest artists.

Into this hiatus stepped Paul Jacquolet, a Parisian ex-
patriate living in a romantic mountain hideout in Central Japan. He had long hair, longer fingernails, an ascetic face
set off by rouge and lipstick and mascara, and a wardrobe
that Cecil B. De Mille would have envied. What was best of
all, he did wood-block prints of exotic subjects much in the
style of Maxfield Parrish. Girls half nude against tropical
flowers remain a strong impression in my memory, but he
was a good deal more than a mere illustrator. His line was
exquisite and his use of color was good. But the important
thing was that Jacquolet immediately created the impression
of "an artist." He was accordingly swept up by the generals'
wives and he became the official kept artist of the Occupation. Just as all good Germans always knew one Jew whom
they befriended, so we all knew an artist whom we supported. (Never mind that a hundred great original men were
starving.) It became fashionable to have Paul Jacquolet at
one's parties. Everyone had a set of his prints, especially
those from the more exotic South Sea islands. Everyone felt
at ease that the United States was sponsoring art. And the
whole damned thing would have fallen flat on its face and accomplished nothing if Jacquolet had not looked like an artist.
He accomplished a great deal more, I must confess, than
Jackson Pollock ever could have.

It should be obvious that I consider image-creation a
totally irrelevant aspect of a life within the arts and I can
therefore have not much sympathy with Gore Vidal's proper
and understandable concern over this matter. One of my
great literary heroes, Balzac, spent a good deal of time and
energy creating an image which he dutifully enlarged and protected. I don't think the less of him for this; I consider it
wholly irrelevant. I retain a high regard for the exquisite
manner in which Truman Capote uses words and sentences
and indeed envy him this subtle skill; as to his work in the
image-creation field I have no opinion one way or the other.
I suppose I tend to feel that if he does it well, I don't have
to worry about it myself, because civilization's minimum
quota for this sort of thing is being filled, and most ably,

by a man who does it well. We have our age's Lord Byron;
the rest of us can get on with the job of being Thackerays.

So far as I can recall, no one has ever recognized
me in public. I would suppose that my image is totally nil,
not even as faintly alive as Robert Penn Warren's, whose
image I would put close to the nil point. In the recent political campaign it was most disturbing to the people who organized one extensive tour to discover that, in the twelve
Midwestern states in which we campaigned with three speeches a day, not one person knew who I was by sight and only
about one in a hundred had ever heard of me in any other
capacity either. (I suspect they would not have known Capote or Vidal either; they would have known Hemingway and
Arthur Miller, but the latter solely as the husband of Mari-
lyn Monroe.) After about five cold and chilly days of this
they switched my identification to "The Man Who Wrote the
TV Series, Adventures in Paradise." It was astonishing how
many people clustered around to talk with me and to assure
me that that was their very favorite television show and did
I actually know Gardner McKay, pant, pant? From these
and hundreds of similar experiences I have come to the conclusion that my image is something that I need never worry
about and that the creation of images had best be left to
others more skilled in the field.

I had strong reaffirmation of this conclusion when I
watched the use being made of Robert Frost at the inaugur-
al. I thought, "Every administration ought to have its kept
poet the way the Hapsburgs used to have kept painters. And
we're so lucky that ours looks like a poet." Later I reflected, "And we're especially lucky that he's too old to
write any poetry, because that might be embarrassing."

To conclude the analysis of my first position, there
remains the question: "Does a man with no image at all
regret his nakedness and does he envy those who are more
fortunate?" I am not conspicuously qualified to answer this,
because I came to writing at a much more mature age than
almost anyone else you know. I cannot therefore speak as
a young man who feels the weight of his full future before
him. Furthermore, I can recall to the minute when I decided to be a writer, and to have such consciousness of an
act of will bespeaks an entirely unique set of values.

I was managing editor of a department within the
large Macmillan Company, which was then owned in large

part by Macmillan's of London, and one of my duties was to
be nice to the visiting authors from London. I suppose our
heads were eager to curry favor with the home office, because whenever an English writer appeared on the scene, we
fell all over ourselves trying to be nice. We gave lunches,
dressed in our best blue suits, bowed and scraped as they
got off the boat, thanked them for bringing culture to our
shores, and arranged teas and parties and radio appearances
and interviews. In other words, we did our damnedest to
build an image of these gifted writers, composed nine-tenths
of clotted cream and one-tenth Oxford accent. Among the
most impressed among the yokels was I, and I can even now
recite the names of fifty such worthies.

One day in the big boss's absence it fell to me to
sign the royalty statement for the year and to my astonishment I found that all these famous authors from across the
water were doing very poorly indeed. Their books weren't
selling at all. We were paying them heavily in compliments;
but not at all in cash. I thought this extraordinary and so
took home a bundle of their books to inspect; and I was appalled at how bad they were. Most turned out to be cozy
little analyses of one or another village in the Cotswolds,
but there was never a Middlemarch amongst them, and I
recall very clearly banging the table and crying, "Hell, I
can write better than this." And it seemed quite clear to
me that night that I was engaged, as a publisher, in a hilarious, harmless but not altogether honest racket. We took
people of no conspicuous talent, published their novels, and
then set about callously to make them "feel like authors."
Every publisher I know has a young girl out of college whose
job it is to make ordinary men and women "feel like authors,"
if it can be done without costing the publisher any money.
Interviews are arranged, parties, radio and television appearances, photographs, and what-not. It is both ridiculous
and inconsequential. I suppose it does no harm; I'm fairly
sure it sells few books. It does keep the author happy and
it keeps the publisher in a properly cynical frame of mind
so that he can keep his attention sourly on the business aspects of his operation.

Early in my writing life I looked back upon this
sleazy aspect of publishing and decided that whereas as a publisher I had been forced to further the innocuous racket, as
a writer I would have little to do with it. I have kept to
this commitment. I know almost no fellow authors, no
critics, few publishers. I attend no seminars, give no lec-

tures, participate in none of the hoopla.   I do what is necessary to see to it that my books are well received, but at almost every publication date I am out of the country.   I have
never spoken to my publisher about more advertising and I
have refused permission to many in the business who have
wanted to give me public parties.   I do not work in Hollywood and I review the absolute minimum number of books
that I can get away with.   My one great weakness is that I
love all who try to make a living in the arts and I am asked
to do a positively unconscionable number of prefaces to
books; when the requests come from close friends I am powerless to say no; I reason, "If there is anything I can do to
pry a living loose from an indifferent public I'll do it."   I
find it hard to believe that my prefaces do any good and I
think my friends are wasting their time and mine, but publishers feel otherwise.   I suspect, however, that they know
it's a racket, but a relatively harmless one.

If I had an image that could be peddled, I might think
otherwise; but I have none and I think I can say with some
honesty that as a man who started writing only in his forties,
I have much preferred it this way.   Were I younger I might
think otherwise, but it would be through ignorance of the
facts . . . in my case.   I have therefore been relatively
true to a position I laid out for myself a good many years
ago.

Yet even as I reach this conclusion I am beset by a
gnawing doubt, and I may call this my "second position."
It seems to me that the most significant event in literature
to have occurred in the past ten years was the manifesto of
the French intellectuals in which they protested the actions
of their government in Algeria.   I was staggered by the bold-
ness of this statement, its obvious disregard of consequences,
its high moral ground, and its ultimate influence upon French
thought.   Had the statement been made in the United States
by citizens of this nation, I suspect the law would permit
the shooting of the signatories on the ground of giving overt
air and comfort to an enemy of the state.   What impressed
me most was such a statement could have been made in
Paris, and perhaps in Rome or London; it could not conceivably have been made in the United States.   Men like me
would not have signed it, and we would not have signed it because we would have known that in the United States the opinions of people like ourselves were not of any great consequence, whereas in Paris and London they were.

In no major country of the world is the moral significance of the artist of less importance than in the United
States. We make a living; we are able to save a little
money; we are moderately well received in a wide variety of
milieu; and after we are dead we play a substantial role in
forming the public conscience. But that any of us should
play a major role during his lifetime in helping the nation
formulate its scale of values, its aspirations, or its public
conscience is unthinkable. I suspect that from long habit the
people of France actually listened to the protest of their intellectuals and thought that a problem had been ventilated
which merited their attention. I cannot visualize the people
of America doing the same, and their indifference must stem
from a similarly long habit of disregarding what their intellectuals say.

I am therefore driven to this dichotomy: either the
people of France and England are different in some specific
way from the people of the United States; or the writers of
the first two countries are different in some specific way
from the writers of our country. Since the former alternative seems unlikely, I am forced to conclude that over the
centuries the writers of the Continent have done something
right, whereas our writers have done something wrong. I
accept this conclusion and I am even willing to specify what
it is that we have done wrong. Our error has been twofold.

We have not insisted upon our legitimate place at the
council tables of the Republic and we have so far not produced a single writer competent to sit at those tables. We
have settled for a second-class citizenship and have consequently been relegated to a second-class status within the
Republic. Men like me, who should have known better, were
the chief offenders because we might have fought the ghetto,
but we did not. I would hold men like Warren, Faulkner,
Cozzens, Hawthorne, Melville and Crane particularly vulnerable to this charge. They never carried the social burden
for which they were equipped, and all of us--writers and society alike--have thereby suffered a diminution. If Faulkner
today were to make a statement on anything it would be particularist, signed by him alone, and far off to one side from
the mainstream of discussion. The same is true for all the
rest of us, so we slide with our nation from one chance position to the next.

The second error we made is chargeable to the image-
makers. By and large they have been content to create im-

ages of themselves which have been exhibitionistic and yet at the same time recondite.   Perversely, these people have taken themselves out of the mainstream of American life and seem to me to have willed it so.   Suppose that tomorrow Ernest Hemingway and Truman Capote teamed up to make a statement on something of concern to them; could anyone take it seriously?   From Poe on down to the present, the possessors of images in our artistic legions have consciously taken themselves off to one side.   They have been the symbol-servers of a society that did not want artists but did want some kind of cabalistic reassurance that it had artists among its people.   It seems to me that Norman Mailer has woefully fallen into this same trap.

I therefore conclude, somewhat against my own initial judgment and much to my surprise, that Gore Vidal was correct as reported by you in wanting an image, for the one that we would want would not be of a particularist or exhibitionistic sort, but one which had the strength of a popular image and the intellectual underpinning of a real, hard, well-thought-out moral position.   In other words, he would want precisely what the French writer has enjoyed for more than a century, a blend of Zola, Proust, Malraux and Céline, so that when something required to be said we would have a body of writers with images so powerful that they could command attention and yet so firmly rooted that what they were about to say could be counted on to make sense.

We do not have such a group in the United States, and Arthur Miller has written wisely on why not.   Looking back, it seems to me that I was too afraid of the meretricious elements that surround the average image-making and not sufficiently aware of the urgent need of our society for the kind of artist's position that is possible in either France or Great Britain.   I am sure I was right in shying away from the nonsensical operation of the average publisher's helper in the United States; but I also suspect that I was dead wrong in concluding that that was the most important aspect of the problem.   It seems to me now that it was at best a regrettable excrescence that beclouded a fundamentally sound consideration.   I remain wryly amused at the ridiculousness of blowing up a transparent little talent like Françoise Sagan into what the bullfighting world calls a figura; but I was totally wrong in not sensing that sometimes this has to be done so that later on, when France faces a moral crisis, there is someone like Miss Sagan at hand to utilize the creation for good purpose.

In that respect we in the United States have created only trivial figures that can be used to no effective purpose. (Can you imagine Edgar Allan Poe commenting on the Mexican War?) I hope that men like Vidal and Miller and Ellison and Mailer will correct that basic error.

Most warmly,
Jim Michener

Author and Reader

By Monica Dickens, great-granddaughter of Charles Dickens and a best-selling author in England.

From Focus on Indiana Libraries 20:82-91, December 1966. Published by the Indiana Library Association. Reprinted by permission. Part of a speech given by the author at the ILA Conference at Indianapolis on November 4, 1966.

I am particularly pleased to be here today because my husband comes from Indiana. It was in fact the place of his birth. It was also, I must say, the place he ran away from. At the age of fifteen, he jumped on a freight train, went to Florida, lied about his age and joined up in the Navy.

There is an even more important reason why I am delighted to be here and that is because I am always so very pleased to be invited by librarians, because they are really my favorite kind of people, and it is simply marvelous to meet so many of you, captive as it were, all together like this.

It is like that zoo in England where you can see a whole herd of hippopotamus, instead of just the usual one or two, you know. Because librarians, you see, next to a firm rubber cushion to sit on, are one of the most important things in an author's life. We couldn't exist without you; of course, you couldn't exist without us--you are never going to get a librarian to admit that!

Although I must say that librarians are a bit stingy. They will buy one copy of your book and then let everybody who is too mean to buy it, have a free go at it. They do us the very vital service of bringing the author and the reader together.

Now authors and readers enjoy a rather peculiar relationship, as you may have noticed if you have ever seen a

reader meet an author.   Authors always go out of their way
to try to be nice to readers, and readers, unfortunately, say
some very embarrassing things to authors.   There are several stock remarks, and I have compared notes with other
authors and I find they get the same sort of thing.

The first one is the opening gambit of the conversation at a cocktail party, or whatever it is: "I have never
read any of your books."   That is a statement to which there
are no answers at all, and you find yourself saying groggily,
"Why should you."   I think of a marvelous retort on the way
home like, "Well, it is a little above your head," but I never manage to bring it out.

Another one is "I was given your book for Christmas.
I keep meaning to start it."   You can bet they are lying
when they tell you this.   And then there is the gushing host-
ess who introduces you with great pride and says, "Now I am
going to give you a real treat, I am going to introduce you
to a real live author!   This is the treat of your life, folks,
here she is--Mrs. Monica Dickens," and the guest she introduces you to, polite, if not impressed, says, "Why, yes.
How do you do, Miss Dickens.   What name do you write un-
er?"   That is another one that I always think of a good retort to, but only on the way home.

And then there are the people who go through the
whole bit about "Oh, you are really his great granddaughter.
I think that is so marvelous.   I was brought up on David Cop-
perfield, and we read the Christmas Carol to our chidren
every year, and I do think Mr Pickwick is the best novel."
This goes on and on, and they invariably say, "Well, goodbye, Miss Dixon."

And there are the people who will tell you with great
pride, as if they had struggled their way through the whole
book of Leviticus, "I read your last book," and then add, "I
got it from the library," and expect you to be absolutely de-
lirious with joy and rush out and buy yourself a fur coat.

In its way that is better than nothing because, although
you may not have had a sale, the library has got you a reader, and this is what librarians do for authors--they get you
readers.

"What shall I read?" people ask, wandering into their
local public library rather as they wander into the mobile

chest X-ray, you know, because it is free.   Or they have
a sneaking suspicion that this may be where some of their
tax money went.

"What should I read" and the darling librarian, or
one of her delightful assistants, presses on them, if you are
lucky, a copy of one of your books.   While you may think
there is not much gain in that, the library has bought the
book, you have had a teeny-weeny royalty from it, whether
one person reads it or 100.

Though incidentally, we are going to put that right in
the near future, authors are, you know.   When somebody
writes a song, or eats potato chips for a television commercial, or like the man in Time this week who makes the
"bleep, bleep," for the Maxwell House coffee machine.   Every time it is shown they get royalties, and the day will
come when you are going to have to collect a fee, or something like 1/8 of 14 percent--some simple figure like that--
for every 100 words of every book you issue.

Meanwhile the gains for us in libraries is, if the
reader likes your book, if he likes it, there is always that
faint, that 1000-1 chance that when your next book is published that they just might go out and buy it.   They discover
you through the library.

Now you might think that book shops ought to serve this
purpose for authors, but I am afraid that book shops both
here and in England have gone sadly down hill.   They have
become rather like a supermarket; if you don't see what you
want on the shelves and grab it for yourself, it is awfully
hard to find somebody in the book shop who is ready and able
to discuss with you what it is you really do want.

Only last week in Boston I asked this girl if she had
a book on surfing, and she handed me a copy of the Atlantic
Monthly!

When my last book was published in England, the manager of Selfridges (I am sure you know Selfridges don't you,
it is an enormous department store rather like Macy's) had
made rather a nice display for me with a great stack of my
books and cards and photographs and everything and I spent
a nervous hour hovering around and being bumped into by
shopping baskets and children.   People asked me the way to
the rest rooms, but I never, never saw anybody look at this

pyramid of books, much less buy one.

This is a curious thing about book business, that no matter how long you have spent skulking nervously around book stores, and you would be amazed at how many even secure authors do it, because I have met them myself, nervously rearranging their paperbacks, putting their own on top, and anyone you see doing that at an airport terminal is an author.

But you never actually see anybody buying a copy of your book, any more than you ever see anybody reading one. Although I did once, I saw this woman in a hotel in England and she was reading One Pair of Feet and so I picked up my courage and went up to her all smiles and a little humble-- not too humble--sincerity must have been dripping off me like sparks in a steel foundry. I said, "I see you are reading my book." And she said "Oh, is this yours? I am sorry. I just picked it up."

Anyway after I had stood there at Selfridges among the crying children and the dogs, you know Englishwomen take dogs shopping much as American women take their husbands, I finally got the nerve to go up to this young sales clerk who was standing there by me in a Beatle haircut and a pair of Rolling Stones boots which obviously pinched his toes, and I said, "That looks like a rather interesting book. Do you think it will sell?" pretending to be very casual about it. He said "Nah," shifting his gum to the other side of his mouth, and added "No pictures in it. See, it's got all words in it."

But there is one country in this world where book shops are every author's dream of what a book shop ought to be, and that is a place where they not only sell books, but read them themselves and talk about them, make friends with the customers over them and that is Australia.

I did a tour in Australia and New Zealand last year and I was thrilled to see how the book shops are crammed with people. They go in every lunch hour and have a free read. The manager once told me about this man who was reading his way through a book, turning the pages down every day to mark his place. One day they got a new assistant in and she sold the book. The man was furious. He never came back again.

While I was in Australia and New Zealand, down under, as we call it, I had to sit in many stores and autograph copies of my book. This was the deal, and that is always torture. You are made to sit there in the store with
piles of your books, which you begin to hate the sight of before too long because they don't sell. People either ignore
you completely, passing on their way to another shop or they
give you that sort of filthy look that they used to reserve for
people in the stocks. Autographing parties, they are called
in this country, but they don't do that so much any more,
fortunately, either here or in England. People got sick of
them really, they were quite overdone. After all, I mean,
who would go around the corner to meet a real live author.

Authors are so boring now, quite out of style because
they take so long to produce what they do produce, whereas
a painter! Now a painter can spill a can of paint, ride a
bicycle over it and he's got a picture, done in ten minutes.

But in Australia, in all sincerity, they don't have too
many authors of their own and they don't see very often the
English and American authors whose books they read. So
there I was, exposed to public ridicule and to the predictable
traumas that do crop up every time you have to do this sort
of thing.

And the first ones are the people who will pick up a
copy of somebody else's book and bring it up to you to wrap
and give change, which you really do give, even if you have
to give change out of your own purse.

The next ones are the people who think I am Charles
Dickens, and they bring me his books to sign.

Hard on their coat tails come all the people who are
distantly related to my great-grandfather, or whose grand
aunt's cousin's mother's chauffeur's uncle's piano teacher
once sat on his knee when she was a child. They come thick
and fast in Australia because two of Charles Dickens' sons
emigrated there, in spite of the fact that one never married
and the other one had two daughters only, neither of whom
ever married, the country seems to be half populated with
his descendants. They come absolutely flocking into the
store, not to buy books but just to see me and to go away
disappointed because they know more about Charles Dickens
than I do, which would not be difficult.

Then there come the people who come not to see
what you have written but to show me what they have written.   They come staggering into the store, with a manuscript of this two hundred thousand words book which has
gained the world's record in rejection slips.   They want you
to help get it published.   Or if it is not that, they want you
to write their life story, and these are always the people
with the dimmest life story who for reasons think it should
go down to posterity.   The deal is always that they will tell
you the story, you will write it, and you will go fifty-fifty
on the proceeds.

And then there come the people who come out of curiosity really, to be able to tell their friends, "Oh, I didn't
think much of her."   I had two of them in Brisbane.   I saw
them come into the shop.   I was sitting there trying to sell
books and they came in and sort of stalked around behind
shelves.   They stalked me around a pile of maps and then
stood half hidden behind a stack of low-calorie diet books,
giggling and pushing each other.   I said, "Did you want to
buy a book?"   It is extraordinary how brazen you get under
these circumstances but somehow there is a subtlety.   "Did
you want to buy a book?" always sounds a little less brash
than "Do you want to buy?"   It is amazing that you sometimes have to ask it, for there are people who come to a
book store from fifty miles by bus or train and then forget
what they came for when they get there so I said, "Did you
want to buy a book?"   "Book?" said one, as if I had offered
a pair of water skis.   "Well, what it was," she said, "my
friend and I, we were just standing here thinking that picture
of you on the back of your book must have been taken years
ago."

And if people do buy books they always say, "Oh, it's
not for me.   It's for my poor old grandma, or for my
daughter (she reads you know) or for my wife," in case you
might flatter yourself that they are going to read it themselves, and if you ask them what the wife's name is they always get in an absolute tizzy--they can't remember.   I have
autographed more books "To my darling wife" or "To the
sweetest mum in all the world, from Monica Dickens."

In Brisbane a woman came up and she bought a book to
give to somebody and I said, "Well, would you like me to put
somebody's name in it?" and she said, "Yes, Emma Chisit."
So I duly wrote "E-M-M-A C-H-I-S-I-T," and I found out too
late she was merely asking me, "How much is it?" . . .

How to Write Your First Book and Stay Sane

By Burt Zollo, Senior Vice President, The Public Relations Board; President, Public Relations Network International.

Reprinted from the Public Relations Journal by permission, copyright May 1967 by the Public Relations Society of America, Inc.

With the book business booming, peripatetic public relations people are moonlighting their share. Some are writing novels. Others are working on business and industrial books which include, of course, books about public relations.

Many a somewhat jaded if not downright cynical author of the latter may ask the public relations man embarked upon his first public relations book, "Why?" Whether, like Somerset Maugham, he writes to "disembarrass his soul" or because he has something he believes is worth saying or simply because the typewriter and paper are there, the "Why" is disconcerting.

It not only asks for personal motivation; it also suggests to the public relations man that writing a book, even one on a subject that he should know best, is no cinch. Some authors find the effort--and it is an effort--worth it: a book about public relations forces the writer to reappraise his own convictions about his livelihood, to explore the convictions of others, to articulate conclusions. A good book may be a gratifying personal graduate course in public relations.

Other public relations men find the experience frustrating. Writing the book becomes a dull, compulsive, burden, an exercise as exhilarating as a day at the dentist's. In fact, the writing of the book may seem as endless as the questions of well-meaning associates: "How's the book? You mean you're still working on it? When will you finish it?" The author then wonders if the book isn't finishing him.

After having recently gone through the manic-depressive experience of writing a book about public relations myself, some pitfalls now seem obvious. They also may appear obvious to the experienced author, less so to the novice. But, whether master or neophyte, every author faces them. Here are the main ones to avoid.

Pitfall #1: Writing the book first, getting a publisher second. It's good to prepare a chapter-by-chapter outline of the intended epic, and it makes sense to write a few chapters. The former reveals the structure, the latter your talent. But it's wise to go no further without the advice of a literary agent, a contract with a publisher, or both. The sure course to complete frustration is to produce a complete book that, perish the thought, is not salable.

Pitfall #2: Being vague about your audience. When a publisher gives a contract to an author, there's no question about the primary and secondary audience--so far as the publisher is concerned. But what about the author? In his eagerness to get his first book published, he may agree to direct it to marketing people when, privately, he has to admit he isn't quite sure who they are, what they think, what they want to know. Unless he's sure about his audience, sure that he knows it as well as the publisher thinks he does, he may find he's submerged even before he gets his feet wet.

But even when he does know the audience for his book, let's say it's the businessman, he's wise to make sure he has the same businessman in his sights as does the publisher. Is it all businessmen? Is it the small businessman? And if it's the former, does the author have the experience, the savvy, the courage to tell such a variegated group the score? Unless these questions are answered precisely and positively, the author will produce a book that's almost as stirring as a Sigmund Romberg concert is to a group of Beethoven buffs.

Pitfall #3: Being vague about your approach. It's vital for the author-to-be to make certain his approach is clear and consistent. Is this to be a "how to" book or will it be a report on current conditions? Without a clear approach, without a defined attitude or point of view, writing problems are inevitable. The editor may be delighted with the author's knowledge but he'll be critical of the author's "tone." In short, because the author hasn't decided whether he's going to be instructor, critic, or chronicler, his writing will be without smoothness, without incisiveness, without a page that doesn't demand revision.

Pitfall #4: Waiting for inspiration to strike before striking the typewriter. This pitfall--almost a bromide-- nevertheless prevents some authors from completing a book in a reasonable time. McGraw-Hill editors wisely tell part-time authors how to plan their schedules. "Write at least an hour every night, " they say, in effect.

Surprisingly, it works. A book about public relations seldom demands inspiration. But it does demand thought and after a full day of public relations tasks, thought may seem harder to start than an old flivver in a Chicago winter. However, even the family man usually can find an hour-- usually after 8:30 p. m. --when he can push along on his book. Eventually, a work rhythm is developed and some authors even admit that their late-hour labor has a definite therapeutic value that even beats viewing their favorite TV program.

Pitfall #5: Believing that a business book can't entertain. Non-readers of the Wall Street Journal often are amazed to learn that its writing is literate, many of its articles amusing.

The "first book" author, eager to pontificate, may forget that a book is worthless unless it's readable. While a volume about public relations may not aim to amuse first, inform second, it's a common mistake of the neophyte business writer to believe that a weighty subject must be weighted down with ponderous prose. Some humour, some brightness, some style may enable an author to expand his audience-- and, happily, increase his sales.

Pitfall #6: Writing without organization. Some great novelists have admitted writing without precise plan; some current novels, clearly and unfortunately, reflect this difficult approach; but writing a book about public relations is not comparable. The author who proceeds without a clear idea of where he's going, and an organized way of getting there, is going to spend twice the time necessary to complete his book as he would have otherwise.

Methods of organization vary. But it includes outlining individual chapters; a file system related to chapters so

that research is not wasted because it's misplaced; a listing
of all research sources so that individual quotations can be
attributed to the right parties.

Pitfall #7: Maintaining an unreasonable pride of authorship. Most public relations men recognize early in their
careers that few of their articles can't stand editing, few of
their phrases can't stand improvement. The same is equally true of a book. That an author should care about what he
says and how he says it is unquestioned. But he must be
flexible.

If the book's a long time in the writing, revisions
may be necessary simply because conditions have out-dated
some of the author's comments. It's also possible that other books have been published in the meantime and, if the
author is to offer something fresh, he may be forced to rewrite.

Unless he's aware that such contingencies are likely,
he'll be fighting criticism, fighting his editor. The weak
and indecisive author isn't worth his salt; but the stubborn
author who refuses to acknowledge his own inadequacies or
respect his publisher's advice may never see his book reach
the bindery.

Pitfall #8: Failing to obtain written permissions.
Obtaining written permission to use quotations is an annoying
routine, but it's a necessary one. To wait until all chapters
have been accepted and then get the necessary permissions
often proves doubly troublesome for the author because of
the quantity of work involved and for the publisher who may
have to delay the book's introduction.

Waiting until the book is almost ready for the printer
before securing written permissions also may prove expensive to the author. He may find that some of his sources--
particularly if they're other writers, syndicated columnists
or newspapers--charge a fee even if only a single quote from
an article is used. If learned in time, this can be avoided
by using a different, "free" quote. However, when the book
is ready for printing, the author may find it's necessary to
pay the fee to prevent delaying publication.

Pitfall #9: Believing the job is done when the writing is completed. The novice author is overjoyed when the
publisher informs him that all chapters have been accepted.

But his happiness may be short-lived when he realizes
there's more work ahead: preparing an index (the author's
job), citing all acknowledgments (more detail work) and filling out a hefty marketing questionnaire that will help the
publisher promote the book.   Lack of interest in such pedes-
trian tasks means fewer sales, less eagerness on the part
of the publisher to go after the author for another book.

        Pitfall #10:   Talking about "the book" before it's
completed.   Besides appearing annoyingly pompous to friends,
family, and associates, the new author may do his book a
disservice by constantly bringing it into discussion.   He's
bound to be given well meaning advice, and successful books
seldom are the result of group effort.   Too much advice
leads to doubt, confusion, revision, and frustration.   The individual effort--supported by agent and editor--usually is suf-
ficent; if it's not, the idea of a book must be regarded only
as an idea.

        It's possible that this pitfall also should relate to
writing about books before they're published.   However, as
William Manchester learned, it's not always the author alone
who stimulates pre-publication discussion.   An article like
this one alone might suggest that if this author is not pompous he, at the least, is not adverse to calling attention to a
book that he hopes will prove worth his effort.   But once a
business book is completed, it's unlikely that the business
community--including the public relations people--will casti-
gate an author for trying to make sure his book contributes
to the booming book business.

How to Write a Best Seller

By Leo Rosten, author of The Education of Hyman Kaplan,
The Joys of Yiddish, Captain Newman, M.D., and other
books.

From Look 31:12, August 22, 1967. Copyright © 1967
by Leo Rosten. Reprinted by permission.

Cinderella Laminated Shims, Inc.
83 Wacker Drive
Chicago, Illinois

Dear Leo:

I bet you're surprised to hear from me after all these
many years, but it certainly is great about your new book,
A Most Private Intrigue, being such a best seller. I bet you
stash away $1,000,000. You know, I used to be a writer my-
self and at Theodore Roosevelt H.S. had 6-7 stories in the
Roosevelt Bully, which was the name of our school paper.
You'd be amazed how people came up to me crying, "Hey,
what have we in our mist, another John Steinberg?" The
people on my father's side were even more enthusiastic.

So why didn't I go into authorship? The reason is
because I married this girl Florence you never had the pleasure of meeting, whose old man owns Cinderella Laminated
Shims, and with no help from anyone I became Asst. Manager of their Midwest Sales, which is why I am now living
in Chicago, the largest city in Illinois. But frankly, Leo
(and I hope you keep this to yourself) my heart is not in
laminated shims.

Being as I'm only 39 years of age old, and with plenty
of zing to go around, it's not to late for me to crack the big
time as a Writer. Only last night, "Flo," which is what I
call Mrs. Klitcher, cried, "Why don't you ask a 'Pro writer'
like your old friend Leo to tell you the 'inside' tips on how
you can do a bestseller? Because if you are going to adorn

213

the literary seen you should concentrate on writing best-
sellers and not waste time on just any type book!" Which
is true. So I certainly would appreciate the "inside" dope.

I'm ready to give two nights a week and every Sat.
aft. to knocking off a best-seller. This is not just spitball-
ing, Leo, because I want to write badly.

If you wonder what do I have in mind plotwise, here
is one I know would ring the bell: A war-hero from Vietnam arrives home in Waukegan, Illinois on leave, and sees
his kid brother has this gorgeous and beautiful girl--which
the hero falls in love with! But he don't want to break his
kid brother's heart by stealing his girl from him, so he says
nothing but suffers. Now, here comes my twist! The kid
brother is drafted! And he goes to Vietnam where he falls
in love with this nurse! So our hero has to tell his kid
brother's Intended, which makes her cry, and through her
tears and confusion which is understandable she lets something slip out which gives him the right to come right out
and blurt, "But I love you to!" So they get together. You
have to admit a story about two brothers in love with the
same girl is surefire!

How much money should I ask the publisher to advance? I hear some publishers take the lion's share of the
stick leaving the Author the short hair.

Well, Leo, I hope you make a mint on your new book,
and if you want to send me and "Flo" an autographed copy
we won't complain ha, ha, ha. Answer right away! Because I'm raring to go! And will be watching these good old
U. S. mails!!!

> Your old pal,
> Herman ("Herm") Klitcher

Dear "Herm":

It sure was a surprise to hear from you, after 26
years. My book does look like a best seller, but to be frank
about it, "Herm," $1,000,000 is actually $13 more than I
expect to earn. This is just one example of the many disap-
pointments a "pro writer" runs into--coming within a few
cents of a fabulous fortune.

Your wife "Flo" was certainly smart to tell you not

to write just anything but to concentrate on best sellers, because careful research proves (and this is confidential) that best sellers sell more copies than any other type of book! I don't mind telling you the "inside" secrets, so long as you don't go around telling them to other people. After all, "Herm," we don't want every Tom, Dick and Harry knocking off a best seller whenever they feel like it, too. So here is what you should do:

1) Get a romantic, alluring title--something like "How to Avoid Probate." That was not written by a "pro writer" but by an innocent bystander like you, a fellow who wrote only on weekends and Yom Kippur. Another good title is "Sex Is the Most Fun You Can Have Without Laughing," but that's not original, ha, ha.

2) Choose a clean, wholesome plot--about children's toys, say, like "The Valley of the Dolls." Or write up life in a typical small town, like "Peyton Place." And there's always room for a folksy story of an average American marriage, like "Who's Afraid of Edward Albee?"

3) Choose a jazzy pen name. I don't want to hurt your feelings, "Herm," but to be perfectly frank about it, "Herman Klitcher" is not the best name for a writer of best sellers. That might go with a title like "You and Your Flywheel," but not for the type book you'll do. Many big-time writers use pen names, you know: for instance, John O'Hara, whose real name is Sol Rabinowitz. (I hope you will not let this get around.)

I have found a pen name that will guarantee you a best seller: "Dr. Spock." Some people think "Dr. Spock" is the pen name Bobby Kennedy uses, but that's not true; Bobby's nom de plume, as we pros call it, is "William Manchester."

4) Use a typewriter where the carriage moves from left to right, not from right to left. You have to watch out for that these days, "Herm," because the Egyptian Government is smuggling Muslim typewriters into our stores like crazy. One writer I know was tricked into buying an Egyptian typewriter recently and his book laid an egg in the U.S. What he can't figure out is why it was such a smash in Cairo.

5) Write by daylight or electricity. Don't use candles,

except when writing ghost stories. Never write by flashlight, because they have to have their batteries changed every
so often, and few writers are handy enough to change the
batteries in a flashlight without cutting their fingers to the
bone. A writer who has cut his fingers to the bone finds it
just that much harder to ring the bell with a surefire best
seller.

6) At the end of your book, be sure to write "The
End." This is very important. If you don't say "The End,"
many a reader will read right on into the blank end-pages
and will think you did not have anything more to say. That
could ruin your chances for a best seller. You have to remember that women readers like to stick shopping lists and
overdue bills in the back of whatever book they're reading,
and if they go past the end and read them, thinking them
part of the story, they get pretty confused. My Aunt Jenny
was devouring a novel about a missionary in the South Seas
who, instead of converting the natives, becomes a cannibal
himself. But the author had not told the printers to put
"The End" at the end, and my Aunt had stuck a bill in the
back for a manure spreader from Sears, which she read,
thinking it part of the story. She told me she just loved the
story right up to the conclusion, where the author dodged
the real issue.

7) About publishers' advances: You have to realize
that publishers are very kind men who hate to give a writer
a large advance because this only puts the writer in a higher
tax bracket. My publisher nets only 2 cents per book, which
he donates to the Xerox Corporation. My share is 1 cent.
When I asked him, "How come I only get a penny a copy?"
he answered, "That's a good question."

That about wraps it up, "Herm." Once you've written
your best seller, you and "Flo" will get a big kick out of all
the fan mail--for your autograph, money, a lock of hair, a
donation to the Home for Tuba Players Who Fall Down Dry
Wells, or from psychiatrists who think the noise made by
morning cereals is making our children neurotic. You will
even receive letters from old friends who say they want to
write badly--and do.

Well, "Herm," I hope you won't forget your old friend
when you hit the best-seller list. If you don't, just send me
some autographed laminated shims. The ones I own burn a
lot of oil. I don't have to tell you how a creative writer

hates the smell of burning laminated shims.   It keeps him
from writing another best seller.

Sincerely,
LEO ROSTEN

Publish and Perish!

By Jerry H. Gill, Associate Professor of Philosophy, Florida Presbyterian College.

Copyright 1968 Christian Century Foundation. Reprinted by permission from the September 25, 1968 issue of The Christian Century.

It is, of course, possible to perish by virtue of not having published. Nothing need be said about such a fate. Much, however, has been said about the possibility of not perishing by virtue of having published. Such achievement is indeed praiseworthy. Highest praise, however, should be reserved for those who publish and still manage to perish.

The shelves are crammed with books and manuals on "how to succeed in publishing without really trying." What is needed is some advice on "how to fail at publishing while trying your hardest." I offer the following suggestions in partial fulfillment of this need. They represent ten years of successful failure in the casino of learned journal publication.

It is not necessary to be poorly educated, but it helps. At the very least it is imperative that one does not learn to write in school, since being a "late bloomer" brings a great advantage. Take my own case: my master's thesis adviser was obliged to tear up my first draft because it was so poorly written. To this day he is convinced that he wrote more of the final draft than I did. "Keep 'em guessing"--a handy motto.

The best way to get off to a flying start is by submitting reworked term papers, book reports and the like to conservative religious periodicals. It helps a lot if you take a definite stand against the platform of the periodicals you submit to. Such a procedure is guaranteed to collect a large number of rejection notices, which in turn make excellent scratch paper and paper airplanes. Sooner or later, however, that first acceptance notice will show up, and then you are "hooked"--from then on you are an addicted pen-pusher.

My first acceptance notice came in connection with my (and my adviser's) reworked master's thesis. The first journal editor to whom I submitted it rejected it as "quite poorly written." The second rejected it because it was "not quite our sort of thing." But the third editor said it was "very well done." From this experience I refused to draw the logical conclusion that the whole publishing game is based on the subjective opinions of a few biased editors. Instead, I drew the conclusion that success goes mainly to those who persevere.

Once you have tasted success it is essential to begin keeping a record of your hits and misses. First, the practical advantage: it's something of a waste of time to submit the same manuscript to the same editor over and over again. Besides, the art of perishing while publishing depends upon maintaining a delicate balance between the Rational and the Absurd. Second, such a record serves at once to challenge and to humiliate the young writer: the acceptances challenge while the rejections humiliate. Or is it the other way around? I can never remember which does which.

One important element in the publish-perish syndrome is that of editorial correspondence. A would-be writer of journal articles will neither fail nor succeed until he has learned the ins and outs of postal gamesmanship. I have compiled the following noble truths for the guidance of the neophyte author.

1. Speed is of the essence.
Editors are busy and tremendously efficient people, and they expect you to be the same. Editorial efficiency accounts for the great dispatch with which your correspondence and manuscripts will be treated. The editors are well aware of the high responsibility they bear for the advancement of scholarship.

Three facts clearly substantiate and illustrate the importance of speed in the minds of journal editors. First, it never takes more than a year to receive your rejection notice, and usually only half that time. Second, after acceptance it is only one or two years until your article rolls off the press. Third, a glance at the discussion notes and book reviews in current journals makes it reassuringly clear that they are

only two to three years behind the original publication in
question.   And, as was shown above, the original publication
is only two to three years behind the original writing.   The
logic in all these statements is tricky, but I trust that the
point is obvious.

2.   There is no substitute for thoroughness.
All correspondence directed to editors should be ex-
haustively thorough.   Editors are very interested in knowing
all about prospective authors; where you went to school, your
interests, dreams, etc., etc.   Moreover, if you do not hear
back from your editor as quickly as you think you should, be
sure to write asking how your manuscript is progressing.

The importance of thoroughness has been driven home
to me by the almost solicitous quality of most of the rejection notices I have received.   Many actually come on personal, previously printed letter forms.   Often these notices will
begin--and end--by stating: "Sorry, we cannot use your
manuscript.   Thanks."   Sometimes an editor will even become unduly specific and indicate that your manuscript "does
not fit into the journal's present publication plans."   I have
in fact been fortunate enough to receive several rejections
which included reports directly from the critical reader.   The
most helpful was the one which said: "We have rejected in-
numerable manuscripts from this guy."   It's this kind of
thoroughness that teaches the would-be author to revise his
work effectively.

3.   Scholarship is its own reward.
The would-be author must be sure that his motives
are pure.   Far too many aspiring writers seek rewards other
than the joys of scholarship.   Some are confident that publishing in learned journals will bring fame, speaking opportunities, promotions and the like.   Fortunately, such dreams
are not fulfilled, even though the learned journals have a fan-
tastically large circulation.   Others hope that publishing will
bring them a pile of money, either in honoraria and royalties
or in salary increases.   Fortunately, college and university
administrators do not read learned journals at all.

Fortunately again, the editors themselves have taken
steps to ensure that such false motivations are dispelled.
For one thing, most editors steadfastly refuse to mention
anything about the author of an article, beyond his name,
rank and serial number.   Some won't even print enough information to allow the reader to contact the author.   Of

course, there are always "nonunion" editors who publish
such personal items as where the author was educated, his
other publications and his present position.   And--shocking-
ly enough--there are writers so fame-conscious that they
actually smuggle references to their other works into their
footnotes.

Journal editors also see to it that love of money does
not hinder scholarship in any way; they make it unavailable.
To begin with, very few journals offer any sort of honorari-
um for articles they publish, and those that do are careful
not to send it until after publication.   By then the true scholar has forgotten all about the connection between the check
and his article.   In addition, the journals charge exorbitant
prices for the minimum number of reprints of published articles.   Moreover, the subscription rate for most journals is
outlandishly high.   There may be a lack of fame in the publishing game, but the lack of money makes up for it.

After kicking around the minor leagues of article publishing for several years, every true scholar deems it necessary to try for the "big time" by writing an important
book.   He should bear in mind that all the principles stated
above are applicable to book gamesmanship--and with a venge-
ance.   Speed is of the essence, so naturally everything takes
longer.   There is no substitute for thoroughness, so more
correspondence is called for.   Scholarship is its own reward, so never complain about slave-labor royalties.

My first effort at writing a book was an abortive success.   My field of specialization is philosophy of religion,
and I had worked out what I thought was a sound philosophical basis for Christian faith.   I entitled the manuscript Christian Empiricism, sent it off to a top university press and
waited for a big fat contract to arrive.   Since this was before
I had learned the "noble truths," I did not write so much as
one letter to the editor asking why many months had gone by
without my hearing from him.   This failure undoubtedly was
my undoing, for when I finally received a reply it was a very
thorough "No, thanks."

The editor was kind enough--or cruel enough--to en-
close the critical reader's report for my edification.   It was
ten typewritten pages long, and it left nary a bone unpicked.
In order to avoid problems of censorship, I will quote only
the kind things the reader said.

> In my judgment this manuscript does not add up
> to a book at all, but is a collection of pieces of
> analysis more or less loosely related. Its central
> thesis, that Christianity can be shown to be the
> most probable interpretation of reality, is not
> really shown, nor, strangely enough, is it really
> argued for with any awareness of what the real
> problems are . . . . This is a book on the
> empirical approach and it ignores this vital
> movement, it proceeds as though the author
> were unaware of his predecessors, as though he
> thought of this approach before. . . . If the
> manuscript is to be rewritten I suggest a total
> rewriting, excision of large blocks of material,
> focusing on the central problem; but the pre-
> requisite for this is a thorough rereading of
> the literature he uses, and some historical
> perspective gained through an acquaintance with
> the literature, pro and con, on the earlier em-
> pirical movement in theology.

After returning from the sanitorium, I came across an advertisement from a company which expressed genuine interest in publishing books by young, as yet unknown authors. So, after making several minor revisions, I shipped the manuscript off to them with more than average speed. In a couple of weeks I wrote the editor a letter, telling him all about myself and asking how the reading of my manuscript was progressing. I was confident that the quality of my work, together with the employment of such speed and thoroughness, would bring unbelievable results. I was right. Quotes from this second critical reader's report clearly illustrate the superiority of both my book and his intelligence.

> . . . Christian Empiricism is a thoughtful,
> balanced and completely compelling evaluation
> of the relevance of religion to contemporary
> life . . . . From first page to last his book
> is a challenging, enlightening and rewarding
> reading experience. . . . That this should be
> a book of vast intellectual scope and in every
> conceptual subtlety painstakingly researched and
> documented, is indeed admirable but hardly sur-
> prising considering the author's academic back-
> ground. . . . In short, Christian Empiricism
> is a work of stature and moment, one that
> should be warmly received by the discriminat-

ing reading public.

The contract which this editor offered me made it
very clear that he was not going to let money interfere with
my scholarship. In fact, he wanted to revert to the good
old days when men were men and scholars were scholars--
when the author paid the publisher to publish his manuscript.
A quotation from his letter makes clear the true worth of
both my book and the publisher's offer:

> Under normal circumstances, a book of this
> type would require a subsidy of around $6,000.
> However, because of our great enthusiasm for
> this work, we have gone over every item of
> cost and cut them to the lowest rock-bottom
> level that would yet enable us to get out a book
> adhering to top publishing standards. By doing
> this and by increasing our own investment in
> the project, we were able to reduce the subsidy
> to the amount shown in the contract: $3,000.

Since this first success I have been increasingly busy
constructing and peddling other first-book manuscripts. My
wife has been impressed with each of them, and several are
even now in the hands of various editors who are serving as
my literary executioners.

Among the greatest benefits to be derived from a life
of literary scholarship is that of becoming acquainted with
world-renowned scholars. No longer do you encounter them
only from afar at professional meetings; you can cultivate
their acquaintance by exchanging reprints with them, and often you can establish a growing sense of rapport with the top-
level scholars who serve on the editorial boards of learned
journals. Above and beyond the esprit de corps that you feel
with such front-line thinkers stands the fact that it is in the
editorial correspondence that the real "nitty-gritty" of scholarship is to be found.

I have been able to establish an intimate relationship
with one such international scholar--the editor of one of the
world's more influential journals, a man who will one day be
counted as a very important contributor to the development
of his particular field. Although the correspondence between
us is rather personal and pointed in nature, I share it with
you at this time in order to encourage and challenge would-
be writers everywhere.

In 1962 I submitted my first manuscript to the journal of which this scholar is the editor. The manuscript
dealt with the interpretation of a single aspect of one philosopher's thought. The rejection notice read, in entirety:

> Dear Professor Gill:
>   This is a judicious account of the position
> in question. However, you have couched all
> your criticism in the form of rhetorical ques-
> tions. This is a very invertebrate way of
> raising questions.
>   Cordially, _____

Two years later I submitted another manuscript, this
time one dealing with the construction of an original philosophical position. The rejection notice read, again in entirety, as follows:

> Dear Professor Gill:
>   This is very clearly and accurately written.
> Unfortunately you seem to have the idea that
> one can make-do with a little bit of this and
> a little bit of that. One cannot.
>   Sincerely, _____

The disappointment I felt over these two rejections
was partially relieved by the letter of acceptance which I received about a year later. I had submitted a discussion note
in which I attacked an article in an issue of that journal. My
editor friend wrote back:

> Dear Professor Gill:
>   Yes, I'll use your discussion note, I hope
> before too long.
>   Yours sincerely, _____

Note the shift in closing phrase from "Cordially"
through "Sincerely" to "Yours sincerely;" the friendship is
progressing. More was to come.

This past year I submitted another full-length manuscript which my friend the editor accepted with the following
rather lengthy comment:

> Dear Gill:
>   I have been quickly through your article,
> and shall want to use something like it, though

I have some modifications to suggest. Meanwhile, have a look at the book I have listed
below.   I think the author is saying the same
thing you are saying in one place, perhaps
rather too briefly.

Yours, _____

Note how the very heart of scholarship begins to appear in
such correspondence; and note the shift to the intimate "Dear
Gill" as salutation and "Yours" as closing phrase.

As I have been emphasizing all along, it is vitally important to seize the initiative.   Only by meeting challenges
head-on can one hope to become a real success in the publishing business.   With this truth clearly in mind, I wrote
my friend the editor a return letter in which I asked whether
his journal would like me to write a review of the book in
question.   His answer was both prompt and to the point:

Dear Gill:
No!

Yours, _____

D.   Other People in Publishing

W. W. DENSLOW
The Wonderful Wizard of Oz
Dover Publications

Illustrating Children's Books:
Professional Practice

By Henry C. Pitz, award-winning illustrator of more than
160 books and many magazines and author of seven books
and 70 articles for magazines and newspapers.

Text from pages 187-203 of Illustrating Children's Books:
History--Technique--Production, by Henry C. Pitz; copyright
© 1963 by Watson-Guptill Publications, Inc., New York,
New York; reprinted by permission. Illustration by Henry
C. Pitz from Twenty Thousand Leagues Under the Sea, Junior Deluxe Editions, Nelson Doubleday, Inc.; reprinted by
permission. Illustration by W. W. Denslow from The Wonderful Wizard of Oz, Dover Publications, 1900.

Handling An Assignment

Illustrators tend to be individualists, and neither in
their finished pictures nor in the stages that lead to completion do they conform to a set pattern. And yet, fully aware
of their thousand-and-one personal idiosyncrasies, they do
have their methods and procedures and, in a general way,
they move from conception to the finished book in pretty
much the same ways. There are certain procedures that are
inevitable and which they share in common. The novice illustrator has not had the time or experience to work out an
individual system but he can benefit from some basic suggestions.

An illustration assignment begins with a letter or telephone call from an editor. The illustrator has been picked,
presumably because he or she is not only competent, but because the subject matter is congenial, because he or she is
at home in the age group that is indicated, and because of
general dependability. The text is summarized, the number
and style of pictures indicated, the delivery date stated, and
usually the fee set.

If the assignment is accepted, a text will be sent on.
This may be in typewritten manuscript form or it may be
set in type and appear in the shape of galley proofs--long,
snaky strips of paper on which the text is printed in columns.

Every illustrator grinds his teeth at the inevitable
and repetitive question, "Do you read the stories you illustrate?" The answer is, "Yes." Probably the first time the
manuscript is read quickly for information and flavor but
then is followed by a more careful reading in order to find
the most likely spots to be illustrated. These are marked
on the margin, sometimes with little notes. If the text is at
all fruitful in a picture-making sense, at the end of this
reading there should be more picture possibilities than space
provided for them. A third scanning should produce some
order of distribution and some elimination by the artist of
superfluous situations.

The incidents selected are now ready for sketch clarification. Most illustrators make their first sketches of the
thumbnail variety, small and rapidly executed. Their purpose is to quickly explore and bring some clarification into
the inviting images that up to then have only existed in the
mind's eye. Each selected situation may require several of
these quick sketches. Sometimes a situation is tantalizing in
the number of solutions it suggests and elimination is difficult; other situations seem to call for one answer. It is general practice to carry the whole series of compositions
through the thumbnail stage before moving on to more detailed work, for it enables the artist to visualize the whole
set of potential pictures and to decide such things as whether
the sketches of the series are too similar, too inconsistent,
or if some important aspect of the text has been ignored.

The next stage is the larger sketch, usually the same
size as the finished illustration. It may be drawn on tracing
paper first, because changes and revisions can be made
easily. By slipping one version under a clean sheet, you can
trace off the wanted parts and add the new forms; when the
revisions have reached the point of satisfaction, the composition may be readily traced on the final drawing paper or
board for the finished rendering. During this stage, it may
be necessary to refer back to the text from time to time to
clarify details and facts.

At this point, when the full-size sketches are mar-

The stages of an illustration. First, small, quick sketches to crystallize a pictorial idea, then a drawing working out the forms and details from which the finished picture is traced.

HENRY C. PITZ
20,000 Leagues Under the Sea
Junior Deluxe Editions
Nelson Doubleday, Inc.

shaled and approved, it might be well to pause and point out
that the character and purpose of the intended book have a
great deal to do with the procedures. If the book should be
the picture-book type destined for very young children, almost certainly the artist has to construct a dummy showing
the placement of pictures and type. If the book is of the
teenage type and all the pictures are planned to be full pages,
there is no need to prepare a dummy.

A dummy is a sketch facsimile of the book to come.
It is the same size, of course, with each page laid out the
way it will appear in the finished volume. The type lines
will be indicated by ruled lines or, if the text has been set
and printed in galley form, by pasting the relevant amount
of text in its proper place. The pictures are indicated in
sketch form in their proper areas. Sometimes dummies are
finished with a great deal of care and precision, especially
when illustrators and authors are trying to sell a new picture-book idea to a publisher or when the dummy is to be
used as an exact guide for the printer. At other times they
may be very sketchy and abbreviated, when it is only necessary to project the general idea.

Dummies can be made up by cutting suitable paper to
the proper size, folding and forming signatures. The signa-
ture may be sewn or stapled at the folded edge. Publishers
usually will provide the illustrator with his dummy, having
them made up by a printer or paper house.

In the picture book for the young, the text is very
short and should be set in large size, fourteen point or more,
with a picture usually appearing on every page. Very little
text will be on each page, sometimes only a line or two, but
the type space should be accurately drawn or pasted in. The
picture fits above, below or around the text. With color or
halftone pictorial material, the text may be imprinted over
part of the picture, provided this portion of the picture is
light in tone and does not contain active or important forms.
The text should never be illegible for young eyes.

With the completion of the dummy, the illustrator has
an accurate idea of how the finished book will look. It will
show how the pictures will look in relation to each other and
the general impression the book will make as one turns the
page. It will also furnish accurate sizes for each picture, no
matter how oddly shaped they may be. Undoubtedly, the editor will want to see it for approval or suggested changes.

Finally, the printer may want to use it as a guide in printing.

When the time arrives for embarking on the finished pictures, procedures become varied. Most illustrators finish the pictures one at a time; others start several and flit from one to the other, keeping a number of them in progress at the same time; some tackle their favorite compositions first while others horde them up until the home stretch. This is where temperament and experience dictate.

Theoretically, with composition, drawing and other factors worked out in preliminary sketches and clearly charted in full-size master drawing, the final stage is one of technique, rendering what has been already completely planned. Sometimes things work out that way but there are always the imponderables. Can one maintain a fine creative edge throughout a long series? Can one guard one's time against ruinous interruptions? The physical and mental tides do not always flow consistently. Interest may flag toward the end of a long series. A problem of the conservation of creative energy faces the artist and only he can solve it, for it must be answered in terms of his own creative energy and temperament. Since the illustrator is harnessed to a definite delivery day, he has little or no time to spend waiting for a favorable mood. He usually is at his drawing board or easel, regardless of the inner weather. And, all in all, this works out very well. No creative talent works completely smoothly and unremittingly. The hypochondriac artist who is constantly taking his creative temperature will soon have time for little else. The persistent worker has the advantage. There will be days when everything will be dropped in the wastebasket, but other days beginning with misgivings will end up in triumph.

As the series progresses toward completion, it is well to pause for comparisons and revaluations. Are the key characters who appear in picture after picture consistent? Do they seem to be the same person? Are the important accessories, machines, buildings, uniforms, boats and other objects correctly enough visualized to satisfy the sharp eyes of many children?

Finally, the finished drawings should be cleaned and protected with a paper flap. The captions with their page numbers should be written legibly on each drawing. If color separations are necessary, they should key with the necessary

register marks, and the color swatches of the wanted colors
should be painted in beside the drawing. A neat package of
splendid drawings should be delivered on time.

Getting Work

The artist aspiring to work in the children's book
field is usually a young person just out of art school; but
whatever the age, ability or background, the question of getting established is the dominant one.   Ninety-nine out of a
hundred professionals have followed the same path in their
novice days: they peddled their wares.   Ever since publishers have needed illustrations, artists have been knocking at
their doors with portfolios under their arms.

A personal interview, with a display of one's work,
is the accustomed practice, but there are two other ways
which we will mention and dispose of, for they are of minor
value.   One is to have an artist's agent who will take over
the leg-work of selling talent.   The agent is quite an important figure nowadays in the advertising and magazine fields
but there are only a few who concern themselves with book
illustration.   The smaller fees do not attract them; their
commission is usually twenty-five percent.   Nor are they
likely to be interested in the green artist unless the talent is
exceptional.   Although a competent agent could do a great
deal to launch a promising talent, the artist would be deprived of a very valuable experience--the knowledge that
comes from taking part in the give and take of publishing.
Another method would be to prepare promotional material--
cards, folders, photographs and reproductions of one's work
--to be mailed out to possible clients.   This could be a very
valuable way of following up one's personal visits and keeping in touch with interested editors, but it is doubtful if any
career has been launched by this method alone.

Personal visits are the traditional answer but they
could be harmful if not carefully planned and thoughtfully prepared for.   The stock in trade is one's portfolio of work.
Personality counts for something but it is pictures that will
elate or bore the editor.

A haphazard collection of pictures is of little value.
Editors have decided ideas about the kind of pictures they
can use and they quickly dismiss material that is remote
from their own problems.   It is the duty of the young artist

to find out all that he or she possibly can about children's books, their needs, their message, their contents, their appeal, and their physical make-up. Long hours should be spent in the libraries and bookstores, not just idly leafing through the books that happen to suit the artist's taste but examining everything. The idea is to get some feeling of the entire field and not just a small corner of it. Notes should be taken of publishers' names, together with the kinds of books they produce, so that the climates or personalities of publishing firms will emerge. Then the artist is able to discern what to take where, and neither his own nor the editor's time will be wasted.

The bulk of the work should attempt to solve concrete problems in the children's book field. The problems could range from an age-old children's classic to an inventive tale that the artist or a friend has worked out. In the last case, an excellent idea would be to show a sketch dummy of the entire book with two or three of its illustrations finished to the limit of the artist's ability. It is well to show different types of book problems: jackets, end-papers and text illustrations. If the artist should have a few unusually good pieces that are not directly concerned with illustration, they may be included; but the run-of-the-mill type of art school problems such as regulation model studies, still-lifes, landscapes, wallpaper designs and acre-wide abstract "expressions" should be kept for other audiences. If there is anything of great value in any of these, it should be incorporated into the illustrative material shown.

Portfolio Presentation
Presentation is important. Even superlative drawings look better if tastefully and cleanly matted and mediocre things look less so. Presentation need go no further than cleaning up the borders of all drawings or suitably matting them. Tidy paper flaps or cellophane will keep them fresh. They may be carried in the usual artist's portfolio or, if smaller, in the now popular sample books with transparent pages.

There is a point of balance between showing too few and too many items and this could be governed partly by the kind of illustrations shown. Less than seven or eight reasonably ambitious pieces may seem poverty-stricken, and more than fourteen or fifteen might be boring, particularly if they are much the same. Besides, it is wise to save something for a second or a third visit, for this is not a single battle but a campaign.

Drawings made for line reproduction (pen, brush, and ink), are portfolio staples. These are the kind of drawings that most beginners will be given to do for their first assignments. At least one of them should be designed for use, with one or more flat colors and the separations attached to the master drawing, to show the editor that the necessary know-how is present. Almost all novices prefer to work in full color and the best of these efforts should be included-- but only the best. Full-color assignments are not likely to be given to beginners but full-color samples may contain an idea that could be translated into black and white.

The great majority of book publishers are concentrated in New York with a sprinkling in Philadelphia, Boston, and Chicago. The yellow pages of the telephone directories will furnish names and addresses. If the research in the libraries and bookstores has been well done, the aspirant will have some idea of the kind of things used by each publisher. The children's book editor in almost every case will be a woman and her assistants will also be women. One can travel from office to office, in the hope of finding an editor available or one can telephone and make an appointment. Editors are almost all uniformly kind and considerate, but very busy. They cannot be expected to give very much time to any one person; in fact, the aspirants are often screened first by an assistant. There is one large area for children's illustration that is often overlooked: the educational or text book field. A large proportion of this work is for children and their textbooks are usually lavishly illustrated. These are handled by a separate editorial staff, the educational editors.

The visits to editors should be done with some system and notes should be kept. When editors are interested, they will want your name and address. This information should be available on neatly printed cards. They may also want reproductions of some of your pictures for their files. The young artist seldom has photoengraving proofs of his work but he should have photographs or photostats made and sent promptly.

Great hopes should not be set upon the first visit. Not many are given work the first time. After all, there is a certain amount of chance in these visits. Not only must the work be of a kind and quality to be desired, but one must arrive when an assignment has become available. The first visit should be considered a preliminary exploration which will be followed by many others if the ground looks favorable.

Notes should be kept for these visits, and if an editor should suggest a return in a month or two, that should be complied with. Editors will almost never suggest a return unless they are interested.

The thought of continually making the rounds of publishers' offices may be distasteful to some. It is not as much fun as making pictures, but is a necessary part of the illustrator's education. He or she will have a lot of things to learn besides picturemaking; contact with editors is not only necessary, but interesting and stimulating. It is the kind of apprenticeship that can pave the way to a long career of fruitful work.

After one has begun to do professional work, it is sometimes amazing what a potent publicity force one's reproduced work becomes. Book illustration is seen by other editors and, if it kindles their interest, they may wish to have the artist work for them. New assignments often come out of the blue, a reward not only for good work, but for the leg-work to publishers that made possible the first assignments.

The Field Today

Looking out into today's world of children's illustrated books makes one blink and strain to comprehend the dazzle and scope of it. It is an empire now, busy and effervescent, drawing talent from sources never before tapped, bursting with ideas and ambitions, organized, competitive and highly competent. It has lost some of its sense of wonder; the amateur and tentative touch is gone and on the horizon is the threat of an over-confident professionalism. Pedantry did not disappear with the Victorian Age, nor sentimentality, although they take other guises. Moralizing and propaganda are still present, although they are not called that, because they are the moralizing and propaganda of our own time and inclination.

More books mean more dollars and we hope, more education, more delight and more awareness. If the writing,

illustrations, and design of children's books is an art, it
will not be obedient to push-button expansion. It will not be
likely to flower under clinical eyes and automation techniques.

The field has been remarkably fortunate in the people
it has drawn to it. Its writers, artists, editors and librarians come from the same imperfect stock that inhabits
the rest of the globe, but all in all they can be counted upon
for a vocational devotion greater than most, an allegiance to
a sector of human activity they believe in and love, and an
unusual endowment of brains and talent. The financial rewards for this devoted company have tended to be modest,
so the field has not tempted the fortune hunters. But publishers' profits have taken wings in many cases, and little
has been done to share these with those who have made success possible. The excellence of today's children's books
has come to pass because of the lavish care and anxious affection of a body of talented and concerned individuals, and
if giantism overtakes them it may perform its usual magic
of changing individuals into cogs.

But today's children's books are an achievement--
something we can be proud of. Many countries, chiefly those
of Western Europe, have and are producing works of high excellence; others with limited publishing facilities are strug-
gling, improving and satisfying their growing appetites by im-
portations from the more prolific countries. Conditions have
conspired to give the United States, however, not only an
enormous advantage in volume but an all-over superiority in
design and execution. Our best books are no better than the
best of other countries, but there are more of them. Our
average is higher. With allowances made for the many--too
many--weaknesses in American production, the total impression is of strength, variety, inventiveness, and competence.
Future observers may look back and call ours a "golden age"
of children's bookmaking.

It would be easy to expect large volume from our
great population and high degree of industrialization. The excellent quality of so much of our writing, design and illustration might be less predictable; but there is an eagerness in
the land to write and make pictures, and the writer and artist
are no longer oddities. In fact, they have taken on glamour
in most people's eyes. Besides, there is both stability and
ferment in our large population and a rich diversity of racial
strains. It is a good background for the recruiting of talent

for the book arts.

In addition to our rich pool of native talent, is the fertilizing effect of so many foreign talents that have adopted us. They come to us because we promise a freer life, opportunity and an ample livelihood. Besides this, we publish the work of many foreign artists and introduce them to our large public. Our alert and sharp-eyed editors now have a regular practice of scanning the foreign fields and buying the American rights for some of the finest foreign work. So, by and large, American children are seeing the best illustration that the world has to offer.

In return, some of our best books are translated and sold abroad, so that one can have the experience of searching the foreign bookstores for finely illustrated books and being offered the foreign edition of a book that has already appeared at home. But our poorest books are exported also; the cheap comic sheets and the gaudy, badly printed, and atrociously pictured board-bound books designed for the discount and five and ten markets. We may deplore this, for it shows others our discreditable side, but we have not forced these things on the foreign reprint houses; they buy them to satisfy a hunger in their own countries. It can be said with considerable truth that the American publishers supply the home public with much of the best foreign material and little that is poor, while the foreign market takes from us much of our worst.

Within the past two decades, the sense of competition among our publishers of children's books has intensified. They have discovered what a gold mine a children's book department can be and, in certain cases, it has saved the year's figures from going into the red. So there is more snap and crackle, and more tension in the editorial offices of the children's book departments than there used to be. The search for variety has been very fruitful but sometimes it becomes a scamper after mere novelty. The bizarre and extreme modes of contemporary art, the inept and clumsy, disguised under the name of modernism, the trivialities of the latest, chic fad have had their innings and there are signs that they are fading. Too often the stuffiness of the old has merely been replaced by the inconsequence of the new. But the mistakes and failures can be brushed to one side, and we can count our blessings for the yearly bulk of creditable books. Never have so many handsome and worthwhile books been offered to the young of any nation.

The young artist who is ambitious to become part of this world has the odds on his side if he has something to offer. Intelligence, earnestness and a genuine impulse to belong to it can be the foundation. On this can be built the gifts which talent bestows, and accumulated know-how that time and experience should bring. The children's book world is not fenced in. The powers that rule it are dispersed and not despotic. They are used to and expect young blood to be pushing in. This is not to say that the young artist will be immediately embraced and made a member of the fold. Occasionally this happens, but usually the novice is treated kindly and if his pictures are worthy he is invited to come back. If he is persistent enough to return for a second, third, or fourth visit with fresh material of excellence, one or more editors will begin to feel that he is worth a trial.

With the first hurdle passed, the artist may have begun a lifetime career. The book field is less at the mercy of fad and fancy than the magazine and advertising fields. The better illustrators tend to become institutions, serving generation after generation of young minds. So the children's artists are both young and old and in between. Perhaps it might be better to describe them as young artists of all ages.

No one knows if there is a saturation point for children's books. Children's appetites for texts and pictures have grown from year to year; parents' and relatives' pockets have grown too, so the future seems to promise more children, more dollars, and more books. We have become so accustomed to the experience of constant growth and expansion that we almost believe it to be preordained. A change in the economic climate could alter all this but regardless of whether we print more or fewer books, it is vastly more important that they be beautiful than merely numerous. In the midst of congratulating ourselves on the large number of superior children's books we produce every year, we will be laying plans to surpass ourselves in beauty and quality.

The Literary Agent--
His Function, Life, and Power

By Paul R. Reynolds, veteran New York City literary agent;
author of The Writing and Selling of Fiction and other books.

From Saturday Review 49:113-4, October 8, 1966. Copyright © 1966 by The McCall's Corporation. Reprinted by
permission of Paul R. Reynolds, Inc. , 599 Fifth Avenue,
New York, N. Y. 10017.

Once a month six men and one woman--seven of the
leading literary agents of New York City--lunch together. In
business they are rivals, but they are scarcely conscious of
the competition. They are close friends who like to exchange news and gossip of the literary market. Collectively,
these agents sell in excess of $12,000,000 worth of literary
material each year. Collectively, they represent some
1,500 writers. Some of their writers are literary figures
such as John Dos Passos or Conrad Richter. Others write
drivel or the so-called non-book. The agents represent enormous money makers such as Irving Wallace, H. Allen Smith,
Daphne Du Maurier, Morris West, William Shirer, and Ag-
atha Christie; and they represent first novelists whose books
may sell fewer than 2,500 copies and may earn less than
$1,500.

What do these agents do?

The primary function of the literary agent is to obtain
for an author as much money as possible. Authors often are
not good businessmen: They are poor judges of their own
work, and in their modesty they may underrate it, or in their
egotism they may overrate it. The agent sells the manuscripts of his clients, negotiates the price and the details of
the contract, collects the money from the buyer, retains a
10 per cent commission, and remits 90 per cent to the author. Or in the case of a manuscript with sensationally high
sales potential he may conduct an auction before one word is
written. He may offer a dozen copies of the manuscript to a

241

dozen potential buyers asking for bids.   Or he may have a
single manuscript which he assiduously offers to one publisher after another.   The agent may fail to sell such a manuscript, or may find a buyer only after many declinations.
In one case, an agent made a sale only on the sixty-sixth
submission.

An agent deals in many rights.   He may make a contract with a book publisher for book publication, then another
contract with a magazine for first magazine publication, and
a third contract for the motion picture or television rights.
He also may do a substantial foreign business, making contracts for publication in London and in translation on the
Continent.   The agent for The Rise and Fall of the Third
Reich, by William L. Shirer, made more than twenty individual contracts for separate rights to the book.   Agents, of
course, also handle many short stories and articles and, occasionally, screenplays.   Fewer than 4 per cent of the published novels are sold in the movies, but the revenue from
such sales may be enormous: An author such as James
Michener or Irving Wallace may get a quarter of a million
dollars or more for the picture rights to a novel.

The leading New York agents employ from eight to
twenty people, including a bookkeeper, an office boy, secretaries, etc.   Large agencies are somewhat compartmental-
ized: One person may handle nothing but translation rights,
and one or two others may do nothing but negotiate magazine
sales.   Such an agency may make from 150 to 300 book contracts a year and sell an equivalent number of short pieces
to magazines.   It also has an extremely large number of
minor transactions such as reprints and sales in translation
for small sums.   The Japanese, for instance, buy rights to
many American books, paying from $150 to $300 a book.

In practice, the agent is more than merely a businessman.   At times he has an editorial function, although this activity is not nearly as extensive as the publisher's.   For the
name writer, the agent gives little, if any, editorial help.
For relatively new writers, the agent may offer suggestions
as to cutting of a manuscript, expansion, greater development
of a character, etc.   The agent also may assist in the editorial packaging and promotion of books--pressure for a good
"selling jacket," more advertising, etc., as well as helping
obtain agreement between author and publisher on a title that
will help the sale of the book.

Not the least important function of the agent is that
of father-confessor. Authors have doubts as to what to
write next: fiction, non-fiction, books, or short pieces.
They may be undecided between two or more ideas, or which
publisher or publishing arrangement is most desirable. They
can discuss these doubts with their families or friends, but
neither usually is sufficiently knowledgeable to be helpful.
They can talk to an editor or publisher, but it is hard to
confide one's doubts to an editor with whom one expects to
bargain. The agent, however, is experienced in publishing
matters; he may have known the author and his work for
many years; and agent and author have a mutual interest.
One of the agent's functions is simply to listen, to make suggestions, and to express opinions. Thus, the author-agent
relationship may result in strong personal friendship--one
agent has had more than twenty books dedicated to him.

The yellow pages of the New York telephone book now
list eighty-seven agents. Of these, some specialize in selling plays or motion pictures, and some act primarily as employment agents for actors, directors, and producers. No
license is required to become an agent, and there are no
formal qualifications to be met. As a result, every year
individuals enter the occupation, sometimes with no office
other than their apartment, and every year people fail and
leave the business, almost unnoticed.

A number of the people listed as agents are not really
agents, but predatory sharks. These so-called agents advertise extensively in writers' magazines and obtain an ava-
lanche of manuscripts. But they do not make their living
from commissions; they make their living from charging reading fees to unpublished writers. These fees may range from
$10 to several hundred dollars. (In the latter case, the
pseudo-agent probably would promise to have the manuscript
rewritten.) In exchange for the fee, these self-styled agents
then may give or pretend to give criticism, or they may offer or say they will offer the manuscript to buyers. But
these so-called agents may not be competent to criticize, and
most of the manuscripts they receive are so hopeless that
they cannot benefit from criticism, and, of course, cannot be
sold or published. Thus the author receives nothing of value
for his fee. Yet these advertising sharks milk the writing
trade of hundreds of thousands of dollars each year. It is a
shocking racket.

Who are the legitimate agents? There is a Society of

Author's Representatives, an organization of legitimate literary agents and legitimate play brokers, all of whom make
their living from commissions resulting from sales.   The Society requires of its members certain standards of business
practice and ethical conduct.   With two or three exceptions,
every literary agent and play broker who has a substantial
business and a reputation for integrity and competence is a
member.

How does the legitimate agent obtain his clients?   He
does not advertise.   The professional code holds that it is as
unethical for an agent to advertise as it is for a lawyer or a
doctor to do so.   The agent obtains clients by recommendation of his own client authors, or editors, or publishers, or
perhaps by attending a writers' conference.   Obtaining a client often means being in the right spot at the right time, and
the agent never knows in advance what spot or time is right.

One agent on a business trip, for example, stopped in
Dallas, Texas, at 9 p. m. to see an author whose first novel
he admired and had just placed with a publisher.   Bad weather delayed his departure until 2 a. m. the next day.   By mid-
night, the agent had filled the author full of information a-
bout the literary business.   The author then told him of a
friend who was a brilliant writer, although unpublished.   The
agent, delighted to break the conversational monotony, went
with the author to the friend's house, woke up the friend by
throwing pebbles at his bedroom window, and had a long conference over highballs.   The first author ultimately gave up
writing but his friend became a valuable client.

A legitimate agent receives many unsolicited manuscripts from acquaintances of his clients or from people who
somehow have heard of him.   But he accepts few, if any, of
these manuscripts, for these unpublished writers usually want
an agent for the wrong reasons.   They think of an agent as
someone who can sell manuscripts which the author cannot
sell.   They are unwilling to believe what, in nine of ten
cases is the truth: that the manuscripts are poor and, hence,
unsalable.   Every author, however, published or unpublished,
should realize that no agent can sell anything which the author
on his own cannot sell, provided the author offers his work
assiduously.

Authors often change their publishers, but once an author retains an agent, the author rarely leaves him.   Joseph
Wechsberg, Paul Gallico, Catherine Drinker Bowen, Thornton

Wilder, Frank Slaughter, and Ogden Nash all have been with their own agents for more than twenty-five years. Yet each has had more than one publisher through the years.

Agents make mistakes. One agent received an offer of $1,000 from a motion picture company for the rights to an obscure short story published in Argosy magazine five or six years previously. The agent cabled the author that the offer was for $10,000. What caused the mistake the agent still does not know. He just knows that he should have had his head examined. The author cabled back, "Delighted at motion picture offer. Please accept." When the agent's idiotic clerical mistake was discovered, the author quite naturally was furious and refused to accept $1,000, and the story never was sold in pictures. Had the agent's cable given the true figure of $1,000, the author probably would have accepted. In another case, the agent for Native Son, by Richard Wright, failed to insert in the book contract a simple sentence that would have saved the author thousands of dollars in taxes.

Then there was the instance involving the agent for the great best seller, Captain from Castile, by Samuel Shellabarger. Prior to publication of the book the agent received an offer of $40,000 from Paramount for the picture rights. The author, in need of money, told the agent to accept. Twentieth Century-Fox had also expressed interest in the book, and the agent gave Fox twenty-four hours to buy the rights for $100,000. Fox purchased at that price, the agent was pleased with himself, and the author was in raptures. A year later, an executive of Fox, who was a friend of the agent's, told him that Fox had authorized the executive, if necessary, to pay up to $150,000. The author was out $50,000 because his agent was not a better guesser and better bargainer.

The other side of the coin is that agents can ask too much money and never sell a property. One agent, for instance, received from Metro-Goldwyn-Mayer an offer of $25,000 for rights to a novel written by a well-known literary figure. The author insisted on $35,000 which Metro refused to pay. When the novel was published, it had only a modest sale, and the picture rights never were sold.

Agents occasionally find themselves caught in the midst of extremely curious gyrations. Once, an author, who shall remain nameless, wrote three romances which had only mod-

est sales in book stores.   He delivered a fourth novel that
the agent thought extremely poor, and the publisher, much as
he liked the author, regretfully declined to publish the novel.
The agent offered the novel to eleven publishers without success.   He then offered the book to Appleton (now Appleton-
Century-Crofts).   Appleton lost the manuscript.   The author
had no carbon copy, and nothing but three or four pages of
notes.   To the agent's amazement and pleasure, Appleton,
remorseful for its error in losing the manuscript, offered a
contract with money down if the author would rewrite the
manuscript.   This the author did in the next year.   The
agent thought the rewritten novel was, if anything, worse
than the first version.   Appleton, too, was unhappy about the
book, but the firm published it according to its contract and
sold some 1,400 copies.

Appleton, having lost substantially from this publication, thought it should have the chance to publish the author's
next work.   If that were good, perhaps it could recoup its
earlier loss.   But the author, furious at Appleton, first, for
losing his manuscript, and, second, for selling only 1,400
copies of the rewritten work, insisted upon a new publisher.
Houghton Mifflin published the author's next novel, which was
a Book-of-the-Month-Club selection and a best seller.

In Hollywood the agent is omnipresent.   Several agencies are enormous.   The largest, William Morris & Company, has more than 200 employees.   Not merely writers,
but actors, directors, and producers use agents.   A person
writing for motion pictures or television cannot handle his
own work [see "The Hollywood Screen Writers," SR, July 9].
Studios and producers will not read scripts offered by authors
directly.   Fortunately, this is not true in the print media in
New York.   There the agent is never obligatory.

Sometimes it is said that it is more difficult for the
author of a good manuscript to find a good agent than to find
a good publisher.   This may well be true.   An agent is busy
and has a large overhead to carry.   He cannot afford to sell
to the minor magazines.   He cannot afford to handle a writer
who does not make substantial money each year.   Thus most
authors make their first sales themselves.   Only then can
they obtain the services of a legitimate agent.

Literary Agents

By James Oliver Brown, President of James Brown Associates, Inc., a literary agency in New York City.

From The Writer 80:15-7, July 1967. Copyright © 1967
by The Writer, Inc. Reprinted by permission of the Author.

I speak on occasion to writers and aspiring writers,
and the assumption is that I have a special knowledge of the
questions such audiences ask. A few questions have been
singled out as most recurring and this piece is devoted to
them.

There is a lack of understanding on the part of inex-
perienced writers, and some experienced, of the functions of
the East Coast literary agent who, while handling all rights
and forms of writing, concentrates on the selling of rights to
books and magazine stories and articles. The image of these
agents is of rather grasping, ill-mannered, ill-bred parasites,
who resist seeing and handling the works of writers, and who
make the rounds of publishing houses, manuscripts in hand,
persuading publishers to publish books. If females, they
probably smoke cigars. I know of no such East Coast "book"
literary agents.

A writer doesn't need an agent to sell a book for him
here in this country. On the other hand his book will get
closer attention if it has on it the imprint of a good agent.
It might even sell bearing the agent's imprint where it would
not have sold without such imprint, but such a sale would be
rare, because manuscripts get read, regardless of who sub-
mits them. Reactions to writing are emotional, and the endorsement of an agent who is known for his taste and success
might push the emotional scales in favor of the work. If I
started telling an editor why he should like and buy a book,
the editor would assume I was trying to get rid of a dud. The
editor knows the James Brown imprint and for what it stands.
He pays attention, in relation to that standing, whatever it
might be in the mind of that particular editor.

The agent for "talent" (performers) and for all phases
of the performance side of our business (stage, motion pictures, television) has a job of presentation different from
that of the "book" agent, and the image of this kind of agent
has had greater presentation by playwrights and novelists to
the general public.   Partly as a result of this exposure, the
public has a wrong image of the "book" agent.   In the performance side of the business, the buyer more than often
has to be told.   He has to be made to see how to blend
everything together, the writing being only a part of the
whole.   The added factors are things such as casting, directing, stage designing.   The "book" agent, on the other hand,
usually presents the finished product.   Ordinarily it doesn't
need to be spoken about; it speaks for itself.   I don't know
of any of the literary agents on the performance side who
wear hats and smoke cigars.

Functions and relationships
         The literary agent performs a complex and varied
function, which can't be too well defined.   His function depends upon the kinds of writers he represents.   I can speak
only for my own operation.   I'm a business manager-adviser,
coordinator, protector of rights, exploiter of all rights to all
writings of the writers I represent, such rights including
book, magazine, dramatic, motion picture, radio, television,
recording, translation.   My important function as an agent is
bringing in money for the writer, getting the most money possible in the interests of the writer, from every possible
source.   When an agent starts to work on a piece of writing,
a story, an article, a book, whatever, he thinks of it in
terms of all rights and gets it to the people who buy the
rights, here and abroad.   He is an expert in knowing the
markets and having the organization to get to them.

The practices of the members of our agents' professional society, the Society of Authors' Representatives, are
prescribed by reasonable and rigid rules.   We don't advertise, and we don't live on reader's fees and editorial fees.
We get clients from recommendations of people who know us,
writers, editors, and others, and we live on a percentage
take of the amount we take in from a sale.   Theoretically, at
least, if we don't sell we don't eat.   Many, and I suspect,
most "book" literary agents have independent incomes or some
other subsidy such as rich or working spouses.   A few of
us actually live on 10% of our writers' earnings.   This is not
enough for much more than just modest non-caviar, non-Rolls
Royce living.

I feel that if a written contract with one of my clients is necessary, I probably shouldn't have him for a client. On the other hand, if a simple letter agreement is signed stating what the relationship is anyway, I think it is in everyone's interests. I usually send such a document (if I happen to remember to do it) to a new client and leave it up to the client. They usually sign. Except in some situations where the interests of the writer were to be protected by doing it, I advise against the signing of an agency contract which goes beyond stating what the agent-client relationship is. An agency contract, for example, may provide that the agent will continue to handle the unsold rights to a property the agent has handled, should a writer leave the agent. This is not what would happen without the contract, and a writer should know this. Except in extraordinary cases, an agent should cease being the agent when the agency relationship ends. Rarely, if ever, is it in the writer's interests to have two agents working for him on different properties. The deserted agent is a deserted agent, alas, and has left only the right to receive monies and be paid under contracts with book publishers, etc. , that he negotiated before the desertion. (Who cares about a deserted parasite?)

We members of the Society of Authors' Representatives feel that a writer does well to limit his search for an agent, to fit his particular needs, to the Society's membership of almost forty agents of the eighty-seven listed in the Manhattan Telephone Directory. There are at least one or two, and perhaps more, perfectly good agents, not members of the Society. One can consult a nationally known book publisher or magazine or The Authors Guild. By correspondence the author and agent can proceed to get together. I like to meet the people I take on, but not until I have read what they write to see whether they can write.

I consider it not in the writer's interest to be handled by different agents for different rights, but this is because in the operation of my office we handle everything and every right for our clients. We are represented abroad and on the West Coast by agents who carry on our work in these areas for us. We do not take on writers who divide their representation. Some perfectly reputable agents do, I am told. This is a matter of policy, having nothing to do with ethics; rather with efficiency. Commissions are 10% on U.S.A. rights and 15% on British and 15% and 20% on translation rights.

Commissions

I have been asked whether a writer should pay his
agent a commission on something the writer happens to place
himself. If a writer questions the payment of a commission,
but the agent feels he should receive this commission, I suggest a termination of the agency relationship at once since
the agent should have his commission regardless of who
makes the sale. A dispute of this sort sets up bad feeling
not in the interests of the writer. A writer who questions
the value of his agent by wanting to withhold his commission
obviously is with the wrong agent. I cannot conceive of representing someone who thought I was not earning every commission on every sale. We are underpaid for the services
we perform as it is. We can exist only by taking the low
and high commissions on everything. Asking about obligation to pay a commission indicates a bad agency relationship
or a misunderstanding of the agent's function. Agents often
have little to do, for example, with the conferences which
result in assignments to their writers of nonfiction articles
by editors. Sometimes they don't know until a check arrives
that there has been a conference. The agent earns his commission even here by the over-all services he performs in
the over-all writing career of the writers on his list. The
agent even earns it in the case of the arrived check by being sure that the pay is what it should be and that the contract of purchase is proper.

Most experienced professional writers indoctrinated in
this country have a good relationship with their agents. Occasionally one runs into a writer who feels that he must be
with an agent with whom he has no social life and, in fact,
has an arm's length, challenging relationship. I'm sure
these are fine relationships for the parties concerned.
There's nothing wrong with them, ethically. The interesting
thing is that the best agents, the most successful, those with
the best reputations, seem not to have this kind of relationship with their clients.

New writers, new clients

Most agents of all kinds like writers and like to see
manuscripts. A writer does not have to be published to get
a hearing from most of the very best agents. Some of the
largest successes I have had on my list have been first novels by previously unpublished writers, and an important part
of my list is made up of successful writers with whom I

have worked from the beginning of their published careers.
A professional writer can be unpublished. He must know
how to write and have that dedication which compels him to
write and to consider writing as a primary function, even if,
until he gets underway, he has to have a job to eat. We
agents have a special sense of who is and who is not a
"pro." One lady agent (and I'm told she is not being face-
tious, although I hope she is) claims that she can spot a
writer by observing his wrists and ankles!

I'm looking now as I write this at a list of the members of the Society of Authors' Representatives. I know
most of them, some better than others. Most of us are
close friends. I once was an editor with a publisher, as
several of us were, and got to know most of the members
then. We also meet together regularly to discuss mutual
problems. You can't go wrong with any of them as far as
their qualifications and ability are concerned. You can go
wrong as to personality. We all are pretty much alike in
our attitudes toward the business, but we differ very much
as people. It would be good if every writer deciding on an
agent could meet several before making a decision. It saves
a lot of trouble for both parties.

Good hunting to all of you. When you find the agent
who inspires the best work from you, let him or her carry
the ball. They will do it better than any writer can for himself. The agent knows his area of operation. And he can
take the blame for any difficulties with a buyer of the writer's
product. The agent is better equipped to get the buyer (publisher, producer, whatever) to do more for his client. One
of the great functions of the agent is to act as a buffer and
to see that love is maintained between the principals. Most
people function better when they feel they are loved and that
what they are doing is being appreciated. The wise writer
will let his agent be the non-loved.

Beyond Sales
       When I get to the end of my talks to writers, I get
the questions. Down in one of the first few rows is a young
man who asks the question, "If I can place my novel myself, why do I need an agent?"

My reply, "As long as you ask that question, you
don't. It's when you don't ask it that you will need an agent."

What do I mean?   When this young man, I hope not
too much later in his career, discovers that his career isn't
as far along as it should be and realizes what a good agent
can do for him, he's ready for an agent.   The writer is a-
lone in the world without an agent.   He may be the kind of
person incapable of working with an agent.   There are some
of those, and, alas, they usually don't get as far in the commercial world as they could if they were working with the
experts in the competitive market place.   The young man,
now older, in trouble with contracts he has signed, checks
with unread endorsements he has signed, out on too many
tangents and limbs, without direction and proper counseling,
without anyone to fight the battle for money, respect, proper
promotion, proper printings and advertising, acceptable salable titles to his work, feeling alone and unwanted, realizes
why placement of his work is a minor part of the function of
the agent.

Journalism's Stepchildren:
The Book [Review] Editors

By Nona Balakian, Editorial Staff Member of The New York
Times Book Review and Co-editor of The Creative Present:
Notes on Contemporary American Fiction.

From the Columbia Journalism Review 6:40-3, Winter 1967/
1968. © 1968 Graduate School of Journalism, Columbia
University. Reprinted by permission.

It is indicative of our rapidly changing times that as
recently as 1959 the critic Elizabeth Hardwick could create
a small sensation by writing an article in Harper's on "The
Decline of Book Reviewing." By announcing that "Sunday
morning with the Book Reviews [meaning The New York
Times and the late Herald Tribune] is often a dismal experience," she not only caused heads to topple but inspired the
idea for a new book review designed to correct this unhappy
situation--namely, The New York Review of Books, which
began publication in 1963 during the extended New York newspaper strike.

Nine years deeper into the age of mass electronic
media, I have no illusions about creating a similar sensation
by reporting on the state of book reviewing outside New York.
Miss Hardwick's tirade against soupy, innocuous reviewing
was directed exclusively at the New York scene. She was
attacking the sources of power: The New York Times Book
Review, with a current circulation of 1,506,000, the Herald
Tribune, dead since 1966, and the Saturday Review (circulation 491,000). To find out what existed apart from these
powers, I decided to look out of town.

Statistics alone told part of the story. I discovered
that outside New York City there are seventeen large-circu-
lation Sunday newspapers (500,000 or over) that carry Sunday
book sections--most often on a single page, tucked into a
general entertainment section. There are only two supplements comparable in scope to that of the Times: Book World,

253

shared by The Washington Post and The Chicago Tribune, and
the even newer Book Week, in the Chicago Sun-Times.

Some papers, like the Oregonian of Portland (circulation 398,000), have no separate book page but review books on
politics or regional subjects on editorial pages.   In the case
of the Portland Sunday Telegram, Maine's largest paper (circulation 107,000), books are reviewed weekly only in summer,
and bi-weekly and tri-monthly in winter--the logic being, I
suppose, that book reviews are for tourists!   Some, like the
Sunday Detroit Free Press (580,000) find a whole page too
much for books and add a column on art on the same page.

I made a list of two dozen representative newspapers
of varying Sunday circulations, ranging from The Los Angeles
Times's 970,000 to The Providence Journal's 205,000.   I
wrote to their book editors for sample pages and brief reports on their methods of operation.

The response was quick and warm.   With avid curiosity, I attacked the reading of a stack of the book pages submitted.   All too soon my interest turned to disbelief and dismay as I observed how little space there was for reviewing,
how poorly the reviews were displayed, how sloppy the editing was, how incredible the choice of books reviewed--all
this in newspapers that had circulations in the hundreds of
thousands.

It was hard to avoid concluding that book reviewing on
many newspapers is to all practical purposes the lowliest
form of journalism (certainly in terms of compensation) and
the editorship of a book section falls into the category of un-
sung heroism!

The reasons for this are multifarious and, understandably, essentially economic.   Presumably there are not so
many book readers outside New York (even in Boston, Chicago, San Francisco, and Philadelphia) and certainly far too
few book stores.   The publishing industry, moreover, is cen-
tered in New York.   But beyond these deterrents, book reviewing by its very nature presents a difficult problem to
newspapers.   It is a luxury.   Where the circulation is large,
there is the problem of adjusting a non-mass product (for
how many best-sellers are there, after all?) to a mass medium, the newspaper.   And for the smaller newspapers, there
is the financial hitch: you need advertising to make space for
reviews, and publishers are reluctant to spend for ads outside

New York.

Newspapers have tried to solve their book-page problems variously. To make books palatable to mass audiences,
book news is emphasized over reviews. Critical judgment is
abrogated, and in its place we are likely to be given material prepared by a publicity writer. On papers with small
budgets, a syndicated column presenting the views of a single
man may take the place of diverse bylines. This man's
views are repeated in dozens of papers throughout the country. Finally, no one has yet been able to discover how to
find qualified reviewers for books in special fields when all
one can afford to pay a reviewer is $15 or less, or some-
times nothing at all! Under the circumstances, it is a wonder that we have the numerous instances of excellence that
exist. Those I will discuss later.

First, here is what my correspondents had to say a-
bout their jobs as book editors:

Book pages are frequently placed in the hands of general reporters and editorial writers with some literary background who are often engaged in other work on the newspaper. Theirs is often a labor of love, to which, in the larger
cities, a few fringe benefits are attached. As one editor put
it: "There are the extracurricular activities, such as getting
authors to come for book and author luncheons, dinners, etc.,
prowling around book stores to find out what books are going
and which are not, yakking with publishers' sales representatives, and all that jolly, jolly bit." Occasionally the editor
of a book page is a professor who drops into the newspaper
office once or twice a week; one is a professor of philosophy
at the University of Cincinnati, and another teaches English
literature at Los Angeles State College. Others, like the
book editor of The Chattanooga Times, may be librarians.
("I am not at the Times frequently," this editor wrote me in
apology for his late answer.) Or one may be, as in the case
of the editor at The Hartford Courant, a retired school teacher.

An editor from a newspaper in the Northwest with a
circulation of 276,000 writes:

> As you can see, I am given ten tabloid columns
> to fill each week. I have been doing this for 25
> years, and all, believe me, in my spare time.
> I put in a full day as a news editor on our eve-

ning editions.   Mostly I write the pages myself
since I have no budget for paying reviewers.
Sometimes I use a Times Service review and
occasionally someone will do a particular review just for the book.   Except in politics, I
am given latitude with my weekly column and
often write on non-literary subjects ranging
from hunting and fishing to rose gardening and
redecorating our home.

Harriet Doar, the enterprising and talented book editor of a much smaller Southern paper, The Charlotte Observer, reports that she receives 3,000 books a year, of
which only 10 per cent are reviewed.   Here are telling passages from her report:

I am surprised and touched at the writers
[she names Lillian Smith and Harry Golden]
who will take time to review since we cannot
pay them anything. . . We have a new university branch here, and the professors are good
about reviewing.   Housewives are often good,
particularly those who do a little writing . . .
I would like to have more reviews of books
dealing with international problems but I find
these hardest to get done well.   Those with
specialized knowledge want to go on forever,
and I don't feel competent enough to cut and
edit those properly.

The previously mentioned editor who was going to all
those jolly parties also had his headaches, and he wrote:

Newspapers would have better book coverage
if they could get more book advertising and
vice versa.   Your New York Times is not only
villainous but a really malicious influence on
American journalism in this respect.   Rates
for Book Review are so high and the publishers
are so impressed to see their ads there that the
Times consumes most advertising budgets before
they can be placed elsewhere.

Absence of space, of staff, of advertising, of adequate
reviewers--these are the major complaints.

There are other problems.   The first thing that strikes

you in reading the book pages is the conglomeration of books
reviewed. While some papers review a major book like
Truman Capote's In Cold Blood promptly, most review books
that came out perhaps three months ago, and in 500 words
or less. Considering the meagerness of space, one regrets
that so much space is given to third-rate novels, to such
miscellany as books on Yoga, wine drinking, love and marriage, Celtic myths, or movie stars. If on occasion a literary title or an important book on world affairs creeps in, it
is almost swallowed up.

This choice, one might point out, is not completely
the editor's. It is partly dictated by the books that publishers are willing to send him. Since they rarely advertise
their books in these newspapers, publishers are reluctant to
send all their best titles, and they make arbitrary selections
based on preconceived notions of what will sell in St. Louis,
Omaha, or Dallas. As for the time lag, whereas The New
York Times receives its books six weeks before publication
date, the out-of-town papers often receive their copies after
the book has been published.

Book publishers, moreover, show little regard for
special regional interests. The book editor of the Dallas
Times Herald writes:

> Publishers never seem to realize that a Texas
> newspaper is interested in all Texas items . . .
> My chief complaint is that the book industry is
> so confined to the isle of Manhattan.

To return to the book pages. Most of them, as mentioned before, consist of a single page, usually tucked into
the final portions of the entertainment section. (The Boston
Traveler calls it "Show Guide.") In a few instances (like the
Los Angeles Times and the San Francisco Chronicle) the reviews are spaced over a few pages and appear alongside art
and music notes or large movie ads. Generally there is a
columnist and, though he will title his column something like
"The World of Books," books merely provide an excuse, it
seems, for airing views that are ultimately not very literary.
Sometimes he may review a book simply because it caters to
a special taste or interest of the columnist, or sometimes,
possibly, because the author of the book is a friend. The
kind of columnist who gets around will often interrupt his
comments on the book at hand with such asides as "at lunch
the other day the author of this book told me . . ."--which

doesn't leave much room for critical comment.

    The reviewing, at its worst, is catastrophic: mere puffs based on publicity releases, but more poorly written and edited. Even when the reviewers are not identified as housewives (in some cases their addresses are given--so the author can protest?), even when the reviews are by academics, professionals, the critical caliber can be very low, with the emphasis placed less on the book's meaning and art than on its author. It would seem that most usually the author with a striking personality or reputation gets the most attention. Thus, even with a thinker like Paul Tillich (if his book is reviewed at all), what is emphasized is Tillich the man and his life, rather than his philosophy.

    Perhaps what is finally most disheartening is the feeling one gets that books are regarded as a mere commodity. When a frivolous book by Patrick Dennis (author of Auntie Mame) is given equal space with a Cambridge historian's biography of the Earl of Southampton, one wonders if the juxtaposition of these reviews was dictated by anything more than the fact that the Earl and Mr. Dennis sport similar beards!

    Yet I do not want to leave the impression that all is hopeless. Quite the contrary. Editors are generally aware of shortcomings and eager to do something about them. There is growing recognition that reviewing must be raised to a professional level, and more and more academic people and creative writers are being used as reviewers. Finally, one can single out at least half a dozen editors who are doing outstanding work--some of them despite limited resources and inadequate compensation or recognition.

    Thorpe Menn of the Kansas City Star, A. C. Greene of the Dallas Times Herald, Robert Cromie of The Chicago Tribune, and Robert Kirsch of the Los Angeles Times make a careful selection of material and reviewers, try to reflect literary trends with understanding, and themselves write with authority. Edwin Tribble of the Washington Star edits a lively page, and there are others of varying degrees of success, such as The Providence Journal, Detroit News, San Francisco Chronicle, Denver Post, The Christian Science Monitor, The Milwaukee Journal, and The National Observer. Among smaller papers, the Riverside (California) Press-Enterprise runs a solid and literate section.

Still more hearteningly, one encounters on occasion
fresh talents and provocative points of view. The writers
often have little or no sacrosanct feeling about literary reputations and take slowly to literary vogues. This is how a
reviewer in Kansas City approached Edmund Wilson:

> I recall reading with great pleasure many of
> Edward [oops!] Wilson's essays in "The Bit
> Between My Teeth" when they first appeared
> in New Yorker magazine, but they do not stand
> up well upon second reading. This collection
> of his pronouncements over the last 13 years
> strikes me as long and rambling, unified by
> nothing but the author's increasing vanity and
> dogmatism . . . Wilson is ungracefully aging
> into a victim of the too common American as-
> sumption that the whole world should get
> worked up over the crochets of talented indi-
> viduals . . . he resembles in his latest work
> the resolutely independent grocer in a world of
> faceless supermarkets--a still admirable but
> somewhat obsolescent figure.

This is not only candid but expressed in a colorful,
individual manner. It would probably never have been published in New York. And from the same city recently came
the best assessment of John O'Hara as a moralist that I have
ever read.

There is a free and breezy manner that one also wel-
comes. This is how a Dallas critic greeted Susan Sontag's
Against Interpretation:

> Freud is dead. So are Fromm and Marx.
> So is tragedy, the novel, and the theatre.
> And God, of course. What isn't dead? Susan
> Sontag. And what's Susan Sontag? She's a
> young female with an awesome intelligence
> whose book, "Against Interpretation" puts her
> in the front ranks of intellectualism. She is
> the mortician in charge of the funeral serv-
> ices for the 19th century and all that it em-
> bodied. She is the Apostle of the Now.

And there is fearlessness. The San Francisco Chronicle's critic, for instance, minced no words when writing a-
bout Capote's In Cold Blood. In a review as long as the one

in The New York Times Book Review, Evan S. Connell, Jr.,
presented one of the most effective dissenting views on this
book, his final verdict being that it was "as powerless and
empty of ominous significance as a dead snake." When a
book is being heralded on every side as a masterpiece and
is earning the author a cool million, it takes courage to go
out on a limb.

There are disadvantages to being away from the center of power. But there are important compensations, too:

1. Far from New York's promotional hullabaloo,
there is less danger of drifting with the tide.

2. The style of writing can remain fresher because it is less at the mercy of professional editing,
which can, and often does, destroy individuality of
expression.

3. Because little in the way of personal power is
at stake, it is easier to be dissenting and completely
honest.

Book World, the new supplement in The Washington
Post and The Chicago Tribune, by aiming to be "a national
outlook," may further tend to weaken the expression of diverse regional interests and opinions from which ultimately
the richness of our culture derives. That is always the danger of consolidation. But it should take some of the power
away from New York--which is all to the good.

If we want to raise the quality of literary journalism
in the country at large--and at the same time utilize all our
creative and critical resources--we cannot, it seems to me,
continue to center our attention on a single geographical area.
Because New York is the publishing center, we have allowed
it to dominate the literary scene. I think it is time to take
a longer and larger look at the reviewing scene. Let us not
flatter ourselves that as New Yorkers we lead the nation.
Let us, instead, keep our ears cocked to hear what the rest
of the nation is saying. It is an education we can use.

They Say No News Is Good News

By Haskel Frankel, columnist for the Book Section of Saturday Review; Theater Critic for the National Observer; free-lance writer.

From Saturday Review 47:32-3, March 7, 1964. Copyright 1964 Saturday Review, Inc. Reprinted by permission.

Book columnists write about new books being published. Book-publicity people disseminate information about new books being published. The bringing together of these two groups is a business fraught with occupational hazards. Cauliflower ears blossom from too many phone calls; livers turn to sponge at endless cocktail parties; hips spread, paunches swell, and ulcers twinge during overly rich, three-hour lunches; eyes redden and grow dim over the daily ton of material ground out in praise of best-sellers-to-be which only the author's relatives will read and then on condition that they are given a free copy.

Knowing all of this, you can imagine my joy at being invited to the monthly luncheon of the Publishers' Publicity Association. Here, in one room and over but one luncheon, I could surely gather enough news to fill at least a half-dozen columns. How could I miss with all of those lovely publicity people packed in together? I had merely to walk around with ears open and pencil at the ready.

The luncheon of the PPA, as its membership cozily calls itself, took place at the Advertising Club on New York City's Park Avenue. The day I attended, the group had two rooms at its disposal, a long rectangular dining room and a small boxlike room with a makeshift bar at one end. The rectangle opened off the box, in which, at the time of my arrival, some fifty or sixty men and women were jammed and gabbing away. Before I could grab my pencil, someone grabbed me. "Get yourself a drink. Get yourself a drink," he said. I did. I did.

"Ninety-five cents," the bartender said.

Ninety-five cents lighter and one drink heavier, I pushed into the crowd and headed for the friendly face of Mr. A., top publicity man of a very large publishing house. I had at least five inside tips I wanted him to confirm. "Hi," I said. "Now, what's this I hear about a new novel about . . . . "

"You didn't pay for that drink, did you?" Mr. A. asked.

"I did," I said. "Now about that novel by . . . ."

"You're not supposed to pay. You're a guest. I'll get your money back. "

Mr. A. disappeared into the mob. I turned and introduced myself to Mr. B. "Have you any news for my column?"

He thought a moment, "Say, why don't you talk to ----? He's got a new book out next month, a sure best-seller, bigger than his last one. I'll give you his number. It's long distance. You call and get him to tell you about how he . . . ."

A lady cut in. "Here," she said. "Mr. A. told me what happened. I got your dollar back. "

I told her that I had only paid ninety-five cents. She ignored that. "You're a guest so you're not supposed to pay. Just tell the bartender that from now on. "

I took the dollar and thanked her. Over her shoulder I saw Mr. B. drift away. The lady smiled at me. "I guess there's no point in introducing you around. You must know everybody," she said. She waved to someone beyond me and walked off.

A man with a camera worked through the room. "Who's he taking pictures for?" I asked the nearest person, a Mrs. C.

"I don't know," she said.

We introduced ourselves. She represented a quality

publishing house I wanted to talk to.   I fished out the pencil
again.   "I want to ask you. . . ."

"I hope you didn't pay for that drink," she said.
"You're a guest and guests aren't supposed to pay."

"So I've heard."

"You know what I'm going to do when I stop working?
I'm starting a club called the Ex-Career Women's Association.   It will be like Alcoholics Anonymous, only with alco-
hol, see?   Suppose you've been staying home too long and
the kid is getting on your nerves and your husband's a
grouch.   Well, you begin to think about going back to work.
Immediately, you call up a fellow E. C. W. A. member and
she rushes over and before you do anything rash you both go
out and get loaded and remind each other about all the terrible days at the office.   That way you don't make the mistake of getting another job.   Great idea, huh?"

"Well," I said cautiously and polished off my drink.

"I think so too," Mrs. C. said.

Mr. A. was back.   "You want another drink?"

I looked at my glass, and my empty note pad.   "Why not?"

"Don't pay," he said.

"I won't," I said.   "I'm a guest and I'm not supposed
to pay."

Mr. A. pushed his empty glass at me.   "I'm a member and I have to pay, but you're a guest, so why don't you
ask for two drinks--I'm having Scotch and water."

Luckily, luncheon was announced at that moment.   After a decent roast beef, the PPA got down to business.   A
new member was proposed.   The lady in question had left her
firm and was now handling free-lance publicity assignments.
"Does anybody not want her?" Madame President asked.
There was silence.   "Then I guess she's in."

A gentleman arose to plead for volunteer workers at
a publishing function.   "We have seven volunteers but we need
five more.   That way we can rotate people at the reception
desk and no one gets stuck too long.   Huh?"

He looked around. One hand went up. The lady gave her name. "And she's not even a member!" he said, hoping to shame four more volunteers to their feet. You could hear wrist watches in the silence.

The president took over and introduced the guest speakers. I said a few words about my need for news for this column. In desperation, I gave out my home phone number. No one bothered to write it down.

The two main speakers were in the travel field. They spoke on cooperation between book publicity people and travel men. At the table directly in front of the dais sat seven people, four men and three women. Two of the women napped.

At the conclusion of the luncheon, the photographer took pictures of the guests. "Who are they for?" I asked the nearest person. "I don't know," he answered.

The room emptied in seconds. I picked up my note pad. There was a roast beef stain on the page and nothing else. I put it away and started for the elevator. A hand tapped me on the shoulder. It was Mr. B. "Hey now, don't forget to call ---. You could get a great story out of it. See ya."

The lady who had returned my dollar two hours ago was in the elevator. "I hope you didn't have any further trouble at the bar," she said. "You're a guest and guests are not supposed to pay."

I wrote down the phrase so as to have something to show my editor. And that was when I finally learned something I hadn't known before. My ball-point pen won't write through beef gravy.

The Why and How of Publishers' Library Promotion

By Lois Myller, Vice President, Educational Library Department, Simon and Schuster.

From Top of the News 21:48-51, November 1964. Published by the American Library Association. Reprinted by permission.

The dramatic growth of the school and public library market for trade books in recent years has made both publisher and librarian eager for greater cooperation and the development of a closer working relationship. Charged, as both are, with the serving of the diverse needs and tastes of the student and the general reading public, publishers and librarians have broadened their scope of publishing and purchasing areas to meet the challenge.

Concurrent with the expansion of their general publishing programs, publishers have come to recognize the special needs of the library field, not only in terms of the content and physical make-up of the book, but also in terms of methods of book selection, purchasing, and processing. To better serve the needs of the librarian most publishers have established school and library service departments and employ specialists who maintain close contact with educators and librarians throughout the country. Historically, these departments were first established on behalf of children's books through the efforts of the children's book editors, but recently the departments have been extended to serve the full academic and public library field in relation to the publisher's complete publishing program of trade and technical books for children and adults. The special requirements of the school and library children's book selection programs account for the fact that library promotion departments still concentrate the major part of their activities in the children's book field.

Librarians often ask, "Just who is a library promotion specialist and how is he trained?" Some are former teachers and librarians; others have backgrounds in book-

stores and editorial departments; still others have been college travelers or trade book salesmen.   All of them are
trained by you, the librarian.   Trained by reading your journals and attending your conferences, talking with you in your
schools and libraries about your special programs and problems, trained by talking with you about books and learning
your reactions, your experiences, and your criticisms.
They are trained by their correspondence with you and with
the readers whom you serve.   They are also trained by the
editors, and by the authors and illustrators, and the many,
many other professionals who are involved in the creation of
a book and the making of it into a real and physical thing.

In order to fulfill their function as liaison between
editor, publisher, and librarian, the promotion specialists
make frequent field trips to visit schools and libraries
throughout the country.   They are anxious to learn from the
librarians, to share with them the things they have learned
from other librarians, and to discuss the new ideas which
are developing from within the world of publishing itself.
Happily, librarians generally like to talk with them.   They
welcome the opportunity to discuss a publisher's books or the
library's specific needs.   They want to make publishers a-
ware of curriculum changes and of the need for books in special subject areas.   Library specialists can often be useful,
too, in arranging for authors to give book talks, providing
interesting display material and biographical information on
authors and artists, as well as in solving problems of billing
and delivery, and arranging for participation in such programs as the Greenaway plan.   Both the editors and design-
ers of children's and adult books seek out the returning library traveler.   They are anxious to hear of new developments in the library field and are eager for information
which will help them to serve the library's needs more effectively.

Field trips, valuable as they can be, are only a small
part of the publisher's effort to reach librarians.   From the
publisher's office, the library department maintains an active
and diversified program of book promotion.   The activities of
the department are concentrated in the following major areas:
direct mail promotion, advertising, professional exhibits and
conventions, submission of books for review and to selection
committees.

Direct mail promotion ranges from the seasonal catalogues announcing new publications to special circulars and

newsletters on forthcoming and backlist books. Largely through the influence of librarians and teachers most publishers' catalogues have undergone drastic changes over the years to make them more useful as book selection tools. New catalogues have been expanded to include annotations and recommendations by nationally recognized book selection guides for the complete backlist, as well as additional biographical material on authors and illustrators, curriculum values, format, type size, binding, and other specific information which librarians have indicated is important.

The newsletters which most publishers mail on a regular basis seldom are about a single title but more often cover a group of books at a particular grade level or in a single subject area such as books suggested for purchase under the provisions of the National Defense Education Act, or adult books which have been recommended for teenagers. These mailing pieces generally are simply and inexpensively prepared, for publishers feel that the librarian is more interested in the content of the book, the author's qualifications, and the professional reviews the book has received than he is likely to be impressed by the flowery phrase or the full-color broadside.

Advertising is another way in which the publisher can identify and publicize his books which are of particular interest to schools and libraries. The professional journals of these fields receive the major portion of a publisher's advertising budget for children's books as he seeks to arouse interest in new titles and maintain awareness of those already published. Here, too, a serious effort is made to present clearly the information needed by the book selector. Teaser ads are unknown, as copywriters vie with each other not to be clever or "offbeat," but rather to be clear and professional, with honest evaluations of the usefulness of each book.

A most important task of any library promotion department is the distribution of review copies to professional reviewers and the submission of new books to committees engaged in the compilation of recommended library and supplementary textbook lists. Unfortunately, from the publisher's point of view, the methods of book selection vary greatly from city to city, county to county, and state to state, not to mention the "special" situations such as reading circles. In fact, the distressing thing about the submission picture is that nearly every situation is "special," requiring special forms, special handling, special processing, and heavy correspondence.

Ideally, it seems that every librarian would like to examine every book before purchase, especially books intended for children and young adults. This, of course, is impossible, but the publisher can and does make every effort to have his books available for examination, professional review, and evaluation within reasonable economic limitations.

Today the average publisher of children's books sends out between three hundred fifty and five hundred copies of each new book for review. An additional one hundred fifty to two hundred are made available for examination through the program of the State Traveling Libraries, sponsored by the ALA-CBC Joint Committee and the program of E. G. Wood's Books On Exhibit. These exhibits travel on pre-arranged schedules throughout the states giving teachers and librarians in large and small communities an opportunity to hold the book, examine it, and determine its suitability for their needs.

Through the Combined Book Exhibit and similar display services, and by his own attendance at school and library conferences at the state, regional, and national levels, the publisher makes an additional fifty to one hundred copies available. The actual cost of the books themselves, the fees, and the miscellaneous expenses of correspondence, handling, and shipping make exhibiting a costly undertaking for the publisher, though no publisher would dream of abandoning this important service. He must, however, choose carefully among the many thousands of requests received annually to make certain that the limited number of books he is able to send out will receive the widest possible use and serve the greatest number of interested book selectors.

For this reason, publishers concentrate the distribution of evaluation copies of books at the time of their publication, before they have been widely read, reviewed, and discussed. Once the book has been in print long enough for the established reviewing agencies at the national, state and local levels to have reported on it, publishers must assume that librarians can be guided in their book selection and purchasing by these professional judgments, and that there is no further need to sample an established title. It should also be mentioned that the author of a book does not receive a royalty on gratis copies and that he is, therefore, penalized if sample copies are unwisely distributed or if they are put into circulation in regular library collections.

Conventions and exhibits and our reasons for attending them have already been discussed.   Little more need be said except that we are grateful when the convention schedule allows ample time for the delegates to spend time at the exhibit booths.   We are, after all, involved in our joint and separate endeavors for only one reason--books.   The books which lie on our tables for examination are what the conference is all about and why both you and we are there.

Both publishing and librarianship begin with the book, and though our professions lead us in many directions, the bringing together of the book and the reader remains our raison d'etre.

The Truth About the Best-Seller List

By Walter Goodman, Contributing Editor, <u>Redbook Magazine.</u>

From <u>McCall's</u> 94:89+, November 1966.   Reprinted by permission of the author.

Each year, a gross of books find their way into the
best-seller lists featured by newspapers and magazines a-
round the country.   A handful of these books, by dint of their
eminence and durability on the major lists, become the best
sellers of the year.   Some of them are born best sellers--
like the Kennedy books by the Messrs. Sorensen and Schlesinger.   Some achieve bestsellerdom, like Ralph Nader's
<u>Unsafe at Any Speed</u>, which so distressed somebody at the
General Motors Corporation that a firm of private eyes was
put on the author's trail.   And some, like Jacqueline Susann's <u>Valley of the Dolls</u>, the number-one hit of 1966, have
bestsellerdom thrust upon them.   However attained, the higher reaches of the best-seller list bring their occupants a certain amount of celebrity, a substantial amount of money and
no literary distinction whatever.

The two most important national lists, the ones you
are likely to find displayed near the cash register in your
bookstore, are those that appear in the <u>New York Times Book
Review</u> and in <u>Book Week</u>, a Sunday supplement to the <u>New
York World Journal Tribune</u>, the <u>Washington Post</u> and the
<u>Chicago Sun-Times</u>.   The main difference between them is
quantitative.   The <u>Times</u> collects information from 125 stores,
while <u>Book Week</u> makes do with 35; but neither is a model
of the science of poll taking.

For one thing, most stores do not maintain the kind
of inventory control that enables a manager to say with certainty how many copies of any book he has sold during the
past week.   "When the man from the <u>Times</u> called," explains
a former assistant manager of one large New York City store,
"we just sort of looked around and gave him the titles that
seemed to be doing well."   Store owners and managers, be-

270

ing subject to the temptations of commerce, have been known
to look around and report as best sellers books that weren't
selling well enough, considering the number of copies they
had been talked into stocking. Experienced publishing hands
agree that Truman Capote's In Cold Blood remained high on
lists for quite a time after sales had fallen off simply because the stores were overstocked. For similar reasons,
store owners prefer to report a $6.95 book rather than a
$3.95 book--the return is better. Beatle John Lennon's In
His Own Write sold more than 225,000 copies, yet received
only scant acknowledgment on the lists. Book lovers among
store clerks may slip in a title out of sheer affection. A
young woman at Bloomingdale's book department regularly
nominated Joseph Heller's Catch-22, because she was taken
with the novel and felt that it was being ignored.

Since the stores used by both the Times and Book Week
are the most respectable in the country, there are some
books that do extremely well yet are never to be found on a
best-seller list, either because they are purchased at such
unprestigious places as drug counters, discount houses and
shops that sell false whiskers or because store managers
are too fastidious to report them. Thus, despite well-meant
complaints that the best-seller lists do an injustice to America's taste, if the lists were more accurate, they would undoubtedly contain even more wretched works than they now do.

The bloody volumes of Mickey Spillane and the inspirational efforts of Billy Graham have both been slighted by
best-seller compilers. The Reverend Dr. Graham, whose
World Aflame sold 250,000 copies in six months without being officially designated a best seller, complained to his editor about the snub. The editor complained to his firm's publicity man--"Can't you get it on anywhere?"--and with the
help of the sales figures, the publicity man prevailed upon
Publisher's Weekly, the book industry's leading trade publication, to list World Aflame one week and give Dr. Graham
the satisfaction he sought.

Whatever doubts one may have about whether the titles
on the best-seller lists are invariably the best sellers, there
is no question that a book's appearance on the upper half of
the list is a vigorous spur to its sales. We are not a nation
of book readers, and the lists allow those hundreds of thousands of nonreaders, who pay scant attention to reviews, to
see at a glance what is available for the difficult hours when
even television palls. The nonreader's standards are not

rigorous; he is impressed with popularity, in books as in
beer; and it is for his sake and the sake of the publishers
who wish to enjoy his favors that the best-seller lists exist.
Occasionally a publisher allows his eagerness over the lists
to carry him away. After a highly respected New England
publishing firm called the business department of Book Week
to inquire when a new novel of theirs might be expected to
make number one, so they could buy a full page advertisement to celebrate the event, Richard Kluger, Book Week's
first editor, took the best-seller list out of the hands of the
business department and entrusted it to the editorial department, in the faith that editors are less susceptible than
salesmen to the power of advertiser suggestion.

Now and then, a book like Games People Play--which
started with a printing of 3,000 copies, got no major reviews and little advertising, yet sold 300,000 copies in upward of a year on the lists--attains best sellerdom on its
own steam; but usually the steam is generated by professional machinery. This process begins well before publication
date, with two key decisions--how many copies of the book
to print and how much money to spend on advertising. If the
first printing is not sufficiently impressive, the publisher's
salesmen will not strain themselves to get stores to stock up,
and if stores do not stock up, the chances of a given book's
becoming a best seller are grievously diminished. "The
best way to make a best seller," says a vice-president of a
major publishing company, "is to have fifty thousand copies
in the stores."

Having won over the stores, the publisher's next effort is aimed at the professional book community, reviewers
and hangers-on who are in a position to carry the word to
the outer world. A single quote by the Herald Tribune's
Maurice Dolbier, to the effect that Up the Down Staircase was
"the funniest novel published in America since 'Catch-22,'"
started Bel Kaufman's collection of anecdotes on its sensational course.

All that prevents a publisher from trying to make
every book a best seller is money. As many writers discover to their pain each season, most books are put out in a
modest printing of a few thousand copies and are sent into
obscurity with a minuscule advertising budget. Walker
Percy's first novel, The Moviegoer, published by Alfred
Knopf in 1963, received typically scant support until it won
the National Book Award. Mr. Percy took his second novel,

The Last Gentleman, downtown to Farrar, Straus & Giroux.

Publishers nowadays do well to break even on hard-cover books and so are reluctant to throw good money after bad. They know that advertising alone will not sell books. One of our former Presidents, turned memoir writer, had this fact impressed on him some years ago when, disappointed at the sales of his work, he gave his publisher $15,000 of his own money for advertising, on the condition that he would get back ten per cent of the net price of every book sold thereafter. It was a bad gamble; only 500 more books were sold, and he lost $14,700.

The big profits where new books are concerned come from reprint sales, and how much money a publisher can expect from this source is tied in with the best-seller potentialities of the work up for auction. Reprint prices have soared in the past decade--sometimes embarrassingly so. In its eagerness to get reprint rights to Kathleen (Forever Amber) Winsor's latest novel, Wanderers Eastward, Wanderers West, New American Library paid Random House $500,000 before publication. N.A.L. could have saved some money; the next bid was a mere $260,000 and to add injury to injury, the book did not take off in the hoped-for manner.

The overriding importance of paperbacks has led to some peculiar publishing arrangements in recent years. Pocket Books has created a hard-cover division called Trident Press, one of whose main functions would seem to be to lose money on the works of Harold Robbins. His novels, however, are reprinted by the parent concern, which makes money, a great deal of money, on them. The hard-cover edition of The Carpetbaggers, albeit a best seller, reportedly lost $20,000 for Trident; but sales of the Pocket Book edition have gone over five million copies and are still going.

Since Harold Robbins cannot write best sellers for anybody but Trident these days, other publishers are obliged to seek blockbusting novels of their own. One way to do this is to woo best-selling writers from other publishers. New American Library, which seems to have more cash to throw around than anybody else, took Ayn (The Fountainhead and Atlas Shrugged) Rand from Random House with a $250,000 guarantee on a still-to-be-written novel.

Another, cheaper if chancier, method is to keep an eye out for a book with that certain something by an unknown,

hence less costly, writer.   Just what that certain something
is, unfortunately, remains elusive.   Many successful books
have suffered rebuffs from experienced editors before going
on to glory.   O Ye Jigs and Juleps, Virginia Cary Hudson's
slender volume of reminiscences, which sold hundreds of
thousands of copies during its time as a best seller, was
rejected by several of the most eminent firms in New York.

Roderick Thorp's hit novel, The Detective, was picked
up by Dial Press for a pittance--a $1, 500 advance--after it
had been turned down by eight publishers; indeed, a rejection letter had already been formulated by Dial's managing
editor when another member of the staff salvaged the manuscript.   After a year's rewriting to the specifications of the
folks at Dial, during which time Mrs. Thorp supported the
household, the book was named a full selection by the Literary Guild (which called for some more rewriting, in def-
erence to the Guild's family audience) and was bought by
Twentieth Century-Fox for $75,000, plus $1,000 for each
week it remains a national best seller, and by a reprint
firm for $250,000, after spirited bidding.   Since the paper-
back rights were sold to Avon, a subsidiary of the Hearst
organization, the book gained certain fringe benefits.   It was
plugged by a Hearst newspaper columnist, and it was arranged that two chapters would run in Cosmopolitan, a
Hearst magazine.   Mr. Thorp, who used to live in a low-
income housing project, has had to engage an accountant and
a lawyer to handle his suddenly complex financial affairs.

Needless to say, in reprint, movie and book-club ne-
gotiations, the literary quality of the work in question is not
of the first moment.   The editors who turned down The Detective were not necessarily poor judges of fiction.   The
Detective's virtues for the business-wise were a strong plot
(a homosexual murder), a healthy heft (almost 600 pages)
and a dialogue-dependent style that would present no difficulties to impatient readers.

Some novels of distinction do, mysteriously, manage
to climb high onto the best-seller lists--the most notable case
of recent years being Saul Bellow's Herzog.   The book trade
is in perfect agreement that Herzog was the greatest unread
best seller of the decade.   Less mysterious and much better
read best sellers are those like Jacqueline Susann's Valley
of the Dolls ("A piece of junk," says an envious publisher,
"but a salable piece of junk") and Harold Robbins' The Adventurers, which occupied the number-one and number-two

places, respectively, for many weeks of last spring and summer. The Adventurers offered sex, violence and a central
character who brought to mind Porfirio Rubirosa. Valley of
the Dolls offered sex, pep pills and a central character who
brought to mind Judy Garland.

Mr. Robbins, from all reports, writes his books by
himself--a heavy burden, critics agree, for a man to bear
alone--but Bernard Geis, publisher of Valley of the Dolls,
believes in close collaboration between author and publisher.
"A lot of people criticize us for overdirecting authors," he
concedes, "but manuscripts are not engraved in bronze. We
feel we have enough taste to guide a writer." Mr. Geis and
his editors put their taste to Miss Susann's service as they
guided her in cutting, inserting a new key scene and bringing
her characters into sharper focus. "She's the best trouper
I ever worked with," says Geis. "She turned out a new chapter in a week, and it was perfect."

Since Geis Associates put out only a dozen books a
year, each one is expected to be "a potential blockbuster."
Explains Mr. Geis, "We can't afford to take a weak book,
regardless of its merits." Among the books that, regardless
of their merits, have borne the Geis imprint are Sex and the
Single Girl, Harlow and Lita Grey Chaplin's Life with Chap-
lin--An Intimate Autobiography. Random House, which ordinarily distributes Geis' books, declined to have anything to
do with this last number. But Geis publicists are delighted
with it. "Some book!" proclaims one. "He seduces her in
a steam bath."

To protect their investment in Miss Susann, Geis and
his editors have already helped her get through a first draft,
typed on pink paper, of her next novel, due to be published
in the fall of 1967. It will be entitled The Love Machine,
and we are promised it will do for the TV industry what
Valley of the Dolls did for show business, whatever that was.

Miss Susann is not the only novelist in America who is
enjoying the assistance of the house of Geis in creating a best
seller. Up in New England and down in Washington, D.C.,
are two young writers who have also contracted to turn out
novels to the publisher's specifications. The young woman in
the capital is working on a "historical." The young man in
New England is working on a "contemporary."

The latter relates how it all came about. Mr. Geis,

having admired some reviews of his, went to him with a
straightforward proposition: "How would you like to have
tax problems?" Our young man, who thinks of himself as a
poet, had never anticipated such problems, but decided, upon reflection, that he had no really big objection to them,
and so joined Mr. Geis for an expensive lunch in midtown
Manhattan.   There he was given Xerox copies of essays by
Mary McCarthy and Norman Podhoretz on the virtues of "the
novel as news"--that is, in the Geis interpretation, a novel
based on a recognizable character (like Porfirio Rubirosa or
Judy Garland) who is not likely to sue.   "It saves having to
invent characters," observes the writer.   At first, the new
collaborators lighted on Jerry Lewis as a suitable subject--
"The Last of the Movie Comics"--but soon switched to another subject, suggested by the writer's wife.   Who this is
remains a secret for the time being, but he or she has something to do with Italy.   Our author turns out fifty pages every
two weeks and ships them to New York, where his help-
meets at the publishing house scrutinize them and send back
specific suggestions for changes, along with words of encour-
agement--"We're not ashamed to reach for the brass ring on
the merry-go-round."

"I think they're grateful to be able to work for a
change with somebody who can put together a grammatical
sentence," says our young man.   "It's pleasant writing in a
feebleminded sort of way--like those kids' puzzles where you
have to connect the numbers to make the picture.   I have
fifteen or twenty semisensational   pieces of action, and all I
have to do is connect them with a line that is called narrative.   That's eighty-five per cent of the job.   The other fifteen per cent, which will make the difference between moder-
ate success and big success is a shtick.   Jacqueline Susann's
shtick was pills.   When I think of her, I think, if she could
do it, why can't I?   Then I think, But if she could do it,
why should I?"

The answer to this question is at hand.   For approximately six months' work, the writer is getting a $7,500 ad-
vance, plus up to $2,000 in expenses, which he will use, in
the interests of authenticity, on a trip to Venice.   If the book
sells anything like Valley of the Dolls, his additional royalties, plus a healthy paperback sale ("It can't be less than
fifty thousand dollars"), plus a likely movie sale, will transform him into an exceptionally well-to-do poet.   As Geis' energetic young director of promotion, Letty Cottin Pogrebin,
says, "Our authors can rest assured we'll do our part.   Other

publishers live in an ivory tower. They think mass communications are a nasty business. But the rest of the world is
watching TV."

Geis put $50,000 into the campaign for Valley of the
Dolls, which featured such gimmicks as sugar-filled cap-
sules, sent out before publication with a message: "Watch
for the sensational truth about the glamour set on a pill
kick," and took the attractive Miss Susann to some 250 television and radio shows, press parties, autographing sessions,
and so forth around the country. "It's not enough to seek
the habitual book buyers, a few thousand urban sophisticates,"
says Mrs. Pogrebin. "We reach out to the people who read
gossip columns and women's pages. We present the author
as a celebrity in her own right."

Not all publishers have experienced total triumph in
attempting to transform an author into a celebrity. A few
years ago, a small firm decided to bring to this country
from England the author of a mystery novel for which it had
high hopes. Numerous interviews were set up--but all unfortunately, had to be canceled when the gentleman arrived
and turned out to have difficulties getting through public appearances coherently, since he was drunk most of the time.
The book flopped, and the firm underwent a major personnel
shake-up soon afterward.

But to return to the happier story of Valley of the
Dolls; A tie-in with a hotel chain gave Miss Susann free
suites in exchange for the honor and publicity of having her
stay at the hotels on tour, and Twentieth Century-Fox, which
bought the movie rights, chipped in with a sizable advertising
budget of its own, to help its property remain on top of the
lists as long as possible.

Movie companies customarily meet the publisher's advertising budget dollar for dollar. "You can smell the movie
money," says an agent of long experience. Occasionally, as
with The Detective, the film studios offer a bonus to the author if his book stays on the best-seller lists for a specific
number of weeks--which has in the past led authors' agents
to hire publicity men to go out and simply buy the book in
the reporting stores. This, the movie people figured out,
they could do themselves, and do it they have.

Hollywood's emisssaries are not renowned for their
subtle natures, and at least one man from a large studio has

openly approached an editor at the Times Book Review about
getting a certain book on the list.   He was turned down.

Otto Preminger's purchase of the outsize novel Hurry
Sundown, in 1964, reaped an unexpected crop of publicity,
owing to a misunderstanding.   Preminger was keeping details of the purchase secret, so an enterprising Times reporter called the publisher, Doubleday, and inquired of the
woman who took the call, "Do you know the cost of Hurry
Sundown?" "Sure," she replied.   "Seven ninety-five." The
reporter, in the belief that he had just been awarded a scoop,
instead of the book's retail price, led off his next day's report: "One of the highest prices on record, approximately.
$795,000, has been paid for screen rights to Hurry Sundown."
This figure was $595,000 too high.

Although there is no doubt that the best-seller lists
are mighty aids in the selling of books, bookstores have not
found them an unmitigated blessing.   The trouble is that as
soon as a book makes the list, discount outlets stock up on
it and undersell the conventional shops.   In New York, last
summer, for example, Korvette's was selling The Last Battle, the number-one nonfiction best seller, published at $7.50,
for $5.29.   All $5.95 books, including The Adventurers,
Valley of the Dolls, In Cold Blood and Papa Hemingway,
were priced at $4.19.   "Why is it called the best-seller
list?" asked a New Jersey bookseller after the discounter
had moved in.   "Worst-seller list is the correct name for
this cutthroat list."

Theodore Wilentz, president of the American Booksellers Association and co-owner of the exemplary Eighth
Street Bookshop in New York's Greenwich Village, has refused invitations to participate in what he feels is an iniq-
uitous project.   "The best-seller lists have a destructive influence on book selling.   They encourage discount operations,
which stock only a handful of titles and drive real bookshops
out of business or force them to devote space to such side-
lines as greeting cards and stationery.   This, in turn, limits
the range of books available to the reading public."

Objections to the lists are by no means exclusively
pecuniary.   In August, 1961, the Chicago Tribune, which sums
up reports for the Chicago area, announced that it was sending its weekly list to the cleaner's.   "Recently and tardily,"
explained the editors of the Tribune's Books Today, "we have
become aware that some of the best sellers that have ap-

peared on our list were sewer-written by dirty-fingered authors for dirty-minded readers." From that hour on, the
Tribune's list would be called "Among the Best Sellers," and,
promised the editors, "We will not knowingly include in it
any book that is intended to make money for its author and
publisher by being nastier than the next. . . . We aren't
any longer going to draw attention to gutter literature." And
in 1966, the Tribune list never acknowledged The Adventurers,
although it did make weekly obeisance to Valley of the Dolls.

When Richard Kluger took over Book Week, he discussed with his associates the possibility of doing away with
the best-seller list, which had for years been carried by the
Herald Tribune, and substituting a list of "recommended"
books. This was decided against, partly because news of
what other people were buying seemed to be legitimate news,
partly because Book Week's withdrawal would have left the
Times list without a major competitor, and mainly because
book publishers demanded it as a merchandising device. A
compromise of sorts was reached when the newspaper editors added an introduction to their list, saying the books
named therein were "the most popular in the U.S.--not . . .
the best." A gay little mark was placed beside those titles
deemed by the editors "to be of special literary, social or
historic interest." In a similar spirit, the Times takes note
of "New and Recommended" books beneath its list of unrec-
ommended best sellers.

Mr. Kluger thinks that best-seller lists are uncondi-
tionally terrible: "Most people who are capable of reading
subliterary best sellers are capable of reading literary best
sellers, so by promoting the worst stuff, we diminish their
lives. I didn't feel that I was contributing to the cultural
well-being of the country, to say the least, by plugging best
sellers."

In his disdain for most best sellers and all best-seller
lists, Mr. Kluger undoubtedly speaks for the small number of
Americans who care about books. But the way of the publishing world seems to be with Bernard Geis, who says, "I don't
think we should judge books too quickly. I say, let the
people decide, let time decide." And, indeed, it is a comfort to entrust Valley of the Dolls to the hands of time--or it
would be if we did not already know that 1967 will bring The
Love Machine.

PART II: THE PUBLISHING OF . . .

A. Trade Books

The Revolution in Books

By Robert Escarpit, author, critic, literary historian, Professor of Comparative Literature, Faculty of Letters and Humanistic Sciences of Bordeaux, France.

Reprinted from UNESCO Courier 18:4-10, September 1965, by permission.

The appearance of the mass-circulation book is probably the most important cultural development in the second half of the twentieth century. Although people everywhere have at last begun to show an interest in this event, no one has yet clearly grasped its significance nor fully realized that it is taking place. English-speaking countries, for instance, often misname this type of book "the paperback," although some paperbound books are high-priced articles with a very low circulation. Elsewhere, as in most European countries, it is called, even less appropriately, "the pocket book" or, quite absurdly, "the pocket-size book." It would be as reasonable to talk of "cheap books" or "bulk-printed books."

Mass-circulation books are not distinguished by their specific appearance nor by the number of copies printed nor by the retail price. It is easy to find examples of all these characteristics, sometimes more than a century back, whereas the mass-circulation book is a global phenomenon whose constituent elements cannot be separated, a new type of publishing venture which first took shape in 1935 with the appearance of the Penguin series in England.

The obvious features of mass-circulation books (sometimes wrongly regarded as fundamental characteristics) all combine to enable them to play their role, a role which consists of changing the scale on which publications are distributed, by providing new processes which open up still unsatisfied areas of readership, ethnic groups or social strata.

What is involved is not the adaptation of books to new conditions, but a genuine mutation. The mass-circulation book

283

is as different from the classical book as was the printed
book from the manuscript and the manuscript from the clay
tablet.   This mutation, in fact, will eventually change the
content of books, just as it is already transforming the dialogue between author and reader which constitutes the reality
of literature.

In other words, the whole of written culture as we
have known it for two or three centuries past is directly
challenged by mass-circulation books, and the cultivated
classes of our time are only wrong in feeling disturbed over
this development to the extent that such perturbation reflects
a niggardly attachment to values which have become inadequate for the new dimensions of mankind.

To begin with, viewed as manufactured items, books
have at one bound caught up with other products of modern
industry; the book has been simultaneously adapted to the demands of mass production and modern design.   There was
virtually no technical difference between Gutenberg's books
and books produced at the end of the eighteenth century;
printers carried out identical operations and editions remained
about the same size, rarely exceeding a few thousand copies.

Then, within ten to fifteen years, or roughly the
length of the Napoleonic era, everything changed.   Printing
was mechanized and the book which had editions of from between ten thousand and one hundred thousand copies made its
appearance.   Editions of this order were still being printed
130 years later between the two world wars, and they are
still produced in the traditional sector of publishing.

At the same time, however, mass consumer demands,
emerging from and affecting social advancement, penetrated
the cultural field.   By the 1870s, these demands, which exerted pressure on the whole complex of trade and industry,
were also affecting the media serving the field of culture,
and especially books.

As everyone knows, one of the first effects of mass
production in all fields was a decline in the aesthetic and
functional qualities of the product manufactured.   Because of
their dual nature as physical objects and vehicles for the
communication of thought, books proved particularly vulnerable to such debasement.   "Mass produced" reading matter
became a by-product of the newspapers and hawkers' books
that were the only mass media of the time.   Such "poor

man's books" often sacrificed either content or appearance, and mostly both. At the beginning of the century the working class reader in city or village could only escape from the most stultifying type of reading by his sheer determination to rise above the ugliness and unsuitability of the reading material normally available to him.

It is not surprising, therefore, that such media of mass communication as the radio and the cinema, which from the outset had an aesthetic adapted to their function, should have proved irresistible rivals to books. Indeed when the 1930s came bringing restlessness and more demanding standards, it might well have been thought that books had lost the battle.

Such was far from being the case. Although no one realized it at the time, a genuine revolution occurred in the mid-1930's in the thinking of our industrial civilization. Raymond Loewy then wrote in the United States The Locomotive, Its Aesthetics, which anticipated his famous book on industrial design, Never Let Well Enough Alone. A new type of functional beauty entered everyday life. In Western Europe it was introduced by the "one-price" stores, and in Moscow a similar function was fulfilled by the newly-opened underground railway. Though this beauty may not have been to everyone's taste, it nevertheless suddenly lit up and humanized the dismal atmosphere of a mass consumer world.

Industrial design, which thus became part of our accustomed pattern a little before the Second World War, has been defined as "a technique connected with the creation of products, and aimed at studying the products devised by a firm on the basis of such criteria as suitability for use, beauty, ease of manufacture and reduction of cost price."

Consciously or unconsciously, Allen Lane applied these four criteria to book production when he founded Penguin Books in England in 1935. Penguin books were the first in the world to unite all the specific features of mass-circulation books. Pleasant to look at and convenient in form, they enabled works of real quality to be distributed in huge quantities and at a very low price. It should be repeated that none of these various elements can be considered separately; each depends on the others and the whole secret of mass-circulation books lies in achieving the right balance.

For the modest price of sixpence, the Penguin series gave the public books that normally sold in a hardback edition for ten shillings and sixpence--more than twenty times as much. Such sensationally low prices are now a thing of the past, but one of the requirements of the mass-circulation book is still that it should be sold at rock-bottom price.

This price can be worked out very accurately. The price at which a book is sold to the public is dependent on the cost price of each volume in the original edition, and is established on the basis of a simple formula. Some of the costs of printing a book (type-setting, going to press, etc.) remain the same no matter how many copies are printed; others (such as paper and binding), are linked to each individual volume and thus increase with the size of the edition. In terms of cost price per volume these expenses are incompressible. Fixed costs, however, decrease proportionately as the size of the edition increases, since they are spread over a greater number of copies. The cost price per volume thus diminishes accordingly.

There comes a moment, however, when the fixed costs are spread over such a large number of copies that the effect on the cost price is insignificant, and the latter, along with the retail price then becomes stabilized at the lowest level. The publisher's first concern must be to determine this point, since only when it has been reached can he benefit completely from the effects of mass production.

How far the publisher should go beyond this point remains to be seen. For the purchaser it makes no difference at all whether a book is published in 50,000 copies or in one million since the rock-bottom price has already been reached. But the situation is altogether different from the publisher's viewpoint. On the one hand his financial investment is larger and the risk correspondingly greater; on the other hand, despite the reasonableness and stability of the price, he cannot expect to distribute a mass production book by the same methods he uses for smaller editions.

This brings us to a third requirement of the mass-circulation book: new distribution outlets must be found. In the most developed civilizations cultural patterns are still more or less marked by the stamp of a civilization based on a cultural elite. The bookshop network in particular serves only a small fraction of the population--those social strata or classes which produce the "cultivated" individuals.

In a highly developed country where the reading population (those capable of choosing and using reading matter)
represents 70 to 75% of the population, the real public
(those who make regular use of all types of reading matter)
represents at most 15 to 20%, and the cultivated public
(those for whom the bookshops cater) barely 2 to 3%.

It is out of the question for the moment to reach the
whole of the reading population.   But mass-circulation books
must spread far beyond the cultivated public and penetrate
the real public where they will have their most effective social impact.   This is what has happened in the United States,
where before World War II best sellers rarely sold 100,000
copies, while editions of more than a million copies are now
commonplace.

Books are not distributed solely through bookshops,
but from an infinite number of sales points, including drug-
stores, self-services stores and bookstalls, with the backing
of extensive advertising.   Certain countries, and especially
the U.S.S.R., have developed direct distribution methods
through offices, factories and the postal service.   Finally, in
the years ahead we will see an extension of book vending machines which will increase the bookshop's distribution power
tenfold.

It is in this way that the boundaries of the "cultivated"
public are crossed.   It should be noted, however, that high
sales figures do not necessarily mean that those boundaries
have been crossed.   Many publishers, especially in Europe,
believe they are publishing mass-circulation books because
they have adopted the form and style of such books and have
increased their printing runs ten or twenty-fold.   All they
have done in many cases is to saturate the market offered by
the cultivated public through the inducement of reduced prices.

The whole operation takes place within the old socio-
cultural frontiers, and this is especially true of countries
which have a large and active, though poorly-off, intelligent-
sia.   There are countries where mass circulation starts with
sales of from five to ten thousand copies and others where
sales of between 50,000 and 100,000 still represent limited
distribution within the cultivated sector.

In short, the entry of books into the mass market can affect them in other than material ways. Their content is affected and, along with it, the use which readers make of that content. The dialogue between author and reader which constitutes the basic literary reality is being profoundly altered in its nature and in its machinery alike.

The reading of the cultivated person is marked by an active and conscious attitude. He reacts to what he is reading by judgements, observations and reasoned conclusions, whether the work in question is "literary," in the true sense, or functional. All these reactions combine to form a "literary opinion" whose image returns to the author through various channels: conversations, contacts between publishers and booksellers, literary reviews and so on.

This feedback to the author is the specific and distinctive feature of literary reality. It implies, incidentally, an extremely delicate balance. If the feedback signal is too strong, in other words if the author is too conscious of his public, his work may deteriorate.

If there is no feedback the author can only choose between the sterile seclusion of the literary coteries and the no less sterile use of mechanical techniques for capturing and retaining the attention of the anonymous public like any demagogue.

In mass circulation as we know it today, however, there is no cultural feedback. The literary opinion of the "masses" has no personal contacts, bookselling networks or literary criticism through which to express or transmit itself and often has not even the opportunity to take conscious form.

The publisher of mass-circulation books is thus confronted with a difficult problem. On the one hand, in view of the substantial capital involved, he must reduce the risks of the operation by programming his production to the maximum; on the other, he must offset the disadvantages of having no feedback to guide him. The problem varies according to the types of books he publishes. Here we need only consider three types of books.

First of all, there are the functional books which represent a known and recognized need. This to some extent guarantees the sale of a considerable number of copies. The typical example is the cookbook which contributes to rank a-

mong the best selling paperbacks in the United States.   Eating is a function which can always be relied on and love of
good food is one of the commonest of all impulses.

The same applies to books needed by school and university students.   In recent years the paperback has invaded
the American universities.   This has revolutionized research
and teaching methods.   Scientific textbooks, for example, are
no longer rare and expensive works to be placed on library
shelves where set timetables restrict their usefulness and
where they slowly grow out of date.

They are now cheap, attractively but unpretentiously
produced books which can be purchased for a modest sum
and which students are therefore ready to purchase.   Even if
a student does not buy a book himself, the library can offer
him several copies without worrying unduly over the possibility of their wearing out or being lost.

It is always possible to reprint, bringing the book
up to date at the same time.   In this way it benefits from a
genuine scientific feedback that expresses the views of its
users.   In France this system has been employed for many
years in the Que Sais-le?   (What Do I Know?) series.   In
their special field of scientific popularization and explanation, these little books had already discovered the formula of
the mass-circulation book in pre-war days, although they
were probably unaware of it at the time.

Another formula adopted in mass-circulation publishing is to reprint a literary work which has already proved itself in the cultivated sector.   It may be one of the classics
or a book that has been outstandingly successful in an ordinary edition.   The formula of the classic is obviously more
convenient since the number of titles of works retained in a
country's historical consciousness is strictly limited . . .
roughly about one per cent.   Reprinting the classics, therefore, presents few hazards and this explains why in most
countries paperbacks have produced an unhoped for and reassuring flood of reprints of all kinds.   Texts which have disappeared from circulation now enter the public domain and
can be purchased at any bookstall.

At the same time, there is a limit to this wealth of
material and disadvantages in this practice.   The number of
classic works which a literature can offer is not infinite, a-
mounting perhaps to a few thousand, and one can reasonably

foresee a point at which mass-circulation books in the more
developed countries will be offering scores of thousands of
different titles.   A time must come then, which is not far
off in certain countries, when saturation of the market will
cause a slump in books of this type, and when the only reliable outlet for these huge editions will consist of the normal cultural consumption of schools, universities and similar institutions.

But it is also possible to take up a best seller while
it is still enjoying a success, before it becomes a classic
and when the only process of selection it has undergone--one
far less stringent than that of historical selection--is the
test of normal sales through bookshops.

This may be a very profitable practice, but unfortunately many publishers have not yet understood the machinery
of this kind of sale.   They wait too long after the book's
success in an ordinary edition before prolonging that success
in a mass-circulation edition.

They imagine that the book's success in an ordinary
edition must be exhausted before launching it among what they
believe to be an extension of the same public.   In actual fact
experience proves that the ideal moment for switching a book
from the ordinary to the mass-circulation edition is at the
height of its success in the former edition.

Far from interfering with its success in that form,
the mass edition provides a fresh impetus, exerting an influence on the ordinary edition at the same time as it builds up
its own success through the interest the book arouses in the
cultivated sector.

In advanced twentieth century societies, the cultivated
public and the public at large come into contact daily, often
sharing the same media of communication and expression.   A
book discussed in the literary columns of a newspaper is not
overlooked by readers of the paper who are primarily interested in the sports pages or the crime reports.

The solitary disadvantage of the system, therefore, is
not an economic one.   It lies in the fact that the switching of
a book from the ordinary to the mass-circulation edition is a
unilateral operation.   The book in question has been lifted up
and stimulated by a cultivated literary opinion.   Now it is imposed on the mass readership which unfortunately has no feed-

back circuit through which to bring its opinion to bear on
subsequent productions.

   This brings us to the third type of mass circulation
book--the one produced directly for the mass market and
under pressure from that public.   These are, broadly speaking, the new literary books in the usual sense of the expression.   Unhappily, experience demonstrates that such books
are extremely rare.   Publishers have not yet clearly understood the nature of the instrument they possess.   Still less
do they know how to use it.   They are handicapped by obstacles of an institutional kind, unsatisfactory distribution channels, the indifference or hostility of critics, representing the
opposition of the cultivated sector to the mass-circulation
book.

   Even so, and this should be emphasized, the mass-
circulation book will never destroy books in ordinary editions or even the semi-de luxe book.   On the contrary, by
giving unlimited scope to the bases for literary communication, by transforming reading into a true, everyday activity,
and one which is an integral part of man's existence, it will
awaken a new interest in and a new enthusiasm for books.

   Those who fear that the semi-de luxe book and the
handsome, top-quality book are doomed to be ousted by the
mass-circulation book are mistaken.   The desire to own
books published in beautifully finished editions, solid and
lasting, pleasant to contemplate and to touch, represents on
the part of the reader, a final choice which can only be the
outcome of a long experience of reading.   If so many imita-
tion deluxe editions are now being distributed by various
clubs and if books are often regarded as decorative elements
or status symbols, this is because in such cases the possession of a book is unrelated to the act of reading, because
there is a breach between the book and its purpose.

   As living standards rise throughout the world, the
quality book becomes accessible to more and more deeper and
deeper strata of the population; but reading, in the sense of
conscious reading, what we call literary reading, remains the
prerogative of a minority.   Thanks to the mass-circulation
book, this situation is changing and we may fairly hope that
in the course of the next fifty years this type of book, the
"reading machine," will make its full contribution to the life
of the new societies which will inherit our world.

The Wonderland of Subsidiary Rights

By Paul Nathan, author of the column "Rights and Permissions" in Publishers' Weekly.

From Saturday Review 46:58-9+, December 14, 1963.
Copyright 1963 Saturday Review, Inc. Reprinted by permission.

Literature has always had its business side--ever since blind Homer traded an evening of epic for a place at table and a corner to nod in. And that genteel occupation, publishing, has generally been conducted in hope of profit. In our era, however, books have turned out to have so many previously undreamed-of possibilities for commercial exploitation that it's getting harder all the time to distinguish the world of letters from the world of high finance.

Today, a killing in the stock market has nothing on a killing in the literary market place. And author futures are just as much a matter for manipulation and trading as cotton futures. Reprint rights to Irving Wallace's next novel, The Man, were recently sold to Fawcett for $325,000. While this promises to be a fairly sensational piece of merchandise (the title character is a Negro elevated by extraordinary circumstances and the rules of succession to the Presidency of the United States), $325,000 is still an impressive amount of money to be riding on a work of fiction still unwritten at contract-signing time.

Harold Robbins, whose popularity is attested by the record of such best-sellers as Where Love Has Gone and The Carpetbaggers, has disposed of hard-cover, soft-cover, and motion picture rights to something called The Adventurers for a total of more than $1,000,000. This is another book that was only a gleam in various eyes when the checks were made out.

Plodding along in the old-fashioned way, James A. Michener waits till he has something to show before his agent

292

puts it up for grabs.   But Michener's been doing all right,
too.   Movie rights to Hawaii went for a down payment of
$600,000 against 10 per cent of the film's gross.   Although
the purchasers got so much story for their money that
they've run into trouble trying to reduce it to normal super-
colossal-screenplay size, it begins to look as though the picture will be made.   And if, in this age of boom-or-bust
spectaculars, Hollywood's Hawaii doesn't do a nosedive at
the box office, it could certainly gross close to $20,000,000.

Movie rights and reprint rights happen to be two of
the most conspicuously lucrative of the so-called subsidiary
or secondary rights of books.   There are many others that
can contribute to authors' and publishers' economic well-being.   Among these are first and second serial rights (magazine and newspaper publication, domestic and foreign), book
club, foreign book publication in hard and soft covers, comic book, dramatic, television, commercial--and probably one
or two I've forgotten.

Commercial rights?   If you've ever snuffed out a
cigarette in an ashtray bearing one of those garbled transla-
tions from the book Fractured French, or if, a dozen years
ago, you bought some youngster a Hopalong Cassidy gun-and-
holster set, you've seen these in profitable operation.

Simply printing and selling books seems to be regarded by most publishers these days as the least part of their
job.   Many of them are on record as saying that if it weren't
for the income from subsidiaries, they couldn't keep afloat.
One young man, Sol Stein, set up a new publishing house--
now in its second year--on the premise that in order to qualify for his list a manuscript must also be a prospect for book
club distribution, reprint, magazine sale, or some other form
of secondary exploitation.   With few exceptions, Stein has
stuck to his rule--and the firm of Stein & Day achieved the
considerable feat of winding up its first year in the black.
The Day of the company title is Mrs. Stein.   Between them,
along with all their other responsibilities, husband and wife
take care of the major details involved in the disposition of
subsidiary rights.

At the other end of the scale, Doubleday, one of the
biggest in the business, keeps a staff of twenty fully occupied handling subsidiaries.   There are special people to deal
with syndication of Doubleday books, with granting permissions for material to be included in anthologies, and with

commercial rights, foreign rights, and reprints.

When a book like The White House Years: Mandate
for Change 1953-1956, by Dwight D. Eisenhower, comes a-
long, virtually the full man- and woman-power of Doubleday's subsidiary rights division is mobilized to get the most
mileage out of it. This is a work that all the big magazines
were waiting in line for. Doubleday sent the top six mass-
circulation slicks copies of the manuscript, requesting that
bids for serialization be submitted by a specified date. The
offers came in on time, but none, in the publisher's estima-
tion, was adequate. Consequently, it was decided to explore
the possibilities of newspaper syndication.

Six hours of telephone calls around the country produced assurances from major newspapers in two dozen cities
of quite a bit more money and much more enthusiasm than
the magazine bids had promised. So, although it represented
a reversal of the usual way of doing business, Doubleday gave
first serial rights to the newspapers; and now that the book
is on the stands, it plans to approach medium-sized and
smaller dailies and offer them a second go at the twenty-
four instalments.

Commenting on the newspapers' response so far, from
the New York Times down the line, a Doubleday executive
observed: "It was as though they welcomed the opportunity
to show they still had some fight left where the magazines
were concerned. I think we have a field here we ought to
return to more often."

Mandate for Change was the November selection of the
Literary Guild and is to be distributed to members of the
Family Reading Club. (Both these organizations, by the way,
are Doubleday-operated.) Newspaper, periodical, and book
rights have been sold throughout the world. And contracts
for such other rights as motion picture, television, reprint
and documentary records have been, or soon will be, under
discussion.

A writer doesn't necessarily have to achieve the celebrity and best-seller status of a Robbins, Wallace, Michener, or Dwight D. Eisenhower to enjoy a lively spin on the
subsidiary-rights merry-go-round. Take Arthur Hailey and
his Flight into Danger. Originally conceived as a television
play, Hailey's modest but nervewracking little melodrama a-
bout an airliner in distress was given a series of produc-

tions by NBC in the U.S., CBC in Canada, the BBC in England, and ABC in Australia. All this stir attracted film-industry attention; a movie version, for which Hailey was signed to write the script, was released by Paramount. The picture crystallized publishing interest; with an assist from a collaborator, Hailey turned the story into a novel for Souvenir Press of London. Doubleday picked this up for American readers, bringing it out as Runway Zero Eight. A paperback reprint by Bantam followed, while foreign-language editions were proliferating all over the map.

Next, Ladies' Home Journal ran the book as a one-shot, and since then it has been serialized or published in abridged form in England, Australia, Belgium, France, Norway, Germany, and a few other places. Like the Flying Dutchman, Hailey's airplane with its crew incapacitated by food poisining is probably on the go somewhere at this very moment.

Broadway may be a book's open sesame to the fabled riches of Hollywood, besides constituting a potential source of lush subsidiary income in itself, My Sister Eileen traveled a path that led from publication as a series of bright New Yorker pieces to collection between book covers; thence to smash-hit stage adaptation; ultimately to films. In due course, someone had the idea of refurbishing the saga of the sisters from Columbus with songs and dances for another whirl in the theatre. Again, a bull's-eye. There was, in addition, a second cinematic Eileen, also with tunes. For good measure, the girls have been seen on TV and have enjoyed a flourishing career in summer stock, in music tents, and on the amateur circuit.

If Enter Laughing finally reaches the screen, as now appears likely, it will be thanks to the successful stage comedy derived from Carl Reiner's novel. The book about a stagestruck Bronx boy had been around and open to movie bids for several years. Similarly, picture producers became aware of the possibilities in Richard Bissell's 7 1/2 Cents and Douglass Wallop's The Year the Yankees Lost the Pennant after the Broadway boys had turned them into the musicals Pajama Game and Damn Yankees.

A typical printed publishing contract provides for the publisher to share to some extent in practically all of an author's subsidiary income. If opposition is encountered, the publisher will sometimes yield a point here or there. On

two specific clauses, however, there is enormous stubborn-
ness.   These are the clauses covering the division of reprint and book club proceeds.   Traditionally, such earnings
are split 50-50.   But lately, certain authors and agents have
been protesting.   Fifty per cent of, say $100,000 is an aw-
ful lot of money--and they ask if a publisher becomes entitled to $50,000 merely by virtue of accepting, printing,
advertising a book, and putting it up for sale.   Even conced-
ing that the publisher really may depend on his subsidiary
cut to stay in business, why should they, the successful
writers, subsidize the weak sisters--and if they must do it at
all, why give away so much?

     Publishers counter by reminding authors how they have
helped build their reputation, often at some initial loss to
themselves--and at cost to other authors who participated in
the same kind of 50-50 split.   They stress the commercial
values which hardcover publication confers upon a manuscript.
After all, without such publication how could there be any
reprint or book club rights to dispose of?

     The argument proceeds apace; but in spite of seeming
intransigence, change has been occurring.   One agent tells,
for example, how he negotiated a deal that netted an author
substantial extra income while permitting the 50-50 fiction to
be maintained.   The hardcover publisher simply paid the
writer $20,000 for the privilege of being allowed to do busi-
ness with him!

     Other special arrangements have been made with top-
selling authors that give them either the full amount of income from reprints or the equivalent thereof in some concession.   There is, as has been frequently remarked, more
than one way to flay a feline.

     In a well-nigh insatiable market the author of proved
appeal has become an object of wild competition among pur-
veyors of mass entertainment who need products.   A fancy
parlay in which Evan Hunter was the key figure set a pattern
a couple of years ago for much that has happened since.   Two
unwritten novels were at issue.   Simon and Schuster committed themselves to publishing both books in hard covers, paying a $25,000 advance for each and guaranteeing to spend an
equal amount, or more, on advertising.   Pocket Books closed
for reprint rights for another sizable sum.   Columbia Pictures bought in, to assure itself of screen rights to both novels should it want them; the price would be $100,000 apiece

plus a percentage of profits from the films if the books
showed up for a specified number of weeks on the New
York Times best-seller list.   Also, Columbia could avail
itself of Hunter's services as adapter of his book, at a pre-
agreed salary.   Additionally, a London publisher, Constable,
signed for both novels at L 2,000 advances.   All this without anyone--including, conceivably, the author himself--
knowing what the second of the two books, at least, was going to be about!

In the Publishers' Weekly column in which I broke the
news of Fawcett's deal for The Man, I reported also the
first noteworthy result of Dell Books' recent purchase of a
controlling interest in Dial Press, a hardcover house.   Acting in concert, the two companies contracted for Norman
Mailer's upcoming novel.   Dial will publish the original edition, which Dell later will reprint.   The agreement was
signed without any editor seeing a manuscript because there
was no manuscript to see.   Mailer's advance is a tidy
$125,000.

Hard- and softcover houses working in tandem represent ways in which publishers are endeavoring to keep valuable material out of rival hands.   Trident Press and Pocket
Books are so aligned that whatever Trident publishes in cloth
covers eventually ends up in paper under the Pocket Book
imprint.   These all-in-the-family arrangements, of course,
mean that there is no bidding in the open market on soft-
cover rights.   One can be pretty sure that contracts are so
drawn that no author feels he is losing money by disposing
of both hard- and softcover rights in a single package.

Largely because of the golden flood pouring in on them
from various subsidiary sources, a number of authors have
found it useful to form corporations.   This improves their
tax situation.   John O'Hara, one of the select company of the
corporate, has found it fiscally feasible to set a flat cash
price of $1,000,000 on Appointment in Samarra.   Someday
he may get it.   He has also placed a tag of $750,000 on the
three novellas comprising the set known as Sermons and Soda
Water.   In an idle moment I made some calculations that indicated that he was asking approximately $11.50 per word,
not excluding "and" and "the," for his little triptych.   Meanwhile he has sold a short story, "It's Mental Work," to television for what is coyly described as the highest price ever
paid by that medium.

While on the subject of corporations, note that a corporation calling itself Manuscripts, Inc., has set up shop under the umbrella, so to speak, of one of the largest publishing houses, McGraw-Hill Book Company, Inc. An author may sign over his rights in a book to Manuscripts, Inc., and become its "employee," starting off the relationship with a fat advance. Earnings from the book go into a "pool," from which corporation and author each receives disbursements. To qualify for employment by the corporation the author has to have a record as a top money-maker. In return, he becomes eligible for special benefits--whopping tax savings, in particular, if he chooses to live abroad--and a degree of financial security not built into the ordinary book contract. (There is provision for a pension, for example.)

Samuel Johnson undoubtedly spoke for a large element of the contemporary writing fraternity when he proclaimed: "No man but a blockhead ever wrote except for money." In our own time Niven Busch, author of Duel in the Sun, is on record with the assertion that "the writer who doesn't angle his books for film sales is an idiot." Expanding on this in a letter to my PW column, Busch said: "I don't mean that you have to distort or degrade your work to get it into some form that movie companies will buy. If you do that they generally won't buy it. What you have to do is select a subject, out of the many which pass through your mind, if you're worth anything as a writer--a subject which will appeal to a wide audience and hence merit, and probably get, exposure in films, television, and whatever electronic devices for communication the future may provide . . . ."

Sounding almost like a reply to the words I've italicized is E. B. White's statement in The Elements of Style: "The whole duty of a writer is to please and satisfy himself, and the true writer always plays to an audience of one. Let him start sniffing the air, or glancing at the Trend Machine, and he is as good as dead, although he may make a nice living."

Details of that million-dollar deal for Harold Robbins's The Adventurers, mentioned at the beginning of this article, were made public at a press conference. Trident Press, Pocket Books, and Embassy Pictures all were represented and identified as co-signatories with Robbins. It was indicated that the author planned to start work on the new novel and movie script together and ride the two steeds neck and neck, crossing the finish line on both at approximately the

same time.   He acknowledged that while it had indeed been
a pleasure to sign the contracts, he rather dreaded the next
step, the actual writing.   And who can blame him?

As the rights race gathers speed, it looks more and
more as though what goes into a book is less important than
what's to be got out of it.

Paperback to Front

From the Times Literary Supplement no. 3300:425-6, May
27, 1965.   Copyright by Times Newspapers Limited.   Reprinted by permission.

The starting point of this article is the end of the paperback revolution.   Three years ago the total volume of
paperbacks sold had risen by four times from 1952 to a figure of 80 million and the expansion has not slackened in pace
since then.   The years of amazement at the industry's
growth; the years where article after article showed a "national cake" with Penguins having this share, Pan having that
share and the rest of the cake distributed between Corgi,
Panther, New English Library and others--these years are,
or should be, over.   This contribution is both argument and
prediction.   It begins with the present place of the paperback
and the economic reality of that place, and it is confined to
two fundamental points of general interest for reader, publisher and author.

The present place of the paperback can be simply
stated: wherever there is a consumer need or a producer's
opportunity for cheap, reasonably durable communication on
any subject and at any level, there a paperback will be found,
very much cheaper than a hardback book and more durable
than a Sunday newspaper supplement or a magazine.   It is a
sign of the times that the Honest to God controversy started
and has continued in paperback.

Where thirty years ago Sir Allen Lane's Penguins were
a marginal novelty, his and his competitors' books are now
the centre of the nation's book trade.   Cheap hardback editions, the lending libraries of Smiths, Boots and The Times
--all these are either going or have already gone.   Specialist
paperback bookshops are growing rapidly in number, and the
turnover from university students supports a steady issue of
"egghead" paperbacks, both by traditional hardback publishers
and by established paperback houses.   The growth of the egghead market, to examine that end of the trade for a moment,

can be seen in terms simply of production and print runs.
Ten years ago most eggheads were manufactured in America
and distributed marginally in Great Britain. Five years ago
the market had grown to the point where a hardback publisher with a suitable back-list could afford to produce an egghead series by either simply binding up surplus stock in paper covers or by spreading the load of a reprint between the
libraries and the student market. Now in 1965 the Peregrine
series has, according to the spine numbering at any rate,
produced nearly fifty titles in something like three years.
The market is now able to support a print run for paperback
alone.

As the range of the paperback has extended over every
area of general publishing, so terms offered by paperback
publishers have moved dramatically upwards. It is no secret
that the terms for the first Penguins were near a 5 per cent
royalty with a very modest advance. In 1965 popular best
selling fiction titles will easily command from every interested paperback house a 12-1/2 per cent royalty on the published price and from many houses an advance of up to and
over £15,000. Advances in the £3,000 to £10,000 range no
longer amaze. This dramatic change in the income to the
author, from a marginal cheque to a sum that will buy him
a house, heralds the first fundamental shift that this article
examines. The prime source of income for author and agent
must sooner or later become the prime economic power. At
the moment the author licenses to his hardback publisher
both hardback and paperback rights and receives in return a
royalty on the hardback edition that rises from 10 per cent
of published price. If the hardback publisher manages to dispose of paperback rights then he passes to the author only
50 per cent of proceeds from that edition. The Publishers
Association Standard Guide to Royalty Agreements unabashed-
ly equates revenue from a best-seller paperback edition of a
novel with revenue from permission to put a few paragraphs
of it in a work of criticism; in each case the hardback publisher retains 50 per cent of the proceeds. This position
has been strenuously held by hardback publishers but under
pressure from authors and agents a split of proceeds that
gives 60 per cent to the author and 40 per cent only to the
publisher is now considered possible for exceptional cases.

This marginal concession cannot, however, satisfy
either author, agent or paperback publisher for long. A split
that did not matter because of the small amount of revenue
twenty-five years ago begins to look rather unreasonable

where the market value of the author's work has risen so
much that sometimes the hardback publisher can subsidize
the whole of his edition by his share of the first half of the
paperback publisher's advance. Nor can the paperback publishers be long content with a situation that denies them direct access to the people for whose work they are paying
such high sums, nor indeed can they be happy at being ma-
nipulated against each other by hardback publishers in what
amounts to a perpetual auction of leading authors.

The key figure here may be the author's agent who is
in a stronger position than a disparate force of individual
authors. He wants, and rightly so, the best possible return
for his author in terms of money and personal service and
if the economic return shifts over to the paperback publisher
then it is with the paperback publisher that the agent, sooner
or later, will directly deal.

If the author can get substantially more money direct
from the paperback publisher than the 50 per cent or even
60 per cent from the hardback publisher at present brings
him, and if his revenue from a run in hardback covers on
licence from a paperback publisher could bring in as much
or even almost as much as his present direct revenue from
the hardback publisher, then it follows, as night follows day,
that agents and paperback publishers will sometime in the
next decade stand the present trade practice on its head.
There is, after all, nothing sacrosanct about it.

What difference does it make to the reader whether
the hardcover book he buys for money in a shop is controlled
ultimately by the hardback publisher or by a paperback publisher? What difference does it make to the author whether
he derives his income directly from the hardback publisher
and indirectly from the paperback publisher or directly from
the paperback publisher and indirectly from the hardback
publisher? The only differences may increasingly be in favour of control of volume rights being placed in the paperback
publisher's hands. The crucial factor will be the ability of
the paperback publisher to satisfy the author's agent that returns from the paperback royalty will be high and that hardback returns will continue near the present rate.

The possibility may be looked at in terms of the cherished argument of the hardback publisher that he is a vital
servant of literature since he chooses talent and supports it,
knowing full well that his author may never come out in pa-

perback at all and may need support for three or four novels. If current practice is reversed, are we not in any danger of losing books that are of high quality, but which are
not suited to mass exploitation? The answer is two-fold.
First, the concept of the paperback market as an exercise
in mass exploitation only is breaking down. As the range of
paperback has expanded so the economic possibilities in paperback have expanded. Who could have foreseen five years
ago that volumes of contemporary poets would sell in the
twenty and thirty thousands? Yet, if the copyright pages of
Penguin Modern Poets are accurate, these are the numbers
in which this series now sells. The second part of the answer lies in the spread of production costs that paperback
printing allows for both a paperback edition and a hardback
edition, manufactured from the same type.

Let us look in terms of these two answers at a particular problem--the first novel of promise by an unknown
author. This is a problem in fiction which bedevils the trade
and for which even the ingenuity and courage of Hutchinson's
New Authors Idea have not really been sufficient. Which of
the following alternatives better serves both author and consumer?

(a) Publication (as at present) in hardback of
     1,200 copies at 18s.--no paperback contract--
     good reviews--complete oblivion within three
     months.

(b) Publication (as foreseen here) in hardback of
     1,200 copies at 18s.--good reviews--complete
     oblivion within three months, redeemed by a
     short paperback edition when the book can still
     be recalled by the public and when the paper-
     back can be run off on the same print run as
     the hardback edition.

One must not overweigh the argument. The unknown
first novelist will always be a publisher's headache but at
least under (b) consumer and author have a better chance of,
respectively, reading and being read, and--not least--the
publisher is able to spread his risk. He acquires volume
rights from the author or from his agent and makes an advance in respect of both hardback and paperback editions.
He sets up the type and manufactures a hardback edition
which is frankly for libraries and reviewers in the main.
This is published, most probably by a separate hardback

house, in order to establish the book in public libraries
and, through the review columns, as a work of literary merit. The paperback publisher retains only a small percentage
of these royalties since he regards a hardback edition as
mainly a shop window device (which is not far from the
present reality). After an interval, dictated by the nature
of the book, the paperback edition, which may be as low as
7,500 copies, is bound up for the shops. The type may be
further used perhaps for a paperback book club edition, for
again the structure of the present book club trade is not
sacrosanct. The demand for paperback books is enormous:
the outlets for paperback books cannot match the demand:
therefore, has the time not come for a paperback book
club? Into this club, and from the same type again, first
novels of promise could be fed together with more established books.

This example shows how the spread of production
costs by concentration of rights in the paperback publisher's
hands meshes in with the lowering of the maximum paperback run that the market can now stand. Together they suggest a new pattern of fiction publishing that might offer the
author and the public a better service than the present structure of the trade allows. Indeed the present structure is
showing a gradual shrinking of fiction publishing. Some senior firms, e.g., Methuen, seem virtually to have abandoned
the first novel altogether and others, e.g., Chatto and Win-
dus, must surely find the issuing of good quality first novels
a losing, if bravely fought battle. The argument for reversing current trade practice at least deserves consideration in
the author's, if in no one else's, interests.

The second fundamental shift over the next decade will
be the invasion of the traditional educational market by the
paperback. Whatever change in practice there may be for
the general trade, the fact is that turnover from such trade
alone is not sufficient to give a reasonable return to a type
of business whose overhead costs of distribution and promotion are very heavy. Indeed, the additional staff that the
change foreseen above would involve would make some di-
versification essential. If we were living in the 1930s with
a wealth of talent in fiction the situation might be different,
but there are no more major back-list authors to be plun-
dered and there are too few current bestsellers. The paperback publisher must diversify and there can be no doubt
where he is going. From Newsom to Robbins the road to the

educational market is clear.   The fundamental shift will be
to the direct commissioning of paperback textbooks. These
textbooks may range from books in primary mathematics to
books for final-year degree courses in English literature,
but the trend is unmistakable.   Pergamon Press have been
energetic for some time and neither the Signet Shakespeare
nor the Penguin/Nuffield project in science is a by-product.
The Signet Shakespeare is clearly aimed directly at students
and its considerable success in Great Britain, set against
its American origins and overtones, clearly points the way
to student paperback editions on an immense range of subjects by indigenous publishers, both hardback and paperback.
That Penguins, the senior paperback firm, will in some way
follow up the Nuffield project is not hard to guess (presumably one of Sir Edward Boyle's attractions to Penguins is
that he is a former Minister of Education), but more in-
triguing, perhaps, is whether traditional hardback educational publishers will move to some form of paperback publication.   As the techniques for binding and toughening paperback covers improve, one of the diehard classroom and com-
mon-room arguments against the paperback will lose force.
Simultaneous publication in hard and paper covers is now
considered feasible for the university textbook market and
sooner or later the paperback textbook will surely cover a
great range of school work.

If, with whatever minor reservations, the two fundamental shifts outlined above take place, what is left for the
hardback publisher?   Three tasks would remain.   First and
obviously a hardback house would act in fiction as a pace-
maker and window dresser for the paperback.   It could either
link up financially with a paperback house or else, given sufficient money and energy, expand its own paperback distribution to such an extent that it acts as window dresser for itself.   Pace-making and window dressing will be a necessary
part of the structure of publishing for many years to come
both in fiction and in certain types of non-fiction.

The second task follows on naturally from the invasion of the educational field.   However advanced paperback
techniques may become there must be some lower limit to
the number of copies that have to be produced to make economic sense.   As higher education expands, so the market
for specialized non-fiction at university and technical college
level will expand and areas that the paperback cannot touch
can be explored in depth by a hardback.   This type of publishing is, of course, already familiar in imprints such as Rout-

ledge and Kegan Paul, Methuen, and Allen and Unwin. More
recently the Faber and Michael Joseph series on sociology
are portents of things to come.   The flood of publishers visiting new universities will clearly not abate.

        Thirdly there is a whole area of general publishing
particularly in memoirs, biographies and what might be
called the "elegancies of history" at which hardback publishers are particularly adept and in which the paperback seems
curiously impotent.   Whatever, for example, happened to the
Penguin Biography Series?   In a special cover and with a
special by-line, this series made a brief appearance at the
end of the 1950s and has not been heard of since.   The author who is writing a hefty readable study of an historical
figure or a period in history may be advised by his agent to
contract still with a hardback publisher from whom the returns on a selling price of up to 42s. may well outweigh any
direct arrangement with a paperback publisher.   The immense success of the Collins/Eyre and Spottiswoode edition
of Lady Violet Bonham Carter's Winston Churchill As I Knew
Him could probably not have been achieved directly in paperback.

        There is, then, no need for the hardback trade to
despair, but the two shifts that this article foresees may increasingly force the smaller houses to streamline editorial
policy and make the larger ones clarify their relationships
both with paperback publishers and with paperback imprints
of their own.

Art Book Publishing Today

By Thomas G. Rosenthal, Managing Director, Thames and
Hudson International Ltd.

From the Times Literary Supplement no. 3460:646-7, June
20, 1968. Copyright by Times Newspapers Limited. Reprinted by permission.

As with many other subjects it is, inevitably, much
easier to say what a subject is not, rather than what it is.
Art book publishing is not, nor was it ever, the same thing
as coffee-table book publishing, a confusion which does exist
in certain places . . .

The other confusion that exists is between books that
deal with the fine arts and those which deal with other subjects which lend themselves to copious illustration, such as
archaeology, architecture or history. This is a more understandable confusion, like that which, for years, caused people
to refer to all paperbacks as Penguins. Let us assume,
therefore, that the terms "art book" and "illustrated book"
are interchangeable and refer to any book on a serious non-
fictional subject where the illustrations are essential and of
more or less equal importance with the text.

It should not be necessary at this moment in time, and
for readers of this journal, to expand on the international aspects of art book publishing, since most people are by now
familiar with the concept of printing the illustrations simultaneously for several countries at once, thus enabling a heavily illustrated work to be published at a price which a general, instead of a select, monied public can afford. This is now
so well established as to need no comment. What, unfortunately, seems to be almost equally well established, is a series of false ideas about the international process.

The most popular of these ideas, perhaps because it is
the most appealing in a world where Mogul and The Plane-

makers dominate public taste more than one might care to
admit, is that of the publishing super-tycoon, a kind of literary Sir John Wilder who pulls an idea out of his briefcase
and before you can say "remainder!" has sold it to publishers in seventeen different countries, collected a small fortune in advances, and only then goes home to execute (I
choose my word carefully) the product.   Serious art book
publishing simply does not work that way; the method just
indicated, if it exists at all (I suspect it is a creation of
the gossip columns rather than an actual publishing method),
is only applicable to books of trivial importance and value,
which probably ought not to exist and when they do, often
tend to produce, among the participating publishers, burnt
fingers which stretch well up to the elbow.

If a large, or small, illustrated book is worth doing
at all, the publisher backs his judgment, since that, after
all, is his raison d'étre as a middleman of literature and
scholarship, and goes it alone.   Having, therefore, made an
irrevocable decision to go ahead, he commissions his authors and his outside editors; his academically highly qualified picture research staff do their vital and imaginative
work and, in close collaboration with the author, he prepares
the layout and makes a dummy.   Having done that, he then,
and only then, whirls round the world selling what is, in effect, a completed book to publishers in as many countries
as possible.

This brings one to the second and related international myth, that of co-production and publishing consortia.   Co-
production is, of course, a useful shorthand term to describe
the international publishing process.   It should, however, be
applied only to the question of simultaneous production of
physical material, i. e., the illustrations only or, sometimes,
the complete book.   When it becomes a matter of editorial
content, publishing goes out of the window and is replaced by
a kind of richly aromatic literary stew.   If you have a consortium preparing the "product," as opposed to a single publisher creating a book, then the inevitably too many cooks
equally inevitably spoil the book.   Publishers, fortunately,
are highly differentiated individualists, who spend their working lives pitting their editorial tastes against those of their
competitors.   They all know, or at least think they know,
what their books should contain.   Consequently any member
of a publishing consortium, particularly if he has, as the
Americans say, put his money where his mouth is, will want
to make his contribution to the contents of the book.   The re-

sults are all too easily imaginable in the case, for example, of a history of modern painting, pre-sold to a dozen countries. Each country will want its own folk heroes in, to please its own public, regardless of their actual status in any objective international survey. The result of this kind of thing is, almost invariably, one of those grey, spineless books which offends no one and, therefore, pleases no one. (Incidentally this principle works, alas, all too well in the field of literature; the preceding sentence could equally well apply to those books chosen to receive international literary prizes before publication--to the best lobbyist the spoils.)

It may no doubt sound arrogant to say that the best international publishing works on the good old-fashioned principle of take it or leave it; but that, quite simply, is true. But then, whoever heard of a serious novelist deliberately inserting a scene set in Outer Mongolia in order to capture the reading public there? The two most successful books ever published by Thames and Hudson are Herbert Read's Concise History of Modern Painting and The Dawn of Civilization, edited by Stuart Piggott. Both have been translated by, not adapted for, every major publishing country in the world, with the usual exceptions of Russia and China. The Dawn of Civilization was written by a team of exclusively British scholars and deals with a field, pre-history, which is studied, and taught by experts, all over the world. But it was conceived for, published for, and bought by a completely international public.

Herbert Read's book is probably the most extraordinary case of all. As one would expect of any book on this subject, containing less than ten thousand pictures and a million words, it is highly personal, subjective and even, on occasion, eclectic. Yet it is, I think, precisely for these reasons that this remarkable book, tailored to no man's taste other than its author's, has appeared in all the usual languages, and in Japanese, Hebrew, Hungarian, Serbo-Croat, &c., and has sold over half a million copies.

Naturally, to be able to produce a sales figure like that is music to any publisher's ear, and he who denies it is merely a hypocrite; but the pleasures are more than financial. In the first place, when sales figures like that are normally achieved only by the Harold Robbins and Irving Wallaces of this world, it is heartening that such an intellectually uncompromising book can also be sold on such a scale. Sec-

ondly, the book is a triumphant vindication of the principle
of illustration and its natural corollary, international publication.

It is, of course, perfectly possible that Read's book
would have sold as many copies if it had been either unillus-
trated or accompanied by a few pages of plates separated
from the text. Possible, but unlikely, since to read about a
work of art without having at least a small reproduction of
it in front of you for reference purposes, is both frustrating
and unnecessary. On the other hand, to provide nearly 500
illustrations, in a book that was first published at 28s., is,
without international support, either ruinous or quixotic.
But, by the time the dummy of the whole book had been
shown to publishers in America and Europe, the total first
printing came to more than 100,000 copies, and what had
seemed at first to be an enormous risk became financially
as well as aesthetically valid.

Not all art books can be printed in such quantities,
nor are they all, in the sense of multiple editions, international. Occasionally a book will be printed in only one language and in a very small edition. However, it is the function of the art book publisher to publish virtually any book
which deserves publication on grounds of the scholarship of
the author and the interest of the subject matter. Clearly it
would be difficult to publish commercially a monograph on,
say, the misericords in a particular parish church. That,
clearly, is work for the local antiquarian society or, possibly,
a university press. But most art-historical subjects not as
esoteric as that last example can, and should, be worth publishing.

And then, to use a platitude, if a book is worth publishing it is worth publishing properly. If the book is going
to appeal to only a limited number of people then one should
budget accordingly. A typical case is the recent Catalogue
Raisonné of Daumier by K. E. Maison. After careful market
research it became clear that this massive piece of scholarship would appeal only to a limited number of libraries, private collectors and art dealers. Consequently it was decided
to print only 1,500 copies in English for the whole world,
and it was further decided that, within reason, price was not
a vital consideration. The book is thus very expensive
(which should not be confused with poor value; Rolls Royces
are not cheap). This does not mean that the publishers are

making a huge profit; probably the publisher's profit is lower than usual since the book consumed far more in overheads, in terms of time spent on layout, proof-reading &c., than many of our best-sellers. But it does mean that the author could be paid a reasonable royalty, at least partially to compensate him for the work of a quarter of a century; although, such is the situation of some scholars today, in terms of hard cash Mr. Maison would probably have done better to sweep the streets. It also means that we could spend a great deal of money on the production of the book, so that its physical quality could match its distinguished scholarship.

This, naturally, is an extreme case, but it does make the point that not all art book publishing is a matter of huge multi-lingual editions. Every year many distinguished art books are published in small editions in English, French, German and other languages and are not translated because the academic and institutional community, to which they appeal, is a small one which will buy the book in its original language. Both the time interval, and the cost factor involved in translation for the even smaller separate national markets, render separate publication both uneconomical as well as unnecessary. English publishers are, naturally, better off here than their continental counterparts, because of the American market, and we are often able to publish distinguished works of scholarship on, say, Archaic Greek Gems, whose market in the Commonwealth alone would not be adequate, but when combined with an American publisher, often a University Press, becomes sufficient for successful publication.

I have dealt mainly with questions of quantity since these, ultimately are any publisher's greatest problem. Yet for an art book publisher the quantity problem takes no longer to solve than for the fiction publisher. Market research is rarely performed and the vital factor is, almost invariably, inspired guesswork, with some publishers being more inspired than others. What makes the publishing of illustrated books different from, for example, novels or technical books, is a variety of aspects ranging from the contribution of the publisher to the attitudes of the public.

By referring to the publisher's contribution I am not, of course, belittling that of the author. The author stands or falls by the quality of the text alone and, apart from the normal editorial function of unsplitting the odd infinitive and spotting an inaccurately typed date, the publisher does not have much effect on the text beyond that of his detail initial briefing in the case of a commissioned, as opposed to a spontaneously generated, book.   Where the publisher's real function lies, in addition to the obvious marketing and promotional skills which apply equally to all kinds of books, is in the provision of the illustrations and the design and layout of the book to make it a useful tool rather than a merely decorative object.   This function is, in its way, as complex as the writing of the text and, when well done, is entirely complementary.

Good picture research for an illustrated book is far from simple.   One cannot just use a picture because it is attractive; it also has to be relevant, functional and not over familiar, and usually as much time is spent on this by the publisher's staff as is spent by the author in writing his text. Only when all the words and pictures are ready can the publisher begin the layout and relate the two parts of the book to each other, so that the reader can use the book with as much ease and rationality as possible.

Here one comes to the somewhat controversial questions of size and production quality.   Different books, to use another platitude, are created for different people.   A paperback on Impressionism is aimed at the really general public and the student, whether sixth-former or undergraduate. They all want a comprehensive, but reasonably brief, text, with a lot of pictures in colour and black-and-white, for very little money.   Therefore one has to use a cheap printing process and relatively low quality paper, and one must print a lot of copies.   Inevitably the pictures are small and, because of the limitations of printing and paper quality, neither wholly accurate nor wholly beautiful.   Yet the purpose of these pictures is not to substitute for the experience of looking at a work of art--nothing can do that--nor to act as decoration.   Their purpose is to act as points of reference for the reader, which is why one makes great efforts to put the picture on the same page as the text which describes it, and to illustrate the thesis of the author.   Perhaps none of this needs saying; but there does seem to be a feeling about that many illustrations are just so much window dressing and commercial flummery, without relevance to the matter of the book.

Another misconception that exists is the feeling that

big books are unnecessarily big.   Perhaps they are, but it
is surely somewhat wide of the mark to complain that they
are not easily read on a railway journey or in bed.   How
many people actually want to read something like The Flowering of the Middle Ages between London and Crewe, or as
a suitable soporific after Late Night Line Up?   Books like
this are meant to be read in a clean, well-lighted place, at
either desk or table (unstained by coffee cups).   They are
large so that they can accommodate within a reasonable number of pages a text the length of three average novels, and
a large number of relevant pictures, maps, chronological
charts, line drawings, &c.   The pictures themselves are large
so that they can, as is both author's and publisher's intention, adequately communicate both images and ideas.

Such books are also frequently accused of being glossy,
as if glossiness were a crime.   They are indeed glossy, both
inside and out.   The outside, that is the jacket, is glossy
because a laminated jacket is stronger than an unlaminated
one and, also, does not get dirty in handling.   The inside,
that is the illustration sections, is glossy because one gets
a far better looking, and more faithful reproduction of the
photographs on shiny paper which does not absorb too much
ink.

Readers who have persevered this far might have noticed a somewhat defensive note creeping into this article.
This is because the publication of illustrated books is something of an uphill struggle in this country, not commercially
(although obviously the risks are greater) but intellectually.
There is, I think, a clearly discernible prejudice in the Ang-
lo-Saxon mind against books with a lot of pictures--a prejudice which, like other prejudices, is simultaneously irration-
al and based on reasons with their roots in the national psyche.   Most, it seems, go back to the more than vestigial
Puritanism which is so strong still.   The best knowledge is
hard-won knowledge and, if the story is partially told in pictures and is thus more readily assimilated, then that is a
bad thing.   Also, what is beautiful tends to be, at worst, sin-
ful and, at best, frivolous.   In other words, heavily illustrated books are not serious.   They can be bought as presents for Aunt Edna, but not for use by oneself.

This is clearly reflected in the way in which such
books are reviewed in the British press.   Naturally in the
technical journals they are soberly and lengthily assessed.
A reviewer in the Burlington or Antiquity will deal compe-

tently with text and pictures, taking both in his stride as
natural bedfellows; but the non-specialist press tends to treat
the illustrated book as a poor relation.   The one notable exception is this journal which for all the occasional viciousness
which is apparently endemic in anonymous reviewing, does at
least take illustrated books seriously and regards the texts as
more than an appendage to the pictures.   In the general
press, however, the situation is radically different.

Naturally all of a publisher's geese are swans, since
even Barabbas was human, but most publishers, I suspect,
would rather see one of their books honestly attacked than
coolly nodded at en passant.   What is so profoundly depress-
ing is the relegation of a book, representing years of hard
work by author and publisher, to the Christmas round up of
"gift books."   Worse still is the habit of taking a striking
picture from a book and putting a two or three line caption
underneath it.   Naturally one appreciates the reason for this.
A page of solid type is thus brightened and a book which
would otherwise escape mention is brought to the attention of
the public.   For the publisher it does not make all that much
difference.   If it is a bad book it will not sell anyway and,
if it is good, it will.   What is so galling is the wording of
the captions, which, neglecting to pass a verdict on the text,
regularly resound with phrases like "another sumptuous album
from" and "a glamorous picture book published by."   The
reductio ad absurdum was reached not so long ago, when one
of the Sunday "heavies" printed a picture and caption to mark
the publication of a series of thoroughly sober and unglamor-
ous books dealing with various aspects of Greek and Roman
life, half of which are not even illustrated at all.

The real victim here is not the publisher but the author, who might well have spent up to five years writing
100,000 words or more which are thus summarily dismissed
with the word "album."   Possibly a definitive study of, say,
Chagall would be more circumspectly treated if it had no pictures, and perhaps the publisher is at fault in adding 1,000
pictures to the text.   But what use is a text about a painter
without reproductions of the works listed and referred to?

The fact is that by supporting a text with copious illustrations one runs the risk, in this country, of depriving
the author of serious criticism in the more influential newspapers and journals.   Fortunately, one does, at the same
time, know the presence of the illustrations helps to ensure
that serious works of scholarship have a much greater chance

of being translated into several languages.

The review media apart, however, the current illustrated book publishing scene is extremely encouraging. As our society and its educational system become increasingly more visual, publishers can take advantage of improved printing techniques and graphic design to produce more adventurous books and, unquestionably, the art book revolution has had effects on public taste which, if not as far-reaching as those of the paperback revolution, are, nevertheless, particularly important in the history of ideas and their reception. The much greater appreciation of the previously neglected Baroque and Mannerist periods owes a great deal to the publishers who first took the risks involved in producing handsome books on what was previously unfashionable.

The good art book publisher should and can act as a patron, both in the present and retrospectively. Working closely with art historians and critics, he can help to make and reassess reputations. Sir Anthony Blunt has revolutionized our knowledge and understanding of Poussin; Graham Sutherland owes much of his current reputation to Douglas Cooper's monograph; the interim assessment of Francis Bacon by John Rothenstein and Ronald Alley helped to focus attention on an artist at that time not yet occupying his present peak. For some reason, doubtless connected with the nature of the visual as opposed to the verbal image, such books seem to be more influential more rapidly than the equivalent pioneering works of literary criticism.

Perhaps art books and illustrated books on history, &c., do occupy an honourable place in the culture of our society. Certainly they seem to be essential for the proper communication of ideas and for the true understanding of certain subjects. As Hugh Trevor-Roper has written in his introduction to the forthcoming The Age of Expansion:

> This is the seventh volume in a series which
> seeks to illustrate as well as to describe the
> history of civilization, and by its illustrations
> not merely to enliven but to deepen the study
> and understanding of that history. . . . Faced
> by the vast expansion of our field, we have
> called in the new world of photographic repro-
> duction, which informs through the eyes, to
> redress the imbalance of the old, purely literary

method, channelled exclusively through the
mind. "

Are Business Books Really Necessary?

By Thomas O'Hanlon, Senior Editor, <u>Dun's Review and Modern Industry</u>.

Reprinted by permission from <u>Dun's Review and Modern Industry</u> 85:44-5+, April 1965. © 1965 Dun and Bradstreet Publications Corporation.

The way to protect your business in the event of a nuclear attack is to set up a line of executive succession, build bomb shelters and decentralize facilities.

You can succeed in the mail-order business by finding out what the other fellow is doing successfully "and follow suit."

To cheat on personality tests, simply answer "as if you were like everybody else is supposed to be."

Success in company politics comes from impressing "the right people."

If you want a job with an American oil company in Arabia, it is preferable to be a married man with grown children rather than a "drunk, wife dodger, gambler, troublemaker or confidence man."

A successful salesman must do "what Diamond Jim Brady did for steel railroad cars."

Companies who want to sell to Negroes should hire Negroes.

Of all the ways to enter the advertising business, the best way is just to "butt in."

Profit-conscious executives can surmount the greatest challenge by turning the managerial staff "into a real team."

317

The scientific method of selecting executive personnel is to establish qualitative standards against which to
measure the candidates.

When starting a new job, free your mind from personal affairs.

White collar unions can be held at bay by "treating the
clerks better than the production workers."

Tautology?   Of course.   Yet each of these pieces of
information has been padded into a book in recent years.   Indeed, despite the fact that less than half of the American
population ever reads a book, and only one in five ever buys
one, the business-book market is, to say the least, booming.   This year more than 1,000 titles will be added to those
already in print, and not a single job classification, it seems,
not even the most arcane area of industry or management,
has been overlooked.   Whether the subject is applied operational planning, supervisory training, controlling of finances
of a foreign subsidiary, taxes, technology, automation, cy-
bernation, motivation or executive stress, there are a dozen
or more books to choose from.

The most emphasized field of all appears to be management, which is broken into a constellation of categories.
There are books on top management, middle management, office management, industrial management, manufacturing man-
agement, factory management, field sales management, dis-
trict sales management, sales management, materials manage-
ment, maintenance management, small-business management,
line management, project management, safety management,
management science and risk management.   The variations
are endless.   Author J. D. Batten has followed up his Tough-
Minded Management, a best seller according to the American
Management Association, with Developing a Tough-Minded
Climate . . . for Results.

In the event that even the most voracious reader might
be daunted by this outpouring of prose, it is hardly surprising that one trade association is selling an expensive executive course "to help improve reading skills."   Among other
bric-a-brac, this course provides booklets of instruction,
reading tests and quizzes, and myriad gadgets all designed to
help the harassed businessman get through the flood of words
other businessmen are trying to sell him.

What all this adds up to, of course, is an insatiable public appetite for specialized knowledge. As critic Dwight Macdonald puts it: "The fact is, the country is in the grip of a how-to mania comparable to the dancing mania that swept over Europe in the fourteenth century."

This condition is fueled in part by what Princeton economist Fritz Machlup calls "the knowledge industry." Machlup asserts that this particular segment of American business has been expanding at a rate 2.5 times faster than the Gross National Product, and that "knowledge workers," those engaged in technical, professional and managerial occupations, will constitute half the American work force by the 1980s.

Since the knowledge workers' stock-in-trade is the possession and interpretation of facts, it is hardly surprising that the publishing industry has reaped rich rewards by simply binding sets of facts between hard covers. But the demand for how-to books is far broader than the engineer's need for a textbook, or the actuary's dependence on a statistical tome to tell him the life expectancy of a 45-year-old nonsmoking laborer of Balkan descent. The fact is that 80% of all knowledge workers, according to a survey conducted by Dr. Gerald Gurin, get ego satisfaction from their work, compared with 39% of clerical workers and 29% of unskilled workers. They are, therefore, from the publisher's point of view, prime prospects for books about themselves, their jobs and business in general.

The publishers seemingly are hard put to keep up with the demand for this specialized form of literature, which ideally should afford a vicarious pleasure to the knowledge worker without the guilt hangover that would follow, say, reading a Mickey Spillane thriller. And the ideal book in the genre, as far as the publishers are concerned, is something that combines the Puritan attitude towards money-making, such as Benjamin Franklin's The Art of Making Money, in Every Man's Pocket, with the current demand for facts. Thus we have E. Joseph Cossman's How I Made $1,000,000 in Mail Order and Nicolas Darvas' How I Made $2,000,000 in the Stock Market, books incorporating a technique that one editor calls "particularizing the generalization."

Most authors, however, find it hard to write in this split-level, best-selling style. More of a bread-and-butter item in business-book publishing is the inspirational tract--

although today the unctuous rhetoric of the Twenties and
Thirties is toned down.

A model of its kind is The Golden Book of Selling by
Eugene Whitmore, a collection of stories about salesmen who
were not "just snagging random orders," but whose ingenuity
and selflessness saved many a business from bankruptcy.
For the salesman on the run, who might not have time to
draw his own conclusions, Whitmore has added, at the end of
each of the fourteen short chapters, ten pensees on the meaning of salesmanship. Particularly striking is this observation: "American Indians built their tepees above rich coal
deposits, fabulous oil fields, veins of gold and fertile soils.
Trouble was, they didn't know how to sell. They just traded."

Because inspirational books such as Whitmore's are
aimed at a mass audience, and are often bought in job lots
for distribution at conventions, or given as prizes, they
must have universal appeal. Thus the characters who come
alive on the pages of The Golden Book of Selling form a mi-
crocosm of society, a kind of melting-pot sales force with
all ethnic groups democratically represented. Marcus Wein-
baum sells clothing; Carl Bauer, fertilizer; J. L. Holt, se-
curities; Ted Grady, paper; Frank Lando, office equipment.

When judging a salesman, says Whitmore, appearances
can be deceptive. He recalls one man "who worked a few
counties in southern Virginia and North Carolina," but whose
sartorial appearance was not up to snuff. "Boy," recalls
Whitmore, "did I get a shock when I met him! Looking like
the theatrical version of the country doctor, he was six feet
tall, round-shouldered and so loosely jointed that he walked
in a shamble."

Pushing on to Nashville, Tennessee, Whitmore was
even more surprised: This salesman was a born clown. He
was short, bowlegged, had overlong arms, a sandy-freckled
face with wide mouth and large eyes--all seeming to spell
out comedy. His laugh made you think a giant was roaring.
His deep bass voice had a commanding note, and I later
learned he had been a first sergeant in an infantry company
in World War I. . . . Yes . . . his nickname was Shorty,
and I never heard anyone call him anything else."

Whatever their physical characteristics, salesmen are
human, says Whitmore, "and at times become involved with
attractions--women, booze, gambling--which wreck many a

sales career. They may occasionally go daffy over baseball, football or other laudable sports."

Summing it all up, Whitmore says: "Medical Men
boast about the conquest of disease by miracle drugs. Yet
who was it but salesmen who took these drugs and taught
medical men how to use them?" To drive home the point,
he concludes: "Countries where people do not understand
creative salesmanship are the impoverished, underdeveloped
areas of the world."

A proven formula

Since creative salesmanship, inspiration and how-toism
have proven salable commodities by themselves, it seems
logical that a combination of all three ingredients would prove
irresistible. A promotional brochure might read something
like this:

> Now . . . the Masters of Success . . . the
> truly GIANT Motivators and Salesmen of the
> twentieth century give you a lifetime of Ac-
> quired Knowledge . . . the secrets of how to
> tap your Full Potential . . . how to transform
> generalized dreams into specific reality . . .
> how to materially, spiritually, mentally bring
> the Double Crown of Success and Personal
> Happiness to your life.

This is precisely the way a salesman named Paul J.
Meyer describes his company, Success Motivation Institute,
Inc. of Waco, Texas. The motto of Success Motivation is:
"Whatever you vividly imagine, ardently desire, sincerely be-
lieve and enthusiastically act upon . . . must inevitably
come to pass," a doctrine first propounded by a monk named
Pelagius, who was resoundingly condemned for his error by
the Council of Ephesus in 431.

For $180, Meyer sells a personal success package,
featuring the "International Masters of Success." The roster
includes Napoleon Hill, who spent 25 years "researching" his
book Think and Grow Rich; Charles L. ("Chuck") Lapp, professor of marketing at Washington University in St. Louis,
Missouri, "author of nine successful books in the field of
selling;" Richard Borden, "Mr. Sales Trainer U.S.A.;"
Frank Bettger, author of How I Raised Myself from Failure
to Success in Selling; Dr. Norman Vincent Peale, author of

The Power of Positive Thinking; Dr. Lee H. Bristol Jr.,
"a noted musician;" Elmer Wheeler, who was awarded a motion picture "Oscar" for his noted sales talk, "Selling the
Sizzle;" and Mona Ling, "America's Number One telephone
consultant."

Not a man to put only $180 eggs in his basket, Meyer
has written several books, which sell for $3.95 up. How to
Prospect Your Way to Millions costs $11.95, while How to
Master Time Organization ("in order to average $100,000 per
year") can be bought for only $6.95, which, given the differ-
ence in potential income, seems fair enough.

Meyer says he sacrificed $100,000 a year in commis-
sions to found Success Motivation Institute, but that he is often rewarded by letters like the one from Lawrence K.Y.
Au of the Paul Revere Life Insurance Co. in Honolulu. "I
can conservatively say," wrote Au, "that Success Motivation
Institute is the main reason for my great success in the insurance business. Moreover, it has made me a better man
to my dear wife and three daughters and a more amicable
business associate."

The Reverend C. A. Roberts of the First Baptist
Church of Tallahassee found one of Meyer's courses "a must
for the personal files of any minister," while racing driver
Jim Rathmann rejoiced: "We are happy to welcome this ter-
rific program into the winner's circle."

Since many business books are sold by mail ("Nobody
ever goes into a bookstore and plunks down cash," explains
a publishing executive. "Most of our books are on the expense account or ordered by companies"), the publishers rely
mainly on mailing lists that can be broken down into categories. Prentice-Hall, for example, can tap their list of
corporate presidents, salesmen, real-estate brokers, doctors,
lawyers or personnel directors whenever they need to sell a
book that might appeal to any one of these categories. In
addition, Prentice-Hall runs no fewer than 11 of the 100 book
clubs in the nation.

The success of book clubs seems to bear out Dwight
Macdonald's point about the how-to mania and Dr. Gerald
Gurin's theory on the ego satisfaction of knowledge workers.
Dr. Ernest Dichter, president of the Institute for Motivation-
al Research, describes the typical book-club member. "He
is," says Dr. Dichter, "the average person with no outstand-

ing intellectual interests and achievements; he is a person, however, who is not able to admit this to himself because he lives in a society where people judge each other primarily for their knowledge. He, therefore, tries to play along as far as he can and become what we might call a pseudo-intellectual. In other words, he is out for the appearance and reputation of intellectuality but not for the intellectual food itself."

Intellectual food is a scarce commodity in the company histories and executive autobiographies in vogue these days, ranging all the way from Milton H. Biow's Butting In, an Adman Speaks Out to Alfred J. Sloan's My Years with General Motors. Far meatier is the seven-volume McKinsey Foundation Lecture Series. Among the authors are Chairman Thomas J. Watson Jr. of IBM, Chairman Roger M. Blough of U.S. Steel and President Frederick R. Kappel of AT&T. Here, the how-to aspect (Watson's book is subtitled "The Ideas That Helped Build IBM") is complemented by an attempt to formulate a business philosophy.

Even H. L. Hunt, the legendary Texas oilman, has considered it worthwhile to put his creed on paper. Hunt's magnum opus, Alpaca, is a singular achievement in the field of business philosophy, since it was not only written by the man himself, but puts forward an unfashionable point of view with clarity.

The main course for the reader is an exposition of Hunt's ideal U.S. Constitution, which includes, among other features, no trial by jury, a 25% income tax, depletion allowances on all natural resources and a plan whereby the wealthier citizens would have seven votes apiece, with the right to buy additional votes to put their candidate across. For dessert, there is a love affair between Juan Achala, who is worried about "the inscrutable future of his unhappy country," and Mara Hani, a beautiful creature who takes one look at Juan's draft Constitution and says "We'll perfect the details here and then go back home and show the people what's good for them."

Conscious of the importance of promotion, Hunt turned up at a Dallas bookstore with his wife and daughters Helen and Sewanee to give Alpaca a boost. The festivities opened with the Hunt trio singing to the tune of "Doggie in the Window" a little jingle that went like this:

How much is that book in the window?
The one that says all the smart things,
How much is that book in the window?
I do hope to learn all it brings.
How much is that book in the window?
The one which my Popsy wrote.
How much is that book in the window?
You can buy it without signing a note.

Free spirits like Hunt, however, are rare these days,
and the majority of business books stress the role of the
employee in an organization.   In How to Succeed in Company
Politics, for example, author Edward J. Hegarty advises the
young executive that the old saw, "Keep your nose clean and
vote Republican," is not enough for a man who wants to get
to the top.   There is the lunch problem for example. "You
went to lunch with Poochie every day," writes Hegarty.
"But now you may be expected to go to lunch with men at
your new level. . . . You may not want to lose Poochie as
a pal, but you are planning to move up too."   The answer:
"Try to handle Poochie and other such situations [sic] your
new status brings in without losing the friends."

In business books, the job of the executive is often
compared to the thankless task of a baseball player, who is
expected to perform brilliantly as an individual and yet fit
into the team.   To an executive starting a new job, Hegarty
says: "Now you're in the position of the young ballplayer
that just came up to the big league."   In The Golden Book of
Selling, author Whitmore warns: "Most big-league players
scored a lot of runs on the sandlots before anyone took much
notice of them.   Have you served your sandlot time?   It's
important."   (In a Dun's Review survey in 1951, United States
Steel Corp. President Benjamin F. Fairless compared himself to a playing manager, while President Austin S. Iglehart
of General Foods Corp. said he preferred to manage from the
dugout.)   And to illustrate "how different perceptions may be
understood," Alfred J. Marrow in Behind the Executive Mask
quotes a story by "the noted psychologist Dr. Hadley Cantril"
about three baseball umpires.   "The first umpire says,
'Some's balls and some's strikes.   I call 'em as they are.'
The second says, 'Some's balls and some's strikes.   I call
'em as I see 'em.'   The third says, 'Some may be balls and
some may be strikes, but they ain't nothing until I call 'em.'"
The time seems propitious for a book on management by that
experienced executive, Casey Stengel.

The European approach
In contrast to his American counterpart, the European
businessman tends to isolate himself like a solitary golfer
executing shots for his personal satisfaction. As Gilbert M.
Sauvage, one of the contributors to The Business Establishment, a collection of essays about business ideology, puts it:
"The American team, where responsibility is largely shared
between the president of a large corporation and his vice
presidents, is an exception on the other side of the ocean.
The president-director general does not like to delegate
powers." Nor does he like to write business books.

One reason for this could be that business in Europe
has been forced into a defensive position by public acceptance of socialism, left-wing Christian democracy and the rise
of state technocracies such as the Common Market and the
European Coal and Steel Community. "This creates a more
or less hostile environment," explains Phillippe deWoot, director of research at the Management Training Center of the
University of Louvain, Belgium, "which is, of course, neither overwhelming nor overpowering. It is a typical case of
countervailing powers that have neither destroyed nor de-
feated the fighting spirit of business. They have merely
forced it to rethink its role in society and to adjust itself to
this new environment."

Surprisingly enough, American businessmen are also
rethinking their role in society, even though the countervailing forces here have neither the power nor the public acceptance of their European counterparts. Indeed, the outpouring of books about the corporation's responsibilities to stockholders, employees, customers and the public at large indicates that executives are spending a great deal of time these
days examining the function of business--but having little success in spreading their conclusions. As former GE Chairman Ralph J. Cordiner admits in his book New Frontiers for
Professional Managers: " . . . somehow we have not yet
been able to do it well--to describe this new people's capitalism, and all that it means to the spiritual and cultural life of
the people, as well as to their material well-being."

Yet the failure to come up with a definitive description
has not been for lack of trying. "One of the most important
businesses in our time," says John Kenneth Galbraith, "is
the defense of business. Year in and year out it commands
the energies of a sizable number of lawyers, public relations

counselors, agency chiefs, copy writers and miscellaneous journeymen practitioners." This is a remarkable fact, Galbraith goes on, since other interest groups seem to take their existence for granted.

"Thus," concludes Galbraith, "it is barely possible that one reason for the dissatisfaction of business with the case that it makes for itself is that there is no real audience for its argument. The virtues of cleanliness, as it were, are being sold to a people who already appreciate the value of soap."

The Future of Children's Books

By William A. Jenkins, Professor and Associate Dean,
School of Education, University of Wisconsin-Milwaukee;
Editor, Elementary English.

From Elementary English 42:502-12+, May 1965. © 1965 by
the National Council of Teachers of English. Reprinted with
the permission of the National Council of Teachers of English and William A. Jenkins. Based on an address given at
the Annual Book Selection Conference of the Graduate School
of Library Science, Drexel Institute, Philadelphia, November
1964.

Note: the numbers in parentheses refer to the alphabetical
listing of references which follows this article.

Introduction
What is the predictable future of children's literature?
What will children's reading habits be ten years from now,
and what are the foreseeable changes in publishing trends?
Will paperbound books and book clubs play a greater role in
the children's field than they do now? In what areas do publishers feel they are most successful and where do they feel
they must make the greatest changes to serve better this
very important reading market?   To whom and to what do
publishers credit their successes and their failures in the
children's field?

The Study
In an attempt to answer these and other important
questions about the children's field, publishers--that is, children's and juvenile editors--were polled. As far as they are
willing to reveal their feelings and ideas about their publishing habits and plans, and admittedly publishing is a business
that must be cloaked in some degree of secrecy, here is
their thinking.   The validity of the editors' remarks must also reside in whatever statistical and analytical biases have
been worked into their responses.

The study is based on a questionnaire which was sent to 121 publishers listed as working in the children's and juvenile field in the 1962-63 Literary Market Place.　Fifty questionnaires were returned to the writer, forty-four of which were completed.　Of the forty-four returned, thirty-two of the editors identified themselves and their comments may be verified.　In general the questionnaire was directed to "What predictable changes in the children's book field do you feel qualified to comment on?"

Because of the limited number of returns, the results are open to statistical challenge, but the comments of the various children's editors should be indicative of what the field is thinking and it should provide comments about the field of which librarians and teachers should be aware.　Among the respondents, both the very smallest publishing houses and the largest are represented.

Table I

Number of Children's Books Published Each
Year by Respondents to Questionnaire

Number of Books Published Annually	Number of Respondents
1 - 5	5
5 - 10	5
10 - 25	19
25 - 50	9
50 -100	3
101 or more	1
No response	2

The publishers indicate that in recent years the number of books which they have published has increased only slightly.　Statistics, however, do not agree with their opinions.　The total number of children's books being published each year is increasing considerably.　The Library Journal (3) reports that "In 1962, the number of new titles of children's books published jumped to over 2,000; in 1963 they passed 2,500; and this year [1964] indicates a matching, if not increasing, output."

Most of the respondents indicated that they publish for all age groups but a great many also publish for the middle-

grade child.   The youngest child and the adolescent seem to
be two groups for which a relatively small number of books
are published.

Table II

Reading Levels for Which
Publishers Publish

Youngest Child	7
Middle-Grade Child	16
Older Child	12
Adolescents	7
All Age Groups	23

Teachers have felt for many years that the best books
for children have been written for the middle-grade child.
Analyses of lists of books that have been judged meritorious,
such as the Newbery books, seem to corroborate this feeling.
Books in the adolescent group have tended to lack literary
quality, while many books for the youngest child can only be
called "pretty."   The editors indicate that in the next ten
years they expect the yearly increase of titles published to
remain about the same.

Editors View the Future

In commenting on future increases, the editors pointed
to increased foreign markets, increasing public interest in
children's reading, and expanding school and library markets
and budgets as bases for future, predictable growth.   The
great number who indicated that their business would remain
constant, generally based maintenance of the status quo on
the number of titles which their present staff and sales force
could handle adequately, their ability to find good manuscripts,
and the difficulty in maintaining an inventory.   Several publishers indicated that they have decided on the size of their
children's lists and would devote their time and energies to
maintaining them.

Significantly, the editors were optimistic about the future.   Perhaps this is the way they should feel, for some of
the most dramatic publishing stories in recent years have
come from the children's field.   These include reports of publishing houses that have been kept afloat or blown out of the

doldrums by the vigorous activity of their juvenile departments. The influence of the children's trade field is even more impressive when one recalls that the first children's department in a publishing house was established less than half a century ago (10). Publishers are aware that there are more and will be even more children, that they are reading more and using libraries more, and that their parents are aware of the values of owning and reading books. Perhaps these are reasons only one editor predicted decreased activity for his firm in this field.

Ruth Hill Viguers (13) beautifully expressed optimism about the future of children's books at a library conference last summer:

> This is one thing we can be sure of in the future: the unchanging quality of childhood itself, regardless of place. The child who begins his life in New York City or Nepal, or Johannesburg will need food, love, and security, and will respond to sound and suspense. Knowing this, when we speculate about the future, we need consider only the influence of adults . . . children's librarians will emerge to temper that influence.

Table III indicates that in all six categories listed in the questionnaire there have been increased requests by the purchaser of children's books. Trade books in general show a dramatic increase, but so does the easy-to-read book for beginning readers. The effect of increased purchases is illustrated in Table IV which indicates publishing increases. The relationship between sales and releases seems to be a direct one.

Why Publish a Book?
Attempting to find out what influences publishing firms to publish a given children's book, I asked the editors to indicate from among ten different sources of influence, those factors which have the greatest bearing on their decision to publish certain types of books. From their responses it is quite clear that librarians' requests for a book or type of book influence decisions more than teachers' requests. Market analyses of children's reading habits--the Madison Avenue stereotype--and publishing trends in other countries have little bearing on whether a given title is published in this country.

Table III

Recent Changes in Children's Book
Purchases Noted by Publishers

Type of Book	Number Responses Increase	Number Responses Decrease	Number Responses No Change
Children's Trade Books	25	3	7
Biography	17	4	6
Science	27	1	2
Other Non-Fiction	19	3	6
Picture Books for Young Children	16	5	7
Easy-to-Read Beginning Readers	25	1	5

Table IV

Recent Changes in Children's
Books Published

Type of Book	Numbers Indicating Area of Greatest Increase	Numbers Indicating Area of Greatest Decrease
Children's Trade Books	6	2
Biography	2	1
Science	16	1
Other Non-Fiction	3	0
Picture Books for Young Children	4	3
Easy-to-Read Beginning Readers	10	0

Siri Andrews, editor of children's books for Holt (1), has commented this way on librarians' influence:

> Librarians are the largest book buyers and have the widest influence, through their own buying as well as through their own contacts with a reading and book-buying public.

What seemed so obvious to me as the study was undertaken--that children follow their parents' habits, such as favoring the reading of biography--may be only an illusion. Reviewers of children's books also seem not too influential. The results are summarized in Table V.

Table V

Factors Affecting Publishers' Decisions to Publish a Given Children's Title

Rank		Relative Influence*
1	Librarians' request or comments	202
2	Teachers' request or comments	162
3	Authors-illustrators available	131
4	Manuscripts voluntarily received	115
5	Children's book reviewers	100
6	Market analyses of children's reading habits	79
7	Patterns in adult reading habits	64
8	Trends in other mass media	54
9	Publishing trends in other countries	31

* Based on 8 for first rank, 7 for second, to 1 for eighth place, and 0 for ninth place. This procedure is followed in ensuing tables where relative influence is judged.

Table VI, based on a question which is a corollary to the question which forms the basis for Table V, shows the editors fairly consistent in their opinions as to what affects their decisions to publish or not to publish a given book. Significantly, in both tables librarians' and teachers' requests are rated as strong influences in the decision making process.

Table VI

Factors Which Least Influence Publishers' Decisions to Publish a Given Children's Book

Rank		Relative Influence
1	Trends indicated by popular subjects	

	in other media	21
2	Publishing trends in other countries	20
3	Patterns in adult reading habits	16
4	Manuscripts voluntarily received	14
5	Market analyses of children's reading habits	12
6	Children's book reviewers	6
6	Authors and illustrators under contract to the firm	6
7	Teachers' requests for books	3
8	Librarians' requests for a book	1
	Not marked	24

Table VII is a composite of Tables V and VI.

Table VII

Composite Rank Order Comparison of Factors Influencing the Publishing of a Children's Book

	Rank of Factors Most Influential	Rank of Factors Least Influential
Publishing trends in other countries	9	1
Trends indicated by popular subjects in other media	8	2
Patterns in adult reading habits	7	3
Manuscripts voluntarily received	4	4
Market analyses of children's reading habits	6	5
*Children's book reviewers	5	6
Authors and illustrators under contract to the firm	3	7
Teachers' requests for books	3	8
Librarians' requests for books	1	9

* Although children's book reviewing is generally held in low esteem, Eaton (6) indicates that it began as long ago as 1918. She writes that it began with Eugene Saxton's asking Anne Carroll Moore to review W. H. Hudson's Little Boy Lost for the November 1918, issue of the Bookman. In 1924 Miss Moore was asked to edit a weekly paper of criticism of children's books for Herald-

<u>Tribune Books</u>.   According to Eaton, as Miss Moore watched
the five owls who sat on the weathervane outside of the Children's Library in Westbury, Long Island, three of them flew
away.   Thus was born "The Three Owls" of children's literature: the artist, the author, and the critic.

These responses support the reasons offered by Helen
Jones (8) of Little, Brown for manuscripts being rejected by
her firm:

1)   Anthropomorphic animal tales which are neither
     fact nor fable.
2)   Poor plots which are loosely put together,
     pointless, or contrived; wooden characters;
     or lessons of brotherhood pushed too hard.
3)   Too adultish, with too few child associations.

On the other side, Miss Jones lists these reasons for
accepting a manuscript:

1)   The story's the thing.
2)   A known author whose previous sales record
     indicates that the book will be accepted.
3)   Subject needed for balance.
4)   Thematic interest and author promise.

Predictable Changes
       The publishers were asked to indicate significant pre-
dictable changes in the children's book field of which they
are aware.   A wide variety of changes which are occurring
now were included.   For example, one publisher felt that
there is a definite trend toward good science books for children.   Another indicated that children's books have more realism.   Still another lamented the fact that there is an increasing number of titles available and a decreasing <u>quality</u> in
many books.

An editor felt that more and more paperback books
will be published.   A colleague mentioned the fact that institutional markets are growing faster than trade markets because all ages are reaching for and demanding material beyond their standard age group, influenced by better educated
parents and by television.   Schools are moving away from
one-text teaching, toward a basic skills text in a galaxy of
supplementary trade books and reading materials.

Interesting explanations for this condition have been offered by Vernon Ives (7). He says, (a) publishers prefer to publish authors, not books, for even a bad book by an established author is easier to sell than a new book; (b) when a publisher makes a large advance royalty to an author he is under financial obligation to sell a poorly finished product; (c) orders "from above" in a publishing firm to publish "a delightful little fairy tale" by Joe So-and-So's daughter (especially when a novel by Joe may be put under contract) have to be carried out; and (d) publishers, like everyone else, jump on the bandwagon and publish books, often bad, on topics which everyone is discussing at the moment. Ives feels that the only brake on publishers is increasing costs, but these also prevent many good books from being published. Frank Stevens (12) also has offered reasons for inferior books: (a) books published according to formulas; (b) series books which capitalize on earlier successful efforts; (c) vocabulary books, based on word count; and (d) sales promotion techniques.

One can only hope the prediction that there will be massive overproduction of junk which will reach a saturation point, soon will come true. The hope was voiced that in the near future there will be more books on the arts, books of fantasy, good fiction, and poetry which children will start reading. Several editors felt that there would be less controlled vocabulary, while an equal number indicated that controlled vocabulary in children's books would remain for the foreseeable future.

Design Changes

To this question, "Are there significant predictable changes in the design of children's books?" those answering affirmatively included among the predictable changes "impressionistic" jacket design; improvement in illustrations as new illustrators enter the field from other media; better art along with better quality, more colors, and more "sophisticated" layout and design. These editors also mentioned that teenagers require "adult-looking" books. Contemporary design in illustrations and typography will increase, one editor noted, while another indicated that abstract art work would be within the covers of more books for children.

In various places several editors pointed to the increase in quality of bindings for children's books. They indicated that this would both increase and decrease the possible

flexibility in design of the books. The influence would increase or diminish, depending upon whether they felt innovations were fads or whether they represented genuine changes.
The development of new materials will open up greater design possibilities, they felt, but "the avant-garde-for-its-own-
sake design has about had its day." In general it must be
said that the editors felt that the significant design changes
would occur through an increase in color, better bindings,
and better layout.

The Future of Paperbacks
        In answer to whether paperbound books for children
will develop to proportions similar to those for adult readers
during the past decade, twenty-one editors indicated that in
their opinion they would not, fifteen indicated they would, and
eight did not respond.

        When asked what in their opinion is the most signifi-
cant change occurring at the moment in children's literature,
the editors surprisingly enough pointed to no sensational technological or economic developments. Rather they listed such
things as the great demand for a product which is superior
in every way. They pointed to an increase in appreciation
of the truly literary book, the upswing to literature and away
from the trivial, their awareness of the impoverished vocabulary and content of many books on the market, and the influence of a curriculum which demands related subjects in trade
juveniles.

The Effect of Reading Controversies
        The editors and publishers were asked whether their
publishing programs had been affected by reading controversies which occurred in the past ten years. Twenty-eight indicated that they had not. In a large measure they had foreseen some of the weaknesses in reading and provided materials to meet these needs. They do not publish books with limited vocabularies and therefore were apart from the controversy. Some felt that people are getting fed up with "graded"
readers which are far below the child's level of intellectual
maturity and sophistication. Interestingly enough, one editor
indicated that his firm started the "I Can Read" books when
they found that public libraries were buying primers from
textbook houses.

        On the positive side, an editor indicated that as a re-

sult of the reading controversies his house had sold more
trade books to schools and libraries and had put more and
more of their trade books in sturdy bindings to serve as
readers. Another editor indicated that the frenzy for easy
reading material had led his company to consider vocabulary
more carefully, although as a policy they did not believe in
word lists. An editor decried the fact that his company had
a difficult time selling one of their really fine books to libraries because the purchasing people couldn't decide exactly for which grade it should be bought.

Children's Book Clubs

In the main the editors felt that children's book clubs
will not influence children's future reading fare. This won't
happen because, in the words of one editor, subscriptions to
book clubs are less welcome to children than they were twenty years ago. Another editor indicated that book clubs are
waning and that they have never influenced habits. He views
them as the refuge of the literarily lazy. He pointed out
that adult reading habits are not influenced to a large extent
by reading clubs. Adults who read extensively are more likely to select paperbacks of their choosing than join a reading
club, and this will also be true of children. The results are
shown in Table VIII.

Table VIII

Publishers' Predictions on Future Influence of Children's Book Clubs

Number indicating that book clubs will influence children's future reading fare	13
Number indicating that book clubs will not influence children's future reading fare	19
No response	12
Number indicating that book clubs will influence to a greater extent children's future reading fare	9
Number indicating that book clubs will influence to a lesser degree children's future reading fare	8
No response	27

The Role of Illustrations
          The editors felt that in the future illustrations will
play about the same role in children's books as they do at
the present time.   Several editors felt that a few years ago
more illustrations were demanded for children's books, that
the demand is now being met, and that content is presently
more important.   Great strides have been made in book illustrations, but publishers can afford no more without price
increases that the market would resist.   The quality and kind
of text has been the determining factor in arriving at the
kind of illustrations to be used.   He felt that this practice
would hold true in the future as well.   Illustrating children's
books is a highly competitive business and the increased
complexity of subject matter in areas such as science, requires more and better illustrations.   All in all, the feelings
of the editors about illustrations may be summed up in the
words of one who said, "We cannot afford to do more--and
we dare not do less."

The Future of Illustrations
          The editors were asked whether the illustrators under
contract to their publishing houses recently had shown a shift
in interest in the media that they employ in illustrating children's books.   While it is difficult to categorize their re-
plies, some comments are noteworthy.   A significant number
felt that no change in illustrating media is on the horizon.
Others indicated, however, that artists whom they work with
have long experimented with all media and that they are constantly trying new approaches such as collages, presepara-
tions, and so on.   The medium to be used by the artist is
determined by cost and subject matter, which factors lead
one to believe that many illustrators illustrate books only upon contract and only by a prescription for each book.   Several publishers indicated that they contract an artist whose techniques are most suitable, according to the publisher's interpretation, for illustrating a given manuscript.   Possibly the
most positive conclusion which can be drawn from this question is that most children's illustrators are free lance artists
rather than house illustrators.

Factors Adversely Affecting Reading
          The editors felt strongly that parents' lack of aware-
ness of what is available and teachers' lack of knowledge a-
bout children's books were the two conditions most adversely

affecting their efforts to provide children with good books.
They pointed out that bookstores have a lack of awareness of
what is available and inadequate personnel to sell what is on .
hand; dancing and music lessons, school activities, and so
on, compete with children's reading time; and, parents fail
to encourage children to read and stimulate in them the love
of reading.

Table IX

Cultural Conditions Adversely Affecting
Publishers' Efforts to Provide Children with Good Books

Rank	Factor	Relative Influence	Number Responses
1	Parents' lack of awareness of what is available	168	13
2	Teacher's lack of awareness of what is available	119	23
3	Rising book costs	112	25
4	The flood of poor quality books in supermarkets, etc.	96	24
5	Competition from other media	66	31
6	Children's poor reading habits	51	32
7	Librarians' lack of awareness of what is available	44	37
8	Children's lack of reading ability	38	33

The strongest view, as we suspected, was voiced a-
bout books for adolescents. One editor pointed out that it
isn't easy to find writers who can provide really first-rate
books for this age group. Another pointed out that adolescents' tastes change fast. Their interest in extra-curricular
reading runs a hard second to their social preoccupation with
learning how to look and act grown up, and they simply will
not look twice at anything that smacks of juvenility. The result is that the market for books which would interest them
is too small to publish profitably alone. Adolescents read
adult books because they find writing specifically published for
them inadequate. The "older" child is often in a never-never
land insofar as reading ability goes. For this reason he
wants books as nearly adult as they can be, while a few of
them want nothing more challenging than mystery stories. A
further explanation is that young adult books are knotty prob-

lems to edit and to market.

To a correlative question, "For which age group are
publishers providing the best books?" the editors were equally far from consensus. Fifteen felt that the youngest child
was being given the best books, but twenty-two did not respond to this question. Seven felt that the best books were
being provided both for the middle-grade and for the older
child. (In 1958 De Angelo (5) predicted that editors would
give more attention to books for the middle age group of
children. The prediction, based on reports from juvenile
editors, apparently has not yet fully been realized.)

The Future of Easy-to-Read Books

To the question of whether or not there will be an increase in the near future in easy-to-read books, such as
The Cat in the Hat, the editors indicated by numbers of
twenty-seven to fourteen that there would be such an increase. Three editors did not comment upon this question.

One editor indicated that the number of easy-to-read
books in the future will probably decrease even though there
will be a continuing need. In his opinion, the number presently available in print would continue to be available. A
second editor indicated that the book industry is a great cop-
ier of success. Entertaining, non-formula stories in simple
words are proving attractive to both adults and children.
Since children know more complex words and syntax at younger ages than in former years, and because they are exposed
to television and more adult reading material, the demand
will stay high. Opposing this view was that of an editor who
felt that the market currently had reached the saturation
point.

Learning about Books

The editors were asked which of the various media are
the most effective for informing parents, teachers, and librarians about new children's books. There was an unevenness of response to the question, but they felt clearly that
book fairs and reviews in the lay press are the primary
means for informing parents. Reviews in professional journals and book fairs are the most important means for informing teachers, while librarians receive notice of new books
primarily through reviews in professional journals and advertisements in them.

They felt that exhibits of books, such as state travel-
ling exhibits, convention displays, and readily available review copies also inform librarians.   They point out that at
the ALA meetings and the state meetings of library groups,
publishers have displays which the librarians do notice.   They
also ask that schools of education where future teachers ought
to be made aware of children's trade books acquire, perhaps
for curriculum libraries, holdings for the students to peruse.
They noted that good courses in children's literature also
make future teachers well aware of what is available.   As
far as parents are concerned, they also indicated that television programs which mention children's books are quite influential, as are teachers who strongly urge parents to obtain
books for their children.   Their views of the means of informing teachers, librarians, and parents of new books are condensed in Table X.

Table   X

Effectiveness of Means for Informing
Parents, Teachers, and Librarians
of New Children's Books

Medium	Rank	Relative Importance
A. Parents		
Book fairs	1	73
Reviews in the lay press	2	52
Librarians	3	39
Children's roundtables on TV and radio	4	37
Library displays	5	36
Reviews in professional journals (teachers and librarians)	6	9
Reviewing services	7	7
Ads in professional journals	8	5
B. Teachers		
Reviews in professional journals	1	53
Book fairs	2	42
Ads in professional journals	3	33
Librarians	4	27
Library displays and Reviews in the lay press	5	26
Reviewing services	6	22

Table X (cont.)

B. Teachers (cont.)
    Children's roundtables on TV   7   5
      and radio

C. Librarians
    Reviews in professional journals   1   71
    Ads in professional journals   2   46
    Reviewing services   3   39
    Reviews in the lay press   4   27
    Library displays   5   20
    Book fairs   6   12
    Children's roundtables on TV
      and radio .   7   8

New Bookmaking Processes

To the question, "Are significant new bookmaking or printing processes now being developed which may in the near future greatly influence the children's book fields?" most of the respondents indicated that nothing new and revolutionary will be used in the future. One editor indicated that his firm had just used a new camera for a full-color process picture book which gives a 90 percent reproduction of the original art work at present costs (the cost is high). This is a distinct advantage, however, because the previous method, almost as costly, provided only a 60 to 75 percent reproduction. The Wish Worker was the first hardbound children's book to use this method, according to this editor. Printing on plastic may open up many new avenues of illustrating children's books and influence the design of books.

In this regard, Viguers (13) comments that two major changes in the looks of books are discernible:

> The first is beneficial: consistent effort has been made to dignify good books with appropriately attractive format. The second is harmful: indiscriminate publication of children's books has sponsored the providing of spectacular, eye-catching format to text quite lacking in essence. This deceit has been a cause for the equating of books with dullness . . . .

Manuscript Acceptance

Very interesting results were received from the editors in response to the question, "What are the most important criteria used by your readers and editors in determining whether a manuscript will or will not be accepted for publication?" The most frequent question that the editors asked themselves is whether children will like the book. But they also refer to need of the subject; its honesty; the capability of author; strength of plot; or interest of instruction (for non-fiction) as important questions. One editor put it very simply: "A good story and good literary style." Another editor indicated that he asks himself whether the story has intrinsic merit, whether it will be commercially profitable, and whether it will add prestige to his company's list. A colleague indicated that readability, accuracy, and the fact that the book is not written down to children are his important considerations. Good style and characterization were mentioned frequently, as well as distinguished style characterized by competent plotting and organization of material, leading to good readability.

These responses provide an interesting contrast to a study published in Elementary English in November, 1963. Editors of forty-six publishing houses responded to a questionnaire sent to them by George I. Brown (2). Brown found that editors use 63 different criteria in judging a manuscript, but two are used most often: 1) personal opinion and reaction, and 2) marketability. Some editors were upset by Brown's suggestion that manuscript consideration is not always a unified, studied, systematic procedure. However, Brown found, as did this study, that the editors were very sincere in their desire to publish the best manuscripts. This subjective conclusion must be drawn from their constant references to "quality of writing" and "worthy content."

According to the editors, most companies have publishing programs and whether they publish a given book depends on whether the book fits into that program. Beyond this, they look at originality and good design. Editors indicated that their houses restrict their publications to a few categories, thus making a great many good manuscripts unacceptable to them. One editor indicated that he asks whether the manuscript is better than anything now or soon likely to be available, as far as nonfiction is concerned. With fiction, he asks whether the material is original, artistic, good enough for children, and will children want to reread it. Surprising-

ly enough, another editor indicated that library standards
are one of his prime concerns. He asks himself, "Is this
book needed?" In a more philosophical vein, another editor
asks himself whether the title will make a distinctive and
worthwhile addition to the world of books. A fellow editor
indicated that if he had published seventeen dog stories in
one season he probably wouldn't publish another one no matter how good.

In summary, it would appear that children's editors,
like all other editors, are looking for new, fresh, well-
written, salable material. These are general criteria which
editors everywhere must use. Their feelings reinforce a
thesis implicit in this paper, that children's books are a
part of the mainstream of the world of books.

Changes in Reading Habits
        The editors indicated very clearly that there is a dis-
cernible trend for adolescents to read adult books at an earlier age than formerly. The reasons advanced for this change
include television and other media which are causing a greater awareness in young children and more curiosity about our
world. Furthermore, children today resent being talked
down to and find that in adult books this does not happen.
The editors feel that librarians are encouraging them to do
so and that it is a wise move. They indicate that children
are being encouraged to read adult books, as they have always done in the past. The history of children's literature
is replete with examples of books which have been "appropriated by children," to use Paul Hazard's phrase. Perhaps
another important reason is that teenagers find that books
written for them, as a rule, are rather routine. An editor
pointed to the general speed-up in high school programs
which will have the effect of raising levels in nonfiction as
well as in fiction. "Perhaps children are trying to grow up
faster and faster these days?" asked one perceptive editor.
The opinion was offered that teenage novels are now read by
junior high students, but senior high students have moved on
to adult works, both fiction and nonfiction. This same editor also pointed to better teaching and the generally more
sophisticated world in which we live as effects which make
adolescents move out of juvenile literature much earlier than
they did, even ten years ago.

Children's Books of the Future

The concluding question asked of the editors was this: "As a result of this opinionnaire, our intent is to discuss children's books of the future. In brief, what do you expect to happen in this field for which librarians, teachers, and parents should be aware of and prepared?" The answers ranged over a wide territory.

One publisher indicated that more titles would be published in the future, but that more discrimination on the part of the editors will be needed. He felt, happily, that books will become more a part of growing up and readership will improve in quality and quantity. He sees the push on education spurring this because the country is becoming more mature and all of us will use our leisure time more profitably.

Jean Karl, children's book editor for Atheneum, writing in Library Journal (9), feels that publishers must continue to publish for wide needs:

> Because we do not know tomorrow, but must
> anticipate it, because we must cope with a
> divergence of information to be communicated,
> and most of all because we cannot give chil-
> dren a narrow look at what interests them or
> what they have come to need; because we dare
> not pour children into tight molds, because we
> must encourage diversity, in authors and in
> minds of children, the avalanche [of books be-
> ing published] must exist.

The cost of publishing, as well it might be, was a concern of a great many editors. They felt that they must find a way to educate the buying market in what is best against what is cheap and trivial and then the public should expect to buy the best for their money. Similarly, with the increasing number of children's books being published annually, one editor cautioned that in the future purchases will have to be more selective than ever. The great rash of "easy readers" of low quality, not really balanced by a few books of truly excellent quality, makes the task of choosing children's books a very difficult one. There are vast numbers of mediocre books on the market.

Several editors expressed the hope that children's books will become less expensive in the future, fewer in num-

ber, and of higher quality.   They also indicated that perhaps
in the future children's books will be better planned for the
age group they are to reach.   The great numbers of children's books which are being published make the job of recognizing new and original talent even more difficult.   Some
editors felt that it is imperative that they try not to sift
their reactions to the output of creative people through their
adult experiences.   They must constantly remember that children are brand new, even if they as adults are not.

Again, Viguers' (13) very cogent remarks must be
referred to.   Her views of the future are clear, and, most
of all optimistic:

> The growing interest in poetry today bodes
> well for the future . . . much poetry for chil-
> dren will continue to be drawn from the work
> of the great poets. . . . The making of picture
> books will grow in integrity. . . . Children's
> interest in animals . . . will continue to stimu-
> late the writing of animal stories. . . . In time
> there will not be stories of minority groups as
> such because--hopefully--people will not be
> thought of in groups. . . . Children will always
> enjoy vicariously the accomplishments of diffi-
> cult or impossible deeds. . . . Stories of soli-
> tary survival will continue to be loved. . . .
> Biography, too, will appeal for its glimpses of
> courage and accomplishment in the face of great
> odds. . . . In future adventure and historical
> tales . . . the history of the twentieth century
> will provide action, drama, and certainly trag-
> edy. . . . The forces, constant through the
> ages, are these: what the child wants and what
> the adult thinks the child should have.   From
> time to time in the history of children's books,
> the second has obscured the first.   In the future,
> books will continue to be affected by both
> forces. . . .

Perhaps the most striking aspect of their responses
is the sincerity with which many editors approach their tasks
and their concern for maintaining the present day high quality
of children's books by striving for even greater heights.
Literary qualities, more successful union of texts and illustrations, and ways of getting more children to read and love
reading, are things that seem to occupy their time and ener-

gies. A final quotation from Viguers (13) supports this position:

> . . . in spite of the irresponsible and mass-market production of books, there do exist publishers who maintain high standards in their publishing and who search for originality and distinction in writing and illustrating for children. . . .

As a result of the editors' responses we conclude that the future of children's literature is indeed bright, and that the efforts of these editors, abetted by skillful teachers, sincere librarians, and knowledgeable parents, will make the present prediction a reality.

References

1. Andrews, Siri, "Publishing Books for Youth," in Youth, Communication and Libraries, edited by Frances Henne. Chicago: American Library Association, 1949, pp. 93-104.

2. Brown, George I., "Criteria Used by Editors in Selecting Manuscripts of Children's Books," Elementary English 40:724-8 (November, 1963).

3. "Choosing 'the Right Book' Today," Library Journal 84: 13 (December 15, 1964).

4. Dalgliesh, Alice and Margaret B. Evans, "Designing Children's Books," Bulletin of the New York Public Library, 60:573-7 (1956).

5. De Angelo, Rachael W., "Children's Book Publishing," Library Trends, July, 1958, pp. 220-33.

6. Eaton, Anne Thaxter, "Reviewing and Criticism of Children's Books," Bulletin of the New York Public Library, 60:589-92 (1956).

7. Ives, Vernon, "The New Look in Children's Books," Library Journal, 72:1730-3 (December 15, 1947).

8. Jones, Helen L., "Over the Editor's Shoulder," Library Journal, 32:19-21 (December 15, 1964).

9.   Karl, Jean, "Books for an Uncertain World," Library Journal, 84:14-16 (December 15, 1964).

10. Melcher, Frederic G., "Working Together: Publisher, Bookseller, and Librarian," Bulletin of the New York Public Library, 60:619-21 (1956).

11. Smith, Lillian H., The Unreluctant Years. Chicago: American Library Association, 1953.

12. Stevens, Frank A., "Challenge to the Publisher," Library Journal, 84:16-18 (December 15, 1964).

13. Viguers, Ruth Hill, "Children's Books: Yesterday, Today, and Tomorrow," in The Reading of Children, edited by Doris M. Cole. Syracuse: School of Library Science, Syracuse University, 1964, pp. 7-26.

Do You Remember? Popular Books, 1924-1964

By Alice Payne Hackett, Contributing Editor, Publishers' Weekly.

From Saturday Review 47:109-25, August 29, 1964. Copyright 1964 Saturday Review, Inc. Reprinted by permission.

Titles mentioned in this article appeared on national best-seller lists. The statistics, based on sales in American bookstores, are from Alice P. Hackett's Sixty Years of Best Sellers (Bowker, 1956) and from the annual best-seller lists of Publishers' Weekly.

1924

Forty years ago more people were reading Edna Ferber's first big hit So Big (Doubleday, Page) than any other current novel. Second in popularity to this story of a mother and her son on a farm near Chicago was the then-shocking novel of college life The Plastic Age, by Percy Marks (Century). Along with those two, people were buying The Little French Girl, by Anne Douglas Sedgwick (Houghton Mifflin), romance and adventure by Philip Gibbs, James Oliver Curwood, Zane Grey, Coningsby Dawson, and Rafael Sabatini, as well as Booth Tarkington's The Midlander (Doubleday, Page). In 1924, as in most years since then, the nonfiction best-seller list was dominated by "how-to" books--on cookery, health, etiquette, self-improvement of body and mind, and books to amuse and entertain. The Cross Word Puzzle Books were an innovation, the first best-sellers of the new firm of Simon & Schuster. Biography was an important subject. Papini's Life of Christ (Harcourt, Brace), Maurois's Airel (Appleton), Mark Twain's Autobiography (Harper), and The Americanization of Edward Bok (Scribners) appealed to readers of the day, as did Saint Joan by Bernard Shaw (Brentano's).

1925

Arrowsmith (Harcourt, Brace), which was Sinclair

349

Lewis's third great success and certainly the most intran-
sient of the popular books of 1925, introduced the subject of
medical research into American fiction.   Other remembered
novels of the year are The Constant Nymph, by Margaret
Kennedy (Doubleday, Page); The Green Hat, by Michael Ar-
len (Doran)--daring for its time--and The Perennial Bache-
lor, by Anne Parrish.   Papini, Maurois, and Bok (with a
new book, Twice Thirty, Scribners) reaffirmed the popularity of biography, joined by Lord Grey with his Twenty-Five
Years (Stokes), J. J. Brousson with Anatole France Himself
(Lippincott), and an advertising man's version of the life of
Jesus, The Man Nobody Knows, by Bruce Barton (Bobbs-
Merrill).   Outstanding in 1925 was the appearance of When
We Were Very Young, by A. A. Milne (Dutton), the Christopher Robin verses enjoyed by both children and adults ever
since.

1926

Humor headed the best-selling novels.   Columbia professor John Erskine's The Private Life of Helen of Troy
(Bobbs-Merrill) provided sophisticated amusement in a novel
that told what happened to Helen after she left Menelaus.
The almost slapstick comedy of Hollywood's Anita Loos was
the year's second choice in fiction, Gentlemen Prefer Blondes
(Boni & Liveright).   Only in eighth place then was the best-
known novel of all, Show Boat, by Edna Ferber (Doubleday,
Page).   Sorrell and Son, by Warwick Deeping (Knopf), was a
big hit and made its author one of the most popular novelists
of the Twenties and early Thirties.   Galsworthy's The Silver
Spoon (Scribners) was a best-seller of 1926 as were top well-
known romances by P. C. Wren, Beau Geste and Beau Sabreur
(Stokes).   The first volume of Mark Sullivan's Our Times
(Scribners) pointed up a new interest in American contemporary history, as George A. Dorsey's Why We Behave Like
Human Beings did in psychology.

1927

Sinclair Lewis topped every other novelist with his
story of a hell-fire preacher, Elmer Gantry (Harcourt,
Brace).   The first book of Mazo de la Roche's long-continued
chronicle of a Canadian family, Jalna (Little, Brown), was
also a great hit.   Louis Bromfield made his first appearance
on the annual best-seller list with his fourth novel, A Good
Woman (Stokes).   Such familiar names as Booth Tarkington,
Mary Roberts Rinehart, Warwick Deeping, Edith Wharton,

Anne Parrish, and Anne Douglas Sedgwick filled the rest of
the fiction list. In nonfiction the title most immediately familiar to the 1964 public is Revolt in the Desert, T. E.
Lawrence's abridged account of his wartime exploit in Arabia
(Doran). For the readers of 1927 it was We, Charles Lindbergh's story of his record-breaking solo flight across the
Atlantic (Putnam). Outselling all others, however, was The
Story of Philosophy (Simon & Schuster), foremost of the
many books of the period that popularized specific fields of
knowledge. This was historian Will Durant's first great success. Napoleon, by Emil Ludwig (Boni & Liveright), was a
notable biography of the year, while Katherine Mayo's Mother
India (Harcourt, Brace) awakened a large number of people
to the human problems of India at that time.

1928

Galsworthy, Hugh Walpole, Tarkington, Deeping, and
Bromfield were the popular novelists of the Twenties, titles
by them filling the fiction list of 1928. The leader of the
year, however, was a book by a new writer, Thornton Wilder. His The Bridge of San Luis Rey (A. & C. Boni), reviewed as a modern masterpiece, made such an impact that
the Pulitzer Prize judges for the first time gave the award
for a novel to a book with a setting outside the United States,
in this case South America. As usual throughout this decade,
biography was paramount. André Maurois's Disraeli (Appleton) led nonfiction. Emil Ludwig had a new biography,
Goethe (Putnam). Richard E. Byrd added his account of
North Pole flying adventure, Skyward (Putnam), to the still
popular We. Interesting best-sellers of the year were Eugene O'Neill's long drama, Strange Interlude (Liveright), and
The Intelligent Woman's Guide to Socialism and Capitalism,
by George Bernard Shaw.

1929

The great novel of World War I, appearing here eleven
years after the end of that war, and written by a German,
was the best-seller of the last of the early-century boom
years. The novel was All Quiet on the Western Front, by
Erich Maria Remarque (Little, Brown), whose novels are
still best-sellers. Dodsworth (Harcourt, Brace), one of Sinclair Lewis's most popular works as book, play, and movie,
was second. Interest in regional fiction was reflected in two
distinctive novels of the deep South, Mamba's Daughters, by
Du Bose Heyward (Doubleday, Doran), and Scarlet Sister

<u>Mary</u>, first novel by Julia Peterkin (Bobbs-Merrill), which won the Pulitzer Prize of the year. Leading nonfiction title of the year with respect to sales was French religious philosopher Ernest Dimnet's <u>The Art of Thinking</u> (Simon & Schuster). Classed among nonfiction, a Civil War narrative in poetry was the most notable and perhaps most enduring book on the list--<u>John Brown's Body</u>, by Stephen Vincent Benét (Doubleday, Doran). Newspaper political commentator Walter Lippmann made his first appearance among bestsellers with <u>A Preface to Morals</u> (Macmillan). Prominent biographies were <u>Henry the Eighth</u>, by Francis Hackett (Liveright), and <u>Elizabeth and Essex</u>, by Lytton Strachey (Harcourt, Brace).

1930

Novelists familiar to the reading public dominated the best-seller list in the first full year of the economic depression. Edna Ferber led with her tale of pioneer Oklahoma, <u>Cimarron</u> (Doubleday, Doran). Hugh Walpole published what was perhaps his most popular novel, <u>Rogue Herries</u> (Doubleday, Doran). New names were Margaret Ayer Barnes, who won the Pulitzer Prize with a long novel about the social scene in the early part of this century, <u>Years of Grace</u> (Houghton Mifflin), and Katharine Brush, author of the sprightly and entertaining <u>Young Man of Manhattan</u> (Farrar & Rinehart). Leading off nonfiction was the forerunner of many "doctor stories," <u>The Story of San Michele</u>, by the Swedish Dr. Axel Munthe (Dutton). Will James made a great hit with <u>Lone Cowboy</u> (Scribners). <u>The Adams Family</u> (Little, Brown) was one of James Truslow Adams's contributions to American history and biography, while historians Charles and Mary Beard wrote a serious study for the general reader, a two-volume work, <u>The Rise of American Civilization</u> (Macmillan), which reached a wide audience.

1931

Well known, if by name only, to readers of the Sixties are some of the most popular novels of 1931--books such as <u>Grand Hotel</u>, by Vicki Baum (Doubleday, Doran), and <u>Back Street</u>, by Fannie Hurst (Cosmopolitan Book Co.). A permanent place in twentieth-century literature was also won by the two top novels of the year: <u>The Good Earth</u>, Pearl Buck's story of poverty-stricken China under the war lords (John Day), which was an important factor in her being awarded the Nobel Prize for literature, and <u>Shadows on</u>

the Rock, by Willa Cather (Knopf), a novel laid in seven-
teenth century Quebec.   A memoir of imperial Russia, a
guide to the new post-revolutionary Russia, an exposé of
Washington political and social life, and a volume of poetry
were the features of 1931 nonfiction.   They were, in that
order, Education of a Princess, by the Grand Duchess Marie,
one of the former imperial Russian family (Viking); New
Russia's Primer, by M. Ilin (Houghton Mifflin); Washington
Merry-Go-Round, published anonymously but later acknowledged as the work of columnists Drew Pearson and Robert
S. Allen (Liveright); and Fatal Interview, by Edna St. Vincent Millay (Harper).

1932

Nineteen thirty-two marked the first appearance on a
best-seller list of Lloyd C. Douglas, whose books were to
be great sellers for twenty years or more.   Magnificent Ob-
session (Willett, Clark) was that rarity, the "word-of-mouth"
seller, winning its way by its own momentum.   It was the
first novel written by Lloyd Douglas after his retirement
from the ministry.   A. J. Cronin also made his début on
this annual list with Three Loves (Little, Brown).   Other
popular novels were The Sheltered Life (Doubleday, Doran)
and Inheritance (Macmillan) by, respectively, Ellen Glasgow
and Phyllis Bentley.   In that worst year of the Depression,
the memorable books of nonfiction were mostly about the
past.   Leading was James Truslow Adams's The Epic of
America (Little, Brown), followed by Only Yesterday (Harper), an evocation of the U.S. not so long ago by Frederick
Lewis Allen, then an editor of Harper's Magazine.   Van
Loon's Geography, by Hendrik Willem Van Loon (Simon &
Schuster), and The Story of My Life (Scribners), by Clarence
Darrow, most famous defense lawyer of his time, were books
that won many readers.

1933

Anthony Adverse, by Hervey Allen (Farrar & Rinehart), which set new sales records, was the first popular
novel of great length since Victorian days and swung public
taste back to the historical novel.   The next most-talked-a-
bout novel of the year was that of a German writer, Hans
Fallada, whose Little Man, What Now? (Simon & Schuster)
was a story of depressed postwar Germany.   Looking Forward (John Day), the first book by Franklin D. Roosevelt after he became President, found many readers, but the top

nonfiction of the year was Columbia Professor Walter D.
Pitkin's Life Begins at Forty (Whittlesey House), the title itself becoming part of the American language. Many readers
were attracted to British Agent, by R. H. Bruce Lockhart
(Putnam), an account of a British diplomat's experiences in the
Russia of Lenin and Trotsky. However, in biography and
autobiography Stefan Zweig's Maria Antoinette (Viking) and
The House of Exile, by Nora Waln (Little, Brown) were outstanding. Yet another best-seller, 100,000,000 Guinea Pigs,
by Arthur Kallet and F. J. Schlink (Vanguard), made fal-
lacious consumer advertising its butt.

1934

Again two novels of the South won high places among
best-sellers and, again, one of them won the Pulitzer Prize.
One was Lamb in His Bosom, by Caroline Miller (Harper);
the other was So Red the Rose, by Stark Young (Scribners).
Four women writers reached their first very large audi-
ences: Phyllis Bottome with a story of abnormal psychology,
Private Worlds (Houghton Mifflin); Mary Ellen Chase with a
story of Maine life, Mary Peters (Macmillan); Alice Tisdale
Hobart with Oil for the Lamps of China (Bobbs-Merrill), and
Danish writer Isak Dinesen with her Seven Gothic Tales
(Smith & Haas). Another best-selling novel was directly con-
nected to the top nonfiction title of the year, While Rome
Burns, by Alexander Woollcott (Viking). As raconteur Mr.
Woollcott had one of the largest radio followings of the time;
his recommendation of books was tremendously influential.
It was he who first made James Hilton's books nationally successful, and brought his 1934 tale of an English schoolmaster,
Goodbye, Mr. Chips (Little, Brown), to an enthusiastic audience. Notable biographies and autobiographies were Nijinsky,
by Romola Nijinsky (Simon & Schuster), The Native's Return,
about Yugoslavia, by Louis Adamic (Harper), and Brazilian
Adventure, by Peter Fleming (Scribners). Stars Fell on Ala-
bama (Farrar & Rinehart), Carl Carmer's exploration of
regional history and folkways, also attracted wide attention.

1935

Lloyd C. Douglas's third novel, Green Light (Houghton Mifflin), was 1935's fiction best-seller. Other names of
distinguished authors achieving solid successes appeared.
Ellen Glasgow, an author of recognized merit for almost four
decades, was second on the list with Vein of Iron (Harcourt,
Brace). Third was Thomas Wolfe with his second novel,

Of Time and the River (Scribners), and further down the list
were Franz Werfel's The Forty Days of Musa Dagh (Viking)
and Robert Briffault's Europa (Scribners). Besides Mr.
Chips, now in its second year on the best-seller list, James
Hilton had the much longer novel, also a Woollcott recommendation, which was to prove even more popular, Lost Horizon (Morrow). Both Mr. Chips and Shangri-la became meaningful words in our language. Nonfiction accounted for an
unusually large number of books both popular and critically
well received. Leading all others was Anne Morrow Lindbergh's account of her flight, as navigator, with her famous
husband over the North Pole to Japan, North to the Orient
(Harcourt, Brace). Life with Father (Knopf), also fondly remembered as a play, contained Clarence Day's reminiscences
of his New York family early in the century. Personal History (Doubleday, Doran) was newspaperman Vincent Sheean's
account of stirring events. And along with these came Francis Hackett's Francis the First (Doubleday, Doran), R. E.
Lee, by Douglas Southall Freeman (Scribners), as well as
scientist Hans Zinsser's Rats, Lice and History (Little,
Brown).

1936

Gone With the Wind (Macmillan), Margaret Mitchell's
first and only book, another example of the long historical
novel, began its two-year reign as a record-breaking best-
seller. The speed of its sales gave this gripping narrative
of Southern devastation during the Civil War added publicity.
Philosopher George Santayana wrote of twentieth-century
Brahmin Boston in The Last Puritan (Scribners). Another
new name was added to best-selling authors of historical fiction, that of Walter D. Edmonds, who wrote Drums Along the
Mohawk (Little, Brown). It Can't Happen Here (Doubleday,
Doran) was Sinclair Lewis's warning to Americans because of
what was happening in Germany at the time. Rebecca West
and Aldous Huxley were English writers whose books appeared
for the first time among our best-sellers: respectively, The
Thinking Reed (Viking) and Eyeless in Gaza (Harper). Nineteen thirty-six marked the appearance of the first of John
Gunther's long and famous list of "inside" books, Inside Europe (Harper). I Write as I Please, by Walter Duranty (Simon & Schuster), was one of the most widely-read reporters'
stories of experiences in the USSR. Interest in medical science and research was pointed up by Man the Unknown, by
surgeon Alexis Carrel (Harper), which headed 1936 nonfiction,
and An American Doctor's Odyssey, by Victor Heiser (Norton).

1937

The year's fiction list was packed with substantial novels by such authors as Cronin, Maugham, Bromfield, and Hilton.   Newcomers were Kenneth Roberts with his big historical novel Northwest Passage (Doubleday, Doran), Virginia Woolf with The Years (Harcourt, Brace), and John Steinbeck with his initial big popular success, Of Mice and Men (Covici, Friede).   Nonfiction was, in the main, substantial too.   To be noted were Noël Coward's autobiography, Present Indicative (Doubleday, Doran), Mathematics for the Million, by Lancelot Hogben (Norton), and Volume I of Van Wyck Brooks's critical history of American literature, The Flowering of New England (Dutton).

1938

Most long-lived among the year's popular fiction, still being read today, were the leading best-seller, The Yearling, by Marjorie Kinnan Rawlings (Scribners), the story of a Florida boy and his fawn, and the famous Rebecca, by Daphne du Maurier (Doubleday, Doran), which combined romance, mystery, and suspense in a way that satisfied a great audience and firmly established the author as one of the most popular of contemporary novelists.   Nonfiction provided an interesting list.   First was the work of a Chinese philosopher, The Importance of Living, by Lin Yutang (Reynal & Hitchcock).   Margaret Halsey got off a lively spoof on the English, their manners and mores, in With Malice Toward Some (Simon & Schuster).   There were biographies --Madame Curie, by her daughter Eve Curie (Doubleday, Doran), Benjamin Franklin, by Carl Van Doren (Viking), Fanny Kemble, by Margaret Armstrong (Macmillan).   Both Anne Morrow Lindbergh and Admiral Byrd added to their narratives of exploration, the first in Listen, the Wind! (Harcourt, Brace) and the second in Alone (Putnam), this time about the Antarctic.   Ogden Nash's I'm a Stranger Here Myself (Little, Brown) brought a favorite New Yorker writer to the fore in book form.   The country doctor's story was told by Arthur E. Hertzler in The Horse and Buggy Doctor (Harper).

1939

The greatest novel stemming from the Depression years was 1939's leading seller and Pulitzer Prize-winner, The Grapes of Wrath, by John Steinbeck (Viking).   Like other well-known novels of the Twenties, Thirties, and Forties, such as Grand Hotel, Elmer Gantry, East of Eden, and The Silver Chalice, The Grapes of Wrath is reaching a new generation as a late-hour TV movie. John P. Marquand's first serious novel, The Late George Apley, had been both a popular and critical success when it was published in 1937. Frequently, as with Thomas Wolfe and many other writers, an author's second book achieved greater national popularity than his first; in Marquand's case it was Wickford Point (Little, Brown). More and more fiction as well as nonfiction was being based on the fateful events of the pre-World War II years. Such a novel was Escape, by Ethel Vance (Little, Brown), as its title implies an exciting story of flight from Nazi Germany. Christopher Morley, long prominent in other literary fields, wrote a widely read novel about a modern working girl, Kitty Foyle (Lippincott). The Nazarene (Putnam), reviving the religio-historical theme common to many popular novels over the years, was the work of a writer in Yiddish, Sholem Asch, then new to readers in the United States. Of world significance among the nonfiction best-sellers was Adolf Hitler's Mein Kampf (Reynal & Hitchcock), and a number of outstanding titles mirrored European disorder. To be noted in other fields were Yale Professor William Lyon Phelps's Autobiography with Letters (Oxford), Wind, Sand and Stars, in which French flyer Antoine de St. - Exupéry (Reynal & Hitchcock) added to the poetic literature of flight, and, extending the American grass-roots country doctor theme, Country Lawyer, by Bellamy Partridge (Whittlesey House). John Gunther continued his series with Inside Asia (Harper).

1940

Two new British writers proved excellent representatives of their country insofar as the American reading public was concerned. Leading fiction sales for the year was Richard Llewellyn's moving story of a Welsh mining family. How Green Was My Valley (Macmillan). Jan Struther, who was one of the most frequent and entertaining guests on the top radio show, Information, Please!, proved as popular with the book audience when her Mrs. Miniver (Harcourt, Brace) was published. Most memorable, from a literary standpoint, was the book that finished in fourth place, Ernest Hemingway's novel of the Spanish Civil War and his first really big seller, For Whom the Bell Tolls (Scribners). Two good, and lengthy, historical novels made the grade--Stars on the Sea, by F. van Wyck Mason (Lippincott), and Oliver Wiswell, by Ken-

neth Roberts (Doubleday, Doran). In the first year of the
live war only two nonfiction leaders were concerned with
world political events: American White Paper, by Joseph
W. Alsop, Jr., and Robert Kintner, Washington newsmen (Simon & Schuster), and Days of Our Years, by Pierre van
Paassen (Dial). Top seller was Osa Johnson's record of her
life with her explorer and big-game-photographer husband,
Martin Johnson, I Married Adventure (Lippincott). Self-edu-
cation and entertainment balanced each other in Mortimer
Adler's How to Read a Book (Simon & Schuster) and Oscar
Levant's A Smattering of Ignorance (Doubleday, Doran).

1941

A. J. Cronin, who was to be one of the most popular
novelists over a score of years, hit the top of the fiction list
with probably his best-liked book, The Keys of the Kingdom
(Little, Brown). Random Harvest, by James Hilton (Little,
Brown), a novel of the First World War, was second. This
Above All, by Eric Knight (Harper), was one of the most
highly appreciated novels of early World War II. Mr. Knight
was, incidentally, the creator of "Lassie" in book form.
Again fiction was filled with familiar names--Hemingway, Roberts, Marquand, Ferber, and Mary Ellen Chase. Books a-
bout the war were the most popular in nonfiction. Berlin Diary, by foreign correspondent William L. Shirer (Knopf), and
Winston S. Churchill's speeches in Blood, Sweat and Tears
(Putnam) were highly influential in the months before the
United States entered the war, while Alice Duer Miller's narrative poem The White Cliffs (Coward-McCann) was emotionally moving.

1942

World War II was represented only by one very popular
novel in the year after Pearl Harbor. This was John Steinbeck's story laid in invaded Norway, The Moon is Down (Viking). Religious themes predominated. The year's leader was
The Song of Bernadette, by Franz Werfel (Viking). Lloyd C.
Douglas's most famous book, The Robe (Houghton Mifflin),
made its initial appearance on the best-seller list, to which it
was to return another four times. The humorous saga of the
most popular G.I. of World War II, See Here, Private Hargrove, by Marion Hargrove (Holt), surpassed in sales all other nonfiction of the year. War books--technical, political,
and personal--dominated the nonfiction scene. Perhaps most
to be remembered were W. L. White's They Were Expendable

(Harcourt, Brace), Ambassador Davies's Mission to Moscow (Simon & Schuster), and Elliot Paul's reminiscences, The Last Time I Saw Paris (Random House).

1943

The Robe had become the most widely-read novel of the time. In its second year it was at the top of best-sellers. Following it were such well-known novels as The Valley of Decision, by Marcia Davenport (Scribners); So Little Time, by John P. Marquand (Little, Brown); A Tree Grows in Brooklyn, by Betty Smith (Harper), and The Human Comedy, by William Saroyan (Harcourt, Brace). One World, by Wendell L. Willkie (Simon & Schuster), was most impressive of the many war books that filled the 1943 nonfiction list. Not to be forgotten either were Guadalcanal Diary, by Richard Tregaskis (Random House), and Here Is Your War (Holt), first best-seller by the best-loved reporter of the war, Ernie Pyle. The only civilian books among the first ten of the year were On Being a Real Person (Harper), by Dr. Harry Emerson Fosdick, famed New York pastor and radio preacher, and Our Hearts Were Young and Gay (Dodd, Mead), recounting the madcap European travels of those prewar junior misses Cornelia Otis Skinner and Emily Kimbrough.

1944

Pioneer in its time, Strange Fruit (Reynal & Hitchcock), a novel about Negro and white in the South, was written by Lillian Smith. The hotly discussed book shared with another the ban of Boston, which brought added publicity to both. The other was the first novel by Kathleen Winsor, a story of Restoration England, Forever Amber (Macmillan). Memorable for their quality were two books with war backgrounds in that last full year of World War II, A Bell for Adano, by John Hersey (Knopf), and The Razor's Edge, by W. Somerset Maugham (Doubleday, Doran). Ernie Pyle's second book about the American G.I., Brave Men (Holt), joined his Here Is Your War on the nonfiction best-seller list, which was headed by a book of humorous war experiences, I Never Left Home, by touring comedian Bob Hope (Simon & Schuster). And one of the most popular war reporters, Quentin Reynolds, contributed The Curtain Rises (Random House). With little of the fanfare that was to come later to the story of Anna, Anna and the King of Siam, by Margaret Landon (John Day), reached eighth place on the year's list. Among the popular biographies were Good Night, Sweet Prince, Gene Fowler's life of John Barry-

more (Viking), and Yankee from Olympus, an account of the
Holmes family and Justice Oliver Wendell Holmes in particular, by Catherine Drinker Bowen (Little, Brown). Writing
autobiographically, Ambassador Grew told about Ten Years
in Japan (Simon & Schuster).

1945

New names dotted the best-seller list along with others
well established there, such as Lloyd C. Douglas, Sinclair
Lewis, and James Hilton. Coming to the fore, each with
what was to be one of many popular historical novels, were
Thomas Costain, Samuel Shellabarger, and Irving Stone. The
titles were The Black Rose (Doubleday), Captain from Castile (Little, Brown), and Immortal Wife (Doubleday). Douglas's The Robe, which had been first in 1943, was second in
1944 and again in 1945. New novelists were James Ramsey
Ullman with his book about mountain climbers, The White
Tower (Lippincott), Adria Locke Langley with A Lion Is in
the Streets (Whittlesey House), a novel based on a Southern
political character, and Gwethalyn Graham, Canadian author
of Earth and High Heaven (Lippincott), which was concerned
with the problem of religious prejudice. Ernie Pyle had been
killed in the Pacific war theater early in the year. His best-
seller of 1944, Brave Men, outsold every other title of both
fiction and nonfiction of the next year. Another war correspondent who illustrated his own books, Bill Mauldin, scored
a hit with Up Front (Holt). The leading autobiography was
Richard Wright's Black Boy (Harper). James Thurber took
his first bow on the best-seller list with The Thurber Carni-
val (Harper).

1946

Several authors who are best-sellers today first
reached that status in 1946: Taylor Caldwell with This Side
of Innocence (Scribners); Frances Parkinson Keyes with The
River Road (Messner), and Frank Yerby with The Foxes of
Harrow (Dial). Other new names were Frederick Wakeman,
who added another idiom to our language with his story of the
advertising business, The Hucksters (Rinehart), and Mary
Jane Ward, who performed the same semantic feat when her
picture of a psychiatric institution, The Snake Pit (Random
House), found many readers. The widely publicized, lively
autobiography of Betty MacDonald, The Egg and I (Lippincott),
won first place in nonfiction in 1946. Two biographies of the
late Franklin D. Roosevelt were 1946 best-sellers: As He

Saw It, by Elliott Roosevelt (Duell, Sloan & Pearce), and The Roosevelt I Knew, by Frances Perkins (Viking).

1947

The Miracle of the Bells, by Russell Janney (Prentice-Hall), was an example of the power of publicity and advertising to get great distribution for a book. The author, a theatrical producer, told a story that was good enough, however, to gain more readers in 1947 than did any other novel; it had been second in 1946 (the film is still around on late TV). Besides a roll of historical and modern novels by long-time popular writers, including Lydia Bailey, by Kenneth Roberts (Doubleday), and Prince of Foxes, by Samuel Shellabarger (Little, Brown), there were two books on the problems of prejudice. Gentlemen's Agreement, by Laura Z. Hobson (Simon & Schuster), dealt with Jewish-gentile relations; Sinclair Lewis's Kingsblood Royal (Random House) with those of Negro and white. Peace of Mind, by Rabbi Joshua L. Liebman (Simon & Schuster), which had been second in 1946, led nonfiction in 1947. Another impressive religious book of the year was Human Destiny, by the famous scientist Pierre Lecomte du Noüy (Longmans, Green). John Gunther's first edition of Inside U. S. A. (Harper), which has been revised a number of times since, was third on the 1947 list, while Arnold J. Toynbee's enduring work, A Study of History (Oxford), was also on the ladder. War memoirs continued to be well read.

1948

The Naked and the Dead, by Norman Mailer (Rinehart), was one of the most pervasively-read of World War II novels. In 1948 it was exceeded in sales only by Lloyd C. Douglas's religio-historical novel The Big Fisherman (Houghton Mifflin). Another interesting war novel was by playwright Irwin Shaw, The Young Lions (Random House). A leading first novel, bought by the public and discussed by the critics, was Raintree County, by Ross Lockridge, Jr. (Houghton Mifflin). Not long after his book's success, the author committed suicide. People were also buying Dinner at Antoine's, by Frances Parkinson Keyes (Messner), probably the author's best-known book. Joining Peace of Mind, in its third year, was a layman's self-help book, How to Stop Worrying and Start Living, by Dale Carnegie (Simon & Schuster). His How to Win Friends and Influence People (Simon & Schuster) had been the best-seller of 1937. Dr.

Norman Vincent Peale's first best-seller, A Guide to Confident Living (Prentice-Hall), got around in 1948. And, along
with religion and self-help, came sex. More people bought
Dr. A. C. Kinsey's not inexpensive, serious study Sexual
Behavior in the Human Male (Saunders) than might have been
expected, especially since it was brought out by a medical
publisher that did not push it unduly. However, topping
everything during 1948 was General Dwight D. Eisenhower's
account of the winning of the war, Crusade in Europe
(Doubleday). Also in the field of contemporary history were
The Gathering Storm, by Sir Winston Churchill (Houghton
Mifflin), and Roosevelt and Hopkins, by Robert E. Sherwood
(Harper).

1949

A new author of popular historical fiction, Mika Wal-
tari, headed the list with The Egyptian (Putnam), followed by
the Biblical-historical works The Big Fisherman, by Lloyd
C. Douglas, and Mary, by Sholem Asch (Putnam). John O'
Hara made his first appearance as a top best-seller with A
Rage to Live (Random House). Nonfiction was entirely dominated by books of games and entertainment and by inspirational works. The latter included The Seven Storey
Mountain, by Thomas Merton (Harcourt, Brace); The Greatest Story Ever Told, by Fulton Oursler (Doubleday); Peace
of Soul, by the then Monsignor Fulton J. Sheen (Whittlesey
House), a Catholic rejoinder to Peace of Mind, and, in its
second year, A Guide to Confident Living.

1950

Once again a novel with a religious background was
the most popular of the year with American readers. This
was The Cardinal, by a writer new to the lists, Henry Morton Robinson (Simon & Schuster). Two novels had war backgrounds. In Ernest Hemingway's Across the River and Into
the Trees (Scribners) the war was a minor backdrop for the
love story of an older man and a young girl. The wall that
barred off the Jewish ghetto of Nazi-occupied Warsaw was
the inspiration for John Hersey's great novel. The Wall
(Knopf). In the wake of the numerous topical books of the
war years, most popular nonfiction had turned out to be novelty and "how-to" books. There were few books for serious
readers among the first ten of 1950. The Mature Mind, by
philosopher-psychologist H. A. Overstreet (Norton), stood out
like a beacon, and there were also Thor Heyerdahl's account

of modern sea adventure, Kon-Tiki (Rand McNally), and the
sermons of Washington minister Peter Marshall, Mr. Jones,
Meet the Master (Revell).

1951

After a declining chart of interesting new writers or
achievements by established authors, the public's choice
made 1951's novels a brilliant line-up. At the top was the
first work of a new writer, James Jones, a strong story of
the pre-war Army in Hawaii, From Here to Eternity (Scribners). Excellent stories of the wartime Army and Navy followed it: The Caine Mutiny, by new novelist Herman Wouk
(Doubleday), remembered as stage play and movie as well
as a book; The Cruel Sea, by Nicholas Monsarrat (Knopf),
another writer new to the lists; and Melville Goodwin, U.S.A.,
by John P. Marquand (Little, Brown). James A. Michener,
whose 1947 Tales of the South Pacific (Macmillan) did not a-
chieve, on first book publication, the audiences that did the
musical made from it, took a postwar look at the South Pacific in Return to Paradise (Random House). The nonfiction
list was not so bright, though shining out at sixth place from
among the picture books, health books, and cookbooks was
Rachel Carson's marvelous account of The Sea Around Us
(Oxford). Washington Confidential, by Jack Lait and Lee
Mortimer (Crown), harked back to Washington Merry-Go-
Round of just twenty years before, and started the authors'
series of "Confidential" books.

1952

Standing out from all the popular historical novels of
the year was Ernest Hemingway's short masterpiece. The
Old Man and the Sea (Scribners). The Caine Mutiny was second for the second year, followed by John Steinbeck's East
of Eden (Viking). Also in the running was Edna Ferber, who
had turned to Texas and Texans for Giant (Doubleday). Because it is axiomatic that the Bible is always the best-seller,
sales of Bibles are never totted up each year for the best-
seller list. But in 1952 a new translation, long in preparation, was published, and, as a new book, became the top
best-seller of that year and the following two. This was The
Holy Bible: Revised Standard Version (Nelson). Dr. Peale's
The Power of Positive Thinking (Prentice-Hall) was on the
list as well as another religious book, This I Believe, edited
by Edward P. Morgan (Simon & Schuster). Second in sales
only to the Bible was Catherine Marshall's biography of her

late minister husband, A Man Called Peter (Whittlesey House).
There were other interesting biographies. Two of them, relating to the election year, were This Is Ike, edited by Wilson Hicks (Holt), and Mr. President, by William Hillman
(Farrar, Straus & Young), about the Truman Administration.
Actress Tallulah Bankhead told her own story in Tallulah
(Harper), while, recalling events that come to light in 1948,
the most important figure in the Alger Hiss case, aside from
the principal, told the story of his life and his political activity in Witness (Random House). The author was Whittaker
Chambers.

1953

To coincide with the release of movies based upon
two books of previous years--two very different in subject
matter--cheaper editions of The Robe and From Here to
Eternity were popular features of 1953. The Silver Chalice,
a religio-historical novel by Thomas B. Costain (Doubleday),
which had been 1952's most popular novel, was second in
1953, followed by historical and modern novels by favorite
writers. Among new names in fiction were those of Leon
Uris with the war novel Battle Cry (Putnam) and Ernest K.
Gann with The High and the Mighty (Sloane). Most of the popular books outside fiction were repeats from the year before
or new books in the same vein as their authors' previous successes. They included the Revised Standard Version, The
Power of Positive Thinking, A Man called Peter, and This I
Believe, all in the classification of religion. Dr. Kinsey followed the human male with Sexual Behavior in the Human Female (Saunders). Also in this area of human activity was
Polly Adler's A House Is Not a Home (Rinehart).

1954

From a critical standpoint the most interesting title a-
mong the popular novels of 1954 was The View from Pompey's
Head (Doubleday), with which Hamilton Basso, well-known author, became a best-seller for the first time. His was the
story of a Southern city as seen by a lawyer who was born
there, but who made his first return to Pompey's Head after
many years in New York. John Steinbeck's Sweet Thursday
(Viking) and Mac Hyman's first novel, No Time for Sergeants,
a riotous story of U.S. Army life as experienced by a raw re-
cruit, were both made into successful plays. Top fiction seller was a novel that reaffirmed popular interes in medical
matters, Not as a Stranger, by Morton Thompson (Scribners).

For the third successive year, religious nonfiction proved
most appealing to American book-buyers. Added to the Revised Standard Version and The Power of Positive Thinking
were The Prayers of Peter Marshall (McGraw-Hill) and a
new second volume of This I Believe, edited by Raymond
Swing (Simon & Schuster). Elmer Davis, one of the best-
liked commentators on the air through war and postwar years,
wrote a book on current affairs, But We Were Born Free
(Bobbs-Merrill). Choice in autobiography led to best-seller-
dom sportswriter Grantland Rice's The Tumult and the Shout-
ing (Barnes) and I'll Cry Tomorrow, singer Lillian Roth's
story of her comeback, written by her and by Gerold Frank
and Mike Connally (Frederick Fell).

1955

Herman Wouk, whose war novel had been so enthusiastically received four years before, returned to the fiction
list, in first place this time, with a novel about the problems of a modern New York girl, Marjorie Morningstar
(Doubleday). There were a number of interesting novels by
authors new to the list. Patrick Dennis's Auntie Mame (Vanguard) introduced a delightfully eccentric but well-meaning
character in a book that was turned into a big Broadway hit.
MacKinlay Kantor had been known as novelist and poet for
years; his long Civil War novel Andersonville (World) brought
him fame. A young French girl, Françoise Sagan, intrigued
many readers with ther Bonjour Tristesse (Dutton). The Man
in the Gray Flannel Suit, by Sloan Wilson (Simon & Schuster),
pictured the Madison Avenue man foreshadowed in The Hucksters of 1946. Anne Morrow Lindbergh returned to top the
best-seller list, after seventeen years, with her Gift from the
Sea (Pantheon), a thoughtful essay addressed primarily to
women. The Power of Positive Thinking continued to sell
extraordinarily well in its fourth year on the list, as did A
Man Called Peter in its third. A book combining fine photog-
raphy and science was The Family of Man, by Edward Strei-
chen (Simon & Schuster). In the field of public affairs there
were ex-President Truman's Years of Decisions (Doubleday)
and John Gunther's Inside Africa (Harper).

1956

As in No Time for Sergeants, Mac Hyman's best-seller
of 1953-54, the humor in Don't Go Near the Water, by William Brinkley (Random House), was aimed at martial life, this
time the Navy in the Pacific. The book found more readers

than any other novel of 1956.   The two that followed it were
by a writer new to the list and by a first novelist.   Edwin
O'Connor's first big best-seller was The Last Hurrah (Little,
Brown), story of a once powerful politician in a New England
city.   The first novel was also laid in New England; it was
Grace Metalious's Peyton Place (Messner), which attracted
lots of publicity.   "How-to" books and books of information
surged up on the nonfiction list, which contained only two
books for general reading.   These were The Search for
Bridey Murphy, by Morey Bernstein (Doubleday), a strange
account of a young Colorado matron who under hypnosis assumed most convincingly the speech and character of an eigh-
teenth-century Irishwoman; and, just reaching tenth place,
Kathryn Hulme's moving biography of a Belgian nun, The
Nun's Story (Little, Brown).   Among other popular nonfiction
of the year were Profiles in Courage (Harper), which won
the Pulitzer Prize in biography for the then Senator John F.
Kennedy; The Birth of Britain and The New World (Dodd,
Mead), the first two volumes in Sir Winston Churchill's A
History of the English-Speaking Peoples; and a Civil War his-
tory by Bruce Catton, This Hallowed Ground (Doubleday).

1957

The leading 1957 novel, greatly praised by the critics,
was the story, professional and emotional, of a New England
lawyer, By Love Possessed (Harcourt, Brace).   The author,
James Gould Cozzens, had written many previous books.
This one marked the high point of his career to date.   Meyer Levin wrote Compulsion (Simon & Schuster), fictionaliza-
tion of the Leopold-Loeb case of more than three decades before.   With On the Beach (Morrow), a dramatic and chilling
story of a future atomic war, Nevil Shute, who had written
many popular novels over the years, reached the annual list
for the first time.   Where Did You Go?   Out.   What Did
You Do?   Nothing.   (Norton) was one of the most provocative
book titles ever.   These childhood reminiscences of Robert
Paul Smith proved deservedly popular.   Highly entertaining
also were the personal sketches of everyday suburban life in
Please Don't Eat the Daisies, by Jean Kerr (Doubleday).
And outstanding was the autobiography of Bernard M. Baruch,
Baruch: My Own Story (Holt).   The FBI Story, by Don White-
head (Random House), was also high in the year's sales, while
perennial best-selling writers on religious themes appeared
again--Norman Vincent Peale with Stay Alive All Your Life
(Prentice-Hall) and Catherine Marshall with the autobiographi-
cal To Live Again (McGraw-Hill).

1958

Novels by Russian writers were high spots in the year's fiction. First was Boris Pasternak's Doctor Zhivago (Pantheon), the story of a doctor who was also a poet in post-revolutionary Russia. The Soviet government prevented the author from accepting the Nobel Prize for literature, which was awarded to him in that year. The twelve-year-old heroine of Lolita, by Vladimir Nabokov (Putnam), became a familiar figure, on the screen as well as in the book, though there was little resemblance between movie and novel. From the Terrace (Random House) was a new John O'Hara best-seller. Edna Ferber celebrated what was to become the newest state, Alaska, in Ice Palace (Doubleday). And for the second successive year Art Linkletter's humorous Kids Say the Darndest Things! (Prentice-Hall) outsold the rest of nonfiction, even The New Testament in Modern English (One-Volume Edition), translated by J. R. Phillips (Macmillan). The first best-seller by a commentator on affairs present and past, whose books were to continue to be very popular, was Only in America (World). The author, Harry Golden, is the editor of the paper The Carolina Israelite. John Gunther brought history up to date in Inside Russia Today (Harper).

1959

The history of another new state was incorporated by James Michener in his long novel Hawaii (Random House), which was exceeded in popularity during 1959 only by Doctor Zhivago in its second year, and, at the top of the list, Leon Uris's novel about the modern nation of Israel, Exodus (Doubleday). Washington newspaperman Allen Drury's first novel, Advise and Consent, was also read by a large public. Another book based on political affairs, and causing much comment because of its portrayal of American bureaucrats in southeast Asia, was The Ugly American, by William J. Lederer and Eugene L. Burdick (Norton). D. H. Lawrence's Lady Chatterley's Lover (Grove), first published in 1928 and long an under-the-counter item, became a 1959 best-seller when it was issued here in its original form, and stayed in the headlines most of the year because of various court proceedings. The Status Seekers (McKay), by Vance Packard, whose previous The Hidden Persuaders (McKay) about advertising had gained attention, added "status" as a connotative word in our social and business life. A rarity among top popular books was a little volume originally written as a text-

book by William Strunk, Jr., late professor of English at
Cornell University. Elements of Style (Macmillan) was revised by E. B. White, New Yorker writer, who looked upon
it as a bible of writing style. Playwright Moss Hart's Act
One (Random House) vied with Harry Golden's reminiscences
of his early New York life, For 2¢ Plain (World), for auto-
biographical laurels of the year.

1960

Fiction repeats from 1959, in first and second places
on the 1960 list, were Advise and Consent and Hawaii. They
were followed by the work of a writer entirely new to this
country, an Italian nobleman, Giuseppe di Lampedusa, who
had died before his novel about a noble Sicilian family, The
Leopard (Pantheon), was published here. John O'Hara had
two books on the list at once: a novel, Ourselves to Know
(Random House), and Sermons and Soda-Water (Random
House), containing three novelettes. The first best-seller
by Irving Wallace, whose books and the movies based upon
them were to be among the most highly remunerative of these
years, was The Chapman Report (Simon & Schuster). This
was concerned with the affairs of an interviewer working on
a survey of human female sexual activity. William L. Shirer,
whose Berlin Diary had been one of the most widely read
books of World War II, wrote a notable history, The Rise
and Fall of the Third Reich (Simon & Schuster). Jack Paar,
at the height of his TV popularity, wrote about himself in I
Kid You Not (Little, Brown). A best-seller was The Conscience of a Conservative, by Barry Goldwater (Victor Publishing Co.). But The Strategy of Peace, by President-elect
John F. Kennedy (Harper), did not quite make the top ten.

1961

There were several novelists well known to American
readers who were the most popular of the year--and some
new ones. Longest known was A. A. Milne, whose Winnie
the Pooh appeared in Latin as Winnie Ille Pu, translated
from the English by Alexander Lenard (Dutton). This innova-
tion--translations of favorite stories of both young and old into foreign languages--was one that caught on. John Steinbeck
continued as a longtime best-seller with The Winter of Our
Discontent (Viking); he was to be awarded the Nobel Prize for
literature in 1962. Irving Stone's fine novel about Michel-
angelo, The Agony and the Ecstasy (Doubleday), had the most
buyers of all. Leon Uris wrote a novel about the Warsaw

ghetto in World War II, Mila 18 (Doubleday). J. D. Salinger,
whose The Catcher in the Rye (Little, Brown) had been a
hit in 1951, first appeared in the top ranks with stories a-
bout the Glass family in Franny and Zooey (Little, Brown).
The Pulitzer Prize-winning To Kill a Mockingbird, by Harper
Lee (Lippincott), was the year's leading first novel. Like
Lady Chatterley's Lover in 1959, Henry Miller's Tropic of
Cancer (Grove), long under cover, was brought out in the
open in 1961, to find many readers and many would-be sup-
pressers. As had happened before, a new Bible translation
outsold all other nonfiction: The New English Bible: The
New Testament (Cambridge University Press and Oxford University Press). There were two timely books on political
affairs: The Making of the President, 1960, by Theodore H.
White (Atheneum), and A Nation of Sheep (Norton), about
American foreign policy and public information, by William
J. Lederer, co-author of The Ugly American of 1959. Ring
of Bright Water, by Gavin Maxwell (Dutton), was one of the
delightful books about nature that come to the fore only occasionally. This was about life on the Scottish coast with
the author's pet otters.

1962

The most widely read novel of the year was one long
anticipated by the critics--Ship of Fools, by Katherine Anne
Porter (Atlantic-Little, Brown), a dissection of the people
aboard a ship going from Mexico to Germany in 1931. Anne
Morrow Lindbergh for the first time turned her talent to fiction in Dearly Beloved (Harcourt, Brace & World), the run-
ner-up of the year. Allen Drury's second book, A Shade of
Difference (Doubleday), dealt with politics in the U. N. instead of in Washington. Serious in intent but full of excitement were two semipolitical thrillers, Fail-Safe, by Eugene
Burdick and Harvey Wheeler (McGraw-Hill), and Seven Days
in May, by Fletcher Knebel and Charles W. Bailey II (Harper
& Row). The Reivers (Random House), William Faulkner's
first book to appear on an annual best-seller list, was published just before his death and won the Pulitzer Prize. It
ranked tenth on a fiction list of unusually high quality. Aside
from The New English Bible, Frederic Morton's fine biography of the banking family The Rothschilds (Atheneum), lawyer
Louis Nizer's description of some of his famous cases, My
Life in Court (Doubleday), and John Steinbeck's account of a
trailer trip from coast to coast with his dog, Travels with
Charley (Viking), there was little serious on the nonfiction
list. O Ye Jigs & Juleps! (Macmillan) was a pleasing little

book, a diary recording the manners of the early 1900s
kept by Virginia Cary Hudson when she was a child. Not
quite making the list of the top ten were some outstanding
books: Robert Frost's In the Clearing (Holt, Rinehart &
Winston), which had a greater readership than poetry usually attracts; Barbara Tuchman's Pulitzer Prize-winning history The Guns of August (Macmillan); Rachel Carson's Si-
lent Spring (Houghton Mifflin), and Six Crises, by former
Vice President Richard Nixon (Doubleday).

1963

        Provoking more argument than the novel that outsold
it in 1963 was Mary McCarthy's story of some Vassar
friends as they were ten years out of college, The Group
(Harcourt, Brace & World). Its author had long been a distinguished writer but this was her first top hit. It was first
time on the list as well for the leading popular novelist of
the year, Morris L. West, who wrote about a newly-elected
Pope in The Shoes of the Fisherman (Morrow). Rumer Godden also gained her first place in top fiction with The Battle
of the Villa Fiorita (Viking). There were two other authors
whose first published novels achieved great popularity. One
was John Rechy's story of homosexual life in several large
American towns, City of Night (Grove). The other was a
picture of life aboard a Navy gunboat in China forty years
ago, The Sand Pebbles, by Richard McKenna (Harper & Row).
Along with books by Salinger, Michener, O'Hara, Caldwell,
and Du Maurier, last year's fiction list was decidedly pre-
sentable. Nonfiction featured novelty books and guides for
the homemaker. Reading fare included J. F. K.: The Man
and the Myth, by Victor Lasky (Macmillan) and Bob Hope's
hilarious record of his peacetime travels, I Owe Russia
$1200 (Doubleday). Highly popular, but not among the first
ten, were The American Way of Death, by Jessica Mitford
(Simon & Schuster), The Fire Next Time, by James Baldwin (Dial), Mandate for Change, by ex-President Eisenhower
(Doubleday), and Rascal, by Sterling North (Dutton).

1964

        For the first time a spy story has it hands down. It
is unlikely that any other novel of 1964 will acquire more
readers than will The Spy Who Came In from the Cold, by
John Le Carré (Coward-McCann). Nonfiction is as yet unde-
termined, though it is certain that the many books under the
heading J. F. K. will dominate the list. Some of the most

popular are: Profiles in Courage, Memorial Edition, by
John F. Kennedy (Harper & Row); Four Days, with preface
by Bruce Catton (American Heritage and UPI); A Tribute to
John F. Kennedy, by Pierre Salinger and Sander Vanocur
(Encyclopedia Britannica); A Day in the Life of President
Kennedy, by Jim Bishop (Random House); and The Burden
and the Glory, by John F. Kennedy, edited by Allan Nevins
(Harper & Row).

Report on the Publishers' Weekly Spring List
to the Government of Mars

By Clarence Gohdes, Editor of American Literature; author
of books about American literature; Professor of English,
Duke University.

From South Atlantic Quarterly 64:390-3, Summer 1965. ©
by Duke University Press.   Reprinted by permission.

The special committee appointed by the Martian Con-
federation of States to analyze the "Spring 1964 List" of the
Publishers' Weekly begs herewith to make its report.   It
will be recalled that four middle-time-units ago Your Excel-
lency turned over to us this valuable treasure which was
found in the possession of one of the two prisoners brought
back by our raiding party sent to investigate the planet called
"The World."   The delay in submitting our report is due to
the untimely death of these captives, upon whose supplementary information our interpretation and analysis have in part
depended.

The prisoner who had the "Spring List" in his pocket
when captured asserted that he was the manager of a variety
store which maintained a book department and that he was in
the habit of using it as a means of selecting books to be sold
in his shop.   It is clear that the periodical lists the works
about to be released by the various publishers in a country
called the United States of America.   The issue under survey
consists largely of advertisements and a roster of 9,007 authors and 9,518 titles of books.   (Both prisoners, even when
questioned separately, stoutly maintained that in their country
no one reads a magazine or newspaper unless it is provided
with an abundance of advertisements such as to challenge the
reader's ingenuity in discovering the reading matter.)   It consists of 506 pages bound in paper and has as a decorative device on the front cover a photograph of a large daisy in the
center of which appears the word "Spring."   It weighs one
pound, eight and a half ounces.

The authors or editors of the books listed are, first of all, arranged alphabetically and run from A. Aaboe, author of Episodes in the Early History of Massachusetts, to B. Zwirz, whose lucubration is entitled Compact Book of Fresh Water Fishing. We can draw no safe conclusions from examining the names of these authors or editors and accordingly shall say no more about them except to note a few of the most prolific. Heading the list in the number of titles represented is a person named W. Shakespeare (thirty-two items). The prisoners informed us that the reason for his preeminence is that the four-hundredth anniversary of his birth, in April, 1964, occasioned a surge of reprints of his works. They also stated that the next most prolific author, E. R. Burroughs (eighteen titles), was more nearly representative of popular taste in their country. Most of his books appear to deal with a remarkable person named Tarzan, to whom the titles apply adjectives like "magnificent" and "triumphant." Apparently, this Tarzan has visited cities of gold and, more important perhaps, has penetrated the earth's core. Your committee recommends that on the next expedition to "The World" a special effort be made to secure copies of these works.

The writer responsible for the next highest number of publications (fifteen) is E. Fodor, author of guide books all called "modern." We note a special fondness of this word in the list, for, all told, sixty-six titles begin with this word. In contrast only ten begin with the word "ancient." Two authors are tied for next place, namely, A. Christie and E. S. Gardner (eight titles apiece). The former, we infer, is a popular mortician and the latter a lawyer especially interested in peculiar legal cases, involving calendar girls, daring divorcees, half-awakened wives, reluctant models, and one-eyed witnesses. Following, with seven different books, is M. I. Reid, who seems to address his works to amateur writers; and thereafter come a pair (six each), H. James and H. Melville, undistinguished so far as our information goes.

More consequential by far than the authors' names are the titles, which provide clues to the nature of the people by whom and for whom the books are produced. Generalization, however, is exceedingly difficult. What common denominator exists among the following examples we are unable to decide:

If He Hollers Let Him Go; Teen-Ager You're Dating;

That Happy Feeling of Thank-You; Virgin Luck; So You
Want to Be Psychoanalyzed; Quick Before It Melts; Read-
ings in Delinquency; Passion Flowers in Italy; Normal
Neurosis; Medical Itch; Metropolitan Opera Murders; Little
Dog Gone; Lose Weight with the Stars; Love You Good,
See You Later; I Can't Boil Water; I Was a Male War
Bride; High Cost of Holy Living; The Gods Hate Kansas;
Drinking with Pepys; Escape across the Cosmos; Dog That
Spoke French; Dennis the Menace, A. M. , Ambassador of
Mischief; Chastise Me with Scorpions; Come Dance with
Kitty Stobling; Burning as a Substitute for Loving; Bible in
Pocket, Gun in Hand; All Women Are Fatal; All Over God's
Irish Heaven.

     The above collection of titles selected to illustrate pe-
culiarity and variety suggests, however, a consciousness of
sex which may be revelatory, even though only eleven titles
actually begin with the word "sex" or "sexual." Among these
are Sex and the College Girl, Sex and the Mature Man, Sex
and the Office, and Sex in Business. We note the absence
of sex in science.

     Apparently "black" (20) is favored as an initial word
over "white" (0); "life" (20) over "death" (15); "man" (41)
over "God" (18). "New" appears fifty-two times; "contemporary" (11), "experiment" or "experimental" (16). Geographical favorites in the first words of the titles are "America" or "American" (89), "Russia" or "Soviet" (25), "France"
or "French" (19), "Africa" or "African" (18). While "California" crops up eleven times and "World" seventeen, Mars
does not occur at all.

     By all odds the favorite first word in the titles of the
books listed is "how" (96), with examples like How Did a
Nice Girl Like You Get Into This Business, How Never to
Be Tired, How to Be a Jewish Mother, and How to Buy and
Sell Old Bottles. "How to" is especially favored and runs the
gamut, from How to Make Love in Five Languages and How
to Travel with Children to Europe, How to Study Philippians,
Colossians and Philemon, and How to Pose for the Camera.
In contrast with "how," only three titles begin with "why,"
nine with "when," and four with "where."

     Your committee concludes that the "Spring List" of the
Publishers' Weekly shows no indication that Mars is about to
be invaded, though two titles suggest that the inhabitants of
"The World" may be groping in that direction: Extraterrestrial

Communication and Exploration of the Moon. We recommend that efforts be made to obtain copies of these two
titles when next an expedition goes to that planet. Your
committee would like also to examine copies of I Am an
Adulteress, Sexually Responsive Women, and How to Solve
Your Sex Problems with Self-Hypnosis, if they can be obtained.

                    Respectfully submitted,

                    Clarence Gohdes
                    Professor of Sociological Analysis
                    National University of Mars

B.   Educational Books

Odyssey of a Book: How a Social Studies
Text Comes Into Being

By Ronald B. Edgerton, editor and Head of the High School
Social Science Department of a major publishing house.

From Social Education 33:279-86, March 1969. © by the
National Council for the Social Studies.   Reprinted by permission.

Most of us have used social studies textbooks as students for over sixteen years and as teachers for many more.
We should be experts on this subject, if any.   Especially
since all textbooks, like all women, are pretty much alike.
But are they?   Outwardly and superficially perhaps.   Most
textbooks have covers and bindings and pages and print; and
some, like people, can be quite boring.   But each is unique
in reflecting the ideas of the individual(s) who authored it.
Each is a creation, a brainchild if you will, legally protected by the law of copyright whose date marks its birth.
As one first-time author put it, "Writing a new textbook is
the nearest any man can come to bearing a baby."   And another when queried about his children replied, "One girl,
two boys, and a HIGH SCHOOL TEXTBOOK."   (Note the increasing order of difficulty.)   Yes, textbooks, like children,
are quite common--and as easily understood.   Perhaps this
accounts for the myriad of myths, misconceptions, and naive
notions about them: such as, that they are easy to write,
pretty much alike, and more expensive in hard covers than
as paperbacks.

Believe it or not, new textbooks arise out of needs--
usually dissatisfactions with the status quo.   New times demand new measures (tools and techniques of learning) and
new men (idea people such as teacher-authors).   The new
texts may appear visually on overhead transparencies, orally
on records or tapes, or electronically via computers.   But
irrespective of the media of communication used, all require
authors (idea people), editors (communication specialists),
and publishers (providers of the media used).   Which is to

say that regardless of how ideas are transmitted, they usually have to be authored and edited first.

How Are Authors Obtained?

Contrary to popular belief, authors of high school and
elementary school textbooks rarely appear to publishers with
finished manuscripts and requests to publish them. The task
is a far cry from dashing off a novel to send to a tradebook
house, or having a secretary type up one's lecture notes for
a college text. This does not mean that textbook publishers
are not snowed-under with unsolicited manuscripts. They
are. But most of these "manuscripts" are more appropriately described as bundles of guide sheets, often sadly deficient
in literary merit, scholarship, marketability, or all three.
Yet none can be dismissed lightly. Each requires most tact-
ful handling, for hell hath no fury like a penman or penwom-
an scorned. The editorial accent, therefore, is on the positive, because any teacher who goes beyond the call of duty
to undertake the difficult task of putting ideas into writing is
not an ordinary one. Moreover, a careful assessment of the
material submitted may well reveal the author's flair for
asking especially pertinent questions, or making challenging
assignments, or selecting provocative readings. Would she
care to try her hand at preparing a special feature, or end-
of-chapter exercises, or a workbook, or a set of tests to accompany a new textbook upon which we are now at work?
Who knows what may come of it?

Most potential authors of textbooks have to be discovered and then persuaded to write. How are they discovered?
Heads of editorial departments comb all pertinent educational
conventions for top-notch social studies specialists and teachers who appear to be the idea men and women in the profession. And it is no accident that publishers already count a-
mong their fine authors most of the past, present, and future
officers, directors, committee members, and identifiable doers in the National Council for the Social Studies, the American Historical Association, and similar professional organizations. These leaders have proved possession of the vim, vig-
or, and vitality required in extra measure in any successful
author. For textbook writing requires a tremendous investment of outside hours--week-ends, holidays, vacations, and
so-called "spare" time.

Editors attend dozens of sectional meetings and make

countless inquiries to determine who the innovators and
trend-builders really are. Convention program committee
members, insofar as they gear their programs to the most
provocative topics, practices, and practitioners, do a great
deal of discovery spade-work for us all. Hence as editors
rub elbows with fellow teachers at these meetings, continually asking "What are you doing about this problem in your
school (or college)?", they are heartened by the great variety of pragmatic responses. And once editors have identified
the doers in today's classrooms, they have some of the potential authors of tomorrow.

A second fine source of leads to potential authors is
the feedback provided by publishers' representatives (all
former teachers) who visit the schools and colleges regularly and are forever alert to promising persons and practices.
Interested teachers might well explore this avenue more than
they now do. Another source is regular examination of
professional journals for writers with something to say and
the ability to communicate it. Since most of these writers
have already been under consideration, the reading of their
articles is more a matter of confirmation than discovery.
A fourth source is the staff of the many subsidized "experimental" projects about the nation. At first glance one would
expect that these projects would be most productive of future
textbook authors. They are not. For most of their writers
are bound by the terms of the subsidy and are not free a-
gents. Moreover, when publishers are asked to bid on these
projects, the terms are often so restrictive or so "way-out"
that most will not touch them. When projects are accepted,
however, much work may remain for the publisher to fit the
materials into marketable packages.

How important is the age factor among potential textbook authors? Very. Potential authors need to be old enough
to be considered "experienced," yet young enough to be active
teachers and writers throughout the life span of the textbook.
Most successful high school and/or elementary school publishing projects (including new copyrights and revisions) run
for twenty years or more. Hence, anyone who thinks, "I'll
have plenty of time to write after I retire," will have difficulty finding a market for his manuscript. The teachers who
choose textbooks rightly prefer authors who are still on the
classroom firing line. The "generation gap" is wide enough
as it is. To meet this need, publishers encourage older authors to take on younger collaborators who can become increasingly responsible for revisions and new editions by the

time the senior author retires.   But isn't fame a factor in
selecting an author?   Sometimes.   But fame more often follows authorship than precedes it.

How are potential authors persuaded to become textbook authors?   Love has a great deal to do with it, and the
same driving idealism to build a better world which persuades
people to devote their lives to teaching.   As a "two by four"
teacher I might influence thirty to a hundred youngsters each
year with my own two hands within the four walls of my
classroom.   But as a teacher-author I might reach hundreds
of thousands of pupils in thousands of classrooms.   The fact
that many authors of successful textbooks get royalty checks
greater than their teaching salaries each year is not generally known, and it is doubtful that this is a prime motivating
factor.   But it does help to compensate for the sacrifices involved.   Come to think of it, during fifteen years of editorial work I do not recall ever having to persuade any really
potential author to write a textbook.   The idea was already
there.   Even so, advances against future royalties often help
to keep the bill collectors away while the text is being written.

What About Contracts?

How quickly should an author sign up?   Should one hire
an agent?   Authors of tradebook manuscripts often hire literary agents to negotiate the best possible royalty contract for
them.   But the contract practices of tradebook houses (which
sell to the public through book stores and book clubs) should
not be confused with those of long established textbook houses
(which sell directly to the schools).   Textbook royalties are
pretty well standardized at four, six, eight, ten, and eighteen percent of the net price for elementary, junior high, high
school, and college hardback textbooks respectively.   Note
that the percentages are inversely related to the size of the
markets (enrollments).   How long such standards can be
maintained in the face of intensive competition, especially at
the college level, is a matter of conjecture.   A case in point
is the professor who said, "I have a leave of absence coming
up and would love to write a college textbook for you.   Can
you match the offer of a salaried secretary plus an electric
typewriter while I'm doing the job?"   That was ten years ago,
and any college representative today can top that.   It is only
fair to add, however, that such supplementary inducements
are not the lot of beginners, but rather are the "fringe bene-

fits" which accompany fame.

How quickly should potential authors of elementary and high school textbooks sign contracts? Not very. The temptation is almost irresistible to be sure, especially when one's colleagues are flaunting them right and left and dropping teasing tidbits, such as, "I have to fly to New York over the weekend to see my publisher." But do not rush into signing contracts. The procedure of many publishers is to try to match a specific potential author with a specific publishing need. The initial "courtship" might consume several weeks or even months during which all angles of who might do what, when, where, how, and why are explored. Both parties operate under a "gentleman's agreement," spelled out in a series of letters which provide mutual opportunity for understanding and individualized treatment of problems on a person-to-person basis as they arise. Oftentimes the formal contract per se is not signed until the project is well along.

In contrast, suppose everything is signed and sealed at the start. The project involves, as many do, a series of books and a team of authors of which you are one. Then you get sick, or accept a new position, or are elected to a prestigious but time-consuming office, or have family difficulties, or are offered "the opportunity of a lifetime," or get "fed-up" with your collaborators, or discover that the project isn't worth the sacrifices entailed. Or suppose that after you have turned down opportunities to vacation, to travel, to do research abroad, to teach summer session, and so on, there is a change in administrative policy of the publishing house, or budgetary problems arise, or unforeseen problems of marketability come up, or the completed manuscript is judged too traditional, or too easy, or too difficult, or not in line with a current fad--so the project is postponed, or even dropped. According to "Murphy's Law," anything that can happen probably will--and all of the aforementioned have. In any event they testify to the advisability of potential authors and publishers keeping their options reasonably flexible. If ever there was a field where human values are paramount, it is educational publishing.

Author-Editor Relationship

At the heart of any successful publishing program is the harmonious author-editor relationship. What kind of person is the editor? What does he do? In all probability he (she) is an experienced teacher of the innovative type, with strong preparation in the social sciences and reasonable command of the English language. He not only knows his subject but can put himself in the shoes of the pupils and teachers who will be using the material he is called upon to edit. This quality of empathy (in the author, the editor, or both of them) is essential to the successful communication of ideas which makes a textbook an effective learning tool.

Textbook editing should not be confused with copy editing. The principal task of the copy editor is to see that a manuscript is properly punctuated and grammatically correct. His knowledge of the subject or experience in teaching is not particularly necessary. High intelligence, an excellent liberal arts education, and a genuine interest in critical reading and writing are quite sufficient. Hence, when spring rolls round each year, scores of bright-eyed Phi Beta Kappa-type graduates-to-be from our great cathedrals of culture descend upon publishing personnel offices with high hopes of editorial employment. Tradebook houses and the college departments of textbook publishers welcome them for the excellent copy editing of which they are capable.

The textbook editor, with his command of subject, empathy towards teacher and pupil, and communication skills, goes far beyond copy editing. He is a team leader--coordinating the work of many authors (of texts, exercises, workbooks, tests, filmstrips, tapes, teachers' manuals, et cetera), of editors of art, maps, graphics, plus secretaries, critical readers, and assorted participants. Besides giving inspirational leadership, a good editor provides the authors with objective evaluation of their plans and presentations, specific identification and accentuation of their strengths, early elimination of faulty practices, deadlines and definite schedules, constant follow-up to reinforce their self-discipline, clear statements of the projects' overall philosophy, organization, special features and style, and proof of how the program fits into changing educational needs and policies and how it represents improvements over competing products. He recognizes the significance of the visual plan of the text through early preparation of art and map lists, and arranges appropriate conferences with specialists in art, maps, typography, and design. He is responsible for the prompt and efficient handling of the manuscript(s) through all stages of proof, art, and dummy.

Major Stages in the Preparation of a Text

What are the four major stages through which a text-book must be guided? And what are some of the specific steps therein?

The first, or pre-writing, stage involves considerable research, careful planning, and many conferences. Creating the project requires the matching of some identifiable educational need with an authorship deemed capable of meeting it. Making a comprehensive proposal (usually a package of text and appropriate supplementary materials) includes outlining the project, stating the curriculum need and grade placement, describing the proposed authorship, estimating the probable market, identifying the principal competition, suggesting a desirable format, and estimating probable costs. The project is then presented to the New Publications Committee for approval or rejection. If the project is approved, a writing plan is drawn up. This includes definitive selection of all necessary authors and subsequent conferences with them and appropriate subject matter consultants, psychologists, a graphics team, other staff specialists, and management.

Stage two involves the actual writing and editing. While the author is putting flesh upon the bare bones of his writing outline, the editor is reviewing his conference notes, studying the results of market analyses, examining promising courses of study, curriculum criteria, applicable educational research, and competing materials.

Step (a): As soon as the author sends in several chapters, the editor evaluates the material. This involves critical reading for overall understanding, clarity of style, adequacy of content, plan of presentation, teachability (including appropriateness of vocabulary and sentence and paragraph length and complexity), necessity for permissions for quoted material, et cetera. The principal aim of the editor in this evaluation step is to help the new author set a pattern; to avoid the extremes of writing over the heads of pupils or talking-down to them; to be aware of serious omissions, sweeping generalizations, or imbalance of content; to avoid style mannerisms; and to prevent the necessity for a great deal of future rewriting.

Step (b): When sufficient manuscript is available, detailed editing follows. Each word, sentence, paragraph, and

page is now pored over with a critical eye to check on
meanings, generalizations, exceptions; accuracy of facts,
dates, titles, spellings, citations of sources, cross references; consistency of usage; punctuation, grammar, ad in-
finitum.   As a former teacher, the good editor habitually
asks himself, "Would most of my pupils understand this
point, this paragraph, this direction?   Would a simple example or further proof help here?   If so, what might I suggest?"   If the author's sentences are unusually complex,
they must be simplified.   Substitution of a period for a
semicolon may suffice.   Overuse of dependent clauses often
constitutes a reading hazard, especially when the author
dives into the sea of a sentence and comes up on the opposite bank with the verb in his mouth.   Concepts need to be
cut down to bite size, without either making mincemeat of
the material or evoking the reaction of the man who looked
down at his first plate of hash to exclaim, "The man who
chewed this can eat it."

        Every editor worth his salt must possess a certain a-
mount of healthy skepticism.   For example, when a manuscript quotes Robert Kennedy as the author of a widely acclaimed thought, and cites Bobby's speech plus newspaper
accounts of Teddy's moving eulogy to his brother in confirmation, you are inclined to let it pass.   But then that little
devil of a doubt arises, and a call to the reference librarian
reveals that the quotation is from George Bernard Shaw,
Back to Methuselah, Act I, Part I.   The Serpent talking to
Eve says: "When you and Adam talk, I hear you say 'Why?'
Always 'Why?'   You see things and you say 'Why?'   But I
dream things that never were; and I say 'Why not?'"

        Step (c):   Early forwarding of art and map manuscript
is very important.   This is because pictures need to be ordered and maps and charts drawn to exact specifications--a
process consuming a year or more.   The illustration program for a successful high school history text intended for
use by all students will average about 25 percent--some 200
pages in an 800-page text.   It is the editor's task to decide
how best to use this space, keeping in mind the adage that
one good picture is worth a thousand words.   He would be
wise to have some serious conferences with the art editor,
because the kinds of illustrations have a great deal to do with
their effectiveness as well as costs.   In the end he will need
to answer some very specific questions: How many photographs? drawings? charts? graphs? time lines? maps? black
and white? second color? four colors?   Which should be

quarter page? half page? full page? What picture-essays
(often double-page spreads) or albums (often eight pages or
more) are planned? What maps will be required for the
built-in atlas?

As the editor works through the manuscript page by
page he thinks in terms of how the ideas might best be illustrated and requests an appropriate picture here, a table
of data there, and/or a special map, diagram, or graph
elsewhere. Where a map, graph, table, or time line is
requested, the editor must indicate quite specifically exactly
what places, figures, or other data he wishes thereon. Is
it to be a physical map, a political map, or both? What
size? In second color? Any particular projection desired?
Will extensions or "bleeds" into margins be used? Detailed
lists of all art and map requests with specific manuscript
page numbers are then compiled and forwarded to the art
and map departments. Costs of art and map originals plus
offset positives may well run to $100,000. And contrary to
widespread belief, the publisher does not own much of the
illustrative material in a typical text. He pays for permission to use photos and cartoons and must do so again with
each big revision of the text.

Step (d): Many manuscripts or portions thereof under-
go field testing. This is especially necessary when the text
is designed for "inner city" or other special groups. Many
authors use Xerox or comparable copies for tryout in their
own classrooms. Experiment-minded teachers in appropriate areas about the nation are employed to provide necessary
trials and feedback. Other teachers and specialists serve as
critical readers for the same purpose. In addition, many
helpful suggestions come from the teacher-authors chosen to
write the chapter or unit exercises, to provide the annotated
bibliographies, and to prepare special features such as biographies, condensed readings, "discovery" projects, conflict-
ing interpretations, culture correlations, case studies, time
lines, and the like. Final editing often incorporates hundreds of changes that no one dreamed were necessary when
the author sent in his original manuscript. The task is not
complete until someone has written all titles, captions, or
legends for several hundred maps and illustrations.

Stage three consists of some dozen steps of transfer-
ring the manuscript to print. Forwarding the manuscript includes clearing, recording, coding, scheduling, and routing.
Graphics work involves analyzing, designing, completion of

art and map procurement and editing, preparation of style
sheet, and marking of the manuscript for composition. The
editor has frequent conferences with members of the graphics team to make certain that the design, typography, and
art are all in keeping with the purpose, subject, and grade
level of the text and the needs of the children for whom it
is intended. Large pictures, large type, and generous white
space give an appearance of ease. The functional use of
color can be especially effective. Few illustrations, small
type, and narrow margins connote difficulty. All type chosen
for use in maps, legends, tables, graphs, charts, exercises,
front matter, appendix, and index must be compatible with
the type used in the headings and running text. The layman
would be amazed at the great variety of emphases attainable
through the use of a single type when set in lower case,
italic, boldface, large or small caps, and combinations thereof.

After the manuscript is designed and marked by the
graphics team, bids are taken and it is forwarded with a
style sheet to one of the many composition houses. Here the
manuscript is set in type. The copies of 1R proof (first revision, often called galley proof) are sent to the author(s),
editor(s), members of the graphics team, and others.

The 1R proof is then edited, and all corrections (including those sent in by authors) are transferred to the
Printer's Set. It is the 1R state which requires the greatest
"won't" power on the part of the new author. For seeing his
brainchild in cold type for the first time, he can usually
think of endless ways in which it could be improved by extensive rewriting. But the financial costs of yielding to this
temptation are prohibitive. Correct all errors? Yes. Add
final election returns, or history-making turns of events?
Yes. But treat galleys like new manuscript? No. Not only
are the costs staggering, but when they run above a certain
percentage they are chargeable to authors' royalty.

The graphics editor now takes the 1R proof and pastes
it up in pages on special layout sheets. He leaves measured
spaces on each page for specific illustrations, maps, and
legends--all properly "sized" by art, map, and text editors.
The text editor adjusts "longs" and "shorts"--cutting or adding text where necessary to balance columns and make the
page self-contained. Art is then finalized, and the Printer's
Set goes back to the compositor.

The 2R (second revision), or page proof stage includes making corrections, adjusting type to print pages,
proving and correcting. A cross sectional sampling of the
art and map material is now color-proved to see whether the
various gradations of the second color are as effective as
they might be. The author and editors process 2R as they
did 1R proof. It is often at this page proof stage that copies
are made for authors of the many supplementary items we
shall describe later. It is also at this crucial stage that the
index is begun. As anyone who has prepared an index for a
high school history text can testify, it is an exacting and
time-consuming task. Expertly done, a thirty to fifty page
index contains thousands of items and makes a more effective and time-saving reference tool than many teachers and
pupils realize.

It is at the page proof stage, too, that final decisions
have to be made regarding the use of material for which permissions from copyright owners have been sought. If, for
any reason, a permission has not yet been granted, or the
owner of the copyright has not yet been found, the material
must be deleted and the "hole" filled by other means. Permission costs, which may run to several thousand dollars for
excerpts from the writings of others, are chargeable to authors' royalties. Were this more generally known, publishers
probably would not be deluged with so many manuscripts consisting primarily of collections of what others have written.

If 3R proof is needed, it follows the same plan as
that for 2R. Final corrections are composed; type is carefully locked up; and repro (from reproduction) proofs are
made and sent to graphics to make the dummy. The dummy
process includes positioning of repro pages and color proof
or photostats on pattern pages; insertion of script items;
marking instructions in margins; clearing with the text editor;
and routing the dummy with a set of repro proof, art, specifications, and printing estimates to the production department.

The fourth and final stage, that of manufacturing and
distribution, is not under editorial control. It involves plate
making, offset lithographic printing, binding, and distributing.
The platemaking process includes photographing the art and
repro proof, stripping together film for art and text, and
making plates via a photographic process. The days of letterpress printing of textbooks are largely past. The fabulous
Web press, with its miles of paper swiftly flowing over and

under the plates in a continuous web, has come into its own. Its economies, of course, are best realized on big-volume runs.

After printing is completed, the signatures (multiples of sixteen pages) are gathered and sent to a bindery. There they may be glued, wired, stitched, or sewed together--depending upon state specifications. The textbooks are then cased (covered) either as paperbacks or hardbooks (cardboard and cloth or vinyl) and shipped to the warehouse for distribution to the schools.

Supplementary Items

Keep in mind, however, that the pupil textbook is only part of a larger learning package consisting of a teachers' annotated edition or manual or both, a pupils' workbook, unit or chapter and final tests, filmstrips, tapes, recordings, and transparencies. It is a rare package indeed which does ' not involve a dozen teacher-authors. Hence, as soon as page proof (2R) is available on the pupil text, copies are rushed to the teacher-authors selected to write manuscripts for each of these supplementary publications. And each project requires author-editor planning, conferences, scheduling, editing, art work, design, typography, and most of the stages and steps outlined in detail above.

Let us take a close look at just one of the supplementary items in the package aforementioned. The Annotated Edition for teachers is especially important because it so often determines whether they will even look at the rest of the package. It consists of the pupil text plus everything the teacher might wish for the proper use of it as a learning tool. Its bound-in manual section contains a statement of the philosophy, purposes, and essential features of the pupil text plus helpful teaching suggestions and lists of audiovisual aids and paperbacks. Most valuable (and costly) of all, however, are the pertinent notations overprinted in the margins of each page of the pupil text adjacent to the material to which they appertain. These comments, suggestions, answers, and interpretations are written by especially skilled teachers with the aim of saving time for other teachers.

After all of the annotated material for teachers is set in type, it is photographed and stripped-in on pages of a duplicate dummy of the pupil's edition and then new plates are

made. After each form (several signatures) of the pupil
text (say 80,000 copies) comes off press, the plate for the
same form of the Annotated Edition is substituted and some
20,000 more copies are run. This procedure is repeated
for the entire printing, and then the sheets for the Annotated
Edition are sent to the bindery first. Why first? This is
because free sampling to teachers is the heart of the text-
book-selling process. Teachers rightly insist upon examining new textbooks before ordering, and as many as ten thousand copies of one Annotated Edition ($50,000 worth) may be
gifted to supervisors, department heads, textbook committee
members, and other teachers in the first year. Most publishers can cite cases where more copies were gifted to
teachers than pupil copies were sold. If the pupil edition
were bound first, not only would several precious weeks be
lost, but double gifting would be necessary. The pressure
to receive new textbooks early in the calendar year is tremendous, and when the pupil edition is gifted, most teachers
want a copy of the Annotated Edition when available anyway.

One of the occupational hazards in bringing out a new
social studies textbook lies in meeting attacks from outside
pressure groups. Criticisms from teachers in the field are
not only welcomed but constantly solicited, for the best written and edited new text in the world is certain to contain
muddy passages and "slips that passed in the night" which
use by thousands of pupils and teachers quickly unveils. All
publishers are indebted to the countless teachers who have
thus helped them make good textbooks better. But the criticisms from special interest groups rate the word "attacks"
because they often proceed from the assumption that textbook
authors and publishers are engaged in a conspiracy to sub-
vert the American way of life. Social studies textbooks probably receive more brickbats than all other textbooks combined.
The very term "social" is suspect, for it is obvious to some
critics that the word social is synonymous with socialism.

What will be done about these pressures? They may
be rationalized in the manner becoming intellectuals. As
George Orwell so aptly put it: "Intellectuals are no more
dishonest than other people, but their resources for self-de-
ception are greater." After all, isn't it the aim of all good
business to "give the customer what he wants"? What happens when a publisher refuses to make the changes demanded?
The adoption usually goes to one who does make them. Who
makes the decisions on most of these adoption committees
anyway? The same fine type of people who write, edit, sell,

and use the textbooks--the educators.

Dispelling Myths Concerning Textbooks

In conclusion, let us take a quick look at some of the common myths or misconceptions concerning textbooks which answers to the following questions may help to correct.

Why do textbooks waste so much space on pictures? Because research shows that pictures are far more effective than words covering the same subject, and much more economical of space. You can write page after page about the Taj Mahal at Agra, but a four-color picture plus appropriate legend will put you to shame. We need to train ourselves and our pupils to read the pictures as carefully as we read the text.

Why do publishers change copyrights so often? Because teachers and adoption committees demand it. Some big cities will not allow a text to be listed if its copyright is five years old--even if it is an ancient history text! This editor once polled many American history teachers during the first week of June and found the majority had not yet finished the New Deal. Yet many will buy a 1969 copyrighted text "because it is so much more up to date than that old (1968) one."

Why do social studies textbooks cost so much? Because they cost so much to make. They are larger and more colorful than ever before. They contain built-in atlases, built-in readers, and many teaching aids not demanded a generation ago. The wages paid in print shops are near the highest in American industry. And believe it or not, publishers' profits and authors' royalties are almost equal and together are less than fourteen percent of the total cost. Fewer illustrations and maps and copyrights would cut costs tremendously, but then you'd find the books "too difficult and too old" and wouldn't buy them.

Aren't paperbacks much cheaper than hardbacks? On the contrary, they cost considerably more. Careful studies made in New York City, Los Angeles, and Texas prove this point. A hardback history textbook costing $4.60 net will easily last four years. That puts the net cost per year at $1.15. The same textbook with a paper cover would save you twenty-five cents per copy, but the cover might have to be replaced repeatedly in four years. "Ah," you say, "but paper backs aren't the 'same textbook' and don't cost $4.60 net." That is right. Neither do they generally contain the illustrations, maps, color, and other features that make textbooks our greatest teaching tool. They are mostly print, with a few black and white maps and pictures, if any--and less than a third the length of the textbook. So you would need several paperbacks to cover the same ground as one hardback. And paperback copies get lost, purloined, or damaged so frequently that many are unfit for use even for the second semester--much less the third, fourth, fifth, sixth, seventh and eighth semester.

Why do publishers hesitate to bring out a textbook for lack of a market? Why don't they bring it out and make the market? Some of the biggest financial fiascos in publishing history have resulted from yielding to that very human and idealistic impulse. Probably a fourth of all the textbooks published never bring back what they cost--even when the best market research available led management to believe that there was a market. Remember the widespread talk and prediction about how programmed instruction was going to "revolutionize" education? Publishers lost millions of dollars preparing materials for a market that never materialized.

It's a rare annual convention of the National Council for the Social Studies that does not abound in unique proposals and assorted panaceas crying out to be published. Editors make notes and subsequently investigate as many as possible. Typical reactions, however, are the following: When a supervisor who presented a most provocative idea at a sectional meeting was queried as to how many of the teachers in her own large city system were willing to use it, she replied, "It's very frustrating. I can't persuade more than a corporal's guard even to try it. But if you were to publish it, I'm sure you'd sell a million." Another fine speaker, whose project was warmly received by a group, spotted an editor in the room and with a twinkle in his eye, put the question, "If some publisher brought this out, how many of you would purchase it?" About thirty hands went up. Then the editor rephrased the question, "How many of you would order copies for all of your pupils?" One hand went up. It is quite tragic but true that when teachers say that they will buy a copy the market isn't sufficient to justify the costs of publication. Many will be content with the gift copy. A small paperback without illustrations of any kind might break

even with a life sale of fifty thousand copies, but any really
competitive high school social studies hardback textbook
would require sales of from 250,000 to 500,000 copies--de-
pending upon costs of art and map originals and positives.

Come now, isn't it true that when you've seen one
social studies textbook you've seen them all?   Frankly, no.
They vary greatly in style, readability, organization, ease
or difficulty, content coverage and emphasis, special features,
interpretation, kinds of exercises, supplementary supporting
items, and teachability.

What is the relationship between educational publishers
and educators?   They are first cousins.   Educational publishers consider themselves an integral part of the profession of education.   Publishing personnel, from editorial to
sales, consists of outstanding teachers.   Many read more
journals, hold more memberships, visit more schools, and
attend more educational conferences than they ever could afford to do while teaching.

Expense accounts help, of course, but the number of
"former teachers" who still hear the school bells ring each
fall and to whom each convention is akin to a homecoming
is legion.   The textbook packages which constitute the curriculum in schools throughout the nation are written by
teacher-authors in almost continual conference with these former teachers.   Hence, the wholehearted enthusiasm with
which publishers support educational journals, conferences,
goals, and activities generally, is born of mutual self-inter-
est.   In short, what is good for the schools is good for educational publishing.

Dilemmas of a Textbook Writer

By Henry Wilkinson Bragdon, Instructor Emeritus in History, Phillips Exeter Academy; author of Woodrow Wilson: the Academic Years, and co-author of the textbook History of a Free People.

From Social Education 33:292-8, March 1969. © by the National Council for the Social Studies. Reprinted by permission. Adapted from a talk to the Connecticut Council for the Social Studies on May 3, 1968.

Nearly twenty years ago I signed a contract to write an American history text for senior high school students. A Macmillan officer remarked at the time that this could be a full-time job. And that is almost what it has become. The care and feeding of this text, History of a Free People, is my principal occupation. It took over four years in the writing. It has been revised five times, and I am now working on still another edition. Macmillan has surrounded it with a flotilla of eleven paperbacks; I wrote one and helped to edit the rest. Six more paperbacks and a two-volume edition are in the works. There is a continuous stream of correspondence from teachers and students, usually critical, sometimes angry. There are attacks from both the right and the left. One has to develop a thick carapace. What bothers me most is not the work, nor that I often wish I were back in the classroom, nor the critics, but that I have never resolved certain practical, pedagogical, and moral dilemmas.

I shall analyze these and other problems and deal successively with Publishers, Patriots, Pedagogy, and Conscience.

Publishers

I have sometimes seen in print statements to the effect that textbook writers are simply marionettes, with the publishers pulling the strings, that publishers tell us what to

write, how to write it, and surround us with taboos as rigid
as those that bedevil television.   Here, for instance, is an
article, "Textbooks and Trapped Idealists," Saturday Review
of Literature, January 18, 1964, by Frank G. Jennings, one
of its editors.   According to Mr. Jennings a textbook is likely to germinate in the mind of a book salesman, and then to
be hatched corporately by the staff of a publishing house,
whose first concern is that it shall offend no segment of the
textbook buying public.

All I can say is that this was not the way it was with
this book.   I was approached by a Macmillan Vice President
in charge of the school section, Richard Pearson, and asked
if I'd like to try my hand at a high school textbook.   After
thinking it over, I said yes, but that I was interested only in
a certain kind of book--one with a chronological arrangement
instead of the then fashionable topical approach, one that reduced the colonial period to a single chapter, one that cen-
tered on politics and political ideas.   Macmillan accepted
these and other later ideas presented either by me or by the
coauthor they found to work with me, the late Professor Samuel P. McCutchen of New York University.   We were assigned an excellent editor, Mrs. Dorothy Arnof, and she
worked so closely with us that she became in effect a third
author.   Macmillan advised us about certain technical mat-
ters--whether pages should have one column or two, for in-
stance--and decided on the format.   But in all big things we
made the decisions.   This took courage on the publishers'
part because their initial investment in plates, maps, illustrations, charts, and other production costs was not less than
$250,000.

The text was being written at the height of the Mc-
Carthy era, but Pearson told us to forget it, that this would
have passed by the time the book came out.   He kept sending
me books on civil liberties, such as Alan Barth's The Loyalty of Free Men, and throughout our book civil liberties received emphasis greater than in most texts.   The very title,
selected by the publisher, was meant to be a kind of rebuke
to McCarthyism.   The first title more or less agreed on was
United We Stand--defiant, shoulder-to-shoulder; it was changed
to History of a Free People to get across the idea that freedom was a good to be cherished.

I don't say there were not restraints that irked me.
At first I was expected to submit to a curriculum expert who
tried to get me to write prose according to a series of for-

mulas--I should, for instance, limit myself to the first
5,000 words in the Thorndike word list; sentences must be
short; I should avoid compound sentences, so the semicolon
was verboten.   I soon found I could not stand this, told
Pearson so, and he called off the expert.   And yet she had
done me good in that she forced me to wonder constantly
whether I was communicating meaning to eleventh graders.

I found writing a textbook the most difficult form of
composition I have ever attempted.   This derives partly from
the necessity for compression, which I shall deal with later,
partly from not knowing what course to steer between the
Scylla of writing over the readers' heads and the Charybdis
of underestimating their intelligence.   Then too I was writing
for a most varied audience, composed of intelligent and interested students, apathetic and unintelligent students, teachers, consultants, and in the background my professional colleagues.   Recently while acting as consultant for a publisher
I had occasion to criticize the style of the manuscript of a
projected American history text.   My advice to the authors--
and I admit this is a counsel of perfection--was as follows:

> Don't Write Down! . . . . Write as though you
> were writing for a mature audience consisting of
> at least four persons:
>
> a dull, uninterested person whose attention you
> want to attract and who has difficulty in compre-
> hension;
>
> a bright, knowledgeable person, whose intelli-
> gence you don't want to insult;
>
> a highly respected English teacher, who used to
> tear your schoolboy compositions apart;
>
> an historian who is going to grade you on whether
> you are to keep your membership in the histori-
> cal fraternity.

One taboo Macmillan did insist upon: the Civil War
had to be called The War Between the States.   This concession to the Southern market irritated me, and I demanded
that Macmillan prove it was necessary.   So they polled their
eleven southern sales offices; every one of them solemnly
stated that a textbook that used the term Civil War could not
be sold south of the Mason-Dixon line.   I gave in.   Texas,

I thought, was worth a mass. This is one occasion where
the publishers in effect forced me to do something I disliked.
The only other point at which I was pressured was in just
the reverse direction--I must mention certain members of
minority groups, such as Crispus Attucks and Haym Solo-
mon. But that was all--nowhere else was I told what to put
in or keep out.

It would be disingenuous of me to maintain that I am
not influenced by certain unspoken barriers. I cannot remember offhand any that influenced me in writing History of
a Free People, and so take an example from a book on constitutional rights that a colleague and I have just completed. [1]
In it we put students to close examination of recent Supreme
Court decisions. In discussing right to counsel we chose
Escobedo v. Illinois (1964) over Miranda v. Arizona (1966),
even though the latter was more recent and perhaps more
controversial, simply because Miranda dealt with a case of
rape, while Escobedo was accused merely of being an accessory to murder. According to the peculiar mores of American society, which naturally permeate schools, children may
contemplate any kind of violence so long as sex is not involved.

Furthermore, one cannot get away from the Confucian
proverb: "The superior man knows what is right; the inferi-
or man knows what will sell." I'd be happier about History
of a Free People if it were not so obviously designed as an
article of commerce. Every two years or so there is a new
cover, like the changing radiator grilles on new cars. There
are so many illustrations, chapter-end activities, bibliographies, appendices, maps, and diagrams that students may
complain that the book is too heavy to carry home. But
there is no help for it. Some other texts are horrendously
even bigger, and I am assured that this increases their sales.

The evidence I get through Macmillan salesmen is that
Mr. Jennings is too often right when in the previously quoted
article he wrote:

> Textbooks are accepted or turned down because
> they are profusely illustrated, because they have
> lavishly colored covers, because they are larger
> or smaller than the ones in use, because they
> are written by people with the right kinds of
> names, coming from the right schools, in the
> right part of the country. Sometimes they are

accepted or rejected, because it is very late
on a dreary Friday afternoon.

To give an example from our experience.   An adoption board in a city that shall be nameless was divided three
to three as to whether to adopt our book or that of a competitor.   No compromise was possible.   So they finally decided to test which book was more durable--textbooks are
supposed to stand up to the wear-and-tear of daily use for
from three to five years.   Those who liked our book better
threw the other one at the wall, taking turns with the others
throwing ours.   Eventually the cover came off the other book
and we got the adoption.

Patriots

Back of the idea that timid publishers are constantly
telling writers "You can't print that," is the notion that pressure groups, especially those of self-dubbed "patriots," will
drive from the market any books that aren't a bland, homogenized mixture of pap and uplift.   There is substance to this
notion.   In the 1940's rightists attacked a series of junior
high school texts written by Harold Rugg of Teachers College, Columbia, as being leftist and un-American.   Based on
the idea that students in sixth, seventh, and eighth grade
should know the historical background of contemporary issues and should learn to discuss them, the Rugg texts were
the best in the market.   But in not more than five or six
years the patriots won; Rugg's books disappeared from
schools.

The patriots are still at work.   Look at the illustration from the cover of History of a Free People.   See--
that's the fascist eagle holding the communist sickle.   A certain Congressman Utt from California said so; and students
in Santa Barbara schools were told by frightened parents not
to take the book home.   The same crazy notion turned up in
other California towns, and in other states.   The publishers
had to issue a release to let agitated teachers and school
superintendents know that this eagle came from an index of
American design published in 1840.

More dangerous than the kooky charge by the California Congressman was the one by Holmes Alexander, a
columnist said to be syndicated in 300-odd newspapers.   A-
mong other things, Alexander accused me of "clayfootery"

and to prove it quoted <u>History of a Free People</u> as follows:

> (General George Washington) lost more battles
> than he won . . . (and) sometimes annoyed men
> by his stiff manner and a tendency to talk and
> write as though all were lost.

"This," remarked Alexander, "about the indomitable man who
refused to be beaten!" To show the extraordinary mendacity
of his attack here is the whole paragraph (with Alexander's
quotes in bold type):

> Washington was undoubtedly the greatest Amer-
> ican asset, even though he lost more battles
> than he won. He may have been mistaken in
> training his army in strictly European lines.
> He sometimes annoyed men by his stiff manner
> and a tendency to talk and write as though all
> were lost. But no man did more to win the
> war. While British commanders often returned
> to England for the winter, Washington's devotion
> to duty was such that he saw his home at Mount
> Vernon only once during the war, and then only
> for a few hours. He alone commanded sufficient
> respect to keep the Continental Army in being.
> Often soldiers remained with the army, even
> when they were unpaid and their enlistments
> were up, because, as one of them used to tell
> his grandchildren, "He was a fine man, General
> Washington--he was everything a man should be."

Alexander went on to accuse me of trying to create a
younger generation "without heroes, without respect for their
country, and without emotional patriotism." He concluded by
remarking that "some people in the textbook business are doing the work of our enemies." I consulted a lawyer on this
one. He consulted other lawyers and they thought that I had
grounds for libel. But Macmillan advised against it. They
said I'd lose my shirt in lawyer's fees, that they'd see to it
that Alexander was answered, and that the assault was so extreme it would boomerang.

There is evidence that they were right. Alexander was
rebutted by several letters to the editor (including one by a
former student of mine), and there was no evidence that sales
were adversely affected.

Then there is an evaluation of our book put out by an organization called "America's Future, Inc." On the face of it this is a reputable organization; most of the committee that run it are men of academic standing, including Felix Morley, former President of Haverford College, and professors from Kenyon, Yale, Northwestern, and Minnesota. They have issued an evaluation written by E. Merrill Root, who previously had embarrassed Professor McCutchen and me by praising our text in a book called Brainwashing in the High Schools. Later he changed his mind. He wrote, in part:

> One half of it seems so good that the other half ought to be better. It seems as if two different authors had written a different half, without benefit of collaboration. [He apparently thought that I, from conservative Phillips Exeter Academy, wrote one half, and McCutchen from suspect NYU, the other.] The half that deals with the earlier history of America is excellent, while the half that deals with modern history is weak and fallible. There seems a sort of schizophrenia between the two halves. . . .

Some criticisms of the latter part of the book are that we do not suggest that "people in power" deliberately failed to warn the military and naval commanders at Pearl Harbor because they sought war with Japan; that we do not assert that the Bonus March was "Communist-inspired;" that we entitled a chapter "The Affluent Society," thus revealing a "liberal" slant. So, concludes Root:

> The impact of the book, especially since the first half seems to validate the book, is to lull the student into acceptance and then to indoctrinate him with "liberal" superstitions, a "liberal" mood of anti-anti-Communism, and a soft sentimentality toward collectivism.

Root obviously suspects conspiracy.

The publishers tell me not to worry about the right-wing attacks. There is no appeasing the so-called patriots, who are often paranoid and unreasonable people. There is greater danger, even from an outright dollars-and-cents point of view, in knuckling under to them than in ignoring

them. So I do not feel especially threatened by thunder from
the right. As a citizen I am frightened by the Birchers and
the Minutemen and the Citizens' Councils, because I was in
Germany in 1929 when Hitler was considered a joke, but as
a textbook writer I do not consider myself peculiarly vulnerable.

Pedagogy

So, as I work at successive revisions of History of a
Free People, I do not feel controlled or threatened by anybody. I have only myself to blame if the book is less good
than it ought to be--there are no convenient scapegoats anywhere I look. My present concern lies in two areas--peda-
gogy and conscience.

Regarding pedagogy, there is widespread opinion that
history textbooks and courses taught from them are ipso facto
to be deplored. My friend, the ubiquitous Charles Keller,
expressed this view in a talk to teachers at Manhasset, Long
Island, in September, 1962:

> Current textbooks and their excessive use are
> both bad. . . . Textbooks take the fact-by-
> fact approach. They tell students things in a
> way and an order which the author has decided
> --too frequently with his eye, or that of his
> publisher, on getting adoptions in as many
> school systems as possible. The textbook-
> learning teacher gives students little chance to
> figure things out for themselves.

I have been intermittently engaged in producing new
social studies materials for an organization called Educational Services, Inc. (now Educational Development Corporation).
The very concept of a single text was anathema at ESI (EDC).
We produced games, documents, pamphlets, packets of stuff,
maps, pictures, movies, simulations, artifacts, and I don't
know what all, but nary a single volume that could be labelled
a textbook.

I sympathize with this approach. Textbooks encourage
the idea that history is something to be memorized and re-
gurgitated. Too many teachers never go beyond the text and
simply put students to learning the answers to the questions
in the chapter-end activities. There is abundant evidence,

alas, that too many teachers concentrate on picayune facts. The Macmillan salesmen almost unanimously report that teachers want more military history, and for all I know History of a Free People may sometimes lose out because it minimizes the details of wars. I have seen tests based on my text that demanded nothing but a knowledge of details. All this bears out what Henry Adams meant when he said that "nothing in education is so astonishing as the amount of ignorance it accumulates in the form of inert facts."

As long as the textbook is the chief pedagogical tool in high school history courses, just so long are those courses likely to be a dreary business of read-recite-test, read-recite-test.

Another difficulty with basing a course on a textbook is that it tends to make everything seem equally important, while if you want to excite students about history and give them a real sense of the past, with a sophisticated aware- ness of the complexity of events, it is necessary to do a cer- tain amount of "postholing"--settling down and going into a period or a topic in depth, or setting students to their own explorations.

A textbook does not force bad teaching. A reasonably imaginative teacher or curriculum maker will put it in its place, will use it to give an overview, or simply for refer- ence. Here it is useful. To try to do without it is like moving into a wilderness area without a map.

Furthermore, we have tried to break down the Pro- crustean influence of the textbook in various ways:

1. In a Teachers' Annotated Edition we constantly urge teachers to get students to look beyond the daily assign- ments. In a bound-in set of suggestions we adjure them not to abuse the textbook by treating it simply as a repository of inert knowledge, but instead devise "attack strategies" that will "actively engage students' minds."

2. Dorothy Arnof has edited a book of readings, A Sense of the Past, especially designed to appeal to the aver- age student, as well as to the able one, and to get across the sense that history deals with people. A friend of mine teach- ing slow students in a junior high school found that they en- joyed being read to out of this book.

3.   For able students, we have put out ten paperbacks: Frame of Government, a close textual study of major
constitutional documents, and nine books of Perspectives in
American History, "postholing" and combining lively narrative, documents, and historical interpretation.

But too many teachers will not look beyond the text,
too few school boards will invest in extra paperbacks for history classes, so one is driven inexorably back to the proposition that the textbook itself must contain antidotes to the
pedagogical poison it may transmit.   We have attempted this
in various ways:

1.   In each chapter there is an informal sketch of
some usually minor figure of the time, written in such a way
as to be read simply for interest.   (In the Teachers' Annotated Edition we urge that they do not test on these.)

2.   Each section of the book is prefaced by a little
essay, which we privately call a "Vista," designed to induce
the reader to look up and away from the ordered expository
narrative.   Here is the beginning of a vista entitled "Moods,"
prefacing a section that runs from the First World War
through the Great Depression:

> Perhaps there is no more vivid experience in
> life than the sudden remembrance of things past.
> What brings this on is hard to say--sometimes
> a sound, such as a distant train whistle or the
> song of a bird; sometimes a smell, such as the
> scent of lilacs or a wood fire.   For a moment
> you remember what it was like to be three years
> old and reaching up for the hand of a grown-up,
> or six and getting water up your nose at your
> first swimming lesson.
>
> In the history of nations, as in the lives of indi-
> viduals, different periods have characteristic
> moods.   The progressive period of the early
> twentieth century was one of high purpose.   The
> delegates to the Bull Moose convention in 1912
> chanted "Onward Christian Soldiers," and Wood-
> row Wilson called his inaugural "a day of dedi-
> cation."   The spirit carried on into the World
> War: America was joining in a crusade to
> "make the world safe for democracy."   And there
> was the poignant gaiety of the doughboys singing

"Over There" as they marched to the ghastly
slaughter on the Western Front.

With the coming of the twenties, there was an
abrupt change. A new mood of disillusionment
was reflected in two war plays, "No More Pa-
rades" and "What Price Glory?" The cynics'
prophet, magazine editor H. L. Mencken, never
tired of ridiculing the great American "boo-
boisie." Crazes came and went. . . .

3. We have inserted into the text short italicized
questions that suggest further study or provoke discussion or
at least induce the reader, as I have already said, to look
up and away. Here are two:

Question: Young people who have not reached
voting age are subject to sales taxes, excise
taxes, and income taxes. Have they a legitimate grievance under the principle of "no taxation without representation"?

Question: How near must a person be for
you to be able to see the whites of his eyes?

We have devised still another means of trying to promote active learning, but I shall not detail them further.
For better or worse, these are gimmicks, and I am not sure
that they or anything the writer can do will take the primor-
dial pedagogical curse off a textbook. Perhaps the very writing of a textbook is an immoral proceeding on the ground
that it contributes to the mental delinquency of minors. And
this brings up the last and most difficult set of problems
that I lump together under the heading Conscience.

Conscience

Here I might start with what is on the surface an innocent question: what should be the length of a textbook?
Presumably a school text should be short, so as to leave students free for other endeavors. We had it written into the
original contract that the basic narrative should not exceed
225,000 words--this was 50,000 words shorter than any competing text. But brevity creates a whole series of problems.
To make a text brief you must leave things out. I thought,
for example, of omitting all formal reference to literature or

the arts because these cannot be treated in any really in-
formative way.   But at a dinner of school art teachers I
was persuaded that to omit mention of the arts was to imply they were not important, so I had somehow to work them
in, in a way that I found unsatisfying because so superficial.
And this danger of superficiality runs all through.   To short-
en you must simplify, and you inevitably falsify, since history is never simple.   Simplification, furthermore, may do
students long-time harm by leading them to expect over-
simple explanations for contemporary phenomena, or pat solutions to contemporary problems.

A columnist in the Baltimore Sun took History of a
Free People apart for its descriptions of McCarthyism and
the school desegregation decision of 1954, saying that they
were so brief and colorless as to be worse than useless.
When I went back to the passages involved, I had to agree.
And yet I had not deliberately pulled my punches.   It was
simply that I was writing within a strict word limit that
handicapped me in attempting to give anything like a feeling
for the topics concerned.

In short, I've come right up against the question
whether a one-volume history of the United States does not
have to be so compressed that it cannot tell the truth.

Then there's the problem whether any individual--I
don't care who--is equipped to write a history of the United
States, in one volume or fifty.   No one knows enough.   The
fundamental morality of the historian is that he do his own
digging and make his own assessment of the sources.   But
obviously no man can do that for more than a small fraction
of the whole field of American history.   So the textbook
writer, no matter how much he knows, must rely for the
most part on secondary sources.   He is always in effect
plagiarizing other men's works.   Nor does he always know
which ones to plagiarize.   For instance, when I was writing
the last major revision there was a dispute going on about
the War of 1812.   Some years ago various historians, especially J. W. Pratt, presented the notion that it was a "war
of agrarian cupidity," brought on by western and southern
War Hawks with designs on Canada and Florida.   Now historians pooh-pooh the Pratt thesis but disagree among each
other.   I could not go over all the evidence to find out which
one to follow.   What to do?

When preparing this last edition we did what we could

to remedy the fact that I was a single fallible individual.
We hired scholars of high repute to go through the text and
say where it was lacking and where it was in error, also
to tell me what books to read to overcome my ignorance.
Still, I was always skating on thin ice.

Then there is the matter of commitment, to which
Frederick S. Allis gave his attention in an excellent essay,
"The Handling of Controversial Material in High School Texts
in American History," published in Volume 72 of the Proceedings of the Massachusetts Historical Society. Allis examined in detail three texts, including History of a Free
People, to see how they handled sensitive topics. Our text
emerged with a bit more credit than the others, but it by no
means escaped impeachment for "neutrality and lack of commitment." Even when we did commit ourselves, Allis accused us of doing so by indirection, either by quoting what
others said or by merely emphasis.

I certainly feel free now to commit myself on any and
all issues. And recent editions are more outspoken than
earlier ones in certain areas--such as the three centuries of
injustice to the Negro. As the great-grandson of four mili-
tant abolitionists, I never intended to pussyfoot on this matter, but the Negro revolution has educated us all in this regard and has made us realize the way we have made the
black the "invisible man" in American history. Still, it is
not easy. Take this passage:

> In May, 1963, the Reverend Martin Luther King
> organized peaceful demonstrations against seg-
> regation practices in Birmingham, Alabama.
> Men, women, and children participated. When
> hundreds were jailed violence broke out. King
> and his followers seemed to have won conces-
> sions, but white extremists exploded bombs a-
> mong Negro groups, triggering an outbreak of
> Negro violence. . .

That passage was enough to get our text thrown out of
Birmingham. And in a way there was justice, because I made
one blooper, one unprovable statement, when I said that the
bombs were thrown by "white" extremists. I happen to think
the bomb-throwers were white, probably you do too, but the
Birmingham authorities said I was jumping to conclusions. I
was condemning whites without due process.

The most difficult aspect of the question of commitment is how and how far to make a conscious effort to inculcate values.   It is an inescapable function of an American
history text that it affects students' attitudes toward their society.   A traditional method of doing this is to get across
the idea that everything American is better.   A text that enjoyed a vogue fifteen or twenty years ago opened with a section entitled something like "Our America" which was a
paean of praise to the United States and its superiority over
the USSR.   It told how much better we ate and dressed, how
well we were educated, how we stood in the world as para-
gons of all that was right and just.   This is one extreme,
and I think it self-defeating, since it fails to equip students
with the idea that there can be need for change or reform,
and by inference assumes that foreign nations are inferior.
The other extreme is represented by a sociologist we hired
as a commentator.   He regarded any suggestion that American society might be better than any other in any way as
leading to cultural chauvinism.   Somehow I cannot go along
with this.   I feel that there is a mandate to a textbook
writer to attempt to instill a sense of commitment to this
country, free of condescension or false pride, a patriotism
that looks to the past traditions of America to attempt to
right present injustices.

Up to now what we've done in this text is to present
ten themes of American history, such as economic opportunity, a mobile population, concern for the welfare of others, making clear that these are not necessarily uniquely
American, nor ever fully realized.   "Taken as a whole,"
we say, "the history of the United States has been that of a
bold and exciting experiment in founding a society on faith in
human intelligence, human freedom, and human brotherhood.
So far this experiment has been a success.   Its future success depends on the intelligence, good will, and sense of
responsibility of coming generations."   In the new editions
I have toned this down a bit, and the book ends with an assessment of how far we have achieved our stated ideals and
how far fallen short.   But I'm still uncertain.   Go too far
in the direction of indoctrination, and you lay the ground for
future disillusion: fail to make any effort to inculcate a
sense of what America has meant in the world, and you lose
a good deal of the purpose of studying our past and may contribute to the all too common sense of alienation.   I can only say that my intention runs with what Alfred North White-
head once wrote:

The art of a free society consists first in the
maintenance of the symbolic code; and secondly in fearlessness of revision, to secure that
the code serve those purposes which satisfy
an enlightened reason.   Those societies which
cannot combine reverence to their symbols with
freedom of revision, must ultimately decay either from anarchy or from the slow atrophy of
a life stifled by useless shadows. [2]

Notes

1.   Henry W. Bragdon and John C. Pittenger, The Pursuit
     of Justice: An Introduction to Constitutional Rights.
     New York: Macmillan, 1969.

2.   Symbolism: Its Meaning and Effect.   New York: Put-
     nam, 1959, p. 88.

The Dilemma of Social Studies Publishers

By Margaret B. Wilkins, Assistant Editor, D. C. Heath and Company.

From The Social Studies 58:203-7, October 1967. © Mc-Kinley Publishing Company. Reprinted by permission.

Robert D. Price's article "The Textbook Dilemma in the Social Studies" in the January 1966 issue of The Social Studies touched on the source of many of the shortcomings of elementary social studies texts today. But in his article he was primarily interested in assessing the merit of the criticism and setting these criticisms against the responsibility of the classroom teacher in compensating for these shortcomings.

That is one way of dealing with superficial textbooks in social studies. And if the world of education included only ideal teachers, his solution would absolve textbook publishers from ever trying to improve their products. But there are poor teachers, beginning teachers, and unimaginative teachers who are unwilling or unable to meet the challenge Mr. Price sets for them in dealing with elementary social studies texts. There is another important variable factor in the manufacture of dull, superficial, irresponsible textbooks--the textbook publisher.

Elementary social studies textbooks face a dilemma partially because they reflect the dilemma social studies textbook publishers face. Until this dilemma is more widely understood (the textbook publishers understand it and are trying to break out of it) by professional educators, classroom teachers, and the many people who are vitally concerned with the future of social studies education--until these people begin to understand the dilemma, the future of textbook publishing could look like the past. And many past products of elementary social studies are pallid models to use for the dynamic and robust years of the future.

410

The story of the textbook dilemma has its roots in several basic facts of the publisher's life. A textbook publisher must be a businessman whose function is to make money. If he does not make money, he cannot continue to furnish his product. To make money he has to sell as many books as possible to as many schools as possible. He must manufacture a book that will have the widest appeal and make the least enemies.

The publisher is not always sure who is going to have the final decision on whether or not his book is going to be used in a given school system, for the methods by which books are selected vary widely from state to state. Some systems allow the teacher complete freedom in selection of textbooks; others have textbook advisory committees that select texts, while some advisory committees only advise; some systems are tied to the decisions of state adoption committees. A publisher then cannot be sure if his product is selected by a classroom teacher, a professional educator, or a concerned layman. He must try to appeal to them all.

The publisher also is faced with the curriculum dilemma. There is a wide range of curriculum differences. Some systems have no recommended curriculum at all; the teacher is free to choose what he wishes to teach. Other systems have broad guidelines that allow the teacher a wide range of choices and texts, but other states have a rigidly fixed curriculum. The publisher wants to sell his books in all of these areas and he wants his content to satisfy as many of the systems as possible.

A school system that buys a publisher's product is faced with the fact that a school's responsibility is to serve the community. The awareness of this responsibility occurs in greater or lesser degrees depending on the area, school system, and community. But it is not often the case that there is no communication between the school system and the community. When a school system adopts a textbook for its students (whether the individual teacher or a committee makes the choice is irrelevant) that decision was shaped in part by the demands of the community--sectional interests, prejudices, and myths. Buyers of textbooks must, and rightly so, realize that their responsibility is to the community and not to the pocketbooks of the textbook publishers. And it is to their credit when buyers try to balance the demands of the community, the needs of the schools, and the value of the books in question in making final decisions on textbook adoption.

But the publisher is aware of the demands individual communities make in the area of textbook selection. The newspapers delight in reporting instances of vested interests in small communities asking that certain books be banned from the schools. Thus a publisher realizes that to make money, he should try to avoid alienating vested interests. He realizes that he must appeal to committees that come from diverse areas of the country.

Textbook publishing runs on a fairly small margin of profit. To make publishing worthwhile to his businessman interests, the textbook publisher must appeal to these divergent groups to justify his investment in staff time and printing costs. In making this appeal, the publisher of social studies texts faces the usual problems of being accepted or rejected for logical reasons of structure, content, or presentation.

But social studies are more at the mercies of individual prejudices than many other kinds of texts. Social studies deals with man and the way he interacts with his world; social studies deals with the world today, how it came to be this way, and an analysis of the forces that are moving and shaping it today. There is a great deal of disagreement about why the world is where it is and where we should go from here.

Few people are entirely free from prejudice. Often people we would classify as open minded have very definite views on certain aspects of the history of our country, set attitudes toward different ethnic groups, and preconceived ideas (sometimes springing from their own school days) of the economic and social structures of foreign countries. These subjects are the subjects of social studies. For example, a person who tried to judge legislation today on its individual merit and not the party that proposed the law, may be deeply offended by a social studies text that asserts George Washington may have been an inspired leader of men but was an incompetent general and an indifferent politician. Or a New Englander might be offended by a treatment of the pre-Civil War era that stated that some New England sea captains made a fortune by smuggling slaves into Southern ports. Both of these views could be quite offensive to people with different vested interests, yet their inclusion in a text might make interesting and stimulating reading for a student. Also the views could be defended by historians, yet the book may be rejected by an adoption committee because these views were expressed.

Thus when a social studies publisher decides to print a text, he has several demands to satisfy:

1. His stockholders want the company to make money.
2. He must satisfy teachers and concerned laymen as well.
3. He must satisfy the needs of the curriculum committees.
4. He must not offend sectional interests or prejudices.

Besides realistically facing the demands of the market, most publishers feel that they must meet serious aesthetic and scholarly demands as well. A publisher wants an author who will create a scholarly and precise work that has a reasonably defensible point of view. Second, the text has to have at least passible if not commendable literary merit. Thus the authors and editors must be Janus-like in their writing. They must try to maintain literary and scholarly integrity without losing sight of the market for which they are writing.

This kind of writing is going to demand compromises; veracity is compromised to expediency; unpopular attitudes and beliefs are deleted to satisfy sectional interests. The extent to which compromise takes place is a function of the author, the publisher, the market for which the text is designed, the book itself, and sometimes the editor's digestion on the day the decision is made. The extent of compromise is hardly definable since it is a variable, depending on factors that themselves vary. But in light of the compromises that do take place, some products are going to be shallow, puny, and superficial. In fact, some books, particularly social studies books, are so much the children of compromise that it is surprising how many excellent texts are produced.

Many of the charges Mr. Price listed (and later defended) were the result of economic expediency. Many social studies textbooks contain little mention of God and religion, are unromantic, superficial, and fail to deal with subjects in depth; they contain little critical thinking and challenge for the gifted child because a textbook that would do all or part of these things would not sell well. A book that defends a vested interest makes too many enemies. A book

that deals with depth studies must make choices of subjects
and thus runs the risk of appealing to fewer of the systems
that have a set curriculum.   Textbooks that feature critical
thinking and challenge for the gifted sell to the gifted classroom teacher, but most teachers do not have gifted children.

As Mr. Price suggested, publishers do tend to picture the romantic and unrealistic side of cultures in social
studies texts.   These books often fail to reflect the importance of a country in world affairs today.   The publisher
thinks that a wooden-shoed Holland and a kimonoed Japan are
pictures of the countries that will sell best.   People choose
the texts, and people like pleasant, romantic pictures; a textbook that realistically portrayed the plight of many underdeveloped countries today might so repel the buyers that the
publisher would be punished for his honesty.

Some books are unrealistic and romantic because it
is easier to write a textbook that says many of the same
things other textbooks have said than to pioneer a new approach to an old country.   Some authors are afraid to do the
kind of creative thinking necessary for the kind of book that
would break the old molds and lead to new understandings.
The publisher or editor may fail to demand this kind of work
from the author; in this situation the blame for an insipid
text falls on the publisher.

Textbooks that deal with foreign countries face a peculiar difficulty with the time it takes to manufacture the
text.   A lapse of as much as three years takes place between the conception of a book and its final sales.   While
changes are made in the course of the book's production,
these changes must be limited to updating facts and figures.
It would be too expensive to reorganize or change the emphasis of a text during production.   Thus while a country may
have been strategically important in world affairs when a
book was written, by the time it is published the country may
have passed its zenith.   And when the book has been in use
five years, the treatment of the country may be so outdated
that it is useless.   Publishers try to be prognosticators, but
they do not always succeed.

If a publisher is forward-looking in his policy and
does choose countries well, he still runs the risk of having an
obsolete book in three years.   A book that features up-to-
date attitudes, facts, and materials becomes obsolete faster
than a text that relies on hackneyed pictures and phrases.

For some schools early obsolescence is no shortcoming because they have a large textbook budget and are willing to
spend money every few years for the most up-to-date books.
However, many publishers feel that a forward-looking policy
coupled with a generous budget is the exception rather than
the rule. Therefore, the publisher tries often to tailor his
books to minimize the obsolescence in content. One way is
to retreat to standardized pictures of countries and to choose
the stereotypes.

But the best way to minimize obsolescence from a
publisher's point-of-view is to compromise the past and the
future. Emerging African nations, belligerent China, and
the tumultuous Latin American countries are not good subjects for publishers. Stable European countries with noncon-
troversial pasts and stable futures are more attractive subjects. If a rapidly changing country is mentioned at all, it
is to the publisher's benefit to emphasize the factors that
have remained the same and to de-emphasize the fluctuating
aspects of the culture.

In light of the logic that so often accompanies the publication of a textbook, the future of textbooks would at first
seem quite bleak. The future would be more of the same
kinds of dull and superficial social studies texts, populated
with unrealistic people from unrealistic countries. But the
future does not have to be dark; in fact, there are signs
that the future will not be. But if really significant changes
are to take place, the changes will have to be a co-operative
effort among publisher, school system, and community--the
three protagonists in the textbook story.

Many publishers deplore the economic facts that cause
them to tamper with excellent textbooks. These publishers
are dedicated to producing educational materials that will be
an asset to a teacher's classroom presentations. In fact,
the dedication of some can be measured by the fact that they
have chosen the field despite some of the more frustrating
limitations.

Publishers try to produce some texts that are innovations in the field, realizing that such a gamble may not pay
them back for the paper and time that went into the text.
Few people even write letters of encouragement that would
ease the pain of the figures in the loss column. If the publishers are to overcome the "minimized obsolescence" and
"widest possible appeal" traps, they are going to have to be

more courageous and more confident that a good textbook
will create its own market.   Publishers try to keep attuned
to innovations in education; and social studies publishers will
have to be more willing to publish texts that will incorporate
these innovations.

A publisher is more likely to take a risk on a textbook if he knows school systems want that kind of a book.
Publishers try to survey the market before deciding whether
or not to produce a book.   This is one small and very practical area where schools can do themselves an immediate
service.   If teachers, educators, and adoption committees
devoted more time to making their desires and criticisms
more widely known to publishers, perhaps texts would be
more responsive to the demands for educational innovations.
This kind of communication is the key to any changes. Publishers need to be told if the organization of a text is incom-
prehensible to the students.   Publishers need to know if the
illustrations and text are so poorly correlated that they hinder learning.   Publishers need to know if the text is so con-
structed that it fails to lend itself to effective classroom
teaching.

But publishers cannot experiment if the books are not
sold.   Telling a publisher to try harder is futile if the attempt will drive him out of business.   The buyers have a responsibility to help the publisher ease the economic demands
of the industry.   Textbook committees must be responsive to
the demands of the community, but they must have the courage of their professional knowledge not to be slaves to the
smallest amount of adverse community criticism.   Likewise,
the community must have enough respect for the educators
who select texts, to be willing to defer to the selector's
judgment despite the community's misgivings.

The educators themselves need to take stock of what
they demand in a textbook to see if the very things they demand aren't the source of some of the shortcomings in the
text.   A publisher should not have to produce a book that
caters to unique quirks and petty prejudices.   And finally,
like the publisher, the educators must be willing to take a
risk on a textbook that does not follow the usual formulas;
for a really excellent textbook risks failure in order to a-
chieve success.   And successful textbooks in social studies,
texts that are creative learning experiences for the child,
are the hope for our complex future.

Editing a Scientific Encyclopedia

By David L. Sills, Editor of the International Encyclopedia of the Social Sciences; Sociologist; Associate Director, Demographic Division, The Population Council.

From Science 163:1169-75, March 14, 1969. Copyright ©
1969 by the American Association for the Advancement of
Science. Reprinted by permission.

The thousands of "encyclopedias" written since the age of Greece and Rome have two attributes in common. They have all claimed to provide a comprehensive survey of knowledge (either all knowledge, or one branch of knowledge), and they have all been based upon some explicit or implicit scheme for classifying knowledge.

In their other attributes encyclopedias vary widely. Most of them are multiauthored, but a number of great encyclopedias have been written by one man. Most are multi-volumed, but a number of important one-volume encyclopedias have been published. Most present the articles in alphabetical order, but this fairly modern practice is by no means universal even today.

Because of the claim to be comprehensive and the explicit or implicit schemes used for classification, the study of encyclopedias provides a vast (and largely untapped) opportunity for research into both the history of science and the sociology of knowledge--the study of the relation between the characteristics of a society and the origins and nature of what it considers to be "knowledge." Consider the most famous encyclopedia ever produced, the 17-volume Encyclopédie edited by Diderot and D'Alembert. The very fact that it was prepared, to say nothing of its contents, is often taken as an indicator of the broad social and intellectual movement called the Enlightenment. The aim of the Encyclopédie was to treat all subjects, those related to social arrangements no less than those of the physical environment, in terms of a rational, scientific approach--nothing was to be considered too sacred

417

to be questioned by the rationalist iconoclasts of the Enlightenment.

The Encyclopaedia of the Social Sciences was edited
by two economists, E. R. A. Seligman and Alvin Johnson,
and was published in 15 volumes by the Macmillan Company
between 1930 and 1935. It reflects the prevailing notion of
the late 1920's and early 1930's that social ills can be cured
if knowledge from the social sicences is both widely dispersed among the public and is brought to bear on these ills;
it also reflects the fact that the social science most highly
developed at that time was economics (largely pre-Keynesi-
an). The historicist insight that the Encyclopaedia is a document of its time, not simply a compilation of more or less
obsolete articles, is in part the result of the effort to create a new encyclopedia of the social sciences.

The recently published International Encyclopedia of
the Social Sciences, (IESS) was published in April 1968 in
17 volumes by the Macmillan Company and the Free Press.
As its editor, I am presumably well qualified, perhaps overly
qualified, to tell its story. Nevertheless, I have handicaps,
some self-imposed and some that I cannot avoid. In spite of
Watson's example in The Double Helix (1), I am not willing to
expose all the conflicts and frailties that are part of the story,
even though many of these are an essential component of the sociology of knowledge. Also, my account can be only a partial
one because I obviously did not know everything that was going
on. Each of my fellow editors has his own story to tell, as do
many of our contributors. Finally, this is only a partial
story because we encyclopédistes of the 20th century, no less
than those of the 18th, constitute part of the data that some
future sociologist of knowledge will analyze if he studies the
IESS. The thousands of "rational" decisions we made to
solve intellectual or practical problems may well reveal both
the blind spots and the unwitting prescience of social sciences
of the 1960's.

Background
The story begins with the several efforts, immediately after World War II, to encourage the publication of a new
or a revised edition of the "old" and much-respected Encyclopaedia of the Social Sciences (hereafter called the Encyclopaedia). In 1950, Alvin Johnson prepared a report on the
proportion of the articles in the Encyclopaedia that would have
to be revised or rewritten for a new edition. In 1951, Bert

F. Hoselitz, an economist at the University of Chicago,
prepared a memorandum proposing a new or revised edition.
And in 1954, in response to a suggestion made by Johnson,
Bernard Berelson, then director of the Behavioral Sciences
Program at the Ford Foundation, asked several dozen social
scientists and librarians to comment on the desirability of
a new or revised edition.   The responses to these inquiries
were generally favorable, and Berelson asked his associate
Francis X. Sutton to undertake a study of the feasibility of
such a project.

At Berelson's suggestion, and with Ford Foundation
funds, several ad hoc meetings were held, and a study group
was formed under the aegis of the University of Chicago.
W. Allen Wallis, a statistician and economist then at the
University of Chicago, served as chairman (2).

The study group met during the summer of 1955, and,
with the assistance of Hoselitz and a small staff, it prepared
"A Study of the Need for a New Cyclopedic Treatment of the
Social Sciences."   This thorough report, which examined both
the need for a new encyclopedia and the administrative problems that would be involved in meeting the need, was submitted in August 1955 (3).

The Chicago study group also inquired into the relevance of producing an encyclopedia in the mid-20th century.
"What is an encyclopedia about?" and "What is an encyclopedia for?" were two of the questions examined.   They are
also questions that my editorial colleagues and I discussed at
great length, and our implicit answers are an integral part
of this account.

By 1955, the Encyclopaedia was 20 years old, and the
frequency with which individuals consulted it had undoubtedly
declined.   (The increase in the number of social scientists
may well have led to an increase in total use.)   It is difficult to obtain objective measures of the use made of reference books, although one member of the study group, Frederick Mosteller, did attempt to measure the use of the Encyclopaedia by examining the wear and tear of seven sets lo-
cated in six libraries at Harvard University and the University of Chicago.   Applying a four-point scale ("clean," "well-
used," "heavy use," and "very heavy use"), Mosteller found
the articles that seemed to have been consulted most frequently.   The study demonstrated that the Encyclopaedia had
been used frequently in these libraries, and that conceptual

articles were more frequently consulted than descriptive
ones.

The study group also obtained interviews with 66 social scientists (at 19 colleges and universities) concerning the
desirability of a revised or new encyclopedia. Naturally
enough, there was general agreement about the overall obsolescence of the Encyclopaedia; it would have been quite remarkable if this had not been the case. And a majority (39
of the 66 respondents) favored either a revised edition or a
completely new encyclopedia. By and large, undergraduate
teachers (except for psychologists) in colleges favored the
project, but research-minded university professors did not.
I myself believe that the plan to prepare a revised or new
edition had, at best, the lukewarm support of leading figures
in the social sciences in the mid-1950's, although the study
group was not so explicitly pessimistic in summarizing the
reactions it uncovered.

Given the difficulty of the task of preparing a new encyclopedia that many people thought would not be worth the
effort, the study group considered various alternatives--sup-
plements to the Encyclopaedia, dictionaries, handbooks, and
a new loose-leaf encyclopedia. But none of these alternatives
seemed to have as much merit as another encyclopedia. Although Sutton's many interviews on the subject revealed doubt,
indifference, and a feeling that "the reference needs of the
social sciences in the mid-20th century called for something
radically new--something that would be as typical of this century as Diderot's and D'Alembert's encyclopedia was of the
eighteenth," Sutton found that "no brilliant, modern invention
to supersede an encyclopedia emerged in the many discussions" (4).

Berelson and his immediate superior, William Mc-
Peak, a Ford Foundation vice president, gave sympathetic attention to the report, and the Social Science Research Council (which had sponsored the earlier Encyclopaedia) devoted
two sessions to the subject during its meeting in the fall of
1955. But others in the foundation were cool to the proposal,
and the project lay dormant for 5 years until late 1960, when
the Macmillan Company decided to publish a new encyclopedia
of the social sciences without any foundation or other subsidy.
W. Allen Wallis was appointed chairman of the editorial advisory board.

The story of the developments reported thus far has

already been described (5).   I was appointed editor in the
fall of 1961, and began full-time work in March 1962; accordingly, it is only from this time forward that I have first-
hand knowledge of how the IESS was prepared.   My purpose
here is to review briefly the organizational structure devised
for the purpose of editing the IESS, to summarize the editorial philosophy and policies developed as a result of collab-
orative work among the editors, and to describe some of the
intellectual and technical problems faced by the editorial
staff.

Organizational Structure

            The IESS had an international editorial advisory board
which functioned not as a body but as a group of individual
consultants.   Its members served without compensation.
They were sent two successive versions of the preliminary
table of contents and were asked to submit comments and
suggestions--many replied with helpful suggestions.   Some
helped the editors to identify scholars who might contribute
articles on specific topics.

            Initially, the editorial policies of the IESS were re-
viewed by an executive committee (6) (which became inactive
when the editorial staff was formed).   To ensure strong disciplinary coverage in all the fields of the social sciences,
this committee recommended appointment, for each major
discipline, of an "associate editor" who would have more
duties than an advisory editor but considerably fewer than a
full-time editor.   These associate editors, together with five
"special editors," carried out their responsibilities largely
by correspondence (7).   The disciplines represented were
anthropology, economics, political science, psychology, sociology, and statistics.

            This list reveals what we considered to be the core
social sciences.   Other fields were included to the extent
that their substance seemed to warrant it.   Linguistics and
archeology were included under anthropology; geography was
included because its social and cultural branches are closely
related to anthropology, economics, and sociology; history is
represented by a series of articles on the different fields of
history (economic, intellectual, and others) and on varieties
of historiography; and law and psychiatry were included to the
extent that they embrace the subject matter of the social sciences.

Each of the associate and special editors--who became known as "field editors"--was allocated a quota of
words and of articles: approximately 1 million words and
290 articles each to economics, political science, psychology, and sociology; about half of that to anthropology;
250,000 words and 65 articles to statistics; and 1.3 million
words and 400 articles to biographies. It soon became evident that such fields as geography and history and many general social science topics did not readily fit into our system
of classification; these were picked up by various editors,
according to their knowledge and interests.   Thus, Edward
Shils took responsibility for most of the articles on history
and religion, and I took on geography and a series of articles
on the production, dissemination, and utilization of social
science knowledge.

The field editors used fairly standard procedures for
building lists of articles and potential contributors. They all
consulted textbooks, abstract journals, and colleagues, to
make sure that no important topic was overlooked.   The
process of pruning and adding to the disciplinary lists was
continued until well into 1967 when the production schedule
made further changes impossible.

The field editors continued to serve as consultants
throughout the preparation period. They read most of the
articles and often wrote comments on them; in some instances,
they did a considerable share of the technical editing. They
nominated new contributors for articles that did not arrive or
that had to be rejected. In every sense, they were senior
partners in the enterprise, and each had full responsibility
for the treatment of his discipline.

The field editors, however, could not take a leading
part in the actual editing of the encyclopedia.   They were all
active professors; six of the 12 were also departmental chair-
men or directors of research institutes; three others were
editors of scholarly journals.   In short, the IESS had to compete with many other demands upon their time; in some instances, it competed very successfully, in others, less so.
The actual editing was done by me and a staff of full-time
editors, recruited for this purpose--nine young social scientists who were willing to interrupt their careers for the period necessary to create an encyclopedia (8).   Assisting this
staff were two assistant editors (9), a bibliographical staff,
and a staff of copy editors provided by the publishers.   On
the substantive level the work of this staff involved repeatedly

reviewing the table of contents to make sure that no essential topic was overlooked; locating contributors for hundreds of articles when the knowledge of the field editors had been exhausted; evaluating proposals for new articles that were volunteered by outsiders; upholding academic standards in the face of many pressures from a commercial publisher; and mediating between the "hard" science and the "soft" science wings of the social sciences, a task made complicated by the fact that most of the editors were members of the former. On a different, but also important level, we were responsible for extracting articles from intellectually nervous or overcommitted professors; for negotiating with the publisher several times a year on the budget and the production schedule; for acting as gadflies in keeping some of the field editors attentive to the needs of the encyclopedia; for determining rules for stylistic matters and writing a style book with which to enforce them; for making a policy for quotations, citations, and bibliographies and establishing procedures to ensure their accuracy; for devising procedures to verify the many thousand cross references; for writing guides to related articles to place at the head of articles on broad topics; for instructing the printer on how to set complicated mathematical matter in linotype; and for seemingly endless proofreading.

Contents: Organization
        An alphabetically arranged encyclopedia consists of entries under which articles are placed; in that sense, it differs markedly from such topically arranged social science reference books as the Handbook of Organizations, the Handbook of Social Psychology, or the Handbook of Psychiatry. A reader seeks what he wants to know in these handbooks by consulting the table of contents or the index, whereas the reader of an encyclopedia generally first consults an alphabetically located entry. Two tasks of the editor of an alphabetically arranged reference book are to ensure that articles are placed where readers will look for them and to provide an entry for every topic that a reader might consult. The selection of these alphabetical entries was thus of crucial importance.

        It might be assumed that we simply derived our list of entries from the lists of topics drawn up by the field editors, but this is not what happened. Each discipline has certain widely used concepts which obviously called for entries: acculturation, culture, diffusion, and race--in anthropology;

capital, cost, interest, and money--in economics; administration, decision making, legislation, and power--in political
science; attention, emotion, learning, and personality--in
psychology; community, groups, socialization, and stratifica-
tion--in sociology; and distribution, likelihood, probability,
and estimation--in statistics. But we soon learned that lists
of topics, useful as they were as starting points, and as a
means to ensure complete coverage, could not provide us
with a complete list of entries.

We alphabetized the lists of topics provided by the
field editors and added a number of topics that are either
nondisciplinary (for example, ethical issues in the social sciences; information storage and retrieval), or are from disciplines other than those of the field editors (for example, history; geography). Then each member of the editorial staff
went through the master list, to put like titles together, lo-
cate gaps, and retitle vaguely worded topics. The first preliminary table of contents was distributed to the field editors
in November 1962. A meeting with the field editors was held
in late November, when many articles were added and deleted. A second preliminary table of contents was ready in
February 1963. This also was distributed, and the changes
incorporated into a third version, which was sent in April
both to the field editors and to all members of the editorial
advisory board. This process was repeated (through correspondence and staff meetings) approximately every 6 months;
in June 1967 the 12th (final) table of contents was included
in a printed prospectus.

The changes that took place between the first table of
contents and the published work constitute much of the intellectual history of the IESS. Many articles were added to the
list as new topics came to the attention of the editors, or as
articles received were found to neglect some important aspects of a topic. Biographical articles were added for these
reasons, as well as when death made someone eligible to be
the subject of a biography. Many articles were dropped when
a topic was deemed inappropriate or was covered in another
article, when a suitable contributor could not be found, or
when a contributor failed to submit an article and it was too
late to commission another; and many articles were retitled.

The titles of some articles were changed for the mundane reason that they were not received or edited in time to
be printed in the original alphabetical position, and the titles
of others were changed in order to place them where we be-

lieved they would be more likely to be consulted by readers.
But far and away the largest number of articles was relo-
cated in order to group two or more articles under one heading.   These groupings, which we called composite articles,
are one way that we resolved the dilemma of "alphabetiza-
tion versus systematization"--that is, the question of how
the inter-relatedness of topics in the social sciences can be
reflected in an alphabetically arranged encyclopedia.   Furthermore, they indicate both the degree to which synthesis
was achieved by the editors and the degree to which synthesis was impossible.   For these reasons, composite articles
deserve a brief discussion.

The editors of the old Encyclopaedia adopted as one
of their major goals the achievement of "a more comprehensive synthesis" of the social sciences--to use the phrase in
Seligman's preface.   In his 1952 autobiography, Pioneer's
Progress, Alvin Johnson recalled how it had been hoped that
the Encyclopaedia would serve as a powerful force for unity
in the social sciences.   Yet when Sutton talked to social scientists in 1954 and 1955 about the goals of a new encyclopedia, few such hopes were expressed (4, p. 30)

The editors of the IESS never dreamed of achieving
a "comprehensive synthesis"; our goals were more modest.
We made composites of related articles regardless of their
disciplinary origin; we tried to resolve flagrant terminologi-
cal discrepancies whenever they were found; and we sought to
point out substantive connections between articles by developing an extensive system of cross references.

As the result of the preparation of the 12 successive
tables of contents, a majority (601 out of 1118) of the topical
articles in the IESS was placed within 198 composite articles.
(The term "topical article" refers to a non-biographical article.   The IESS also contains 598 biographical articles describing the contributions of 601 persons; of these, only 12
are placed within composites.)   By contrast, the earlier Encyclopaedia has fewer than one-fourth (424 out of 1966) of its
topical articles within its 102 composites (10).

Many of these composites represent various facets of
a topic from the point of view of a single discipline; for example, the six articles under the heading "geography" are all
by geographers on various fields of geography, and the six
articles under the heading "taxation" are all by economists
on various types of taxes.   But 105 of the composites contain

articles from more than one field. For example, the three
articles under the heading "diffusion" are by an anthropologist, a geographer, and a sociologist, and the four articles
under "conflict" are by a psychologist, a political scientist,
a sociologist, and an anthropologist. By the use of these
strategies, the editors hoped not so much to create a unity
within the social sicences as to reflect as clearly as possible
such unity (and diversity) as exists.

Contents: Substance
          The discussion thus far has been for the most part fo-
cused on the procedures followed in selecting and arranging
the contents of the IESS, rather than on the content itself.
It would of course be possible to tell the story the other way
round; to answer the question "What is the encyclopedia a-
bout?" and then tell how it was put together. But this would
give the impression that the character of the IESS was determined in advance, and that the procedures followed in preparing it flowed naturally from a master plan. This is not what
happened. Several years before undertaking this assignment
I wrote a book in the field of organizational sociology, the
major thesis being that organizational procedures (means)
have an enormous impact upon organizational goals (ends).
On the title page of that book I thought it appropriate to quote
these lines by Ferdinand Lassalle (1825-1864):

                    Show us not the aim without the way,
                    For ends and means on earth are so
                         entangled
                    That changing one, you change the other
                         too;
                    Each different path brings other ends in
                         view.

          Nothing in my experience in editing the IESS caused
me to think less of the cogency of this observation.

          In the first year or two of our work, the editorial
staff and I did develop a fairly clear notion of what kind of an
encyclopedia it was going to be. When a topic nominated for
inclusion was thought inappropriate, or when an article submitted seemed inappropriate (either in its entirety or in part),
the judgment we would make to each other was "Wrong encyclopedia!" This means that we had a rather clear conception of what was appropriate, of what we really wanted to include, but we also had to take into account the differences

among disciplines, the differences in point of view among the field editors and among the contributors, and the quite different motivations that would ultimately bring readers to the IESS. In spite of all these compromises we were able to produce an encyclopedia that conforms, to a large extent, to our conception of what the IESS should be; and because of these compromises, the model may well have been modified to its advantage.

This conceptual model was developed in our staff meetings, in our discussions with the field editors, and in our informal conversations. The "style" and "tone" of the encyclopedia that emerged is partly the result of the reconciliation of our individual points of view; partly a consequence of the fact that the editorial staff had all been graduate students in the remarkable decade of the 1950's, when the social sciences acquired much of their contemporary empirical-theoretical character, and partly a reflection of the "behavioral sciences" orientation of the field editors. But it was also a response to three "outside" influences--the Enclopaedia, the report of the Chicago study group, and the contributors.

It is difficult to assess the influence of the Encyclopaedia on our thinking, but in my own case it was an important one. The very fact that an encyclopedia of the social sciences had been produced before made the task seem plausible and feasible. Also, the Encyclopaedia gave us a point of reference: we knew that readers and reviewers would inevitably compare the two encyclopedias, and the success of the earlier one meant that there was a standard of excellence that we had to meet. Finally, our awareness of the varying rates of obsolescence of articles in the Encyclopaedia perhaps helped us make the IESS a little more obsolescence-proof than reference books usually are.

The report of the Chicago study group contained three major "operational" recommendations that gave us a mandate for seeking (and gaining) acceptance for a conception of the IESS that we found thoroughly congenial. The first was that the primary stress in articles should be on "theoretical contributions and empirical regularities"; the second was that descriptive material should in general be included "only for illustrative purposes"; and the third was that the number of biographies should be far fewer than the 4000 in the earlier Encyclopaedia and should be limited to persons of direct relevance to the social sciences.

The first commissioned articles began to arrive in the late fall of 1962. By June 1963, two hundred forty-eight articles had been received, and by October the count had reached 899. The effect of this feedback from the contributors upon the editors' conception of what the IESS should be like should not be underestimated. Especially in the early years, our practice was to circulate manuscripts widely among the editors, whose reactions to them, positive and negative, affected future editorial decisions. The comments we made to each other went far toward establishing a consensus on the ideal model for the IESS.

Contents: Two Encyclopedias Compared

The question "What is the encyclopedia about?" can also be answered by contrasting its articles with those in the earlier Encyclopaedia. Simply turning the pages of the two encyclopedias gives the largely correct impression that the earlier one places greater emphasis on economics and less emphasis on psychology and statistics; that it includes hundreds of biographies of historical figures (from Alexander the Great to Theodore Roosevelt); and that it contains hundreds of articles on particular institutions (from Christian Science to the League of Nations) and on particular historical events (from the Black Death to the Russian Revolution). A more systematic way is to compare sample pages from the two encyclopedias. This was done.

It is evident from the articles on the sample pages that the editors of neither encyclopedia were able to establish a standard level of abstraction for use in selecting topics; both samples reflect great diversity in modes of organizing knowledge, and both contain articles on many analytical levels. One striking difference is between the number of articles devoted to the different disciplines. The Encyclopaedia is stronger in economics, which is a reflection of the relative importance of economics in the late 1920's and early 1930's and of the fact that both senior editors were economists. The IESS has a more even balance between the disciplines, a reflection partly of intellectual developments in the intervening years and partly of policies established by the editors (Table 1).

Table 1 demonstrates the difference between the topical articles in the two encyclopedias as far as disciplinary balance is concerned, but it does not reveal the equally large differences in content. These differences could be demon-

Table 1.   Major disciplinary relevance of articles on sample pages of two social science encyclopedias.

Discipline	Encyclopaedia of the Social Sciences*	International Encyclopaedia of the Social Sciences†
Anthropology	4	11
Economics	39	14
History	7	1
Information sciences	0	2
Law	2	1
Political science	16	14
Psychology	1	16
Public health	1	0
Sociology	16	18
Statistics	0	2
Totals ‡	86	79

* A sample of 100 pages was drawn by the staff of the Chicago study group (2; the articles that appear on these pages are listed on appendix pages 150 and 151 of the report). The page numbers were selected by using a series of 100 random numbers chosen from M. G. Kendall and B. B. Smith, Tables of Random Sampling Numbers (11).

† A sample of 100 pages was drawn by me by a procedure identical to that used in selecting the sample of Encyclopaedia pages, except that the page numbers were selected by using a series of 100 random numbers chosen from Rand Corporation, A Million Random Digits (12).   D. B. Peizer, statistical consultant at the Center for Advanced Study in the Behavioral Sciences, gave advice on appropriate procedures to follow in drawing the sample.

‡ The totals are less than 100 because pages containing only biographies of bibliographies were excluded from the samples.

strated by means of a content analysis of the sample pages;
alternatively, the articles on the sample pages could be classified according to whether or not comparable articles are included in the other encyclopedia and, if not, to try to discover why not.   This was done.

        The degree of overlap or near overlap between the two
encyclopedias as represented by these samples is nearly the
same: 32 out of the 86 articles in the Encyclopaedia sample
have counterparts in the IESS; examples are articles on agri-
cultural credit, capitalism, democracy, homicide, liberty,
mortality, and social work.   Similarly, 38 out of the 79 articles in the IESS sample have counterparts in the Encyclopaedia; examples are archeology, business cycles, justice,
land tenure, literacy, propaganda, and sociology.   Of greater
interest is the frequency distribution of the reasons for lack
of overlap.   Of the 54 articles in the Encyclopaedia sample
that do not have counterparts in the IESS, 38 are too specific-
descriptive to meet the purposes of the IESS (for example,
company towns; railroads); 12 are too historical-descriptive
(Conciliar movement; Jacobinism); three are not included because the concept is not in current social science use (amateur; decadence; gerontocracy); and one (Islamic law) because
a planned article did not materialize.   By contrast, of the 41
articles in the IESS sample that do not have counterparts in
the Encyclopaedia, 29 deal with concepts not used at the
earlier time (for example, automation, ethology, and game
theory) and 12 with concepts outside the announced scope of
the Encyclopaedia (for example, emotion, psychometrics, and
ramdom numbers).

        These comparisons are suggestive of the kind of sys-
tematic analysis of the two encyclopedias that might profitably
be extended.   Such an analysis would demonstrate the extent
to which and the ways in which the definition of social science knowledge has changed since the late 1920's and early
1930's.

Purpose
        We did not of course plan the IESS so that it could be
used by future sociologists of science; we had much more
mundane uses in mind.   The question "What is an encyclopedia for?" was constantly before us.   We were aware of the
doubts about the need for a new encyclopedia that the Chicago
study group had encountered in the 1950's, and we were almost daily made aware that the need for a new encyclopedia

did not have a high priority among social scientists of the
1960's.   Although the rate of acceptance among invited contributors was very high, partly, we thought, because of the
prestige of the earlier Encyclopaedia and partly because of
the reputations of the field editors, many declined because
they saw no need for an encyclopedia, and many others undoubtedly accepted the invitation only to show faith and good-
will.

Apathy toward a new encyclopedia was by no means
universal.   The older generation of social scientists was enthusiastic, and 60 contributors to the earlier Encyclopaedia
contributed to this one.   Such important older social scientists as Edwin G. Boring, Crane Brinton, Carl J. Friedrich,
Otto Klineberg, Hans Kohn, Harold D. Lasswell, Margaret
Mead, Oskar Morgenstern, Talcott Parsons, Joseph J. Speng-
ler, and Jacob Viner were willing contributors.   Among economists of all ages the prestige of the Encyclopaedia was high,
and their cooperation was generally the easiest to obtain.

A major reason for the general lack of interest in a
new encyclopedia was surely the lowered prestige of encyclopedias generally; it seems that a generation ago scholars consulted the Encyclopedia Britannica more frequently than they
do now, and that for many scholars today an encyclopedia is
an expensive set of books containing third-hand material that
a salesman tries to persuade them that they must buy if they
have the best interests of their children at heart.   Moreover,
in this age of the computer-generated abstract service, how
can an encyclopedia be anything but an outmoded form of publication?

Although these arguments surely have some merit, it
is my hope that the IESS will partly refute them.   The IESS
will have to speak for itself; all that I can do here is to try
to describe the ways in which we tried to make it as widely
useful as possible.

Our awareness that the encyclopedia would have to
create its own demand led to a number of editorial decisions.
An early concern was to try to gauge the audience.   Little is
known about who uses what kinds of encyclopedias for what
purpose.   Our typical users, we guessed half jokingly, would
be "the American graduate student and the assistant professor at the University of Bombay"--the first because of his
need to pass his subject matter doctoral examination and the
second because of his limited access to current American

and European books and journals.   We also guessed that
some undergraduates would use the encyclopedia, and that
mature scholars would use it to explore alien disciplines.
Given the range of potential users, we thought it best not to
insist that our contributors aim at a particular intellectual
level--we let them suit themselves and the subject, and
trusted that the result would in turn suit some segment of the
audience.

A related decision was that of having the IESS consist
entirely of articles written expressly for it.   Accordingly, in
spite of many pressures upon us to include previously published material, nothing in the IESS is reprinted from the
earlier Encyclopaedia or from any other publication.

We insisted that every article be accompanied by a
bibliography, and in some cases we enlarged the bibliographies supplied by the contributors.   We also developed an extensive system of cross references to guide readers to related articles.

In the course of editing the IESS we used the earlier
Encyclopaedia extensively as a source of "facts"--dates, the
spelling of names, the names of political parties and other
organizations, the titles or dates of publication of books--
and we inferred that the IESS would probably be used for the
same purpose.   We took some pains, therefore, to verify the
facts it contained.   And since we thought (and rather hoped)
that the IESS might be referred to for its use of technical
terminology, mathematical symbols, tables, figures, and matters of style generally, we tried to make it a model to be
followed in preparing material for publication.

Our expectations of potential users went even beyond
these.   One further use was as a readily available compilation of new articles by people on topics that the authors
themselves had either created or with which they had become
closely identified.   Examples are: in anthropology, Ray L.
Birdwhistell on kinesics; in economics, Wassily Leontief on
input-output analysis; in political science, Harold D. Lasswell on the policy sciences; in psychology, Joseph Wolpe on
behavior therapy; in sociology, Robert F. Bales on interaction process analysis; in statistics, Herman Chernoff on decision theory; and in other fields, Anatol Rapoport on general
systems theory, and Thomas S. Kuhn on the history of science.

Finally, we envisioned the IESS as being more than a traditional reference book in the sense that it would contain articles on topics that most readers would neither look for nor expect to find in an encyclopedia until word of their existence had been disseminated, articles, that is, on topics which would not appear on a standard list. Examples of articles of this kind are James A. Davis and Ann M. Jacobs on tabular presentation, Erik H. Erikson on psychosocial identity, Lloyd A. Fallers on societal analysis, I. J. Good on statistical fallacies, Nicholas Hobbs on ethical issues in the social sciences, Frederick Mosteller on non-sampling errors, and B. F. Skinner on the design of experimental communities.

Conclusion

Since encyclopedias are potentially useful sources of data for both sociologists of knowledge and historians of science, the basic biases underlying the IESS will eventually be revealed. The most that can be said now is that the editors attempted to be eclectic in their choice of topics and contributors. An effort was made to have as many non-American contributors as possible: 32 countries are represented. The majority of the 1505 contributors, however, are from the United States, the British Commonwealth, and 17 European countries.

Although we attempted to be eclectic, such influences as refusals, propinquity, friendship, ignorance, and intellectual prejudice undoubtedly influenced the selection of topics and contributors. A methodological task of the future sociologist of knowledge will be to sort these capricious influences from the more systematic ones that will reveal more clearly the contemporary state of the social sciences.

In the meantime, the editors of the IESS have considerable grounds for satisfaction. In spite of its many shortcomings, the IESS represents and summarizes much of the best of the social sciences of the 1960's. The initial doubts were overcome, and editors and contributors were drawn from the group of leaders in the field who had had the greatest hesitation. If we were to do it again we would do many things differently, but we hope that the fact that it was done at all will demonstrate that a scientific encyclopedia can be a relevant publication in the 1960's.

Notes

1. J. Watson, The Double Helix (Atheneum, New York, 1968).

2. The other members of the Chicago study group were Kingsley Davis (sociology), University of California, Berkeley; Clyde Kluckhohn (anthropology), Harvard University; Lyle H. Lanier (psychology), University of Illinois; Charles McKinley (political science), Reed College; Frederick Mosteller (statistics), Howard University; Arthur M. Schlesinger, Sr. (history), Harvard University; and Jacob Viner (economics), Princeton University.

3. University of Chicago, A Study of the Need for a New Cyclopedic Treatment of the Social Sciences (mimeographed, 25 August 1955).

4. F. X. Sutton, Amer. Behav. Sci. 6, 29 (1962).

5. No full-scale history or analysis of either encyclopedia has yet appeared. The Chicago study group report (3) is the most comprehensive single source. Brief accounts are given in Alvin Johnson's autobiography Pioneer's Progress (Viking, New York, 1952); by F. X. Sutton (4); by D. L. Sills, Amer. Behav. Sci. 6, 31 (1962); and in the "Foreword," "Preface," and "Introduction" to the IESS.

6. The executive committee for the IESS consisted of Edward Shils, Jeremiah Kaplan, Morris Janowitz, and W. Allen Wallis, chairman.

7. The associate editors for the IESS were: Heinz Eulau (political science); Lloyd A. Fallers (anthropology). William H. Kruskal (statistics); Gardner Lindzey (psychology); Albert Rees (economics); Albert J. Reiss, Jr. (sociology); and Edward Shils (social thought). The special editors were: Elinor G. Barber [(biographies) the only special editor who worked in New York as a member of the editorial staff]; John G. Darley (applied psychology); Bert F. Hoselitz (economic development); Clifford T. Morgan (experimental psychology); and Robert H. Strotz (econometrics).

8. The full-time editors for the IESS were: Elinor G.
    Barber (biographies); Marjorie A. Bassett (economics);
    P. G. Bock (political science); Robert M. Coen (econ-
    ometrics); J. M. B. Edwards (sociology); David S.
    Gochman (psychology); George Lowy (bibliographies);
    J. M. Tanur (statistics); and Judith Treistman (anthro-
    pology).

9. The assistant editors for the IESS were Donna M. Smith
    and Barbara J. Westergaard.

10. The totals given are subject to slight recount variability,
    since there are a few articles that can be counted as
    either biographical or topical (for example, Fourier
    and Fourierism).

11. M. G. Kendall and B. B. Smith, Tables of Random
    Sampling Numbers (Cambridge University Press,
    Cambridge, England, 1939).

12. Rand Corporation, A Million Random Digits (Free Press
    Glencoe, Ill, 1955).

13. This paper is based upon work performed at Crowell
    Collier Macmillan, Inc., New York, and was written
    while I was a 1967-68 fellow at the Center for Ad-
    vanced Study in the Behavioral Sciences, Stanford,
    California. I thank the center and staff for the time,
    perspective, and facilities provided me. Helpful com-
    ments on an earlier draft were furnished by B. Bar-
    ber, B. Berelson, P. G. Bock, H. J. Jerison, W. H.
    Kruskal, D. G. MacRae, F. Mosteller, E. A. Rubin-
    stein, J. M. Tanor, and W. A. Wallis.

New Devices and Old Publishers

By Cameron S. Moseley, Vice President, Harcourt, Brace & World, Inc.

From Visucom 2:9-11, February 1966.   Copyright 1966 by Tecnifax Corporation, Holyoke, Massachusetts.   Reprinted by permission.

> Note from author: "Since the article was written nearly six years ago and published five years ago, it is out of date in a number of respects, even though it still reflects my general thinking fairly well."

A textbook publisher, commenting on the proposed purchase of a publishing company by a large manufacturer of communications equipment, allegedly remarked: "They've got it backwards. The publisher really should be buying the equipment company. But most of us gave up owning printing plants years ago."

This publisher's opinion may well be wrong. Since only a relatively small proportion of the books, magazines, and newspapers published annually is actually first-rate, the equipment manufacturer, given the opportunity, conceivably could do a better job of publishing than the publisher himself. Moreover, the analogy between communications equipment and printing presses is certainly false, or at least inaccurate. The remark does illustrate rather well, however, the feelings of unease and uncertainty with which many publishers regard the present state of affairs in publishing, and particularly in educational publishing.

While textbook publishers are convinced that books, unlike buggy-whips, probably never will be supplanted by advances in technology . . . the concept of the book surely will remain, no matter what form books of the future may take . . . they are not entirely sure what they should be doing

436

about producing materials for the many new devices now a-
vailable to educators.   And they are even less sure what they
should be doing about the devices themselves.   They suspect
they may have to become involved in improving the razor as
well as in sharpening the blade.

The fact that no publishing firm . . . and indeed no
firm of any kind . . . appears to have produced a teaching
machine suitable for widespread use in school classrooms
does not necessarily mean that publishers should confine their
activities to the production of programmed materials in some
printed form, books or otherwise, and should leave teaching
machines entirely to the systems and equipment manufacturers.
Even if computers prove to be the answer to this problem,
publishers presumably should have some role in programming
them, or rather in preparing programmed materials that will,
in turn, be "programmed" for the computer.   (" 'When I use
a word,' Humpty Dumpty said in a rather scornful tone, 'it
means just what I choose it to mean . . . neither more nor
less.' 'The question is,' said Alice, 'whether you can make
words mean so many different things.' 'The question is,'
said Humpty Dumpty, 'which is to be master . . . that's
all.' '")

Eight-millimeter continuous loop films in cartridges
. . . commonly, but inaccurately, known as "single-concept"
films . . . appear to be an important educational aid, but
very few classrooms now have projectors in which such films
can be shown.   Does this mean that publishers should wait
for film-projector manufacturers to sell the schools enough
"standard" eight-millimeter film-cartridge projectors before
developing a really wide range of continuous-loop films directly related to school curricula and textbook programs?
Or should publishers play some role in developing and marketing a "standard" projector?

In recent years "do-it-yourself" overhead projection
transparencies have become established as extremely important teaching aids.   It seems probable, however, that they
can never provide the whole answer to a teacher's needs for
good material to use with the overhead projector.   It also
seems likely that nearly every school classroom in the country will be equipped with, or have easy access to, an overhead projector within the next five years.   Perhaps publishers
should work more closely with the manufacturers of overhead
projectors and overhead-projection transparencies to see what
can be done to bring the price of commercially-prepared

transparencies down to a more attractive level. And perhaps they should start thinking in terms of thousands (and
even tens of thousands) instead of hundreds for their printing
runs of overhead-projection transparencies.

Three questions are of particular importance to publishers in making decisions about the preparation of materials for new educational devices, and about the devices themselves. The first of these questions is well-known, but the
other two have received less attention. First: How does a
publisher retain full control of his copyrighted materials?
Second: What should the publisher's attitude be toward the
development and marketing of useful "hardware?" Third:
How can a publisher make sure the new materials he is producing for new devices are not given away to help sell basic
textbook programs?

As almost everyone, in school and out, now realizes,
publishers are deeply concerned about the proposed revision
of the copyright law soon to go before the Congress. "Although school people do not object to paying for typewriter
ribbons for their typewriters and soap for their washrooms,"
one textbook publisher observed recently, "many of them
seem to feel that the use of copyrighted materials in the
preparation of transparencies, tapes, course syllabi, and so
on should be free and unrestricted, or at least allowable
through some sort of 'blanket permission.' "

The schools quite naturally turn to published, copyrighted materials of various kinds as a convenient source for
the preparation of transparencies, tapes, copying masters,
and other materials (audio and/or visual) suitable for classroom use, particularly if commercially-prepared materials
are not readily and widely available at reasonable prices.
Properly controlled, with proper credits, and in some cases
the payment of appropriate fees, such use of copyrighted materials is highly desirable and should, indeed, be encouraged.
But, if the procedures are uncontrolled, publishers may find
themselves giving away their property (and the property of
their authors) without a reasonable financial return. Carried
to its logical extreme, this could mean the end of the educational publishing industry. Publishers now have every reason to hope, however, that the new copyright law, although
recognizing the important principle of "fair use," will not
sanction the "free use" of copyrighted materials for educational purposes.

The second question, relating to the development and marketing of "hardware," has been alluded to earlier. The textbook publisher traditionally feels that the development and marketing of "hardware" (i.e. film, filmstrip, overhead, opaque, and slide projectors, phonograph-record players and tape-recorders, laboratory equipment, copying machines, closed-circuit television, computers, and the like) are not his proper concern. Obviously, he must concern himself with, or at least be aware of the development and marketing of films, filmstrips, overhead projection transparencies, slides, phonograph records, tape recordings, video tapes, and computer programs. The relation between such materials and basic textbook programs is plain to see. But, when confronted with a new piece of equipment that may be potentially useful in the classroom, he is inclined to say, "When this device is perfected, standardized, and in wide use, then we may well want to produce materials for it, but until that time, there's nothing we can do except be interested." This is not of much help to the equipment manufacturer who wants to be sure good materials for his new device will be available when the device itself is on the market. He tends to think that, if textbook publishers took more interest in the actual development and standardization of new devices, they could help to improve the form in which these devices ultimately reach the schools. The early involvement of a few baseball players certainly would have improved the form in which the Houston Astrodome was first presented to the public!

An interesting variation of this question is the publisher's relationship to the development and marketing of manipulative materials, particularly in the fields of science and mathematics, where the need for such materials is clear and undisputed. A publisher may scoff at the idea of a school's buying a "tornado demonstrator" for twenty dollars. He nevertheless knows that, when his textbooks direct teacher and students to "obtain X piece of equipment, and such-and-such an amount of Y materials" in order to engage in a suggested activity, the teacher (and particularly the non-specialist elementary teacher) who does not have easy access to the recommended equipment and materials when he needs them has an understandable feeling of frustration. This is true even when the equipment and materials are relatively simple and relatively easy to obtain. Does this mean that publishers should "publish" such things as balance scales, pinhole cameras, probability demonstrators, and electromagnets? Does it mean, also, that they should carry bags of sand, Coke bottles, and tubes of glue in their inventories? They can perhaps be forgiven, or at least understood, if they're occasionally heard to observe, "I wish we could get back to making and selling books."

Actually, publishers have had considerable influence in certain areas in the development of "hardware" and technology. They have, for example, worked with printers and binders in the development of new kinds of inks, papers, presses, binding devices, and composition methods. And, more recently, they have exerted some influence on the standardization of tape-recording speeds used in language laboratories, the development (embryonic though it still seems to be) of teaching machines, and the wider use of overhead projectors. But, as a group, publishers tend to shy away from "hardware" and to look on themselves solely as the creators and distributors of materials of instruction, of what might be termed the "software" of the curriculum.

Textbook publishers, with some justification, show a certain peevishness because schools seem to spend relatively more on audio-visual devices than on "printed materials of instruction," and they take a wry delight in regaling anyone who'll listen with stories like these: The school system that spent $20,000 on overhead projectors, only to discover that commercially-prepared materials for these projectors were in short supply, and that the teachers in the system needed considerable special training before they could prepare their own. The textbook committee that adopted a new foreign language program with great enthusiasm only to be told by the superintendent they would have to wait another year to buy the materials, because $25,000 had just been spent on the language laboratory in which the materials were to be used. The superintendent who spent $15,000 on an electronic teaching machine, presented it proudly to his teachers, and then told them to go ahead and prepare programs for it.

Despite their understandable annoyance about this state of affairs, some publishers are prepared to admit that, if textbook publishers took more interest in, and were better informed about, "educational hardware" and its uses, the related interests of schools, publishers, and equipment manufacturers all might be better served.

The third question . . . How can a textbook publisher make sure the new materials he is producing for new devices are not given away to help sell basic textbook programs? . . . has received less attention, perhaps because it is so intimately related to the basic nature of textbook production, pricing, and marketing. The textbook publisher is concerned, fundamentally, with creating a product that will be purchased in relatively large quantities for use on a per-pupil basis. Therefore, he tends to think of materials that will be used mainly, if not wholly, by the teacher for class demonstration, and purchased, at best, on a one-copy-per-classroom basis, as aids to selling the basic textbook program rather than as products that should be marketed in their own right. If giving away a few sets of filmstrips, or records, or transparencies will help nail down a large textbook adoption, why not do it, particularly if competing publishers are giving away their similar products? And, since a textbook salesman gives away dozens of examination copies of textbooks, workbooks, and tests every day, he does not relish becoming involved in the intricacies of handling loan sets, approval sets and demonstration sets of expensive items that are designed primarily for teacher use.

One result of this situation is an increase in the prices of the per-pupil elements in the program . . . textbooks, workbooks, laboratory manuals, and tests. Items that are given away must be paid for somehow, and the only way to recover these costs is to raise the prices of the items that actually are being sold. Another result can be careless editorial, production, and pricing procedures, and superficial selling knowledge and methods. Obviously, it is harder to "get serious" about a product that, even though it carries a price and is designed ostensibly to be sold, is very often given away in order to help sell something else.

Furthermore, supplementary items can divert so much attention from the basic program that adoptions sometimes seem to be decided on the number and nature of the unusual "free extras" rather than on the quality of the basic program itself. This situation sometimes encourages publishers to get on their audio-visual horses and ride off in so many directions at once that publishing schedules are delayed and the various elements in a particular program appear at seemingly unpredictable intervals over a period of two or three years, to the vast and understandable irritation of schools and to the despair of the publisher's salesmen.

Publishers also may become so involved in making sure all the elements in a large program are clearly and properly correlated, so intent on marketing the "complete package," and in general, so intrigued by the "learning sys-

tems approach," that they lose touch with school realities.
One of the best protections a school system has against over-
organization of the curriculum is wide flexibility in the choice
of materials to fit particular local situations.   The "learning
systems approach" does have certain Orwellian aspects!

Furthermore, publishers can become so fascinated by
the ingenuity and attractiveness of the package that they pay
less attention than they should to the contents.   Even the
most ardent advocate of any new device or new materials
will, when pressed, admit that what is presented is more important, in the final analysis, than how it is presented.   A
cheaply-printed, durably-bound, inexpensive collection of good
short stories really is of more value to most students than
a set of full-color filmstrips of the birthplaces of famous
writers, accompanied by a phonograph recording of "litr'y"
commentary.   A relatively crude, but clear and reasonably
accurate, one-color "do-it-yourself" map transparency really
is more valuable than a four-color map transparency that is
crowded with irrelevant details and hard to read.

Although publishers, as a group, may indeed be vaguely uneasy and uncertain about just how they should react to
the current explosion of new educational methods, materials,
and devices, they probably have more confidence than ever in
the marvelous economy and efficiency of the book as a basic
educational tool.   It may be . . . there are some signs the
process has already started . . . that the proliferation of new
devices, new materials, and new methods actually will help
to define what a book is, what it can do best, and what can
be done best in the classroom by non-book means.   If this is
true, then publishers will think less about competing with
television, radio, filmstrips, moving pictures, overhead projection transparencies, phono-records, tape recordings, magazines, etc., and more about designing textbooks to do "book"
jobs and preparing other materials to do "non-book" jobs.

To take full advantage of these developments, however, textbook publishers probably should know more than
they know at present about some of the new educational devices, and about their possible role in developing, standard-
izing, and perhaps even marketing them.   If publishers, with
some reason, tend to regard educational "hardware" manufacturers as illiterate, these same manufacturers, with equally
good reason, regard many publishers as painfully ignorant
about, and strangely insensitive to, what the new devices
really are, what they can do, and what publishers should be

doing about them.   Like many teachers, many publishers tend
to be all thumbs when it comes to operating a movie projector, loading a tape-recorder, or using an overhead projector.
In these areas many publishers are slow-learners, under-
achievers, and culturally-disadvantaged.   There are signs,
however, that, when proper provision is made for their individual differences, and when the limitations of their cultural
backgrounds are recognized, they can learn, and learn fast.
It is rumored that one publisher already has an author at
work on a book entitled, HOW TO TEACH YOUR BABY TO
USE AN OVERHEAD PROJECTOR.

     Of course, when schools have sufficient funds, Federal
or otherwise, for the purchase of necessary equipment and
materials, a greater range of good-quality equipment and materials will become available.   Hardware manufacturers may
go into publishing, publishers may go into hardware manufacturing, and entirely new kinds of educational firms may
emerge, but the ultimate results should be beneficial for all
concerned.

     When considering the proper role of printed materials
of instruction in relation to new materials and devices, old
publishers know that the question is not "which is to be master," but rather which publisher will do the best job, for the
schools and for his firm, in using his brains to help develop
better educational methods, materials, and devices.   Their
recognition of the nature of the question is shown, in part,
by the recent establishment in textbook publishing firms of a
variety of new departments and divisions for "research and
development," "special education projects," "new media in-
vestigation," and the like.   In this brave new world, the old
publisher's lot, though not unhappy, is certainly more confusing and complicated than it used to be.

Federal Aid for Education and the Book Publishers

By W. D. Cole, President, Washington Educational Research
Associates, Inc.; formerly Chairman of the Board, Crowell
Collier & Macmillan, Inc.

From Financial Analysts Journal 22:53-6, September-October
1966. © by The Financial Analysts Federation. Reprinted
by permission.

Federal funds are now available for both book oriented
programs and for programs not book or library oriented but
permitting book purchases. The major book oriented programs are as follows:

a. Title II of the Elementary and Secondary Education Act of 1965 authorizes a five-year program
   beginning with the fiscal year ended June 30,
   1966, under which $100,000,000 has been appro-
   priated for the first fiscal year for the purchase
   of school library books, periodicals, audio-visual and other instructional materials.

b. Title II-A of the Higher Education Act of 1965
   authorizes a five-year program beginning with
   the fiscal year ended June 30, 1966, under which
   $10,000,000 has been appropriated for the first
   fiscal year and $25,000,000 is expected to be
   appropriated for the second fiscal year for the
   purchase by college and university libraries of
   all types of library books and published materials.

c. Title I of the Library Services and Construction
   Act continues a program under which an estimated $22,500,000 will be expended in the fiscal
   year ended June 30, 1966 for library services
   and published materials. In prior years approximately 30% has been expended for books. The

act requires matching in double the amount of
the federal grant with state and local funds.

Major non-book oriented programs include the following:

a. Title I of the Elementary and Secondary Education Act of 1965 authorizes $775,000,000 a year
commencing with the year ending June 30, 1966
primarily for educational programs for disad-
vantaged children of families with incomes below
$2,000 a year. Typical projects proposed in-
clude pre-kindergarten classes for 3 and 4 year
old children, summer school and extension courses
for under-privileged children and bookmobiles to
visit homes. A number of publishers have reported that, initially at least, the orders they are
receiving for materials under Title I of the Elementary and Secondary Education Act are actually exceeding the orders under Title II of that Act.

b. Title III of the National Defense Education Act
continues a program in the amount of $79,200,000
for the year ended June 30, 1966 for the purchase of laboratory equipment and instructional
materials including books (but excluding textbooks), for elementary and high school use, in
science, mathematics, foreign languages, English, reading, history, geography and civics.
The act requires matching of federal funds by
the states.

c. The Economic Opportunity Act of 1964 authorizes
$550,000,000 for the year ended June 30, 1966
for youth projects including the Federal Job
Corps, literary programs for those eighteen
years of age and older to aid them to obtain employment, pre-school programs for 3 to 5 year
old children and the Head Start Program providing an eight-weeks summer program for 5 and
6 year old children preparatory to entering elementary school, through field trips and an introduction to picture books, toys, music and films.
The act requires 10% matching by the states.

d. The Urban and Rural Community Action Programs appropriated $300,000,000 for the year

ended June 30, 1965, and $715,000,000 for
1966.   This requires 10% state and local matching, and under it, all instructional materials are
eligible for purchase.

e. The Vocational Education Act of 1963 appropriated $154,000,000 for the fiscal year 1964,
$180,000,000 for 1965, and $252,000,000 for
1966.   It requires equal matching by the states,
provides primarily vocational educational programs through public high schools and junior
colleges and places no limits on purchases of
instructional materials.

The sharp increase in funds available in the year ended June 30, 1966 under these acts is indicated by the following summary:

	1966 Appropriation	1965 Appropriation
The above three book oriented programs	$ 132,500,000	$ 25,000,000
The above five non-book oriented programs (but permitting book pur- chases) described above	$2,448,000,000	$962,900,000
	$2,580,500,000	$987,900,000

As Congress did not approve until early in 1966 the
appropriation of the $100,000,000 for Title II of the Elemen-
tary and Secondary Education Act of 1965 or the $10,000,000
appropriation for the Title II-A of the Higher Education Act,
they had little effect on publishers' sales until April-June,
1966.   Title II of the Elementary and Secondary Education
Act required the state education authorities to submit plans
to the federal government for the spending of these funds, to
commit all funds not later than June 30, 1966 and actually to
expend them not later than June 30, 1967.   As a result, a
substantial part of the funds provided under these two acts
for fiscal 1966 will be expended in the 1967, rather than the
1966, fiscal year.

Under both the book oriented and non-book oriented
programs, it is expected that a major portion of the funds
expended for books will be for library books rather than textbooks and that juveniles will represent a major portion of

the library books.

Impact on the Book Publishers
The largest amount of federal funds available primarily for book purchases is the $100,000,000 provided under Title II of the Elementary and Secondary Education Act of 1965 for elementary and secondary school library books, textbooks, periodicals, audio-visual and other instructional materials. Analysis of the state plans for the spending of these funds filed with and approved by the U. S. Office of Education indicates how these funds will be expended.

For the first plan year ending June 30, 1966, textbooks will benefit comparatively little from this act because roughly half of the state plans have expressly excluded textbooks from the program for the first year and many of the remaining plans have eliminated the amount that may be expended for textbooks to a maximum 15%. The amount that may be expended for audio-visual instructional materials, other than books, is limited in many of the plans to a 10% or 15% maximum. Based on these plans, one may roughly estimate that $70,000,000 or more of the first year funds under this act will be expended for books and of these books not over 10% will be textbooks and 90% or more will be general educational library books, with emphasis on juveniles.

The limitations placed on textbook purchase in these plans are for the first year of the plan. One reason for such restrictions initially is the recognition of the paramount importance of school libraries and the general inadequacy of current school library resources. Plans to be filed for later years may ease such restrictions on textbook purchase.

The great need of the public schools, colleges and public libraries is shown in a study by the American Library Association of the gap between recommended library standards and actual materials resources of such libraries in 1962-1963. This study reports the actual number of volumes in the libraries at 377,200,000 and the volumes needed to meet library standards at an additional 387,400,000. The cost of the books to bridge this gap was estimated at approximately $1.6 billion. Approximately 60% of the books needed are for elementary and secondary school libraries. It is recognized that at least a decade or more would be required to eliminate this gap. Because of this national library shortage, some authorities are predicting a further substantial increase in federal funds for library expenditures over the next two or three years.

Mr. Douglas Cater, Special Assistant to the President, in a letter of March 12, 1966, stated that during the fiscal year ending June 30, 1967 federal grants specifically earmarked for the purchase of books and other library materials, such as periodicals and audio-visual materials, will exceed $140 million, and that, combined with varying matching funds, the total may approach $240 million.

The book publisher markets which will be chiefly affected by this influx of federally funded sales are the following:

	1963	1964	Compound Annual Growth 1958-1965
	($ Mill.)		%
General Books			
Juvenile books--			
$1.00 & Over retail	72.7	79.0	10.1
Adult hardbound trade	109.7	117.0	8.3
	181.4	196.0	
Textbooks	462.0	508.8	10.4
Subscription Reference (general encyclopedias)--sales to schools and libraries	12.8	19.8	

Source: American Book Publishers Council, Inc. and, for subscription reference books, Stanley B. Hunt & Associates.

Trade Book Publishing
        As the new federal funds will be expended principally for juvenile and other library books, the publisher markets chiefly affected will be the trade publishing segment of the general book market. Trade publishing traditionally comprises the juveniles and adult hardbound books such as novels, biographies, popular histories and other books sold through book distributors to booksotres and by bookstores to consumers. However, the so-called institutional market, public and school libraries, school bookstores and schools, has become increasingly important to the trade publisher. The importance of this institutional market is indicated by the fact that roughly eighty percent of the sales of juvenile books are new to this market and educational books, other than textbooks, now

represent more than fifty percent of trade publishing sales.

The availability of federal funds for books has recently become a significant factor in the developing demand for educational books; and when one considers the sales of juvenile books ($1.00 and over) and adult hardbound trade books, only $196 million in 1964, and the relatively large amounts of federal funds now and prospectively available for such books, it is evident that federal funds are becoming the major factor in the general educational book market.

These developments in educational books have been a boon to trade publishers. So important are they that within the past five years virtually every large trade publisher, including the trade departments of textbook publishers, has launched its own sales force to sell the institutional market and augment its sales to this market through book wholesalers.

These events have not only increased the volume of trade book sales, they have also significantly altered the character of trade book publishing. Traditionally the trade book publisher, as a publisher of popular fiction and non-fiction marketed through bookstores, has depended on product of brief sales life. The sales life of even best selling popular fiction and non-fiction is typically measured in a few weeks or months. The considerable editorial, art, composition and plate costs of a book must be recouped from products with a remarkably short life span; and trade publishers typically have lost money on the majority of books on their trade list. As a result, the trade publisher has depended upon the large profits of the few best sellers or on institutional titles, such as juveniles, to recoup losses on many of his trade titles; and most significantly, he has been under constant pressure to replace his ephemeral product with new product.

To the extent that the trade publisher still publishes popular fiction and non-fiction, these basic economic factors remain. But the recent growth of the market for educational books with a much longer product life has given the trade publisher a longer product cycle, and greater stability in sales and profits. The prospective availability of federal funds, in fact, suggests not only stability, but substantial growth over the near and mid term future. As a consequence, the reputation of trade publishing among investors, which has been tarnished by an undistinguished and fluctuating profit record, may well improve.

Textbook Publishing
        Federal funds will be less important to textbook than
trade book publishing. For a number of years the primary
emphasis of the federal programs will presumably be on
building library resources and social rehabilitation programs.
Many of the state filed plans for spending under Title II of
the Elementary and Secondary Education Act specifically limit the maximum that may be expended on textbooks to 10% or
15%. Further, this textbook market, over $500,000,000 in
1964 and more than two and one-half times the $196,000,000
juvenile and adult hardbound trade book market described a-
bove, is large in relation to the amount of federal funds that,
initially at least, will be available for textbooks.

        Federal funds available for textbooks, however, should
increase and be increasingly important in later years for a
number of reasons. Textbooks are no less essential to education than supplementary and general reading in the libraries. Furthermore, they rapidly become obsolete because
of periodic revisions while general education books, including
many supplementary reading texts, do not. As a consequence,
the pressure for funds to build library resources should les-
sen as the library resources improve, while the pressure for
funds for textbooks will remain constant.

        The termination of the Vietnam conflict will almost
certainly result in a substantial increase in the funds available for education programs. Thus far, only limited amounts
have been available for vocational education and for international education. These are both areas in which substantially increased federal aid should become available after termination of the Vietnam conflict; and textbook publishing should
gain substantial sales as federal funds become available for
programs in these areas.

        While textbook publishing may benefit less than gener-
al trade publishing from federal funds for book purchase, the
present growth and prosperity of the textbook industry is
largely due to the sharp increase in public interest in education over the past decade, and to the federal programs for
textbook improvement, teacher training and educational research. These programs have resulted in the more rapid
obsolescence of textbooks, the development of new texts, and
the increase in the number of texts used per student. These
developments, with the rising student enrollments in the secondary schools and colleges, have caused textbook sales to

grow at approximately 10% a year over the past five years. The effect of the federal funds for textbooks should aid in sustaining, and even exceeding, this rate of growth over the next few years.

This is particularly significant because of the investment characteristics of textbook publishing. The industry is non-cyclical because student enrollments and textbook sales are not dependent on the business cycle. Profit margins are remarkably stable, primarily because textbooks are not price competitive and price-cutting is ineffective in increasing sales. Further, the industry does not attract new competition, except by way of acquisition, because of the long investment cycle in the development of new product, the editorial risk, the high investment in new product, and most important, the considerable expense of developing and maintaining a sales force with inadequate product during the initial years of a new company.

These characteristics and the prospective sales growth resulting from this country's strong interest in and heavy commitment to education account for the current investor interest in this industry.

Subscription Reference Books

Reference book publishing will be one of the prime beneficiaries of federal funds. The major market for reference books (encyclopedias, dictionaries, atlases, etc.) is the institutional market, especially schools and libraries. While sales of reference books generally will expand under federal programs, general encyclopedias, such as those used in elementary and junior high school libraries will be especially benefited.

General encyclopedias are classified in the industry's trade association reports as "subscription reference books" because sales of these multi-volume sets are principally to homes with payment on a subscription or time payment plan. Of the thirty or more U.S. publishers of general encyclopedias, four companies account for over 90% of domestic sales: Field Enterprises (World Book); Grolier (Encyclopedia Americana, International Encyclopedia, and others); Britannica (Encyclopedia Britannica) and Crowell Collier & Macmillan (Collier's Encyclopedia). These four companies dominate the market because of the quality of their product, profits sufficiently large to justify the heavy expense of maintain-

ing their products up to date, the acceptance of their product
by schools and, not least, the effectiveness of their direct
sales forces.

The school and library market, of course, accounts
for only a small fraction of their sales; close to 4% of total
domestic sales for a decade through 1963 and then in 1964
a sharp jump to 6%. In 1966 and 1967 such sales may well
reach 10% of domestic sales due to the availability of federal
funds.

While such sales will have an appreciable impact over
the near and mid term on industry sales and a somewhat
greater impact on profits because of wider margins, the long
term outlook for this industry will depend principally upon
the trend of domestic home sales and exports.

The domestic home market is growing slowly as a result of population growth and the growing affluence of U. S.
families. The four companies who now dominate this market
will presumably continue to do so. There is little likelihood
of new competition arising because of the very great expense
and risk involved for a new company in building an adequate
product and market acceptance. The export market for encyclopedias is growing faster than the domestic, and the long
term outlook of the foreign markets is excellent. In short,
federal funds should provide a near term sharp gain in institutional sales, but the long term outlook will depend on the
progress of other, larger divisions of the subscription book
publishing industry.

Conclusion
In summary, therefore, the availability of federal
funds for book purchases will be greatly increased in 1966
and following years. This increase will be especially significant to general book publishing because of the high ratio of
new federal money to the total industry sales of juvenile
books and adult hardbound trade books. The impact of these
new funds on textbook publishing will be comparatively small
in 1966 but should increase materially in 1967 and the years
following. The subscription book industry should have roughly a doubling of its institutional sales to schools and libraries over the near term and mid term, but institutional
sales should still constitute only about 10% of total subscription book sales.

Federal funds for books are only a minor part of total federal aid to education. This federal commitment to education will certainly continue on an increasing scale, especially after the termination of the Vietnam conflict. Reduction of war spending should be accompanied by a step-up in aid to education and other social programs both domestic and foreign. The effects of these programs will certainly benefit the book publishers, although in ways not now wholly foreseeable.

C.   Scholarly Books

Book Publishing--and Bookkeeping

By Daniel N. Fischel, Handbook Editor, McGraw-Hill Book
Company.

From Science 152:871-5, May 13, 1966. Copyright © 1966
by the American Association for the Advancement of Science.
Reprinted by permission.

Book publishing has often been described as a partnership of author and publisher, and perhaps for this reason one
sometimes notices a certain marital coolness between the
partners. "Learning hath gained most by those books by
which the printers have lost," sourly observed the English
historian Thomas Fuller over three centuries ago. Lord Byron was even more pungent.

"Now, Barabbas," he observed, "was a--publisher."

But time, better copyright laws, and competition have
done much to better the author's position, even in scientific,
technical, and professional publishing. Instead of paying to
have his monograph printed, he is lunched and lionized by
publishers eager to swell their lists. There are still risks
in publishing, but royalties can sometimes assume truly royal
proportions, and the fringe benefits of prestige, advancement,
and job offers seem to accompany even those books that have
modest sales.

The lure of publication has become so great that last
year over 25,000 books of all kinds were published in the
United States alone, and this number represents only a small
fraction of the world's output. But today, although no reputable publisher will deny his authors a share of the wealth
they have created, he may be charged with a more subtle
form of exploitation: encouraging them to write books for
which critics see no need.

Worthless Books?

In their competitive race for manuscripts, technical
publishers send their representatives into research laboratories and college campuses with literary vacuum cleaners,
scooping up questionable as well as worthy projects, proffer-
ing contracts, and urging authorship on those who ought better to be decently dissuaded. "Of the making of many books
there is no end," complained Ecclesiastes, and this bit of
Old Testament wisdom has been echoed by commentators in
our own day--sometimes, as other critics have wryly noted,
in print, and at length.

Despite their zeal, publishers can hardly be blamed
for all the ills of an overarticulate society. Thinking publishers do not willingly publish bad books; it is hard enough
to sell the good ones. But it must be admitted that publishers do not always think before they print. Obviously only a
fraction of last year's 25,000 books were of outstanding merit. And doubtless even the better ones varied widely in quality from chapter to chapter and even from page to page.

Before we concede that most of these books ought not
to have been published, however, we ought to examine what
the standards for publications are, and perhaps also what
they should be. A weak chapter deserves criticism, but it
should not condemn an entire book. Unevenness of quality is
characteristic of all book-length works; even Homer nodded.
Should we not agree, further, that a book may justify its existence by being useful, rather than by being great? Just as
dirt has been defined as "matter in the wrong place," so
many a book seems to be deprecated, not for any intrinsic
defects, but for not being what a reader or reviewer expected.

At times--let me own it candidly--the responsibility
for such disappointed expectations is the publisher's, in allowing his salesmen and copywriters to tout a routine state-
of-the-art summary as an advance into the unknown (which it
probably is, to them) or a sophomore textbook as a practical
guide for the working engineer. Such confusion may simplify a difficult marketing job, and it may even sell some books,
but it also misleads many readers.

Yet again and again the simple truth seems to be that
sophisticated book reviewers have too little regard for the
unpretentious book that does not aim to say anything new.

Caught up by what is fresh and exciting in superconductivity
and laser modulation, they tend to look down on the routine
labors of designing a highway overpass, or improving an al-
loy. To extract a true sense of the book that is disparaged
by the professor of systems engineering at Research Tech,
one often has to introduce a stiff discount for intellectual
snobbery. Surely he also serves who collects what is known
and presents it simply and straightforwardly to those humble
readers (may they always be with us) who are looking for
tools and aids to get on with the job!

What is the test of a valid book? How can the author
shape the concept, the publisher recognize it, and the reader
single it out for purchase? With as many standards as there
are critics--and as many critics as readers--the only fruitful test is the one of currency. Books are instruments of
communication, and the only objective test of their success is
whether they are bought and read.

Still, if you are a prospective author, I give you scant
help by referring you to the judgment of the marketplace,
which is only rendered after the work is done and the book
has been published. Are there no ways to tell the worth of
a book before it is put between its covers?

Obviously, publishers think so, or they would not hire
editors, and authorize them to say "Yes" to some proposals,
"Yes, but" to others, and "No" to the rest. Let's leave a-
side the question of "literary" ability. Anyone who can write
a good business letter has all the talent he needs to write a
good book. Specialized books are read for the useful ideas
they contain; the simpler and more direct the writing, the
better the book. Certainly it helps to write well. But few
published authors have this happy gift, and it would dry up
the channels of communication if the rest abstained.

Recipe for a Good Book
        What writing does take is (i) a competent grasp of the
subject, (ii) good planning, and (iii) some hard work. The
first member of this trio--competence--is of course the pre-
requisite; what can't be acquired on the spot or faked. The
last--hard work--needn't be explained to those acquainted with
it, and can't be to the others. What about "good planning?"

Much could be said about the best way to write a book,
but it is more important to emphasize what not to do. The

worst way to write a book is to sit down and start writing.
In fact, if you want to avoid the booby traps that wreck too
many book projects, don't think of the job as "writing" at
all.

A good book, to be successful, must be built, and you
should no more think of building a 12-chapter book without a
plan than you would expect to erect a 12-story building that
way. The elements of good planning are so simple, and
their advantages so clear, that many editors consider a prospective author's approach to the planning phase a touchstone
of his likelihood to produce. They have unhappily learned
that some men talk excellent books but do not write them.

And yet the muse of the book is courted by musing;
all that is needed is to convert some of that dream into practical scheme. The first requirement is a workable concept.
That is, a clearly focused picture of what the book will cover
(and, of course, what it will exclude), the purpose it will
serve, and for whom it is intended.

A useful trick is to anticipate that brief catalog or
book jacket description. Can you crystallize what the book
will do in a single sentence, and so accurately that no customer will be misled? Will your capsule summary appeal?
Will it promise answers to questions, help to the floundering?
Are you merely going to conduct a pleasant ramble through
your subject, or are you fashioning a working tool?

Implicit in this approach is the idea of the reader as
the target and goal of the entire effort. You may be writing
a book that he will find indispensable, but while you are planning and writing it, the tables are turned, and he is indispensable to you. His needs, his wants, his level of understanding, his interests, his problems--all must be constantly
present to an author, directing his efforts. To make sure
that you will bring your reader along, borrow a concept from
security regulations, and test every topic by asking "Is this
something he needs to know?"

Why Publishers Say "No"

Readers play a key role not only individually, but also
in the aggregate. If there aren't enough of them around, your
book idea will fail for lack of an adequate market. How many
is enough? Leaving aside the book that is extremely costly
to produce--whether because of length, or complicated compo-

sition, or illustrations, or color printing--a sale of five or
six thousand copies will justify the commercial publication of
most technical books.   But it takes a real effort to sell even
half this number.

  We publishers constantly hear that library purchases
alone will support the publication of a given book.   "What libraries?" we ask.   Fewer than 1000 public libraries have
even as much as $10,000 a year to spend on books, and how
far will that sum go toward acquiring the annual output of
25,000 different volumes?   Even the addition of school, research, and industrial libraries, with their specialized interests, does not help appreciably.   In publishing circles, an
appeal to the prospective library sale is considered an ad-
mission that a book has too small, or too ill-defined, a market.   If a book appeals strongly to readers, their libraries
will scramble to stock them.

  The true market is the ultimate user himself.   Often
I've been told by an author that his proposed book on, let us
say, interval engineering, will have a great sale because
there are 10,000 members of the National Interval League,
and "every member will buy one--maybe two." Well, they
won't.   A more realistic appraisal of this particular market
is given by the League's initials--NIL.

  Not even a new edition of the Bible can hope to attain
complete saturation of its prospective market.   To sell
10,000 copies of a book, one needs a core market approximately ten times larger.   To be sure, not all interval specialists are members of the League--but their nonaffiliation
makes them that much harder to reach.

  Suppose we publish the book, however, and send a direct-mail circular to the 10,000 League members.   Perhaps
their journal has praised it editorially, and we had the good
luck to run a full-page ad for the book in the same issue.
What kind of sale can we expect?

  Well, the mail campaign, if we are very lucky, might
produce an excellent 2-percent response--that's 200 books.
Repeated 6 months later, it might just break even with 125
additional books--and indicate that further mailings must be
ruled out as uneconomical.   In addition, all this promotion
might stimulate another 25 orders that are not "keyed" to the
mailings but were sparked by them nonetheless, coming in on
company purchase orders and the like.   Another 50 responses

would come in through bookstores, in addition to the regular bookstore business of 250 copies on publication.

We have a total domestic sale the first year of 650 copies. Add 200 for foreign sales, and double the total for a 5-year projection, and we have a grand total of 1700 copies--not even enough to break even.

Of course, there is still some hope that a really good book on interval engineering might also appeal to the gap specialists, and perhaps even to the hole engineers, both of whom must occasionally cross the borders of their own precincts into interval land. This type of interdisciplinary appeal is much courted by editors, but in fact it is rarely achieved, and in his frantic efforts to tailor a work that will be comprehensible to the gap men and the hole men, as well as his interval colleagues, the unhappy author is likely to be left with pure emptiness. He'll have company, however-- isn't the publisher his partner?

The Clouded Survey

Editors like to think that rejections are always due to an author's faulty conception, but candidness forces me to admit that publishers, too, make mistakes. I am not referring to the spectacular instances of the manuscript that went the mechanical rounds of publishers' offices until it caught one neophyte editor off guard--and then made his fortune. Such sports are notorious in "trade" publishing, where a new trend in historical or rogue novels can take established houses unawares. What afflicts technical publishing is a more subtle evil. Typically, it takes this form:

The editor, after greater or lesser conference with the author, receives a book proposal, and sets about his review procedures. His advisers rave about the book, but his "market survey" is negative. Now, despite what I have said about the real importance of a market appraisal, it must be admitted that the process is not scientific.

Usually what happens is that the editor asks the sales manager for an opinion. That expert searches his memory or his files for the sales performance of the last book published in the same field. Let us say it came out 3 years before and had a submarginal sale of 2300 copies. He shakes his head.

"I can't sell more than 2500 of those," he says, generously inflating the estimate a trifle. "You'd better scratch it." And scratch it the editor does, congratulating the author on his escape from an enterprise that would have been fruitless, had it not been for the paternal wisdom and experience of his publisher.

Now of course this method is not completely absurd. If the book being used as a touchstone is truly on the same subject, and if the treatment is truly comparable, and if the quality is truly the same (to publishers, an unwritten manuscript is always A-1)--then one does have an index, of sorts. It should not be used in its unqualified, raw state, but what do you expect? One good custom does corrupt the world, and creative wisdom cannot always be summoned up at 9:01 on a Monday morning.

As a wise author, you will fortify your editor with a defense in depth against the jaded sales manager. You will give him (in writing! editors are shallow creatures and forgetful) a prospectus that explains how remarkably different this book will be from all other books, specifying the flaws marring each of the others, and the exact reasons for the superior quality and utility of your own. Immodest? Nonsense--if you didn't believe it, would you attempt the job?

Furthermore, you will use a quantitative approach as well, setting down reliable estimates (not of your own invention) of the numbers of people in each of the fields to which your book may reasonably be expected to appeal.

Now, there is a double value to the preparation of such a prospectus. Not only does it protect the editor and over-awe the sales manager, but it can also help you shape your book. Many a proposal has emerged from the prospectus stage in a new and improved version, as the author, compelling himself to be concrete and cognitive, saw the need to sharpen or broaden his conception.

A Price To Pay

A key element in the sales success of any book, of course, is its price. Ultimately, price is a function of the publisher's costs--for editing, manufacturing, royalty, promotion, sales, and overhead. And each of these elements is crucial.

Beyond a certain irreducible minimum, the amount of editorial and other house work required to ready the manuscript for the printer is a function of the author's writing skills and care.   The manufacturing cost depends upon a constellation of factors: the length of the manuscript, complexity of composition, number and type of illustrations, the design and manufacturing specifications, choice of printer, binder, and production methods, and--most of all--the quantity to be printed.

Before a single sheet has been printed, a typical book may have required a plant cost for setting type and preparing illustrations and plates of $15,000.   If the initial printing is a conservative 3000 copies, the plant cost component is $5 per copy.   With a more optimistic printing of 10,000 copies, the plant cost would only be $1.50 per copy.   Is it any wonder that publishers worry so about sales estimates before they price a book--and, indeed, before they even accept it for publication?

My own observations convince me that publishers are and must be optimistic--they more often estimate sales too high than too low, and they survive only if their economic structure is able to absorb a fair percentage of inevitable failures without fundamental catastrophe.   In this high-risk industry, it is not the successes that count, nor the failures, but the averages.

King Royalty

The one element of the financial picture that most directly concerns the author, of course, is his royalty; and this is also the one area where he most sees his interests as being opposed to those of his partner, the publisher.   The truth is, however, that royalties are ultimately paid by the customer, not the publisher.   If the author must be paid more, the publisher will not pay the printer less, nor the binder, nor the papermaker--nor, if he is a good businessman, will he allot less for advertising or the return to his shareholders. Instead, he will increase the price.

Now, since royalties are a function of price, the increase will generate still more royalties, which must be provided somehow.   Thus the price will be increased a bit more, in order to accommodate this additional royalty component, and then, since the pattern is repeated, a bit more still. . . . Eventually Achilles does catch up with the tortoise, but by

this time the price may have ballooned enough to start chok-
ing off sales. So a new chain reaction is triggered, with
smaller sales estimates, smaller printings, higher unit manufacturing costs, still higher prices, and still smaller sales.

Nevertheless, if an author is sought after, and is demanding enough, he can probably find a publisher who will
raise the royalty by a few percentage points. Often such
firms are the newer or smaller ones that are hungry for
manuscripts, but sometimes established houses will forget
their hard-won wisdom in the competitive fervor of bidding.

What happens? Whoever wins in the bidding, the author loses--because the publishers, if they are to survive,
cannot invest in the book that full spectrum of promotional
effort that alone can maximize its sale. Essentially, they
can give the author a higher royalty only by reducing the
share that they will spend for sales promotion. If the book
sells itself, they will not have lost--but no book ever sells
itself so well as when a determined publisher is behind it
pushing. All the publisher can do is try to convince his authors that their earnings must ultimately be measured in dollars, not in percentages. No bank will accept a percentage
for deposit.

Of course it is not always the author whose pressure
for higher royalties unbalances the publishing partnership.
Trade practices vary greatly, and unscrupulous publishers
have been known to take advantage of an author's gentleman-
ly indifference to contractual details. What makes this situation difficult to counter is that royalty terms do differ, not
only from publisher to publisher, but from book to book, and
frequently for quite valid reasons.

For technical and professional books, most royalties
range between 10 and 15 percent of the list price, with the
higher rate applying only after the first 5 or 10 thousand
copies have been sold at lower rates. There will be exceptions in most contracts--lower rates for foreign sales, or
direct-mail sales, which require greater promotion and sales
expense and involve higher credit and damage risks. And a
flat rate of 10 percent of list, or even less, may be needed
to improve the book's chances of commercial success--a publishing variation on the architectural paradox that "less is
more." For example, a smaller royalty may stimulate sales
by allowing a larger discount for the bookseller, or increasing the margin for promotion. Or it may permit reducing

the price in an unusually competitive or price-sensitive market. Or it may improve the outlook for publishing a work that otherwise might be too costly or too restricted in its appeal to be economically feasible.

Some technical and professional publishers base their royalties on net receipts rather than list price, with the most common rates ranging between 10 and 18 percent. To compare such a royalty with one that is based on list price, it is necessary to know both the scale of bookseller's discounts and the "mix" of sales, which determine the average discount. If few books are sold by direct mail at full list, and the average discount is 33-1/3 percent, then a royalty of 18 percent based on net proceeds will yield $1.20 on a $10 book--the equivalent of 12 percent of list. With an average discount of only 25 percent, however, the royalty per copy is $1.35, or 13-1/2 percent of list.

Although royalties vary inversely with discounts on a "net" contract, it does not follow that the author's interests are best served by reducing discounts. Booksellers must be businessmen--many of them refuse to stock a book that does not yield them a discount of at least a third, and some will even refuse to order such books to satisfy a customer's request. It's a wretchedly complex business.

Paperbacks

In their search for ways to increase royalties, or decrease prices, or both, authors inevitably invoke the panacea of paperbacks. Generally they are shocked to learn that to bind a book in paper instead of cloth saves only 20 or 25¢ in manufacturing cost. What shocks them still more is the information that the economics of paperback publication usually requires a lower royalty rate, too--and on a much lower price. With these concessions, the savings begin to be appreciable, but even greater reductions can be achieved when a clothbound edition is being reprinted and original composition, art-work, and most other elements of plant cost can be eliminated.

In theory, all these cost reductions pave the way for a lower price which will enlarge the prospective market and, by reversing the upward spiral described previously, yield the largest possible sales at the lowest feasible price. Unfortunately, few technical books behave the way the theory says they should. While price can clearly act as an upper

limit to a book's sale, it is a rare book that can enjoy progressively wider sales in response to successive price reductions.   Sales of a basic handbook of mathematics might respond to price cuts, but a specialized work on powdered-
aluminum metallurgy will not interest persons outside its
normal area simply because it is cheap.

Extracurricular

There are some observers of the publishing scene who
will remark dryly that not all of the factors affecting sales
success are a function of content in relation to price.   What
is requisite for textbook adoption, they will tell you, is political influence, "pull."   And a sharp letter to the president
of the publishing house, followed by a round of golf, will
channel the sales effort behind your work rather than any of
the four others on the same subject that he's had the poor
judgment and doubtful loyalty to publish.

Of course these knowing insiders are the same persons who, in college, told you that you couldn't get an A from
so-and-so unless you were related to a member of the Board
of Governors.   Still, you wonder.   Is there flame behind the
smoke?

Certainly you as an author can help promote your
book.   Giving talks at conferences, publishing papers, re-
minding magazine editors who owe you a favor that a real
book review, rather than a cursory "announcement," will be
appreciated--these steps, and any others that help keep your
name before the public, are "political," but they are also
ethical and sensible, and they will help your book.   And a
continuing, critical review of the publisher's promotion and
sales performance will protect you against blunders that you
are less able to afford than your partner, however teamed
with you financially he may be.

But in the last, hard, cold analysis, books are bought
because they succeed in meeting the readers' needs.   No a-
mount of advertising, or mail campaigns, nor complimentary
reviews, can persuade a man to buy a book from which he
does not profit.   The influence of friends, the charm of your
personality, the planted compliment, and the elaborate snow
job--none of these will help when that exasperatingly reluctant browser thumbs through a copy on the bookstore counter
(or at home on 10-day approval), and then tests his sales re-
sistance against the price on the jacket flap.

Against that crucial payoff, only the lonely hours spent in search of excellence will count. Every shortcut, every compromise with the definite statement, with the tiresome quest for workable data, will tell against you. If you slackened, if you put out less than your own original concept required, your book will not reach its destination. Nothing your publisher can do has a fraction of the effect of the raw material you give him, or the spoken advertising it generates. A mediocre job of copy editing, unimaginative design and packaging, a dull promotional circular--these will not help, but rarely will they be fatal. What gets your books "out" is the publisher's distribution machinery, and what gets them sold is what was in your manuscript.

Of course, you are entitled to the most help your publisher can give you. If I have any message, any "pitch" for prospective authors, it is this: don't enter into a publishing arrangement blindly. Ask questions, seek the counsel of other authors, talk to editors, learn what they have to offer. Also, inspect related books in your field, and note the presentation that different publishers have given them. Then, when you do sign a contract, do so with the feeling that you accept partnership willingly and unreservedly.

Remember Ben Franklin's admonition: "Keep your eyes wide open before marriage, and half shut afterwards." The author-publisher partnership is not quite marriage, and you should certainly not close your eyes, even halfway, but it does help to expect only the best of your publisher. Your attitude will help him to expect it of himself.

Poet and Publisher

By Jon Stallworthy, an Editor of Oxford University Press;
Newdigate Prize Winner; author of books of and about poetry.

From A Review of English Literature 8:39-49, January 1967.
© Longmans, Green and Company, Limited.   Reprinted by
permission.

I

A publisher may perhaps be forgiven for questioning
the authority for Byron's scriptural emendation, "Now Barabbas was a publisher."   One is forced to admit, however, that
it does reflect an instinctive suspicion all too often present
in the mind of the unpublished author; a suspicion somehow
more deeply rooted than that of the average 'producer' for
the middleman he resents but has to have.   If this suspicion
is not always based on the traumatic experience of family or
friends in a publisher's office (as I like to think it is not),
it can perhaps be accounted for by the author's more intimate relationship with his produce than the market gardener's
with his marrow.   The comparison between authors and moth-
ers is often made, and it is of course apt.   Having lavished
love and care upon their offspring, it is natural that they
should be suspicious of the world to which they must give
them up.   As poets generally produce their work more slowly, more painfully, and more subjectively than novelists, and
for less reward in terms of cash or response, it is hardly
surprising if they approach a publisher's office warily and
with a defensive tightening of the arm around its brown paper
parcel.

Since it is almost impossible to write poetry without
the belief that one may one day write it well, and unusual to
submit a collection to a publisher without the belief that it is
at least as good as other poetry already in print, the rejected
poet will naturally feel the rejecting publisher's judgement is
at fault (as, indeed, it may be).   At any one time there are
more rejected than published poets, so this view will be widely held.   Many published poets, moreover, will feel justifiably
that they have had a poor cash return for their work, and

consciously or unconsciously will blame the publisher for this.
Not that many poets write with the prime objects of making
money--they are unlikely to be good poets if they do--but
they are understandably anxious not to join the company of
those whose work has only made money (for publishers and
anthologizers) when it is out of copyright and they are dead.
Hence the twin myths, for such I hope to show they are, of
the poetry publisher at first blind to the work of genius star-
ing him in the face, then robbing the poet or the poet's heirs
of their rightful reward.

The latter assumption is the easier to challenge since
it involves hard facts and figures: the fact, for example,
that most publishers in the United Kingdom, when all their
overhead costs are taken into account, lose money on the
contemporary poetry they publish.   The few that do not lose
money could make it much more quickly if they put their capital to work elsewhere.   In an excellent article, 'The Cost of
Publishing Poetry' (Guardian, 5 June 1964), Charles Monteith of Faber and Faber set out the basic figures:

> The first printing of a first novel is usually
> about 3,000 copies, while the first printing of
> a first volume of verse is 1,000--or even less.
> The small printing number results, inevitably,
> in a selling price which must seem high for a
> volume which is often fewer than 100 pages long.
> The total cost of setting the type for a book is
> not affected by the number of copies you print.
> Whether you print 3,000 or 1,000 it will remain,
> let us say, L200.   But if you print only 1,000
> copies the cost of setting each individual book is
> 4s. while if you print 3,000 it is only 1s. 4d.
> And to the printing cost you have to add the cost
> of paper, of binding, of jackets; and make al-
> lowance for the poet's royalty and the book-
> sellers' discount [usually one third of the pub-
> lished price].

> Is not the solution--the question is always asked
> at this point--to produce all new volumes of po-
> etry as paperbacks?   The answer, I fear, is no.
> The chief reason for the low selling price of pa-
> perbacks is not that they are bound in paper but
> that they are printed in much larger editions
> than cloth-covered books; therefore the cost of
> setting each individual book is comparatively

> small.   But--and here is the snag--you cannot
> risk publishing a book as a paperback unless you
> are reasonably confident of selling all or most
> of the large number of copies you have to print.
> And, in the case of poetry, that means the poet
> must be reasonably well known and--for a poet--
> widely read.

There is evidence that Penguins, with their Penguin
Modern Poets series, have achieved a notable breakthrough
on this front--as they have in the past on so many others--
in that they have sold tens of thousands of certain three-poet
selections where one poet was previously unpublished in book
form and the other two by no means well known.   Other publishers are already following the Penguin lead, but the problem is not to be solved as easily as it may appear from this.
It is harder to distribute books, especially paperbacks, than
it is to produce them, and few publishers in this (or indeed
any) country have distribution outlets overseas to equal Penguins'.   Nevertheless, they have shown it can be done and
undoubtedly more poetry will in future be appearing in paper
covers, if only to contain the ever-increasing costs of production.

If then Barabbas does not publish the work of living
poets for financial gain--the work of 'poets dead and gone' is
another matter--why does he do it?   The answer most commonly supposed (rather than given) Monteith explores and ex-
plodes:

> The appearance of a few volumes of poetry on
> one's list confers--it is said--'distinction' and
> elevates one from the ranks of the purely com-
> mercial into the ranks of those generally admitted
> to be concerned about literature as well as divi-
> dends.   This, I am sure, is fallacious.   Any
> publisher who decided to publish poetry simply
> as crypto-advertisement for his imprint--almost
> as inevitably as a publisher who decided to do
> it simply to make money--would find himself
> landed with a dud, or at any rate a very second-
> rate poetry list.   And few things could be less
> prestigious than that.

The answer that most poetry publishers would give
first is that they like poetry and they like publishing it.   Unlike the reviewer and literary critic, who are respectively

second and third in the line of attendance at the launching of
a new poet, the publisher stakes money and reputation on his
choice.   That the odds are against his increasing either, let
alone both, makes the gamble the more exciting.   If he does
succeed in laying down good poets in his list, he will be rewarded as they mature.   To change the metaphor, one hopes
that the house of John Murray received adequate prize money
for such winners from their stable as Byron and Betjeman.
These sensational successes are, of course, the exception
rather than the rule, and most good poets and their publishers make as much money from anthology and reading fees as
from the sale of their books.   A poet's royalty will seldom
be more than 1s. 10d. a copy, and may well be 9d. or less,
while an anthology fee for a one-page poem may be worth
L6 to him and a broadcasting fee even more.   Fees and royalties alike cease to be due (in the United Kingdom) fifty
years after a poet's death, though the publisher still continues
to make his modest margin on every copy.   This brings me
to another reason sometimes advanced as an explanation of
why publishers are prepared to lose money in the publication
of contemporary poetry.   It is suggested that, as dynamite
moghuls in their declining years endow orphanages and hospi-
tals for disabled soldiers, so publishers plough back some
(small) part of their gains ill-gotten in the exploitation of
'poets dead and gone' into encouraging the work of younger
poets.   This theory of 'moral obligation' I at one time believed myself, but am now inclined to think it no more valid
than the 'crypto-advertisement' theory.   Publishers, in my
experience, infrequently feel guilty about making money out
of Keats and Shelley.   Most of them--and certainly the best
of them--publish poetry, as I have said, because they like it.
A few will also publish an author's poems if he makes this
a condition of their publishing his text-book or novel: and,
while these may have a good fiction or textbook list, they
will seldom publish much good poetry.

II

        After 'why do you publish poetry?', the question most
commonly asked of a poetry publisher is 'how do you publish it?'   This deserves a more detailed answer than it generally receives.   To start, literally, at the beginning: if an
established firm of medical publishers, say, wanted to initi-
ate a poetry list, they would almost certainly have to overcome an acute shortage of their principal raw material.   The
morning's post would contain no 'unsolicited' poetry manuscripts until they had advertised for them and notified literary

agents. The trickle that might then result would probably
be of poor quality, and in quantity would be but a fraction of
the 500 manuscripts received annually by Faber and Faber.
The best of their bad lot they would very likely have to publish before they could hope to receive better, though no doubt
they would be aware of the great gulf fixed between their
poets and those of Faber and Faber (who 'take on a new poet
only about once every two or three years'). There are few
publishers able to launch their list, like the Hogarth Press,
with writers of the calibre of Virginia Woolf and T. S. Eliot.
Once one is seen to be publishing poetry, however, more
manuscripts will arrive and by the law of averages some will
be better than others. Most, of course, will be hopeless;
sad testimony to the fact that more would-be poets are still
influenced by placid, flaccid Georgians and Hymns Ancient
and Modern than by Eliot and Yeats.

As most of the poetry written at any one time is ex-
ecrable, most of that published is poor. Publishers are not
as unaware of this as reviewers sometimes think. If one resolved to publish no poet of lesser stature than Eliot and
Yeats, one would never produce a book. Beta books must be
published if one is to attract the alpha book. The latter, at
any rate, tends to be the work of matured genius. The
Wanderings of Ossian and Other Poems is not a great book:
indeed, had it been submitted by a poet aged seventy-four,
Yeats's publishers, Kegan Paul, Trench & Co., could hardly
have been blamed if they had turned it down. Coming, however, from a poet of twenty-four it was a work of considerable promise, and first collections--when promising though
flawed--must be published by anyone who hopes one day to
see in his list books like The Tower or For the Union Dead.
Only when that day arrives can the publisher afford to reject
the beta collections submitted to him, though he will continue
to watch for the young poet's alpha-beta or alpha-gamma collection. A special, and painful, problem is posed by the
beta poet who, after a number of volumes, produces a gamma
manuscript, or the alpha poet who produces a beta. Eliot,
whose experience with Faber and Faber may have shown him
some of the latter, but few of the former, wrote in an article on 'The Publishing of Poetry' (The Bookseller, 6 December 1952), that should be read by everyone interested in
these matters: 'And I believe that if the Poetry Editor is
himself convinced of the exceptional merit of a poet he should
stick to him through thick and thin however disappointing the
response of reviewers and readers'. The poets already on
a publisher's list, he went on to say, should have priority

over new poets 'except when they produce something lament-
ably below their level, which isn't often'. The better the poet the more developed (as a rule) his self-critical faculties,
and the less likely he is to present such a collection; though
Eliot speaks for all poetry publishers when he says their
chief troubles are dissuading their poets from publishing too
soon and too often. While obviously a publisher should back
his author as long as he can, it is in the interests of neither
to produce a book of poems patently weaker than its prede-
cessors, unless perhaps it is an alpha-gamma collection.
By accepting a transitional book, one that shows its author
advancing uncertainly into a new subject or a new style, the
publisher may help him to make that transition. If, however,
the new collection simply indicates that the muse has passed
her menopause--a condition not, I think, as rare as Eliot
suggests--it should not be published.

     So much for the general principles underlying the for-
mation and development of a poetry list. To turn to questions
more specific: who are the inquisitors, the poet in search of
a publisher may ask, that will sit in judgement on his typescript; how many of them there; what are their qualifications;
and what are they looking for? There are, of course, no
simple answers. Every publishing house has different readers, and probably a different number of readers. Most likely one will be the 'editor in charge'. He may operate in
splendid isolation or, more usually, have anything from two
to half a dozen editorial colleagues whose opinion he values.
If their tastes are not exactly his own so much the better, as
they will call attention to qualities that he might otherwise
overlook. Whereas there have been good literary magazines
that championed one sort of poem to the exclusion of all others, a good publishing house must be more catholic in its
taste: Fabers did not confine themselves to Eliotelian poetry
in the years that Eliot was on the Board. Of the qualities
essential in a good poetry editor the most important is enthusiasm for poetry. This is not the platitude it may sound,
since only enthusiasm for the good will sustain him in his
weekly marathon through the bad, through the long-hand and
carbon-copy wastes, and leave him at the end still with an
appetite for the little (and the large) magazines. He can afford to leave no page unturned, since that may uncover a
masterpiece or bring him a new voice with a new accent, a
new idiom. He is more likely to detect this if, like Eliot
and Pound, he is widely read in the poetry of the past.
Many of the best poetry editors have themselves been poets,
but it would be foolish to consider this an essential qualifi-

cation. In one sense even it is harder for a practising poet
to be a successful poetry editor, as he will be the more exposed to the pressures and prejudices of literary circles.
It is easier to reject a collection of poems by the editor of
a powerful literary journal if one knows that he will never
have occasion to return the compliment. In the last analysis the only sure way to judge a publisher is by the company
he keeps, that is by the authors he publishes, and by what
those authors say of him.

The short answer to the question 'what does a poetry
editor look for?' is--or, I believe, should be--nothing. If
he is looking for blank verse, or free verse, or rhymed
verse, for concrete or for beat poetry, his judgement will be
blunted to what is good in the other categories, let alone any
new category. He should simply ask of the next typescript
on the pile, as Diaghilev asked of Cocteau, 'Etonne-moi'.
He should seek the astonishment of being confronted by the
new, which is not necessarily the same as the novel or ultra-
modern. Good poetry is that which never ceases to surprise:
and in that sense Chaucer's Troilus and Criseyde is newer,
fresher after six hundred years than a 'once seen, never remembered' poem from a week-old magazine, which may not
keep its colours for six days or two readings. The perceptive publisher will soon learn to distinguish between the technically competent--even the highly competent--and the good,
where the one is not the other. He will encounter collections
whose every poem may have appeared previously in reputable
literary magazines, but whose total impact will be less than
the sum of its parts. Alternatively, he may, if he is luckier, find himself reading a typescript that 'astonishes' by its
freshness and authority, even if technically it can be faulted.
In such a case the cumulative impact may far exceed the sum
of its parts and outweigh its incidental flaws. A book of poetry should be (but seldom is) much more than a haphazard
collection of good poems. Its contents, from the first page
to the last, should be unmistakably the work of one hand,
and should be grouped in a sequence as 'inevitable' and right
as the sequence of stanzas within each poem or the sequence
of words within each stanza. If this is a remote ideal, it is
none the less worth striving for, and here the good publisher
can sometimes help his author.

As I suggested earlier, a poet's self-critical faculty
usually develops in a strict ratio with the quality of his poetry. The better he is, the more 'finished' and organized
his typescript is likely to be: and conversely, the less ex-

perienced and less self-aware he is, the less even his work.
The publisher confronted by a malformed collection, if he is
a good critic and has gained its author's confidence, should
be able to persuade him of its malformation and advise him
on what surgery or manipulation is required.   Pound, in his
famous re-shaping of Eliot's 'Waste Land', was exercising
the function of a skilled poetry editor, albeit as a friend
rather than as a publisher.   The general reader is apt to
underestimate the extent to which a manuscript can change
between its submission and its publication as a book.   For
this reason biographers and critics should not condemn publishers A or B for rejecting the early manuscripts of the
great, until they have established the exact form of the work
rejected.   It will often be found that this bears scant resemblance to what was first published.

III

        A publisher will (and should) be judged in literary
circles by whom and how he rejects as well as by whom and
how he publishes.   A high proportion of the less promising
manuscripts he receives will be accompanied by requests for
criticism, which in all probability he will be unable to satisfy because he does not have time and because he will have
learnt that not everyone who asks for criticism wants it.
The truth about a manuscript is often better left unsaid,
though this is not to imply that untruth is a satisfactory substitute.   Most publishers feel that, as they cannot offer helpful advice to all those who ask for it, they should in fairness
offer it to none, but most will make an exception in the case
of a promising author whose work they are nonetheless rejecting.   He or she, probably and paradoxically, will not have
asked for it, but should find it more constructive and useful
than the author of a bad manuscript would find such criticism
as a publisher could offer.   The poet whose work is seriously considered for publication, but eventually declined, may
find it helpful to know which of his poems were liked, and
for what reason, and which were not.   He may also be interested in suggestions as to magazine editors or pamphlet publishers more likely to accept his work.

        A common fault of poetry manuscripts submitted for
publication is that they are not yet ready for it, though they
may contain some good poems.   In advising the poet to send
these to such a journal, the publisher is not simply implying
'get yourself better known so that one day you have an audience for a book', though this is undoubtedly a factor.   He al-

so knows how publication can 'bring on' an author; how a poet seeing his work in cold print (and hearing what is said
about it) will perceive its strength and weakness more clearly than ever he did in manuscript.   This, of course, is as
true of book publication as of magazine or pamphlet publication, but it is logical that the three stages should follow one
another in a natural progression as the poet accumulates
more material of publishable standard.   In those comparatively rare instances where a publisher accepts a collection
by an unknown poet, or a poet known perhaps in America but
not in England, the publisher may himself send poems to literary magazines on his author's behalf.   If these are accepted, they will win readers for the forthcoming book and,
no less important, engage the interest of an editor who will
shortly be in a position to have it reviewed.   Editors, with
space to review a third perhaps of the volumes submitted to
them, will not unreasonably tend to single out books by poets
they have themselves published.

One occasionally meets a disgruntled writer who refuses to send his work to magazines because, he says, 'they
are all run by cliques'.   Insofar as a clique is a group of
people with similar tastes, his statement is largely true: it
could be applied equally to most publishing houses.   If, however, he is implying (and he generally is) that these cliques
exist to promote the work of their members and suppress
talented outsiders like himself, his implication is largely
nonsense.   Other people simply don't like his poems as much
as he does.

Those who regard literary circles as being ruled by
the law of the jungle too often forget the inter-dependence of
its various species of wild life.   Poets, poetry editors, and
poetry publishers are in equal need of each other, and are
generally aware of this.   The new poet in search of recognition may be given his first audience by a magazine editor and
in time repay him by increasing his magazine's circulation.
In this or in a pamphlet his poems may catch the eye of the
publisher who will help him to make his reputation, and
whose reputation he will help to make.   I suspect that future
historians of this century will show the influence of pamphlet
publishers on the development of poets and their audience to
have been out of all proportion to the often modest size and
publicity of their editions.   To date probably the most prominent have been Erica Marx's Hand and Flower Press, Oscar
Mellor's Fantasy Press, and Howard Sergeant's Outposts
Publications.   These have recently been joined by such prom-

ising newcomers as the Northern House Poetry Pamphlets,
The Review Poetry Pamphlets, and the first of a M[anches-
ter] I[nstitute of] C[ontemporary] A[rts] Poetry Pamphlet series. Such pioneers have a harder task than the book publisher, since they produce what are in fact small books, but
generally lack the elaborate machinery whereby the magazine
publisher distributes his magazines to subscribers and bookstalls, or the book publisher his volumes to bookshops. One
way of solving this problem would be for literary magazines
of book-size format to fill a complete section of one issue
with the work of one poet; to print an extra quantity of this
section; and to bind it up separately to sell as a pamphlet
after the issue is exhausted, or to those who only want the
poems. The cost of producing a pamphlet in this way would
be greatly reduced.

In the past it has been by the book that the poet has made
his reputation, and despite the new media now open to him--
radio, television, films, and records--the book is unlikely to
be supplanted as the medium by which, in the long run, he
is known. The publisher who picks his poets wisely, advises
and encourage them, helps them perhaps to shape their books,
and launches them with the impetus of an established imprint,
has as much power and responsibility as many more vocal
lords of the literary jungle.

Book Selection for Reprints

By Sol Lewis, Publisher, Argosy-Antiquarian, Ltd.

Reprinted by permission from Reprint Expediting Service
Bulletin 9:1-4, Winter 1964/1965. © 1964/1965 by Oceana
Publications, Inc.

The matter of selection of books for reprinting poses
a most interesting if complex problem for the publisher. Obviously it is the key factor which separates the potential
"sell out" from the eventual "remainder." While there is no
universally accepted procedure for selection, there are a
number of useful norms upon which nearly all reprint publishers agree.

1. IMPORTANCE. Is the book under consideration
   authoritative? Did it receive good reviews when
   first issued? Has its pre-eminence in its field
   made it a "must book" for those interested in the
   subject?

2. AVAILABILITY. Not all out-of-print titles are
   scarce, difficult to find or costly even if they are
   meritorious. In some cases an initial large printing, while out of print at the publishers, is readily
   available through antiquarian dealers.

3. DEMAND. Highly specialized books are usually not
   in great demand, as the established librarian,
   scholar or collector, well versed and ever alert in
   his field, obtains a copy of a good book upon its
   first publication. This leaves possible future sales
   of a reprint to the relatively few who for some reason or other had overlooked the work when originally issued, to the new libraries and institutions, and
   to those who became interested and learned of the
   book's existence in their respective areas of study
   or research after the first and perhaps only print-

ing was exhausted. Careful consideration therefore
must be given to the number of copies to be printed
with a long look at the limited appeal of the special
subject.

4. COST OF PRODUCTION AND RESALE PRICE. A
just and profitable ratio between the cost of production and the resale price must be determined by the
publisher. Some fine reprint prospects at first
glance seem "naturals"; however, because of size,
color plates, royalties (if the book is still in copyright), special promotion and other foreseeable
"extras," their choice is often impractical.

How then does the publisher decide if the book he is
considering fulfills these necessary requirements? A number
of methods present themselves. Importance can be ascer-
tained without too much difficulty. The standard critical bibliographies in the field should be consulted. The original reviews should be read. If they are not readily accessible,
they may be found reprinted in that excellent bibliographic repository, The Book Review Digest.

Availability can best be checked first through Books in
Print for the book's current status; then through dealers' catalogs and by personal visits and inquiries in the second hand
book shops. The extent of a particular o. p. book's availability is often reflected in the price the dealer asks for it.
Many good out-of-print books are frequently stigmatized as
"plugs." Because there is no dearth of copies that "turn up,"
they are fated to gather dust quietly on the dealer's shelves
priced far less than the reprint publisher would be obliged to
charge for them.

Testing the Demand is a little more complicated. Here
one must exercise a great deal of caution. One must differ-
entiate between a worthwhile scarcity versus a sporadic or
superficially induced demand occasioned by a short-lived topic-
ality, or a publisher's inspired renaissance of an author who
has at last written a "best seller" in his field. This renaissance usually sends some enthusiasts to the stacks in search
of the author's past efforts which, more often than not, turn
out to be ephemera justly deserving their "forgotten" status.

The most successful procedure for testing the demand
for a book (and one which is used by most reprint publishers)
is the continuous checking of periodic and permanent want lists

of dealers and librarians as they appear in such recognized
trade journals as The Antiquarian Bookman, TAAB, Clique,
etc.   The individual wants of colleges and institutions in their
desiderata lists, plus suggestions from librarians as published in the worthy Reprint Expediting Service Bulletin can
also be a most useful procedure.   However, one must be
cautious in using all want lists.   The identical title or group
of titles may be included in a large number of different want
lists.   These lists should be checked on a regional basis
since the same library and/or collector may have submitted
its desiderata to a number of local dealers to insure wider
coverage.   So although particular wants are found in, let us
say, a half dozen or more New England lists, it may well be
that only one copy of a title is actually needed.   Conversely,
if the same book is called for in diversified geographical
areas, there is a good likelihood that the book is a bona fide
scarcity and that the demand for it is genuinely wide-spread.
Similarly, one must be circumspect in assessing the reprint
suggestions from librarians appearing in the R. E. S. Bulletin
or kindred journals.   One request, regardless of how valid
it may be, does not necessarily make a good reprint candidate.   Librarians are understandably not always aware of the
entire reprint schedules of all the publishers, and as a result occasionally they suggest titles that have already been
reprinted sometimes in more than one edition.   Then too
their selection is at times motivated by emotional attachment
and personal preference bearing no relationship to the intrinsic merit of their choice.   Generally the reprint publisher
either is himself a bookman, or employs a bookman in his
organization, who is also an expert on the o. p. market.
This does not mean that he is infallible, for no one can always "pick a winner."   But his experience gleaned invariably
from many years in the book field (quite frequently as a book
dealer, scout or collector) plus his intuitive instinct about a
book's importance and value, minimizes the risk involved in
his selection.

    Specialization is the one outstanding feature of the cur-
rent reprint publisher's program.   I believe that in no other
field has this practice made deeper and more logical inroads.
I am reminded of a sage bit of advice given to me by the
late Americana dealer, Charles P. Everitt, who admonished
me many years ago to "buy the right book in the right place."
He meant, of course, that the best place to buy Americana
is from a recognized Americana dealer, and so on down the
line in every category.   Because, as he explained, the specialist would in all probability know the book; and if he did

not have a copy on hand, would certainly know where to look
for, and possibly obtain one at the "right price." So it is
among reprint publishers today. In that worthy group there
are those who specialize in Americana, Literature, Drama,
Bibliography, Art, Technical, etc. As a result dealers, librarians and collectors who receive and study reprint catalogs
soon learn where to look for and buy the "right book in the
right place."

Complete objectivity in reprint selection is indeed the
virtually impossible "consummation devoutly to be wished."
The collector's viewpoint that in varying degrees inhabits the
thinking of even the most careful reprint publisher must be
stringently submerged in favor of the more practical if less
sentimental consideration of universal acceptance. Dedication
and erudition notwithstanding, it is axiomatically undeniable
that publishers are in the book business to "make money."
If unfortunately in this cold quest many good books are doomed
to remain and to become premium-priced scarce collector's
items, there is, I suppose, the compensation that the rare
book dealer must also live and prosper. Nevertheless, we
should be thankful for the wonderful job that the comparatively few reprint publishers have done to make available to much
broader audiences the immense knowledge and scholarship
that have enriched our cultural past.

The Antiquarian Reprint Trade

By Bernard M. Rosenthal, antiquarian bookseller.

From Antiquarian Bookman 35:1667-8+, April 19, 1965.
Reprinted by permission.

Antiquarian booksellers can no longer ignore the rapid, indeed phenomenal, growth of reprints. Reprints are
here to stay, and in the present article I propose to discuss
the influence they have on the antiquarian book market and to
examine and criticize a number of practices in which some
reprint publishers have engaged to the detriment of the bookseller.

Naturally I can speak with some authority only for the
field with which I am familiar: reference books in Medieval,
Renaissance and Reformation scholarship, including all related topics such as bibliography, paleography, literature and
the like. From numerous conversations with my colleagues,
however, I understand that the problems and grievances are
pretty much the same in other fields, too.

It is both foolish and unrealistic to deny the usefulness
of the reprinted reference book--we may cuss the $10 reprint
when we have the $45 original edition on our shelves, but we
will bless the same $10 reprint if it happens to be a bibliog-
raphy which for years we wanted on our reference shelves.
It is, in other words, quite obvious that the reprint publishers are performing an enormously useful job; indeed without
them the growth of our libraries and universities would be
well nigh impossible. It is precisely because these publishers
perform such an essential service that we antiquarian booksellers should clearly formulate and publicize some of the
reservations and criticisms we have to make:

When a book is reprinted, the date of the original edition should always be clearly indicated--not hidden on the
verso of the title page or elsewhere in the book (sometimes in
very small type). I have even come across the extreme case
where the date of the original edition does not appear at all,

very small type). I have even come across the extreme case
where the date of the original edition does not appear at all,
so that the uninformed buyer thinks he is getting a book published in 1964 while he is actually buying one published in
1922. I would suggest that the original title page should always come first and that the reprint date should occupy some
secondary place--anything else falls, in my opinion, into the
category of "deceptive packaging."

Almost without exception reprints proudly heralded in
elaborate catalogues and advertisements in trade journals are
accompanied by publication dates which turn out to be entirely unrealistic. An exasperating large amount of time is
spent by the bookseller in answering queries and claims why
a book promised for early 1963 was not yet supplied as of
late 1964. This unreliability is by now almost endemic and
I consider it about par for a reprint to be anywhere from
one to two years behind "schedule."

This situation is particularly galling for the librarian
who has immobilized the necessary funds and finds himself
at the end of the budget year with unspent funds (a fate worse
than death). And this practice obviously hurts the antiquarian
bookseller who happens to have the original edition on his
shelf: his book, probably priced higher than the reprint, may
become unsalable or may have to be sold at a loss--and yet,
if our clients knew how long they would really have to wait
for the reprint they would probably be happy to pay a premi-
um in order to have the book now.

My complaints to publishers have yielded a rich crop
of explanations and excuses: faulty originals which were difficult to photograph, inability to find a copy of the book to be
reprinted [sic!], unexpected delays in obtaining reprint rights,
unreliable bookbinders and, if the reprint is done abroad, you
can always blame it on the mail. One or all of these factors
may be valid but could they not be taken into account before-
hand? The way things stand, I have the impression that these
excuses are actually a sort of camouflage for the real reason: "we're still waiting for more orders."

The situation is even worse in those cases--and they
are by no means rare--where a reprint is announced and
then quietly, very quietly, dropped from the reprint program.
It is the publisher's duty to announce the cancellation of a
title and to give it some publicity; to my knowledge this has
never been the case; the only way I have ever heard of a

title being cancelled was when I ordered it and received the curt reply "title discontinued" or the rather striking note "out of print." Announcing cancellation of a reprint hurts no one; not announcing it hurts all the antiquarian booksellers who have a copy of the original edition in stock.

Too often the announcement of a reprint is nothing but a fishing expedition for subscriptions and it is also a kind of claim-staking designed to prevent others from printing the same book. As a reputable antiquarian bookseller, however, I refuse to act as a shill and a barker for publishers who are looking for guaranteed profits without risks. It would seem appropriate that if the publication of a reprint depends on the receipt of a sufficient number of orders this fact should be clearly stated--again, I can see no shame in this. The only way in which the bookseller can defend himself against this practice and against the losses resulting from the cataloguing of an item which will not be reprinted is to personally check with the publisher and get his written assurance to the effect that those items which he has listed in his reprint program and which the bookseller intends to publicize will actually be reprinted. Even this precaution doesn't always work--but it helps.

The quality of the reprints is, generally speaking, quite good. Indeed, many of them are excellent. There is only one practice which leads to disappointment: a reduction in size of the original. I am told that such reductions are sometimes unavoidable because of economic or technological reasons. This may be so, but why not tell the prospective buyer? Obviously there are cases where a smaller size results in a definite advantage, such as when an unwieldy folio becomes a handy 4to which fits an ordinary shelf; but there can be no excuse for starting with a legible (and sometimes aesthetically beautiful) 4to and reducing it to an eye-watering 8vo.

And now, a word about the catalogues of reprint publishers: I have stated my criticism regarding deceptive dating, unrealistic publication dates, failure to mention changes in format, etc. To this list I should add the grievance that all too often the titles are described with almost unbelievable bibliographical shoddyness: authors' names are misspelled, no collations are given and, let me repeat this once more, the worst offense is the omission of the original date of publication. This is followed by a close second: the failure to indicate that the reprint title is part of a series--an offense

which is further compounded by those publishers who take
such series titles and include them in some new series which
they, the publishers, have created. The result is a bibliographical nightmare for the librarian and an awful nuisance
for the bookseller.

An extreme case is the failure to mention that a reprinted volume is actually part of a set; recently I received
an announcement of a bibliography reprint; the title in question was in my special field, but I had never heard of it.
With wounded bibliographical pride I decided to look into this
matter and I found that the reprint in question consisted of
the 45 pages of the last volume of this particular author's
opera omnia which contain his bibliography! The reprinting
of such bibliographical sections of larger works is, in itself,
an excellent idea--but we must be told where these sections
come from.

Finally, I strongly object to the practice of some reprint publishers to include other firms' reprints in their own
catalogues without specifically saying so--that does seem
rather strange, does it not?

As the obvious works are being reprinted it happens
more and more frequently that, with the field getting so
crowded, several different publishers announce the same re-
print--not infrequently at vastly different prices . . . We
have already witnessed some sorry spectacles of price cutting
but it is hoped that this situation will be remedied by the establishment of a central clearing house.

We now come to a further point, perhaps the crucial
one in the whole business, which can be summarized by this
question: was this reprint really necessary? Only the specialist can give the answer for each individual case; for the
purposes of the present article it will be sufficient to consider only the following two general points: the criticism often
leveled against the reprinting of older works is that this practice revives "dead scholarship" and, secondly, that it dis-
courages the publication of new editions which are so sorely
needed in many cases.

Such criticism does not seem to be justified because
there really is no such thing as "dead scholarship" and the
availability of the hitherto unfamiliar or unobtainable 18th or
19th century bibliography, for example, may give us ideas
and guide us into paths which would not have occurred to us.

The making of new editions, particularly when it comes to certain types of bibliographies, is so difficult that many potential authors are scared away from such projects by the sheer size and cost--not by the reprinting of the book in its outdated form.   One can therefore argue quite convincingly that the reissue of the old edition is beneficial.   The old edition, however, can often be improved--and it is precisely here that the reprint publishers could perform a far greater service than they are doing.   There are a number of ways in which such improvements can be made--I have heard all the arguments against them (chiefly increased cost of production and long delays), but the fact that such improved reprints have already appeared shows that there is nothing impossible about them:

1.   A preface by some specialist can be added in which the reprinted text is re-examined briefly in the light of modern scholarship and in which the reader is given relevant bibliographies or other sources to which he can turn for more recent information on the subject.

2.   The reprint of the British Museum Catalogue of Fifteenth Century Printed Books offers a rather spectacular example of how a reprint can be improved to such an extent that it is actually a new edition; neat and legible manuscript corrections have been entered in the original, photographed, and reprinted; the reproduction of such "working copies" may not always be aesthetically pleasing but the advantages are enormous.

3.   An even simpler expedient, used, for instance, in the reprint of the catalogue of John Carter Brown Library is this: an asterisk marks every entry which needs correction. In the brief preface "users are urged to write to the Library for additional information" whenever they come across such an asterisked item.

4.   Marginal cross references referring the reader to related subjects in other volumes are a great help and can literally save hours of work; a successful example of this type of improvement is the twelve-volume reprint of the Bibliothèque de la Compagnie de Jesus.

5.   Two or more monographs on the same subject could be reprinted in the same volume and unified by means of an index, preface, or cross references.   The resulting creation of a new "bibliographical unit" would bring with it

Book Publishing: Inside Views

some headaches, but they would be well worth it if the material is well chosen.

6. A bibliography can always be improved by incorporating in it all the relevant supplements, additions and corrections published after the appearance of the original edition. This is extremely useful especially in the many cases where such material appeared in periodicals or pamphlets. A case in point is, for instance, the reprint of Melzi's Dizionario di opere anonime.

How have the prices of reprints affected the antiquarian market so far? Obviously, when the price of the reprint is much lower than that of the rare o. p. original the latter's price may have to come down. When there has been no deterioration of the paper and the volume is in good condition, most buyers are willing to pay more for the original than for the reprint, but not very much more. Generally speaking the antiquarian bookseller will find that by being able to sell several copies of the reprint, any loss he may have suffered on the original edition is amply compensated.

Nothing in the world of books is simple, however, and I cannot resist the temptation of adding that some reprint prices are so high that we can happily increase the price of the original edition on our shelves.

Let me close with a word of warning to the antiquarian bookseller who plans to sell reprints on a large scale: it is not a part-time occupation. It sounds simple enough to include a reprint announcement in your catalogue; sometimes it is indeed simple and profitable. But anyone who intends to enter this brave new world of reprints on a large scale without losing his good reputation must be willing to devote much of his own and his staff's time to this activity which, as I have shown in this article, can be fraught with pitfalls and difficulties with which the antiquarian bookseller is seldom equipped to cope. Once all this has been taken into account and the necessary experience has been gained, and once we have realized that no one can keep up with all the reprints in every field, then the antiquarian bookseller can perform a real service to his clients by keeping them informed of the important reprints in his own special field. By sticking to this principle I have, over the past years, built up a fairly large reprint business in the course of which I have dealt with approximately one-hundred-twenty publishers, both here and abroad. I hope that they will not be offended by my remarks and that they will not accuse me of biting the hand that feeds me.   I do hope that they will eliminate the practices which, in the final analysis, endanger the good name of the booksellers who make an effort to sell their reprints. Reprints are here to stay, I said above; now sometimes I begin to wonder: are they?

The Antiquarian Reprint Trade!

By Burt Franklin, Publisher, Lenox Hill Publishing and
Distributing Corporation.

From the Reprint Expediting Service Bulletin 10:1-3, July-
August 1965. © 1965 by Oceana Publications Inc.   Reprinted
by permission.

I have been requested to comment on Barney Rosenthal's interesting article entitled "The Antiquarian Reprint
Trade."   To reply properly would require more space than
is here available.

I would like to suggest, however, that he himself has
provided several answers, the most important of which is revealed by the very title of his article and in his first two
sentences, e.g. "Antiquarian booksellers can no longer ignore
the rapid, indeed phenomenal growth of reprints.   Reprints
are here to stay . . ."

What he is saying in effect is that this is a new industry.   Whoever heard of the term "Antiquarian Reprint
Trade" fifteen years ago or even ten years ago.   The majority of the reprinters have been in business for perhaps five
years.

If, then, this field is new, how harshly may we judge
this infant?   Discipline it--yes, criticize it--yes; for only
through salutary criticism will this new phenomenon grow into manhood and take its place alongside established publishing.
At present conditions are, now and again, anarchic, competition fierce, duplication of titles a way of life, under-capitalization rife, systems of notification often inadequate, etc.,
etc.   I know of several esteemed reprinters whose works are
now controlled by printer-binders.   How interested are some
of the latter in the orderly development of reprint publishing?   Then also I suppose there are the fast 'buck' boys associated with every new industrial development or process.

There are exceptions, of course, but they are with us. Rosenthal's shafts may actually apply in depth to only a very few publishers but probably apply to a certain extent to all. But many publishers are successfully meeting, one by one, the problems common to all: improvement of paper and binding, meeting deadlines, respect for the customers and for each other, etc. I submit that Rosenthal's article which I consider salutary, is, in the main, timely--perhaps even overdue.

There used to be a saying that with one hundred dollars, a little credit and some knowledge a man could get into the book business. In a sense this is what has happened in the "Antiquarian Reprint" trade. Show a printer some orders and he will be likely to take a chance on making a subsidy. It's as easy as that. But obviously under-capitalization can bring on abuses not necessarily intentional or even to be foreseen.

I am confident nevertheless that the business known as reprinting has successfully passed its birth pangs and that it is well on the way to maturity. As always, the strong will get stronger and there should evolve better controls and systems. More printers and binders will in all likelihood apply their resources to short run requirements and to the reprint publishers' needs. This in turn will enable the publisher to give better service and perhaps turn out an even better product. Presently, there are severe limitations at the production end which affect dates, service and quality. For example though there are often offers seemingly not followed by publication there is more to the story than the publishers merely 'waiting for orders'. There are bottlenecks of consequence which often seriously hamper the best intentioned and the most able. Rosenthal, who records many titles published abroad does not tell us whether the domestic or the foreign publishers are the worst offenders.

In several other important respects Rosenthal's article contains its own answers. For example, he posits "Is this book necessary?" I submit that if the book isn't necessary its public will not buy it, the dealers will not list it, and the publisher with resulting financial loss, will have to use better editorial judgment in selecting future titles. Rosenthal doesn't fire buckshot in selecting publisher's titles for reoffer in his catalogue. Why should it be assumed that others lack similar critical discernment?

No one can question the desideratum of improving reprints by bringing bibliographies up to date and otherwise updating where possible.   Of two unsubsidized books that are
mentioned favorably in his article, one happens to be ours
(Melzi, where three supplements were added) but one example
aside, is it fair to compare the canon of a subsidized publisher (The British Museum) with that of the unsubsidized?

I do not mean to be captious in calling my friend for
this unfair parallel and I hasten to add that improvement editorially is certainly the wave of the future--and perhaps contains the germ of the best hope for the future of reprinting.
The general vacuum left by most university presses who tend
now toward a more salable book may well be filled one day
by 'reprinters' who have learned the techniques of the 'short
run. '

I completely disagree with most of what is said anent
concealment of dates.   All standard publishers, reprinters or
not, seem habitually to indicate the original date or dates of
publication on the verso of the title page.   And I believe that
seasoned bookmen, librarian or dealer, habitually turn to the
verso on receipt of a book.   It is an evil, of course, if the
original date is not indicated in the prospectus or catalogue.

As to Series there can be no argument but that the
original series must be indicated.   For the convenience of libraries we for our part have several series of our own, but
always as far as I know have indicated the original series if
such there be.

I think that Rosenthal has himself provided the answer
for another problem.   On balance dealers won't offer, and
libraries won't order books from publishers who don't produce books.   This practice will, I am sure, automatically
cure itself and quite soon at that.

If one may venture a small criticism of one's own.
The retailer is in one business, the publisher is in another.
One of the retailer's problems is his record keeping, his
follow-ups, his claims, etc.   He invests perhaps $2 to $5
in listing a book; the publisher may be investing $2,000 to
$100,000 in the same item.   Delays may not exculpate the
publisher but the retailer has no guarantee of an Utopia either.   Most dealers know the publishers who are producing
books; if they don't there is always the P. W. or L. J. and
other resources.   Those who don't produce won't get their

offerings listed after a time.   It is part of the growing-up process of an industry.

Limited space does not permit a study in extenso of the article.   It is a good article, a needed one and I am sure that one cannot fault too strongly its major premises.   In speaking favorably of the improvement in the quality of reprints I wish Rosenthal could have gone a little further and mentioned that some reprinters are often using paper with a life expectancy of 300 years and, often, as well paper with rag content.

If permitted I should like, in another issue of the RES Bulletin to throw out some ideas that have been of concern to me in connection with the protection against possible budget losses to the library and for the protection of dealers who have been enterprising enough to re-offer publisher's "antiquarian reprints."

Everything Is Not Coming Up Roses

By Curtis G. Benjamin, who, at the time of this writing,
was Chairman of the Board, McGraw-Hill Book Company,
New York City.   He now serves as a consultant to that company.

From Special Libraries 56:637-41, November 1965.   Copyright 1965 by Special Libraries Association.   Reprinted by
permission.   Condensed version of an address presented to
the Science-Technology Division at the 56th Special Libraries
Association Convention at Philadelphia, June 9, 1965.

The informal title of this talk was selected after a
more formal and descriptive one had been discarded as being
a bit too long.   The first title was "What I Would Worry A-
bout If I Were a Young Man in the Technical Book Business
Given to Lying Awake Nights Worrying About Its and My Future."   As a lover of long and descriptive titles, I still think
the discarded one was the better.   It describes precisely the
substance and the burden of my presentation.

Many of the problems of technical book publishers are
problems of librarians as well.   In the endless loop of gen-
erating, stating, publishing, vending, and using technical information, all of us--scientists and engineers as generators;
publishers, printers, booksellers, and librarians as vendors;
and scientists and engineers again as users--are collectively
"a part of the maine," and what diminishes one of us, diminishes all.

My specific frame of reference is the kind of technical books in which special librarians have the most interest
--advanced treatises, monographs, handbooks, symposia, and
series in science and applied science--the kind of books that
have the most importance to special librarians and the people
whom their libraries serve, indeed the very kind of books on
which the health and progress of science and technology in
America have traditionally depended.   We do not have to

worry much, if at all, about technical textbooks, training
manuals, operating manuals, and the like; they will take care
of themselves.   But not so with the advanced technical books
of professional importance.   They, and their writers and
publishers and users, can be hurt badly in the foreseeable future if we fail to have proper care for them.

Reasons for Rising Costs

The nut of the issue seems to be prices--the high
prices of technical books.   We do not have to worry much
about the high prices of this year or next (though some of
us do), but we must worry about the prospect of much higher
prices--prohibitively higher, perhaps--in the foreseeable future, which is to say five years hence at the least and ten to
20 at the most.   I would say we have little to worry about
today and much to worry about in the prospect of tomorrow.

In a recent article in the ALA Bulletin (January 1965,
p. 61-4), I outlined the present causes, as I perceive them,
of the relatively high present prices of technical books.   It
might be well to review briefly the three principal causes,
because they point up the prospect of critical future developments.

The first is a lack of technological innovation to reduce the cost of setting type for printing technical books.   It
is true that some of the new methods of cold-type composition are reducing costs for certain kinds of technical books
(those with a high content of chemical symbology, for example), but for most technical books with high mathematical
and symbolic content, the combination of monotype and hand-
set composition is still the best and the cheapest.   Indeed,
for some books hand-set still is better than monotype and
cheaper than a combination of the two.   Not so long ago Mc-
Graw-Hill lost the opportunity to publish an important and
very prestigious mathematical work to the Cambridge University Press in England because the author felt that the hand
compositors at that venerable press would do a better and
cheaper job of handling the complexity of his elegant mathematical statements.   In this case, it is not important that
McGraw-Hill lost a prestigious book to Cambridge; it is important to note that British handicraft skill won out over
American technology--that the practitioner of the Gutenberg
method of type composition won out, in terms of both quality
and cost, over all other methods that have been invented and
perfected since the 1450s.

The second cause of high costs is the coupling of what
has been called the "twigging" phenomenon in science and
technology with rising production costs in the book industry.
The "twigging" phenomenon occurs in the endless fractionation of interest and knowledge in technical fields, a continuing fractionation that has held markets for specialized books
to the same size they were 15 or 20 years ago--this in spite
of the fact that the total corpus of technical knowledge is at
least five times larger than it was 20 years ago and there
are at least three times as many professional scientists and
engineers, or customers, in the United States. (Thus the
tree is much larger, but the twigs are the same size.) In
this same 20-year period, the absolute production costs of
technical books have gone up about 100 per cent. It takes no
mathematical wizard to see what must happen, and has happened, to prices when increased costs are coupled with static
markets.

The third cause of higher prices of technical books is
the so-called "manufacturing clause" in the United States copyright law of 1891, a restriction which has since prevented
American publishers from taking full advantage of lower production costs abroad. The argument over it between authors
and publishers on the one side and printers and labor unions
on the other--an argument sparked in 1961 by the Register of
Copyrights' recommendation for outright repeal of the manufacturing clause--is well known.

The Register's original recommendation, and the backing of his proposal by authors and publishers, stirred certain
leaders in the printing and labor unions to retaliate by demanding the explicit cancellation of a so-called "loophole"
practice under which American publishers have been able to
reduce composition costs of very complex technical matter by
as much as 20 to 30 per cent. Under this practice, such composition is done abroad (usually in the United Kingdom or Japan), and reproduction proofs are sent to the United States.
Then the true manufacturing processes (platemaking, printing,
and binding) are completed in American plants. Printing
firms and labor unions are now insisting that the "manufacturing clause" must be tightened up so that no part of the
production process may be done abroad without the loss of
copyright protection for American authors.

Most publishers feel that their opponents in this hassle
are taking a very shortsighted position. By having complex
composition done abroad at lower costs, they have been able

to publish many important works that could not have been produced in the United States at going prices. If foreign composition is stopped, much printing and binding in the United States will also stop. And the consequences of possible retaliation by the leading European nations must be considered. About 50 per cent of all advanced technical books manufactured in the United States are now sold abroad. It would be easy and natural for the affected foreign countries to impose retaliatory restrictions on the import of our books. Moreover, the possible provocation of such restrictions is in contradiction to the present international trend toward the elimination of barriers of all kinds to the free flow of books among the nations of the world.

With the heat of the legislative battle rising in Washington, it is comforting to know that the SLA, through the Joint Libraries Committee on Copyright, is firmly supporting the Register of Copyrights' basic position against the restrictions and discriminations of the present "manufacturing clause."

Threats of Photocopying, Automated Libraries, and Mechanized Data Systems

If I were a young man in the technical book business, I could soon give myself many gray hairs worrying about three really serious threats to the economic health of my chosen enterprise. The first is the inevitable increase in photocopying, either with or without permission, with or without payment. The second threat is the inevitable advent of the automated library system in which documents (including book pages) are exchanged and displayed by photocopy, by microimages, or by more sophisticated electronic-optical devices. The third threat is the equally inevitable advent of completely mechanized data systems in many of the major disciplines of science and technology.

As we all know, problems of coping with photocopying are on us today, hot and heavy. The problems of coping with the library automation and mechanized data systems would be problems to worry about later if it were not for the fact that we must today try to anticipate them in the current legislation on copyright revision. I am convinced that both the automated library system and the mechanized data system will become generally operative in the United States within the foreseeable future.

In anticipating automated libraries, I am not referring
to Dr. Licklider's "library of the future," with its procogni-
tive systems and subsystems, which rejects the physical book
as a "passive repository for printed information." I am talking about the library system in which one copy of a printed
reference book will serve the present uses of ten or even 20
or more copies. In the case of the data systems, I am not
talking about a total national system that provides for sophisticated interfaces and interactions between man and the system or between one discipline system and another, a system
that handles both data and "facts" as well as documents. I
am talking about a more simple, yet comprehensive, single-
discipline system such as the projected computer-based Chemical Information System that is being organized by the Chemical Abstracts Service. This system will produce computer
files of compound names, compound structures, physical properties, biochemical properties, and so forth and is sure to
replace many commercially published handbooks and data
books in chemistry and chemical engineering.

In my mind there is no doubt at all that increased
photocopying and the advent of automated library systems
and mechanized data systems will surely and sharply erode
the already thin markets for high-level technical books.
What then? I think the answer is obvious: prices will go
up sharply over already high levels. Instead of 5,000-copy
editions at $10 per copy (which at present is minimal for a
publishing break-even), we shall see, perhaps progressively,
1,000-copy editions priced at $50 per copy, next 500-copy
editions at $100, then possibly even 100-copy editions at
$500 per copy. (The $5,000 per copy price is reserved for
new automated library systems established after the 100-
copy editions have been sold out.) Either we shall have to
publish at such prices, or the advanced and specialized treatises, the monographs, the handbooks of data and tables will
not be published at all. Or perhaps I should say that they
certainly will not be published in printed form or under the
traditional pattern of author-publisher-buyer-user relationship. If published at all, they probably will have to be produced on a subscription basis, with the size of the edition
and the price determined in each case by the number of advance orders. So I emphasize that the prospect of much
higher prices or no books at all is something for all of us
to worry about.

Reprographic Clearinghouse

At this point the thought must have come into
your minds, "What's to keep you publishers from charging
fees for the reproduction of your copyrighted publications?
Why don't you stir yourselves and do what has been so often
recommended? Why don't you set up a system under which
you can collect payments for reprographic rights and thus
compensate yourselves and your authors for the loss of sales
of printed books?"

These certainly are good questions. Most of my answers were given in an article in the Library Journal (August 1963, p. 2837-41) in which I tried to present the position and attitude of technical book publishers generally with
respect to the many hard problems involved in the establishment of a clearinghouse for reprographic rights in copyrighted
works. Unhappily nothing significant has happened in the two
years since that article was written to make me feel less
discouraged about the practicability of establishing a workable clearinghouse of the kind about which there has been so
much theoretical discussion and so little action. In truth, I
think the publishers' situation has deteriorated, and I want
briefly to cite four reasons why.

First, there have been recent reports of new technological developments that promise substantial reductions in
the costs of photocopying. (One of these, a new diazo technique, is promising enough, we are told, to be rightly called
a "breakthrough.") Further, there are reports that at least
two very large manufacturing firms are planning to launch
new photocopying machines and methods that will out-Xerox
Xerox. Thus it seems that the present universal urge to
photocopy, either legally or illegally, will surely be escalated in the near future.

Second, in all the discussion of the urgent need for a
national clearinghouse for reprographic permissions, there
has been no recognition whatever that anyone other than the
publisher has a responsibility in the matter. Scientists, educators, librarians, systems innovators, and equipment manufacturers keep saying to publishers, "We are all of us in
this together and it is up to you to do something about it."
And the tone of voice usually suggests that the "something"
should be designed and operated to solve their problems, not
those of the publisher. Again I ask, "Why should publishers
take the lead and make a special effort to establish a system

which will encourage reprographic practices for which we
have no enthusiasm and from which we chance little gain and
much injury?" I am sorry to say that I have heard no reasonable answer to this question.

Third, one continues to encounter evidence that very
few people are willing to face up realistically to the prospective costs of establishing and operating a clearinghouse system that would serve satisfactorily on a national scale. (Anything less than a total national system would not serve its
purpose.) At the same time, one continues to hear only of
"nominal" charges for reproduction rights. Obviously, the
combination of the two factors makes no economic sense.
Other interests are proposing that publishers should establish
and maintain a facility in which it would cost dimes to collect pennies or dollars to collect dimes. Yet it appears that
the monkey inevitably will be placed on publishers' unwilling
backs. I can only hope that, come what may, we publishers
shall be clever enough to insist on charging what it costs to
carry him, plus a little leftover gain for ourselves and our
authors.

The fourth item in my list of discouraging developments is the recent and unexpectedly strong opposition of organized educators to the Register of Copyrights' position on
the "fair use" section of the new copyright bill. The Division of Audiovisual Instructional Services of the National Education Association recently issued a broadside that has ex-
cited many educators to the belief that the new copyright bill
would deny certain fair-use rights that teachers have always
enjoyed in the exhibition or performance of an educational
work in the course of face-to-face teaching activities in the
classroom. Hundreds of aroused educators and friends of
education have been encouraged to go overboard to the position that any educational use is fair use--and woe unto him
who proposes legislation to the contrary! One can hope that
calm and informed voices will be able to quiet this misinformed attack on the fair-use section of the new bill, but at
the moment it looks as though a nasty fight is brewing. I
fear it will spill over to concepts of fair use of copyrighted
technical works.

Government's Role in Publishing
        There is still another set of problems that has long-
range importance to technical publishing in general and to
commercial publishing in particular. The problems in this

area concern the ever larger role of the Federal Government
as a producer of scientific and technical information and the
attendant question of the copyrightability of literary works
produced wholly or in part with government funds. These
problems have been mounting steadily in recent years, although it cannot be said that they have yet reached a critical
stage. But this is something that must be worried about today rather than tomorrow, because the new copyright bill
provides immediate debate and decisive action on questions
that have been skirted for half a century.

All of us are familiar with the growing dimensions of
federal participation in the total national development of science and technology. To some it appears that this trend may
in time result in government preemption of certain large and
important areas of scientific and technical information. Perhaps this development is inevitable, but if private publishers
are excluded from participation in the production and dissemination of government sponsored works, then much harm
will be done to the total information industry. The extent of
harm will be in relation to the proportion of "in-house" versus "out-of-house" governmental activity, because private industry will certainly be excluded from the "in-house" programs. The extent of harm to commercial publishers will
be in proportion to governmental favor of nonprofit publishing
organizations over for-profit organizations. There is much
for commercial publishers to worry about at both levels.

The Rickover v. Public Affairs Press case set off in
Washington a near-panic line of thinking about the question of
private copyright in government-sponsored literary works.
The U. S. Copyright Office responded splendidly to the challenge by making proper discriminations and qualifications.
Later the Register of Copyrights proposed in his original
draft of the new copyright bill that a governmental agency
should be allowed to take copyright in certain kinds of official publications, provided that this would be done "in the
public interest" and with proper over-all executive-branch approval. Under strong opposition, he again had to retreat
and compromise. Now he holds the position that nothing in
the new law should deny any governmental agency the right to
allow a contractor or grantee to take and hold copyright in a
literary work produced as a part of a government-financed
project. This position is sure to be strongly opposed by a
large body of public opinion that holds that anything and
everything produced in whatever form or manner at government expense should be public property. If this strict pub-

lic-domain policy should prevail in the end, it will spell
double trouble--trouble for government agencies and trouble
for private publishing organizations. Who will print technical works of limited interest that are in the public domain?

This whole category of government-related problems
is capsulated in the Chemical Abstracts Service plan for the
development of a computer-based information system. The
costs of the R & D phase and of the installation of operating
subsystems of this project will be financed, presumably, by
a series of grants by the NSF. (The present estimate of
these costs is over $15 million.) If the system is success-
fully developed, it will give the Chemical Abstracts Service,
a nonprofit organization, what will amount to a practical mon-
opoly of chemical information of a research and reference
character, including print-outs of handbooks of data and technical practice. Thus it appears that a government activity
may in this instance effectively preempt a whole discipline
of scientific information and give it over to a nonprofit publishing organization. What is here happening in chemical
information can, and probably will, happen over and over a-
gain in other disciplines. The long-range prospect of government-financed freeze-outs is understandably disquieting to
taxpaying commercial publishers.

Further, the promise of the Chemical Abstracts Service system will not be so bright for the American Chemical
Society or anyone else if the public-domain advocates have
their way and copyright of the products of the system is
prohibited by the new law. It pains me to think of the many
unhappy consequences of this possible event of copyright legislation.

I sincerely hope that I have not sounded too negative
in some of my references to the bright and very promising
new tools of your profession. Naturally I have an overriding concern for the future of the book. I am concerned lest
we allow ourselves to be too quickly persuaded that the book
can be abandoned, that the motivations for its creation can
be safely destroyed. In short, I am concerned that we be
not tempted to cast aside the old before we can be sure that
the new will serve us better.

AUTHOR INDEX

SUBJECT INDEX

electronic computers see: computer . . .
electronic devices 74-5
electronic media 82-4
Electronics Buyers' Guide 107
Elementary and Secondary Education Act of 1965 444-5
Encyclopaedia of the Social Sciences 418-20, 427-32
encyclopedias, editing of 417-35
sales 35
Encyclopédie 417
Erskine, Albert 19, 350
Eulau, Heinz 434
evaluation of manuscripts see: selection of manuscripts
executives, books about 324

Fairchild Comp/Set 94
Fairchild TTS perforators 90
"fair use" rights 500
Fallada, Hans 353
Fallers, Lloyd A. 434
Farrington scanner 91
Faulkner, William 18, 369
Federal aid for education and the book publishers 444-53
Ferber, Edna 349-50, 352, 363, 367
fiction editor's role 136-7
fiction paperbacks 304
fiction, publishing of 20, 57-8, 67-9
film rights see: motion picture rights
films, "single-concept" 437
filmstrips sold by book publishers 83
flashcards sold by book publishers 83
Fleming, Peter 354
Flexowriters 90, 126
Ford Foundation 419
format and typography control by computers 94-8

Forster, E. M. 27, 138
Forthcoming Books 118, 122
Fosdick, Dr. Harry Emerson 359
Fototronic photocomposition machine 104-5
Fowler, Gene 359
fractionation of technical knowledge 61, 496
Frank, Gerold 365
Franklin, Benjamin 319
Freeman, Douglas Southall 355
Friden Flexowriters 90
Frost, Robert 196, 370
function codes and typography 91

Gallico, Paul 244-5
Galsworthy 350-1
Gann, Ernest K. 364
Geis, Bernard, Associates 275-7
Geisel, Theodor 19
Gibbs, Philip 349
Glasgow, Ellen 353-4
Glazer, Suzanne 147
Gochman, David S. 435
Godden, Rumer, 370
"going public" 49, 66-8
Golden, Harry 267-8
Goldwater, Barry 368
government funds for educational books 81
government's role in scientific and technical publishing 500-2
Graham, Billy 271
Graham, Gwethalyn 360
Grahame, Kenneth 159
Greeley, Horace 142
Greene, A. C. 258
Grew, Ambassador 360
Grey, Lord 350
Grey, Zane 349
Groves-Raines, Antony 154
Gunther, John 355, 357, 361, 365, 367

513

515

517

textbooks and textbook publishing (cont.)
authorship 385-7, 395-409
book contracts 382-3
composition 388-9
copyright dates 392
cost 392
dilemmas 410-6
editing 385-7
graphics work 387-8
illustrations 386-7
manufacturing and distribution 389-90
market considerations 393-4
myths about 392-4
paperback, 305, 392-3
pre-writing of 385
purchases by schools 81
sales 35
selection of manuscripts 385-6
social studies 410-6
supplementary materials 390-1
use in teaching 402-5
See also: educational books and publishing
Thompson, Morton 364
Thorp, Roderick 274
threats to copyright 81-2, 497-502
threats to the technical book business 497-502
Thurber, James 138-9, 360
Toynbee, Arnold 361
trade books
sales 36
See also: specific kinds of trade books and specific subjects related to trade book publishing
translation by computer 121
translation rights, paying authors for 82
transmission of published material 81

transparencies 437
Tregaskis, Richard 359
Treistman, Judith 435
Trevor-Roper, Hugh 315
Tribble, Edwin 258
Truman, Harry S. 365
Tuchman, Barbara 370
Tunis, John R. 27
Twain, Mark 194, 349
"twigging phenomenon" 61, 496
typesetting and computers 120
typewriter keyboards and composition 90-1

Ullman, James Ramsey 360
United States Copyright Law of 1891 496
United States government as publisher of technical information 500-2
United States history textbooks 395-409
university libraries 75, 81
university press publishing 170-7
sales 36
Urban and Rural Community Action Programs 445-6
Uris, Leon 364, 367-9

Vance, Ethel 357
Van Doren, Carl 356
Van Loon, Hendrik Willem 353
Vanocur, Sander 371
Van Paassen, Pierre 358
Vidal, Gore 192-3
Viner, Jacob 434
Vocational Education Act of 1963 446

Wakeman, Frederick 360
Wallace, DeWitt 141
Wallace, Irving 242, 292, 368
Wallis, W. Allen 419-20, 434
Wallop, Douglass 295
Waln, Nora 354